NEIGHBOURS AND STRANGERS

| MANCHESTER MEDIEVAL STUDIES |

SERIES EDITOR   Professor S. H. Rigby

The study of medieval Europe is being transformed as old orthodoxies are challenged, new methods embraced and fresh fields of enquiry opened up. The adoption of interdisciplinary perspectives and the challenge of economic, social and cultural theory are forcing medievalists to ask new questions and to see familiar topics in a fresh light.

The aim of this series is to combine the scholarship traditionally associated with medieval studies with an awareness of more recent issues and approaches in a form accessible to the non-specialist reader.

ALREADY PUBLISHED IN THE SERIES

Peacemaking in the middle ages: principles and practice
Jenny Benham

Money in the medieval English economy: 973–1489
James Bolton

The commercialisation of English Society, 1000–1500 (second edition)
Richard H. Britnell

Reform and the papacy in the eleventh century
Kathleen G. Cushing

Picturing women in late medieval and Renaissance art
Christa Grössinger

The Vikings in England
D. M. Hadley

A sacred city: consecrating churches and reforming society in eleventh-century Italy
Louis I. Hamilton

The politics of carnival
Christopher Humphrey

Holy motherhood
Elizabeth L'Estrange

Music, scholasticism and reform: Salian Germany 1024–1125
T. J. H. McCarthy

Medieval law in context
Anthony Musson

Constructing kingship: the Capetian monarchs of France and the early Crusades
James Naus

The expansion of Europe, 1250–1500
Michael North

John of Salisbury and the medieval Roman renaissance
Irene O'Daly

Immigrant England, 1300–1550
W. Mark Ormrod, Bart Lambert and Jonathan Mackman

Medieval maidens
Kim M. Phillips

Approaching the Bible in medieval England
Eyal Poleg

Gentry culture in late medieval England
Raluca Radulescu and Alison Truelove (eds)

Chaucer in context
S. H. Rigby

Peasants and historians: debating the medieval English peasantry
Phillipp R. Schofield

Lordship in four realms: the Lacy family, 1166–1241
Colin Veach

The life cycle in Western Europe, c.1300–c.1500
Deborah Youngs

NEIGHBOURS AND STRANGERS

Local societies in early medieval Europe

Bernhard Zeller, Charles West, Francesca Tinti, Marco Stoffella, Nicolas Schroeder, Carine van Rhijn, Steffen Patzold, Thomas Kohl, Wendy Davies and Miriam Czock

Manchester University Press

Copyright © Bernhard Zeller, Charles West, Francesca Tinti, Marco Stoffella, Nicolas Schroeder, Carine van Rhijn, Steffen Patzold, Thomas Kohl, Wendy Davies and Miriam Czock 2020

The right of Bernhard Zeller, Charles West, Francesca Tinti, Marco Stoffella, Nicolas Schroeder, Carine van Rhijn, Steffen Patzold, Thomas Kohl, Wendy Davies and Miriam Czock to be identified as the authors of this work has been asserted by them in accordance with the Copyright, Designs and Patents Act 1988.

Published by Manchester University Press
Oxford Road, Manchester M13 9PL

www.manchesteruniversitypress.co.uk

British Library Cataloguing-in-Publication Data
A catalogue record for this book is available from the British Library
Oxford Road, Manchester M13 9PL

ISBN 978 1 5261 3981 8 hardback
ISBN 978 1 5261 3689 9 paperback

First published 2020
Paperback published 2022

The publisher has no responsibility for the persistence or accuracy of URLs for any external or third-party internet websites referred to in this book, and does not guarantee that any content on such websites is, or will remain, accurate or appropriate.

Typeset by Servis Filmsetting Ltd, Stockport, Cheshire

Our dear friend and colleague Miriam Czock, who always had an unexpected insight to contribute and could always make us laugh, died shortly before the publication of this book. We dedicate it to her memory, in gratitude.

CONTENTS

List of figures	*page* viii
Abbreviations	ix
Conventions	xiv
Preface	xvi

1	Questions to pursue	1
2	Setting the scene	19
3	The fabric of local societies: people, land and settlement	52
4	Making groups: collective action in rural settlements	86
5	Shepherds, uncles, owners, scribes: priests as neighbours in early medieval local societies	120
6	Interventions in local societies: lower office holders	150
7	Interventions and interactions	181
8	Neighbours, visitors and strangers: searching for the local	209

Appendix: written sources	226
Glossary	236
Bibliography	243
Index	282

FIGURES

0.1	Scale to show locality, micro-region, region	xii
2.1	Western Europe, physical, with areas of expertise indicated	20
2.2	Later eighth-century Francia and Italy	23
2.3	Mid-ninth-century Francia and Italy	26
2.4	Early tenth-century Francia and Italy	29
2.5	Late tenth-century Francia and Italy	31
2.6	England *c.* 800	34
2.7	England in the reign of Athelstan	35
2.8	Iberia *c.* 950	38
3.1a	General excavation plan of Kirchheim, Bavaria	55
3.1b	Interpretation of the excavation of Kirchheim, Bavaria, after Henning, in G. Ausenda et al., *The Langobards Before the Frankish Conquest* (Woodbridge, 2009), p. 160	56
3.2	Farmstead at Pacé, Brittany: the last phase of occupation, after F. Le Boulanger (ed.), *Pacé (Ille-et-Vilaine) – ZAC Beausoleil* (Excavation report, INRAP Grand Ouest, 2011), p. 123	57
3.3	Excavation plan of Vallange, Lorraine	59
3.4	The hilltop village of Poggibonsi in (a) sixth and (b) ninth centuries	61
3.5	Property in Eimsheim	76
3.6	Prüm's estate of Mabompré (893), after Devroey, in M. Gaillard et al. (eds), *De la mer du Nord à la Méditerranée* (Luxembourg, 2011), p. 206	78
8.1	Eastern Brittany	222
8.2	Northern France/Belgium	223
8.3	Rhineland/Bavaria/Saint-Gall area	224
8.4	Northern Italy	224
8.5	Northern Iberia	225
8.6	England	225

ABBREVIATIONS

BG 'Becerro Galicano de San Millán de la Cogolla', online edition (2013), http://www.ehu.es/galicano/?l=es; see also SM
C *Colección documental del monasterio de San Pedro de Cardeña*, ed. G. Martínez Díez (Burgos: Caja de Ahorros y Monte de Piedad del circulo católico de obreros de Burgos, 1998)
CCCM Corpus Christianorum, Continuatio Mediaevalis
CCSL Corpus Christianorum, Series Latina
CDF *Codex diplomaticus Fuldensis*, ed. E. F. J. Dronke (Cassel: Theodor Fischer, 1850)
CDL *Codice diplomatico longobardo*, ed. L. Schiaparelli et al., Fonti per la storia d'Italia, 62–6, 5 vols in 7 (Rome: ISIME, 1929–2003)
CDMA *Codex diplomaticus Amiatinus. Urkundenbuch der Abtei S. Salvatore am Montamiata. Von den Anfängen bis zum Regierungsantritt Papst Innocenz III (736–1198)*, ed. W. Kurze, 4 vols (Tübingen: M. Niemeyer, 1974–2004)
Cel *O Tombo de Celanova: estudio introductorio, edición e índices (ss. IX–XII)*, ed. J. M. Andrade Cernadas, M. Díaz Tie and F. J. Pérez Rodríguez, 2 vols (Santiago de Compostela: Consello da Cultura Galega, 1995)
ChLA *Chartae Latinae Antiquiores: Facsimile-edition of the Latin Charters prior to the ninth century*, ed. A. Bruckner and R. Marichal, vols 1–49 (Dietikon-Zurich: Urs Graf Verlag, 1954–97) and *Chartae Latinae Antiquiores: Facsimile-edition of the Latin Charters, 2nd Series: Ninth Century*, ed. G. Cavallo and G. Nicolaj, vols 50–118 (Dietikon-Zurich: Urs Graf Verlag, 1997–2021)
CL *Codex Laureshamensis*, ed. K. Glöckner, 3 vols (Darmstadt: Historischer Verein für Hessen, 1929–36)
CR *Cartulaire de l'Abbaye de Redon en Bretagne*, ed. A. de Courson (Paris: L'imprimerie impériale, 1863)

ABBREVIATIONS

HR	*Recueil des chartes de l'abbaye de Stavelot-Malmédy*, vol. 1: 664–1198, ed. J. Halkin and Ch. G. Roland, Commission royale d'histoire, Publications in-quarto 36, 1 (Brussels: Hayez, 1909)
I placiti	*I placiti del 'Regnum Italiae'*, ed. C. Manaresi, 3 vols (Rome: ISIME, 1955–60)
LaC	*La Coruña. Fondo Antiguo (788–1065)*, ed. C. Sáez and Mª del Val González de la Peña, 2 vols (Alcalá: Universidad de Alcalá, 2003–04)
Le leggi dei Longobardi	*Le leggi dei Longobardi. Storia, memoria e diritto di un popolo germanico*, ed. C. Azzara and S. Gasparri (Rome: Viella, 2005)
Li, Lii, Liii	*Colección documental del archivo de la catedral de León (775–1230)*, Volume I: 775–952, ed. E. Sáez; Volume II: 953–985, ed. E. Sáez and C. Sáez; Volume III: 986–1031, ed. J. M. Ruiz Asencio (León: Centro de Estudios e Investigación San Isidoro, Caja de Ahorros y Monte de Piedad, Archivo Histórico Diocesano, 1987, 1990, 1987)
LPW	*Liber possessionum Wizenburgensis*, ed. C. Dette, Quellen und Abhandlungen zur mittelrheinischen Kirchengeschichte, 59 (Mainz: Verlag der Gesellschaft für Mittelrheinische Kirchengeschichte, 1987)
MDL V/2, MDL V/3	*Memorie e documenti per servire all'istoria del ducato di Lucca*, vol. V/2, ed. F. Bertini (Lucca: F. Bertini, 1837); vol. V/3, ed. D. Barsocchini (Lucca: F. Bertini, 1841)
MGH	Monumenta Germaniae Historica
MGH Capit. 1	*Capitularia regum Francorum*, vol. 1, ed. A. Boretius (Hanover: Hahn, 1883)
MGH Capit. 2	*Capitularia regum Francorum*, vol. 2, ed. A. Boretius and V. Krause (Hanover: Hahn, 1897)
MGH Capit. episc. 1	*Capitularia episcoporum*, vol. 1, ed. P. Brommer (Hanover: Hahn, 1984)

MGH Capit. episc. 2	*Capitularia episcoporum*, vol. 2, ed. R. Pokorny and M. Stratmann (Hanover: Hahn, 1995)
MGH Capit. episc. 3	*Capitularia episcoporum*, vol. 3, ed. R. Pokorny (Hanover: Hahn, 1995)
MGH Conc. 2, 1–2	*Concilia aevi Karolini*, vols 1–2, ed. A. Werminghoff (Hanover/Leipzig: Hahn, 1906–08)
MGH Epp.	*Epistolae*
MGH Formulae	*Formulae Merowingici et Karolini Aevi*, ed. K. Zeumer, MGH LL 5 (Hanover: Hahn, 1886)
MGH LL	*Leges* (in folio)
MGH LL nat. Germ.	*Leges nationum Germanicarum*
MGH SS	*Scriptores* (in folio)
OD	*Colección documental del monasterio de Santa María de Otero de las Dueñas, I (854–1108)*, ed. J. A. Fernández Flórez and M. Herrero de la Fuente (León: Centro de Estudios e Investigación San Isidoro, 1999)
Ov	*Colección diplomática del monasterio de San Vicente de Oviedo (años 781–1200)*, ed. P. Floriano Llorente (Oviedo: Diputación de Asturias, Instituto de estudios asturianos del Patronato de José M. Quadrado, 1968)
OvC	*Colección de documentos de la catedral de Oviedo*, ed. S. García Larragueta (Oviedo: Diputación de Asturias, Instituto de estudios asturianos, 1962)
PL	*Patrologia Latina*, ed. J.-P. Migne
PMH DC	*Portugaliae Monumenta Historica a saeculo octavo post Christum usque ad quintumdecimum, Diplomata et Chartae*, ed. A. Herculano de Carvalho e Araujo and Joaquim José da Silva Mendes Leal, vol. 1 of 1 vol. only (Lisbon: Academia Scientiarum Olisiponensis, 1867–73)
PRG	*Le Pontifical Romano-Germanique du dixième siècle*, ed. C. Vogel and R. Elze, 3 vols, Studi e testi 226–7, 266 (Vatican City: Bibliotheca Apostolica Vaticana, 1963–72)

S	*Colección diplomática del monasterio de Sahagún (857–1230), Volume I: siglos ix y x*, ed. J. M. Mínguez Fernández (León: Centro de Estudios e Investigación San Isidoro, Archivo Histórico Diocesano, Caja de Ahorros y Monte de Piedad de León, 1976)
SantA	*La documentación del Tumbo A de la catedral de Santiago de Compostela: estudio y edición*, ed. M. Lucas Álvarez (León: Centro de Estudios e Investigación San Isidoro, 1997)
Sawyer	P. H. Sawyer, *Anglo-Saxon Charters. An Annotated List and Bibliography* (London: Offices of the Royal Historical Society, 1968), http://www.esawyer.org.uk/about/index.html
SJP	*Cartulario de San Juan de la Peña*, ed. A. Ubieto Arteta, 2 vols (València: Bautista, 1962–63)
SM	*Cartulario de San Millán de la Cogolla (759–1076)*, ed. A. Ubieto Arteta (València: Anubar, 1976); see also BG
Sob	*Tumbos del monasterio de Sobrado de los Monjes*, ed. P. Loscertales de García de Valdeavellano, 2 vols (Madrid: Dirección General del Patrimonio Artístico y Cultural, Archivo Histórico Nacional, 1976)
T	*Cartulario de Santo Toribio de Liébana*, ed. L. Sánchez Belda (Madrid: Archivo Histórico Nacional, 1948)
TF	*Die Traditionen des Hochstifts Freising*, ed. Th. Bitterauf, 2 vols, Quellen und Erörterungen zur bayerischen und deutschen Geschichte, 4–5 (Munich: Rieger, 1905–09)
TR	*Die Traditionen des Hochstifts Regensburg und des Klosters St. Emmeram*, ed. J. Widemann, Quellen und Erörterungen zur bayerischen und deutschen Geschichte, 8 (Munich: Rieger, 1943)
TW	*Traditiones Wizenburgenses: Die Urkunden des Klosters Weißenburg 661–864*, ed. K. Glöckner and L. A. Doll (Darmstadt: Hessische Historische Kommission, 1979)
UBF	*Urkundenbuch des Klosters Fulda*, vol. 1, ed. E. E. Stengel, Veröffentlichungen der Historischen Kommission für Hessen und Waldeck, 10/1 (Marburg: Elwert, 1956)
UBH	*Urkundenbuch der Reichsabtei Hersfeld*, vol. 1, ed. H. Weirich (Marburg: Elwert, 1936)
V	*Los becerros gótico y galicano de Valpuesta*, ed. J. M. Ruiz Asencio, I. Ruiz Albi and M. Herrero Jiménez, 2 vols

	(Madrid/Burgos: Real Academia Española, Instituto Castellano y Leonés de la Lengua, 2010)
W	*Urkundenbuch der Abtei Sanct Gallen*, vols 1–2, ed. H. Wartmann (Zurich: S. Höhr, 1863–66)

CONVENTIONS

In view of considerable ambiguities in the use of the term 'local' we have adopted the following convention: we have referred to an area of the order of 10 km diameter as a 'locality'; an area of the order of 30 km diameter as a 'micro-region'; and an area of the order of 80–150 km diameter as a 'region' (see figure 0.1). This is merely a convention and has no intrinsic significance; however, it means that where we use the word 'local' we are thinking of relationships of a 10 km or smaller scale. For regional maps in detail, see figures 8.1 (Eastern Brittany), 8.2 (Northern France/

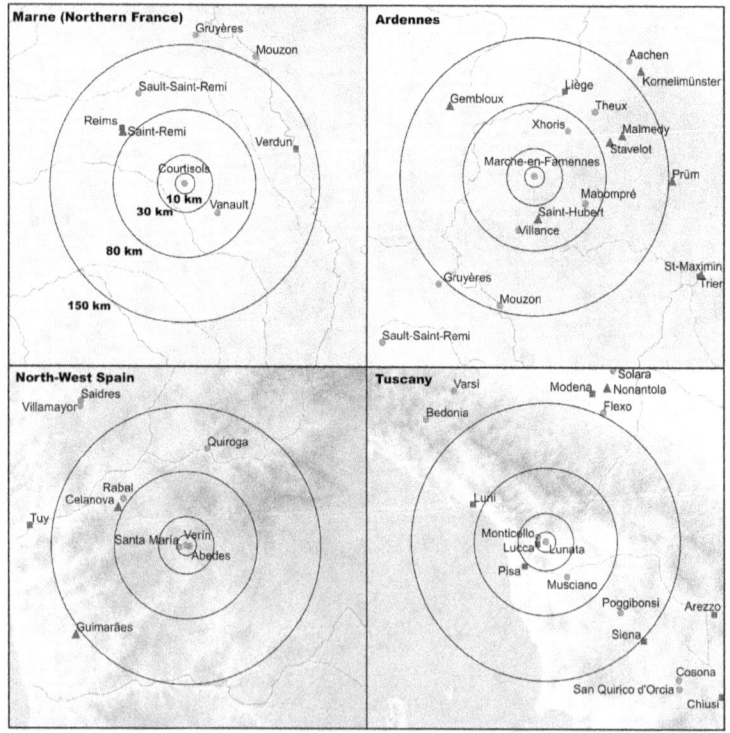

Figure 0.1   Scale to show locality, micro-region, region

Belgium), 8.3 (Rhineland/Bavaria/Saint-Gall area), 8.4 (Northern Italy), 8.5 (Northern Iberia) and 8.6 (England) at the end of the text. In quoting from Latin texts we follow the punctuation and capitalisation of the editions quoted, unless indicated otherwise. We have kept name forms as spelled therein when quoting texts but have used modern forms in discussion and translations where there is a commonly used form. For those unfamiliar with Latin of this period and these areas, note that orthography can be extremely unstable and that grammar often does not follow classical norms.

PREFACE

We have explored the issues considered in this book by bringing together scholars with different kinds and different areas of regional expertise, working closely in a five-year research programme about the early medieval face-to-face group (adopted as an element of the ERC Advanced Grant project 'Social Cohesion, Identity and Religion in Europe 400–1200' led by Professor Walter Pohl, of the University of Vienna and the Austrian Academy of Sciences, a project largely concerned with the 'broad frames of identification for large numbers of people' at a macro-social level). Each member of the group contributed to annual meetings to discuss the major themes identified, with regional presentations on a range of agreed questions. Charles West contributed from his knowledge of local matters in the eastern Paris basin in the early Middle Ages; Nicolas Schroeder from his of southern Belgium; Miriam Czock contributed from her knowledge of the Wissembourg area in Alsace and the Middle Rhineland; Thomas Kohl from more of the Middle Rhineland and also Bavaria; Bernhard Zeller from Alpine regions and the surrounding land in modern Switzerland and south-western Germany; Marco Stoffella from northern and central Italy, with special attention to Tuscany; Wendy Davies from northern Spain and Portugal; and Francesca Tinti from England. Steffen Patzold drew primarily from his knowledge of Frankish capitularies and Carine van Rhijn from hers of Frankish priests' manuscripts. This does not provide comprehensive coverage of western Europe, nor is it intended to do so (see figure 2.1); these are regions which are particularly well documented and also offer a wide range of different material: they make for good comparisons. While other scholars joined us for our first two books (S. Patzold and C. van Rhijn (eds), *Men in the Middle. Local Priests in Early Medieval Europe* (Berlin: De Gruyter, 2016) and T. Kohl, S. Patzold and B. Zeller (eds), *Kleine Welten. Ländliche Gesellschaften im Karolingerreich* (Ostfildern: Thorbecke, 2019)), one or more of the core group took overall responsibility for each topic for this, our final book, drawing the different regional perspectives together into unified thematic chapters; thereby, every member of the group has contributed to every section of this publication and in effect every member has written 10 per cent of it. In practice, Wendy Davies and Bernhard Zeller have done the final editing and taken overall responsibility for Chapters 1 and 2, setting out the questions to pursue and providing some essential background; readers familiar with the period can skip this background on physical geography, political trends and relevant source material. Nicolas Schroeder took the lead on Chapter 3, 'The fabric of local societies: people, land and settlement'; Miriam Czock and Charles West drew together the material for Chapter 4, 'Making groups: collective action in rural settlements'; Francesca Tinti and Carine van Rhijn led on Chapter 5, 'Shepherds, uncles, owners, scribes: priests as neighbours in early medieval local societies'; Thomas Kohl and Marco Stoffella drew together the material for Chapter 6, 'Interventions in local societies: lower office holders', Steffen Patzold that for Chapter 7, 'Interventions and interactions'; and Wendy Davies has provided the concluding Chapter 8. All contributed to the Appendix, which provides some detail about written sources, and to the Glossary, which is a guide to the meaning of terms used in and of the early Middle Ages.

We are indebted to many people and institutions for assistance during preparation of the book. We owe especial thanks to the Institute for Medieval Research of the Austrian Academy of Sciences in Vienna and to the University of Tübingen for hosting and facilitating meetings; and to the European Research Council under the European Union's Seventh Framework Programme (FP7/2007–2013)/ERC grant agreement No. 269591 and to DFG Collaborative Research Center 923 'Bedrohte Ordnungen' for funding in support of those meetings; Walter Pohl and Steffen Patzold, respectively, very helpfully enabled those arrangements. Francesca Tinti's work for this volume is part of the activity conducted within the research project HAR2017-86502-P funded by the Spanish Agencia Estatal de Investigación. We also owe especial thanks to Dr Doris Ebner and Dr Astrid Hansen of the *Bayerisches Landesamt für Denkmalpflege* for their help and for authorisation to reproduce the scan of Rainer Christlein, 'Kirchheim bei München, Oberbayern: Das Dorf des frühen Mittelalters', *Das archäologische Jahr in Bayern* 1980 (1981), pp. 162–3, for figure 3.1a; to Professor Marco Valenti of the University of Siena for permission to reproduce figures 3.4a and b and for providing the images; to INRAP and Franck Gérard for providing material from which figure 3.3 could be drawn; and to Thomas Kohl for providing that from which figure 3.5 could be drawn. With the exception of 3.1a and 3.4ab, Nicolas Schroeder drew all the figures, for which skill and labour we are immensely grateful. Of the many people with whom conversation has been especially fruitful, we would like to thank Jean-Pierre Devroey, Ros Faith, Ernesto Pastor and Chris Wickham. Finally we are very grateful to Meredith Carroll and her colleagues at Manchester University Press for their constructive and always prompt support.

1

Questions to pursue

For all the loose talk about 'community' in pre-industrial rural societies, group action and group identity are not well understood for the early Middle Ages. In this book we aim to investigate groups and group behaviour in rural societies in western Europe in the period 700–1000, before the development of the tighter community structures of the later Middle Ages. We want to discover how far residential settlements constituted units of social organisation and the degree of social cohesion in such settlements. Our focus is on the interconnections and networks of people who lived side by side – neighbours – and their interactions with strangers from beyond the settlement, using evidence from across insular and continental western Europe.

There are many questions to pursue. Was anyone conscious of membership of the residential group or were those who lived in the same place simply residents? Given that a romantic view of agricultural collaboration and cooperation in this distant era has often been expressed, is that view any more than a reflection of post-industrial nostalgia for a supposed harmonious past? Where agricultural cooperation did occur, did it depend on permanent bonds between members of the group or was it no more than simple 'task cohesion', collaboration for the moment? Do surviving source materials suggest the binding force of shared beliefs and values and of formative social memory? How strong was any sense of inclusion and the practice of exclusion? How did a group deal with diversity? How did it deal with intervention from beyond the group? And what was the shape of the residential space – a single settlement, such as a village, or a network of settlements, or a principal settlement with associated hamlets and/or isolated farms, or simply a scatter of farms? We might expect the shapes to vary, depending on climate and terrain: we cannot assume that the village is the only conceivable model for the residential base.

We have no sympathy with the teleological views that see the early medieval residential group as the prototype of the late medieval and early modern structured community. Such an approach ignores the variety of practice indicated by early medieval sources and the complexity of causation processes: local societies were far from uniform and the processes that made and changed them were far from monocausal. Looking at all potential kinds of evidence of social cohesion in well-evidenced localities in Austria, Belgium, Britain, France, Germany, Italy, Portugal, Spain and Switzerland, our investigation is grounded in the land; it is more concerned with the bottom than the top of the social hierarchy, that is, with the people who lived in the same settlement, and it is concerned, in the first instance, with horizontal rather than vertical relationships. Our interest is in the residential group of inhabitants rather than the single household or family. We know from earlier work that it is possible to see some detail of peasant relationships and interactions in Breton villages in the ninth century and to see elements of the functioning of local societies there: residential groups had a clear identity, recognised by themselves and by outsiders; they met regularly and transacted local business in public; they settled local disputes in village courts, with members of the group acting as witnesses, sureties and judges (see figure 8.1).[1] That being so, are similar mechanisms and the same kinds of cohesion visible in other parts of western Europe? Of course, very few rural groups lived in an isolated bubble: the supra-local agents of landlords and rulers elicited a variety of responses from people at ground level, and they themselves, as regular visitors and as strangers, had a greater or lesser impact on the small-scale residential group.[2] Likewise, the values, instructions and demands of the wider literate world of Christianity could percolate down to local level through the actions and ministry of a local priest.[3] This book is therefore also concerned with the reception of these kinds of external impacts and with their variety and intensity.

---

1 W. Davies, *Small Worlds. The Village Community in Early Medieval Brittany* (London: Duckworth, 1988).
2 Cf. M. Stoffella, 'Gli ufficiali pubblici minori nella Toscana carolingia e post-carolingia', in M. Bassetti and M. Stoffella (eds), *Gli ufficiali minori in Italia nell'alto medioevo (secoli VIII–XI)* (Spoleto: Fondazione CISAM, forthcoming).
3 Cf. F. Tinti (ed.), *Pastoral Care in Late Anglo-Saxon England* (Woodbridge: Boydell Press, 2005).

QUESTIONS TO PURSUE

The problems of addressing an issue such as social cohesion in an early medieval context are well known and have been well treated. Chris Wickham set out the parameters: true comparison is difficult when national preoccupations – such as the Arab impact on Iberia, the Norman conquest of England, urban growth in Italy, varying levels of belief in free peasant proprietorship – dominate scholarly discourse; over-attention to legal history has meant limited attention to actual practice and to the way that societies functioned; and the character of available source material varies enormously across space and time, southern European charters, for example, tending to have much more local detail than northern.[4] The perspectives of written sources usually derive from an elite – from landowners and their agents, from rulers and their entourages, from the specialised communities of monasteries and episcopal households – but we want to avoid approaching rural society exclusively through the structures of lordship. It is rare to hear the voice of the peasant, so how can we infer peasant social practice from material of this kind?

In fact, despite the dominant written perspectives, more and more aspects of peasant practice are becoming investigable.[5] The corpus of archaeological data, which has particular relevance for individual settlement size, form and function, and its economic basis, is constantly growing.[6] Recent attention to the processes that lie behind the production of a written text and its transmission reveal practices that were previously hidden and make audible voices that were previously silent. In the last few years a heightened awareness of the potential of records of judicial disputes has emerged: although many of these records deal with aristocratic quarrels, careful sifting can identify cases of peasant conflict and thereby throw light on intra-group relationships, as Lemesle and Albertoni, among others, have demonstrated.[7] A new generation of work

---

4 C. Wickham, 'Problems of comparing rural societies in early medieval western Europe', *Transactions of the Royal Historical Society*, 2 (1992), 221–46. The 'legalism' school has been reinstating the social importance of legal formulations in recent years; see F. Pirie and J. Scheele (eds), *Legalism: Community and Justice* (Oxford: Oxford University Press, 2014).
5 See below, Chapter 2 and Appendix, for detail of written sources available.
6 See below, especially Chapter 3.
7 B. Lemesle, *Conflits et justice au moyen âge. Normes, loi et résolution des conflits en Anjou aux XIe et XIIe siècles* (Paris: Presses universitaires de France, 2008); G. Albertoni, 'Law and the peasant: rural society and justice in Carolingian Italy', *Early Medieval Europe*, 18:4 (2010), 417–45; cf. W. Davies, *Windows on Justice in Northern Iberia, 800–1000* (Abingdon: Routledge, 2016), especially ch. 8.

on the copying and excerpting of legal texts in the early Middle Ages has shown that they are much less the authoritative utterances of a single legislator but rather the outcome both of selection informed by practice and of complex processes of interaction between rulers and subjects, at times reflecting the experience of delegates in the field.[8] Recent research has also identified new types of source relevant for the study of local societies, such as the collections of explicatory material made by local priests. These illuminate the local adaptation of ideas which had been developed at, for example, the Carolingian court.[9] New approaches to the editing of charters, especially private charters, have paid attention to the identity of scribes, thereby revealing that not all charters were the product of institutional scriptoria; rather, some were written by local priests, in close touch with local communities, recording the small-scale transactions of peasant proprietors and tenants; work on the collections of Saint-Gall has been especially influential, but the practice is well evidenced in other collections.[10] In showing that the stories recorded in hagiographical texts – such as miracle collections – may also have originated outside monastic and episcopal centres, new studies have demonstrated the relevance of such texts for investigating local behaviour.[11] Recent scholarly developments,

---

8 D. Liebs, *Römische Jurisprudenz in Gallien (2. bis 8. Jahrhundert)* (Berlin: Duncker & Humblot, 2002); S. Patzold, 'Normen im Buch. Überlegungen zu Geltungsansprüchen so genannter "Kapitularien"', *Frühmittelalterliche Studien*, 41 (2007), 331–50; Ph. Depreux, 'Zur Nützlichkeit bzw. Nutzlosigkeit von Kunsttiteln für Kapitularien (am Beispiel der Nummern 134–135, 143–145 und 178 aus der Boretius-Edition)', *Deutsches Archiv für Erforschung des Mittelalters*, 70 (2014), 87–106.

9 M. Czock, 'Practices of property and the salvation of one's soul: priests as men in the middle in the Wissembourg material', and C. van Rhijn, 'Manuscripts for local priests and the Carolingian reforms', both in S. Patzold and C. van Rhijn (eds), *Men in the Middle. Local Priests in Early Medieval Europe* (Berlin: De Gruyter, 2016), pp. 11–31, 177–98.

10 R. McKitterick, *The Carolingians and the Written Word* (Cambridge: Cambridge University Press, 1989); *Chartae Latinae Antiquiores. Facsimile-Edition of the Latin Charters*, ed. P. Erhart, B. Zeller and K. Heidecker, 2nd ser., vol. 100–111 (Zürich: Urs Graf, 2006–18); W. Davies, 'Local priests and the writing of charters in northern Iberia in the tenth century', in J. Escalona and H. Sirantoine (eds), *Chartes et cartulaires comme instruments de pouvoir. Espagne et Occident chrétien (VIIIe–XIIe siècles)* (Toulouse: Université de Toulouse-Le Mirail, 2013), pp. 29–43.

11 C. West, 'Visions in a ninth-century village: an early medieval microhistory', *History Workshop Journal*, 81 (2016), 1–16; M. Innes and C. West, 'Saints and

then, in which the contributors to this volume have already been involved, make it viable to look into practice at peasant level. Contributors to this volume have received their formation in and from different national contexts, although in collaborating across different traditions we have aimed to move beyond national historiographies. However, it remains relevant to address the major themes that have for a century or more dominated discussions about rural society in the early Middle Ages. National historiographical traditions in western Europe have been formed by distinctive national approaches, reflecting the values and preoccupations of the intellectuals of modern states. As Tim Reuter wrote so powerfully in 1997,

> what we can know is determined not only by the flavour of the sources, but also by the traditional recipes used to cook them ... there is in this [French] tradition – as equally, of course, in the English, German, Italian and Spanish historiographical traditions, all of which tend to avoid eye contact with strangers – a specific way of looking at things.[12]

The attraction of the early Middle Ages for modern scholars has often been a consequence of the search for origins: interest in the local was subsidiary to interest in the growth of the state and the establishment of its institutions, in its multiple forms. In some countries belief in peasant freedom coloured the quality of the perceived emerging national character and its propensity to develop democratic institutions. In other countries the emphasis lay in top-down relationships, that is, in the vertical links between landowners and workers; notions about peasant freedom had less of an instrumental role. Both approaches surface in the several national historiographies and influence their varying perceptions of the local in different ways.

The German tradition is marked by a strong and sustained interest in political and constitutional history, despite its distinguished and widely influential nineteenth-century work on modes of social organisation. Rural society, however, has been (at least obliquely) a consistent interest because of long-standing debates on the nature and quality of freedom. German-language scholarship of the eighteenth and nineteenth centuries generally

---

demons in the Carolingian countryside', in T. Kohl, S. Patzold and B. Zeller (eds), *Kleine Welten. Ländliche Gesellschaften im Karolingerreich* (Ostfildern: Thorbecke, 2019), pp. 67–99.

12 T. Reuter, 'Debate: the "feudal revolution"', *Past and Present*, 155 (1997), 177–95, at 194–5.

assumed strong, stable local identities for ancient and early medieval Germanic villages. Drawing on Tacitus's *Germania*, rediscovered in the late fifteenth century, and also on English writing by Kemble, it was believed that the ancient 'Germans' had been organised in local and regional associations. In these *Markgenossenschaften*, landowning peasant-warriors of equal status held court and democratically decided all matters pertinent to their community. Noblemen – who are mentioned by Tacitus – were only different from other freemen in respect of their prestige.[13]

This view changed radically in the 1930s, when a new generation of scholars, including Theodor Mayer and Heinrich Dannenbauer, advanced the idea that the 'Germans' had always lived in lordship-based, aristocratic societies, in which a small number of noblemen ruled over dependent peasants.[14] Despite the obvious links to contemporary politics in Nazi Germany, this view of early medieval society – known as the 'Neue Verfassungsgeschichte' – continued to dominate German-language works (with the exception of Swiss and East German historiography) in the second half of the twentieth century. Central to this concept was the notion that there was no distinction between the public and the private sphere, with the king being little more than a powerful lord for his dependants on the fisc, with virtually no ties to other non-aristocrats. Since aristocratic lordship was assumed to have been strong, and the public

---

13 See, for example, G. L. von Maurer, *Geschichte der Markenverfassung in Deutschland* (Erlangen: Enke, 1856); G. Waitz, *Deutsche Verfassungsgeschichte*, vols 1–2 (Kiel: Schwers, 1844–47); W. Hechberger, *Adel im fränkisch-deutschen Mittelalter. Zur Anatomie eines Forschungsproblems* (Ostfildern: Thorbecke, 2005). Through Karl Marx, and especially Friedrich Engels, the *Markgenossenschaft* became an important part of Marxist history; see, for example, F. Engels, 'Die Mark', in K. Marx and F. Engels, *Werke*, vol. 19:4 (Berlin: Dietz, 1962), pp. 315–30. For Kemble, see below, p. 8.

14 H. Dannenbauer, 'Adel, Burg und Herrschaft bei den Germanen', *Historisches Jahrbuch*, 61 (1941), 1–50, and 'Hundertschaft, Centena und Huntari', *Historisches Jahrbuch*, 62/69 (1942/1949), 155–219; Th. Mayer, 'Die Entstehung des "modernen" Staates im Mittelalter und die freien Bauern', *Zeitschrift der Savigny-Stiftung für Rechtsgeschichte, Germanistische Abteilung*, 57 (1937), 210–88, and 'Adel und Bauern im Staat des deutschen Mittelalters', in Th. Mayer (ed.), *Adel und Bauern im deutschen Staat des Mittelalters* (Leipzig: Koehler & Amelang, 1943), pp. 1–21; W. Schlesinger, *Die Entstehung der Landesherrschaft. Untersuchung vorwiegend nach mitteldeutschen Quellen* (Dresden: Wissenschaftliche Buchgesellschaft, 1941); K. Bosl, *Frühformen der Gesellschaft im mittelalterlichen Europa. Ausgewählte Beiträge zu einer Strukturanalyse der mittelalterlichen Welt* (Munich/Vienna: Oldenbourg, 1964).

sphere virtually non-existent, local identities were irrelevant, absent or merely the consequence of a lord's domination. As a result, in German historiography rural life has been framed exclusively through the lens of *Grundherrschaft*, land-based lordship, emphasising the pattern of obligations due from dependants to powerful landlords, with a focus on vertical relationships rather than horizontal.[15] Nucleated settlements with communal institutions and a strong local identity (called 'real' villages by Karl Siegfried Bader) were seen as an eleventh-century innovation – a narrative that resembles that of contemporary studies in French by Léopold Génicot and Robert Fossier, albeit with a different derivation.[16]

Since the 1990s there has been a steady decline in the study of large estates;[17] a new interest in, and debates about, ritual and symbolic communication have sustained a focus on aristocratic practice;[18] early medieval local society has therefore until quite recently received little or no attention from historians. Thomas Kohl's work comparing settlements in three regions of Bavaria, however, in cutting across the structures of great estates, shows that a single settlement might be home to the dependants of different landlords, allowing residents sometimes to join together in community action, regardless of the interests of lords.[19]

15 L. Kuchenbuch, *Bäuerliche Gesellschaft und Klosterherrschaft im 9. Jahrhundert: Studien zur Sozialstruktur der Familia der Abtei Prüm* (Wiesbaden: Steiner, 1978); W. Rösener, *Grundherrschaft im Wandel. Untersuchungen zur Entwicklung geistlicher Grundherrschaften im südwestdeutschen Raum vom 9. bis 14. Jahrhundert* (Göttingen: Vandenhoeck & Ruprecht, 1991); H.-W. Goetz, 'Beobachtungen zur Grundherrschaftsentwicklung der Abtei St. Gallen vom 8. zum 10. Jahrhundert', in W. Rösener (ed.), *Strukturen der Grundherrschaft im frühen Mittelalter* (Göttingen: Vandenhoeck & Ruprecht, 1989), pp. 197-246.
16 K. S. Bader, *Studien zur Rechtsgeschichte des mittelalterlichen Dorfes*, 3 vols (Vienna/Cologne/Graz: Böhlau, 1957-73). See below, pp. 10-11, for Génicot and Fossier.
17 See L. Kuchenbuch's programmatic 'Abschied von der Grundherrschaft – Ein Prüfgang durch das ostfränkisch-deutsche Reich 950-1050', *Zeitschrift der Savigny-Stiftung für Rechtsgeschichte, germanistische Abteilung*, 121 (2004), 1-99. A useful study is S. Freudenberg, *Trado atque dono: Die frühmittelalterliche private Grundherrschaft in Ostfranken im Spiegel der Traditionsurkunden der Klöster Lorsch und Fulda (750 bis 900)* (Stuttgart: Franz Steiner, 2013).
18 See especially G. Althoff, *Spielregeln der Politik im Mittelalter. Kommunikation in Frieden und Fehde* (Darmstadt: Primus, 1997) and G. Althoff, *Die Macht der Rituale. Symbolik und Herrschaft im Mittelalter* (Darmstadt: Primus, 2003).
19 T. Kohl, *Lokale Gesellschaften. Formen der Gemeinschaft in Bayern vom 8. bis zum 10. Jahrhundert* (Ostfildern: Thorbecke, 2010).

While English historiography has been much preoccupied with the existence or otherwise of a precocious tenth-century state, and with the extent of royal control of the land surface in the preceding centuries, attitudes to the local have been heavily influenced by nineteenth-century notions of primitive communalism, as articulated by Karl Marx and Lewis Morgan especially.[20] John Mitchell Kemble (1807–57) had suggested that Saxon England was divided into *Marken*, inhabited by communities of free Saxons, associated in the cultivation of the soil and the exploitation of resources under a regime of common property. In his view, the *Mark* 'is the original basis upon which all Teutonic society rests'.[21] Rural societies of the early Middle Ages were thus societies of free equals, making rules and decisions for the whole community, rules by which an individual was bound. Paul Vinogradoff, in particular, focused on the detail of late medieval open field systems of the English midlands, arguing that property rights had been communal in earlier times and shares equal, although by the late Middle Ages the system was in transition with the increase of private property and individual rights.[22] Echoes of this presumed communalism persisted through the twentieth century, although alternative tracks were more concerned with whether or not free proprietorship was ever a norm and, latterly, with the extent, growth and varieties of lordship.[23] However, Susan Reynolds could still write in 1984 that 'all the collectivities which abound in the sources of the twelfth and thirteenth centuries drew their cohesion from ideas and values which were already deep-rooted' and that, in the context of England in the tenth and eleventh centuries, 'where villages existed, the community

20 For the central arguments on royal control, see E. John, *Land Tenure in Early England: A Discussion of Some Problems* (Leicester: Leicester University Press, 1960) and *Orbis Britanniae and Other Studies* (Leicester: Leicester University Press, 1966). For primitive communalism, K. Marx, *Pre-Capitalist Economic Formations*, trans. J. Cohen, ed. E. J. Hobsbawm (London: Lawrence and Wishart, 1964) – notes made 1857–58, published as part of *Grundrisse der Kritik der politischen Ökonomie* (Berlin: Dietz, 1953); L. H. Morgan, *Ancient Society* (New York: H. Holt, 1878).

21 J. M. Kemble, *The Saxons in England. A History of the English Commonwealth till the Period of the Norman Conquest*, 2 vols (London: Longmans, Green, 1849), vol. 1, p. 53.

22 P. Vinogradoff, *Villainage in England. Essays in English Mediaeval History* (Oxford: Clarendon Press, 1892), especially pp. 28, 209–10, 237, 397–409.

23 For 'extensive lordship', see especially R. Faith, *The English Peasantry and the Growth of Lordship* (London: Leicester University Press, 1997).

of habitation [i.e. the residential group] and perhaps of common rights gained some reinforcement from public duties'.[24] The notion is especially persistent in archaeological work, up to the moment of writing, late in the second decade of the twenty-first century: archaeologists writing in English characteristically use the word 'community' to describe the residents of a settlement – although this is no more than a convention, it brings assumptions about the relationships between residents and their practices; and some archaeologists argue that agrarian cooperation 'helped generate a distinct social identity'.[25] Despite this perspective, the amount and quality of data provided by English archaeologists across the last fifty years on the physical nature and economic base of rural settlements are exceptionally important and make their own significant contribution to the historiography; and this is a corpus of data that continues to grow.[26]

Recently an entirely different interpretation has come from Chris Wickham's sustained analyses, especially those published in the decade 1995–2005. In dealing with England before 800 he had to construct a hypothetical village society, which he called the settlement of 'Malling' – hypothetical because documentation was, in his view, completely inadequate to investigate the functioning of local groups. He surmised that inequality was 'structural' – because of inequalities between free and unfree and those between wealthier and poorer peasant households; that agrarian cooperation was limited, although residents ran livestock collectively; that free males attended a local assembly of a dozen or so villages; that the head of one of the wealthier households acted as leader of the residential group and his descendants prospered to become petty aristocrats in the long run; but that vertical relationships were unstable and

24 S. Reynolds, *Kingdoms and Communities in Western Europe, 900–1300* (Oxford: Oxford University Press, 1984), pp. 1, 115.
25 H. Hamerow, *Rural Settlements and Society in Anglo-Saxon England* (Oxford: Oxford University Press, 2012), pp. 99, 163, 166; summarising current views, G. Astill, 'Anglo-Saxon attitudes: how should post-AD 700 burials be interpreted?', in D. Sayer and H. Williams (eds), *Mortuary Practices and Social Identities in the Middle Ages: Essays in Burial Archaeology in Honour of Heinrich Härke* (Exeter: University of Exeter Press, 2009), pp. 222–35, at p. 227.
26 See Hamerow, *Rural Settlements*; R. Jones and M. Page, *Medieval Villages in an English Landscape. Beginnings and Ends* (Macclesfield: Windgather Press, 2006); also H. Hamerow, *Early Medieval Settlements. The Archaeology of Rural Communities in Northwest Europe, 400–900* (Oxford: Oxford University Press, 2002).

impermanent.[27] Although he did not use these specific words, solidarity and cohesion were very limited in this new model.

Both in France and far beyond, the influence of French regional studies has been enormous. Building on the legacy of Marc Bloch's *French Rural History*, Georges Duby's work on the Mâconnais, though focused on the eleventh and twelfth centuries, established the parameters of discussions that still continue and that have had major implications for the interpretation of the ninth and tenth centuries.[28] In northern France and southern (French-speaking) Belgium, the social cohesion of medieval rural settlements emerged as a research topic in the early 1980s. Historians such as Léopold Génicot and Robert Fossier focused on the well-developed rural communities of the later Middle Ages, communities that had a clearly defined geographical expression (a nucleated village) associated with a formalised social group that had a legal status and representatives (the village community).[29] According to Génicot and Fossier, these structures only emerged during the later Middle Ages, as a reaction to the development of local lordships and ecclesiastical parishes. They were imposed from above after the year 1000, providing a framework (*cadre, cellule*) within which rural societies were reorganised into cohesive and compact entities – hence the term *encellulement* for the process.

Rural society of the early Middle Ages was essentially defined in contrast to these later, fully developed communities: for the most part scholars emphasised the absence of the features that characterise late medieval

27 C. Wickham, *Framing the Early Middle Ages. Europe and the Mediterranean 400–800* (Oxford: Oxford University Press, 2005), pp. 428–34.

28 M. Bloch, *Les caractères originaux de l'histoire rurale française* (Oslo: H. Aschehoug, 1931); M. Bloch, 'The rise of dependent cultivation and seigniorial institutions', in J. H. Clapham and E. Power (eds), *The Cambridge Economic History of Europe. Vol. I, The Agrarian Life of the Middle Ages* (London: Cambridge University Press, 1941), pp. 224–75; G. Duby, *La société aux XIe et XIIe siècles dans la région mâconnaise* (Paris: SEVPEN, 1953).

29 L. Génicot, 'La communauté rurale en Belgique jusqu'au XIIIe siècle', in *Les structures du pouvoir dans les communautés rurales en Belgique et dans les pays limitrophes (12e–19e siècle)* (Brussels: Crédit communal, 1988), pp. 17–44; L. Génicot, *L'économie rurale Namuroise au bas moyen âge, 1199–1429*, 4 vols (Louvain: Bibliothèque de l'Université, 1943–95), especially vols 3 and 4; L. Génicot, *Rural Communities in the Medieval West* (Baltimore, MD: Johns Hopkins University Press, 1990); R. Fossier and J. Chapelot, *Le village et la maison au moyen âge* (Paris: Hachette littérature, 1980); R. Fossier, *Enfance de l'Europe. Xe–XIIe siècles. Aspects économiques et sociaux*, 2 vols (Paris: Presses universitaires de France, 1982).

QUESTIONS TO PURSUE

rural communities and the absence of cohesion; consequently, early medieval settlement structures were described as dispersed and temporary. Robert Fossier pushed this approach to an extreme, evoking primitive early medieval societies, living on the edge of extinction in precarious settlements. Since early medieval societies were thought to lack all the forms of local organisation that emerged in the later Middle Ages, scholars tended to focus on large estates (*grands domaines*), as a 'manorial' system, in order to describe the early medieval countryside. The kind of royal and monastic lordship associated with these estates was perceived as a transition between slavery and feudalism: on the one hand early medieval peasants were no longer slaves because they were tenants, who held land from the owners of large estates; on the other hand, they were not yet submitted to the type of local 'political' and 'judicial' lordship described as *seigneurie banale*, involving a capacity to punish and demand extra payments, which was to come later, but only to 'economic' lordship (*seigneurie foncière*), the power that any landowner exerts over his tenants.[30]

Since 2000, these perspectives have changed. First, the considerable increase in archaeological data since the 1990s shows that early medieval settlements were much more organised, durable and stable than assumed by previous scholars working from written evidence alone.[31] Some sort of social organisation may well have existed on a local level.[32] Moreover, historians have started to examine from different angles the written evidence that was produced about large estates, paying more attention to the diversity of local groups in terms of legal and social status and to the several actors – such as *iudices* and *villici* – who moved between local groups and the aristocracy. Thereby it begins to emerge that peasants were not a uniform mass of tenants, but a multiplicity of groups and strata over which aristocratic control could be great or negligible.[33]

30 See Duby, *La société*; G. Duby, *L'économie rurale et la vie des campagnes dans l'occident médiéval (France, Angleterre, Empire IX–XV siècles)*, 2 vols (Paris: Aubier, 1962).
31 E. Peytremann, *Archéologie de l'habitat rural dans le nord de la France du IVe au XIIe siècle*, 2 vols (Saint-Germain-en-Laye: AFAM, 2003).
32 R. Noël, 'A la recherche du village médiéval: hier et aujourd'hui', in J.-M. Yante and A.-M. Bultot-Verleysen (eds), *Autour du 'village'. Établissements humains, finages et communautés rurales entre Seine et Rhin (IVe–XIIIe siècles)* (Louvain-la-Neuve: Université catholique de Louvain, 2010), pp. 3–75.
33 See, pre-eminently, J.-P. Devroey, *Puissants et misérables. Système social et monde paysan dans l'Europe des Francs (VIe–IXe siècles)* (Brussels: Académie Royale de Belgique, 2006).

The distinctive political complexion of Italy in the early Middle Ages has attracted historians of Frankish, German and Byzantine empires, as well as scholars whose primary interest has been Italy itself. Moreover, the presence in Rome of many different historical and archaeological institutes, with their nationally based research programmes and approaches, has significantly influenced the way in which historians in Italy have understood and described medieval society. French regional studies had a major impact on Italian historiography, with Pierre Toubert's study of Latium in central Italy an influential landmark, as was Fossier's *Enfance de l'Europe*, translated already by 1987.[34] This engagement with the local was hardly new, for it followed decades of Italian concern with rural society in, for example, the debates of the early twentieth century on the nature and origins of the rural commune;[35] and the attention to agrarian landscapes, to lower-status freemen and to the socio-economic relationships of cities with the countryside that derived from the studies of Bloch.[36] Toubert and many others highlighted the process known as *incastellamento*, as lords were seen to have built castles on hilltops and to have attracted people into new settlements away from their traditional lowland residences in the tenth to twelfth centuries.[37] Important contributions to this and other aspects of rural history came from the distinguished body of archaeological work of the last two generations – especially from Riccardo Francovich and the Siena 'school' and more recently from Gian Pietro Brogiolo in Padua and Sauro Gelichi (in Pisa

---

34 P. Toubert, *Les structures du Latium médiéval: le Latium méridional et la Sabine du IXe siècle a la fin du XIIe siècle*, 2 vols (Rome: École française de Rome, 1973); Fossier: see above n. 29.

35 Cf. the historiographical chapter in C. Wickham, *Community and Clientele in Twelfth-century Tuscany. The Origins of the Rural Commune in the Plain of Lucca* (Oxford: Oxford University Press, 1998), pp. 185–241.

36 Bloch, *Les caractères*; C. Violante, *La società milanese nell'età precomunale* (Bari: Laterza, 1953); E. Conti, *La formazione della struttura agraria moderna nel contado fiorentino*, 3 vols (Rome: ISIME, 1965-66); B. Andreolli, V. Fumagalli and M. Montanari (eds), *Le campagne italiane prima e dopo il Mille. Una società in trasformazione* (Bologna: CLUEB, 1985). Cf. L. Provero, 'Forty years of rural history for the Italian Middle Ages', in I. Alfonso (ed.), *The Rural History of Medieval European Societies. Trends and Perspectives* (Turnhout: Brepols, 2007), pp. 141–72.

37 A. A. Settia, *Castelli e villaggi nell'Italia padana: popolamento, potere e sicurezza fra IX e XIII secolo* (Naples: Liguori, 1984).

and then Venice), as well as some seminal work from the British School at Rome.[38] Italian historians, such as Tabacco, Violante and Sergi, contrasted *incastellamento* with new kinds of territorial and political lordships (*signorie*).[39] Indeed, much of the historiographical interest of the past two generations has focused on the several and varied transformations of lordly estates (*sistema curtense*) into lordships with associated political powers (*signoria rurale*).[40] The process is not unlike the suggested French shift from *seigneurie foncière* to *seigneurie banale*, with distinctive Italian dimensions in the much greater use of leases and greater requirement of money rents.[41] But the heart of this change lies in the eleventh century and beyond, when post-Carolingian ruling structures declined and new local solidarities and collective actions were seen to emerge in rural communities.[42] For the preceding centuries major themes have

38 R. Francovich and M. Ginatempo (eds), *Castelli: storia e archeologia del potere nella Toscana medievale* (Florence: All'Insegna del Giglio, 2000); G. P. Brogiolo, D. E. Angelucci, A. Colecchia and F. Remondino (eds), *APSAT 1. Teoria e metodi della ricerca sui paesaggi di altura* (Florence: All'Insegna del Giglio, 2011); R. Hodges (ed.), *San Vincenzo al Volturno 1: The 1980–86 Excavations Part 1* and *San Vincenzo al Volturno 2: The 1980–86 Excavations Part 2* (London: The British School at Rome, 1993, 1995). Cf. the recent synthesis by A. Augenti, *Archeologia dell'Italia medievale* (Bari: Laterza, 2016), pp. 82–184.

39 C. Violante, 'La signoria "territoriale" come quadro delle strutture organizzative del contado nella Lombardia del secolo XII', in W. Paravicini and K. F. Werner (eds), *Histoire comparée de l'administration (IVe–XVIIIe siècles)* (Zürich/Munich: Artemis, 1980), pp. 333–44; G. Sergi, 'Lo sviluppo signorile e l'inquadramento feudale', in N. Tranfaglia and M. Firpo (eds), *La storia. I grandi problemi dal Medioevo all'età contemporanea*, vol. 2 (Turin: UTET, 1986), pp. 369–94; G. Tabacco, *Sperimentazioni del potere nell'alto medioevo* (Turin: Einaudi, 1993); G. Tabacco, *Dai re ai signori: forme di trasmissione del potere nel Medioevo* (Turin: Bollati Boringhieri, 2000). Cf. C. Wickham, 'La signoria rurale in Toscana', in G. Dilcher and C. Violante (eds), *Strutture e trasformazioni della signoria rurale nei secoli X–XIII* (Bologna: Il Mulino, 1996), pp. 343–409.

40 B. Andreolli and M. Montanari, *L'azienda curtense in Italia: proprietà della terra e lavoro contadino nel secoli VIII–XI* (Bologna: CLUEB, 1985); G. Sergi (ed.), *Curtis e signoria rurale: interferenze fra due strutture medievali* (Turin: Scriptorium, 1993).

41 Cf. S. Carocci, 'Signoria rurale e mutazione feudale: una discussione', *Storica*, 8 (1997), 49–91.

42 L. Provero, 'Le comunità rurali nel medioevo: qualche prospettiva', in R. Bordone, P. Guglielmotti, S. Lombardini and A. Torre (eds), *Lo spazio politico locale in età medievale, moderna e contemporanea. Ricerche italiane e riferimenti europei*

been the changing status of the peasantry and the growth of large, especially monastic, estates. Historians have tracked both a reduction in the numbers of free peasant proprietors and an increase in tenant obligations across the eighth and ninth centuries;[43] while the tenth century saw such a shift in estate management that labour service declined significantly and leasing was extended, although the terms of leases were much reduced.[44] Rural society has therefore been extensively discussed but has overwhelmingly been viewed in the context of the interests and demands of lords – although peasant resistance has been noted, especially in the ninth century.[45] Recently the idea that rural communities only existed after the eleventh century has been challenged, especially through the investigation of Carolingian *notitiae placiti* (records of judicial cases).[46] The questions raised for rural society therefore focus now not only on the nature and character of horizontal relationships between peasants, but also on the different kinds of rural community or 'collettività locali'.[47]

The past century of historical writing in Spain has been dominated by the fact of Muslim conquest in 711 and its perceived consequences.[48] In the long term Muslim states were replaced by Christian kingdoms, but scholars nowadays acknowledge that there was plenty of interaction

---

(Alessandria: Orso, 2007), pp. 335-40; L. Provero, 'Abitare e appartenere: percorsi dell'identità comunitaria nei villaggi piemontesi dei secoli XII-XIII', in P. Galetti (ed.), *Paesaggi, comunità, villaggi medievali*, 2 vols (Spoleto: Fondazione CISAM, 2012), vol. 1, pp. 309-25.

43 G. Tabacco, *I liberi del re nell'Italia carolingia e postcarolingia* (Spoleto: Fondazione CISAM, 1966).

44 V. Fumagalli, *Terra e società nell'Italia padana. I secoli IX e X* (Bologna: Università degli studi, Istituto di storia medievale e moderna e di paleografia e diplomatica, 1974); V. Fumagalli, 'Precarietà dell'economia contadina e affermazione della grande azienda fondiaria nell'Italia settentrionale dall'VIII all'XI secolo', *Rivista di storia dell'agricoltura*, 15 (1975), 3-27.

45 See Albertoni, 'Law and the peasant'.

46 T. Lazzari, 'Comunità rurali nell'alto medioevo: pratiche di descrizione e spie lessicali nella documentazione scritta', in Galetti (ed.), *Paesaggi, comunità, villaggi medievali*, vol. 2, pp. 405-23.

47 P. Galetti, 'Paesaggi, comunità, villaggi nell'Europa medievale', in Galetti (ed.), *Paesaggi, comunità, villaggi medievali*, vol. 1, pp. 1-22, at pp. 13-19.

48 Claudio Sánchez-Albornoz has been central to this historiography: for example, C. Sánchez-Albornoz, 'Las behetrías: la encomendación en Asturias, León y Castilla', *Anuario de Historia del Derecho Español*, 1 (1924), 158-336 (reprinted in his *Viejos y nuevos estudios sobre las instituciones medievales españolas*, 3 vols (Madrid: Espasa-Calpe, 1976-80), vol. 1, pp. 15-191).

QUESTIONS TO PURSUE

between north and south long before this happened. In considering internal social and political change within the Christian kingdoms, most Spanish historians of the later twentieth century accepted a basic principle of feudal development.[49] In short, they accepted the notion that the world came to be characterised by the domination of private lords over the persons, labour and surplus of a largely servile peasant population. Scholars charted the development at different rates within a tenth- to twelfth-century bracket, and pointed to differences between the Spanish experience and that of the classical Frankish model, although the influence of French scholarship has been considerable.[50] The 1970s and 1980s also saw the emergence, again under French influence, of detailed regional studies, with the systematic analysis of the establishment of great monastic estates – such as the hugely influential works of García de Cortázar on San Millán de la Cogolla and of Mínguez on Sahagún.[51] Younger scholars are now beginning to adopt quite different approaches, however, not only in opposition to the traditional historiography but by using new techniques of analysis and by refusing to take text at face value.[52]

In the mainstream of Spanish historiography, alongside the dominant notion of Muslim conquest lay the equally dominant notion that the central

49 The essential work is A. Barbero and M. Vigil, *La formación del feudalismo en la Península Ibérica* (Barcelona: Crítica, 1978).
50 See especially C. Estepa Díez, 'Formación y consolidación del feudalismo en Castilla y León', in *En torno al feudalismo hispánico. I congreso de estudios medievales* (Ávila: Fundación Sánchez-Albornoz, 1989), pp. 157–256; R. Pastor, 'Sur la genèse du féodalisme en Castille et dans le León, Xe–XIIe siècles. Point de départ pour une histoire comparative', in H. Atsma and A. Burguière (eds), *Marc Bloch aujourd'hui. Histoire comparée et sciences sociales* (Paris: École des hautes études en sciences sociales, 1990), pp. 259–70; J. M. Salrach, 'Les féodalités méridionales: des Alpes à la Galice', in E. Bournazel and J.-P. Poly (eds), *Les féodalités* (Paris: Presses universitaires de France, 1998), pp. 313–88.
51 J. A. García de Cortázar y Ruiz de Aguirre, *El dominio del monasterio de San Millán de la Cogolla (siglos X a XIII). Introducción a la historia rural de Castilla altomedieval* (Salamanca: Universidad de Salamanca, 1969); J. M. Mínguez Fernández, *El dominio del monasterio de Sahagún en el siglo X* (Salamanca: Universidad de Salamanca, 1980).
52 Á. Carvajal Castro, *Bajo la máscara del regnum. La monarquía asturleonesa en León (854–1037)* (Madrid: Consejo Superior de Investigaciones Científicas, 2017); R. Portass, *The Village World of Early Medieval Northern Spain. Local Community and the Land Market* (Woodbridge: Boydell Press, 2017); S. Barton and R. Portass (eds), *Beyond the Reconquista: Essays on the Politics, Society and Culture of Medieval Iberia, 800–1200* (Leiden: Brill, forthcoming).

plateau of the peninsula was depopulated in the eighth century; and that repopulation by 'free' settlers followed in the wake of the Christian reconquest of the later ninth, tenth and subsequent centuries, bringing a free pioneering spirit reminiscent of the colonisation of the American West.[53] It is these 'free settlers' who were long seen to have given rise to a free peasant society in the central Middle Ages, until the enterprise of peasant proprietors was undermined by the growth of lordly powers. The reality of depopulation, however, and therefore of repopulation and colonisation, is very questionable, and has been strongly challenged in recent years. Muslim invasion and campaigning may not after all have sent the Hispanic population of the *meseta* fleeing north into the mountains; most stayed where they were, continuing to farm; and in some parts their settlements were connected through networks of supra-local control.[54] Whether that population was especially and distinctively 'free' therefore remains an open question, although there is a significant literature on peasant resistance (for the most part focused on the eleventh century and later).[55] The nature, completeness and development of lordly powers, and thereby the strength or weakness of vertical relationships, remains a prominent interest.

For all the differences in national traditions, ideas clearly travelled beyond political borders, as evidenced by the direct contact between English and German writers of the early nineteenth century: we can see the widespread influence of German writing of the nineteenth century and of French regional studies in the twentieth. There are also some common themes and preoccupations: free proprietorship and personal freedom and their impact (or not) on emerging institutions; lordship and its many varieties, with a tendency to treat the local through the structures and relationships of great estates; the importance of archaeology, with its capacity to bring entirely new kinds of evidence, as well as its characteristic and

---

53 C. Sánchez-Albornoz, *Despoblación y repoblación del valle del Duero* (Buenos Aires: Instituto de Historia de España, 1966).

54 J. Escalona Monge, *Sociedad y territorio en la alta edad media castellana. La formación del alfoz de Lara* (Oxford: Archaeopress, 2002); I. Martín Viso, *Fragmentos del Leviatán. La articulación política del espacio zamorano en la alta edad media* (Zamora: Instituto de estudios zamoranos, 2002); S. Castellanos and I. Martín Viso, 'The local articulation of central power in the north of the Iberian peninsula (500–1000)', *Early Medieval Europe*, 13:1 (2005), 1–42.

55 R. Pastor, *Resistencias y luchas campesinas en la época del crecimiento y consolidación de la formación feudal. Castilla y León, siglos X–XIII* (Madrid: Siglo Veintiuno de España, 1980).

continuing expansion of the volume of data available; and, more recently, an awareness of the implications of settlement shift and of the significance of nucleation. We need to explore how far those common themes relate to what we now think happened on the ground and we also need to explore which of the issues identified in the several historiographies still have resonance. While primitive communalism and precocious democracy are nowadays unfashionable ideas, we do need to ask about equality, about the free/servile status of rural residents and about social and economic differentiation within the peasant population. Were there many free peasant proprietors or few; were there significant regional differences or just pockets of free peasants here and there? Where there was dependence, what local and regional differences were there and where were there changes in tenant obligations? Lordship may not provide the answer to all aspects of relationships but it cannot be ignored – were vertical relationships always unstable, as argued for early England, or were there regions of long-term stability? And how did different types of lordship impact on neighbours? Nor can we ignore the fact that agricultural cooperation did occur, but we need to explore whether whole groups or subsets of groups were involved in it and whether or not it was characteristic of particular kinds of settlement. Indeed, how much collective action is evident and was collective action community action?

While noting national historiographies and avoiding their constraints, we also want to avoid the master narratives that have largely dominated the study of rural societies until now. This is not to ignore some very fruitful recent work: Chris Wickham's *Framing the Early Middle Ages*, published in 2005, includes plenty of relevant comparative studies of rural societies, but they focus on the earlier period of pre-800;[56] Wickham's *Community and Clientele* develops an exceptionally coherent model of a shift from patronage networks to community structure across the long eleventh century, but is confined to the single region of Tuscany.[57] Thomas Kohl's *Lokale Gesellschaften*, which, in comparing settlements in three regions, cuts across the great patronage networks of aristocratic estates, is confined to Bavaria.[58] Attention to the land between great estates in the Ardennes shows that private landowners

---

56 Wickham, *Framing the Early Middle Ages*.
57 Wickham, *Community and Clientele in Twelfth-century Tuscany*.
58 Kohl, *Lokale Gesellschaften*.

did exist, but again this is confined to a small area.[59] We need to explore how far these regional models have a wider application and how far Wickham's European trends apply when we look at the detailed evidence of the ninth and tenth centuries: he argued that community structures in western Europe were on the whole weak before the eleventh century, especially in contrast to those of the eastern Mediterranean – there were no clear boundaries between different units; people shifted from one group to another; there is no sense that any one group cooperated for all necessary functions. Change came in the west at different rates from the late tenth century onwards, with the drawing of physical boundaries, shifts in burial practice and tighter structuring of community. Do we have evidence that community structures were stronger in some regions or that they sometimes developed before the eleventh century?

While we do consider that some background knowledge is essential for understanding the chapters that follow, those who are familiar with the broad trends of political development in western Europe in the early Middle Ages, and with the written source material that is available, may wish to skip the next chapter and go directly to Chapter 3.

---

59 J.-P. Devroey and N. Schroeder, 'Beyond royal estates and monasteries: landownership in the early medieval Ardennes', *Early Medieval Europe*, 20:1 (2012), 39–69.

2

Setting the scene

Physical geography

Physical context is one of the factors that makes for difference between local societies, and a brief look at the range of landforms in which ours were located is essential. Most of the regions considered in this book lie on the continental landmass of western Europe, a landmass that is cut by the mountain chains of the Alps and Pyrenees and is dominated by a handful of great river systems – the Rhine, running from its source in Switzerland to its delta mouth in the Netherlands; the Danube, running from its source in western Germany to its delta on the Black Sea; the Arno, crossing northern Tuscany; the Loire, rising in the Cévennes and flowing west through central France to the Atlantic; and the Duero, rising in north-central Spain, and crossing the *meseta* to its Atlantic outlet in Portugal (see figure 2.1). Physical and administrative geography, the heterogeneity of documentary ensembles and our various specialisations mean that the regions considered in detail vary significantly in size and nature. The Ardennes massif, for example, covers approximately 11,000 sq km. This is about the size of the contemporary region of Galicia alone, just a small portion of northern Iberia. Tuscany covers more than 22,000 sq km, while early medieval Bavaria was at times an ensemble of the order of 70,000 sq km. These differences in scale do not prevent meaningful comparison, but they need to be kept in mind.

The regional ensembles are also heterogeneous in their physical geography, both from one region to another and internally. Bavaria, for example, has several sub-regions: its southern part is dominated by the high mountains of the Alps; on their north, the Alpine foothills are characterised by hilly landscapes, large lakes and moorland. Farther north, the basin of the river Danube presents a less tormented relief; the

19

Figure 2.1 Western Europe, physical, with areas of expertise indicated

north-eastern part of the region, however, is covered by the Bavarian Forest, a mid-size mountain range with characteristic steep slopes and more amenable valley bottoms. The region surrounding the monastery of Saint-Gall is also typical of the Alpine foothills: the Rhine and its tributaries have generated a landscape marked by the contrast between steep hills and the calm surface of the several bodies of water that form Lake Constance.

Farther down the river, Alsace and the Upper and Middle Rhine consist of a low-lying rift valley surrounded by several upland massifs, such as the Black Forest, the Vosges, the Odenwald and the Pfälzer Wald. The Rhine valley offers very fertile arable land. The surrounding foothills are either strongly dissected or form a landscape of rolling hills; their fertility, influenced by relief and soil quality, varies significantly. The uplands are moderately high (1,424 m for the Vosges; 1,493 m for the Black Forest) or low (626 m for the Odenwald). With the exception of the lower valleys, their soils and relief are generally not suited to arable production.

Similar environmental conditions prevail in the Ardennes. This extensive upland massif lies between the Lorraine and Champagne plains to the south and the Meuse valley to the north. The central Ardennes have a gentle relief and stretches of relatively fertile soil; however, the outskirts of the massif have deeply carved valleys and abrupt rocky slopes. The highest areas are the plateaux on the north (plateau de Saint-Hubert, 589 m) and north-east of the region (High Fens, 694 m), whose strong slopes rise into extensive flat surfaces covered with peat bogs, moorland, grassland and woodland. To the south-west, Champagne is a sub-region of the Paris basin. This area is less than 300 m above sea level and has a succession of *cuestas*,[1] gentle undulating relief and shallow, chalky, soils. Farther west, the Île-de-France presents extensive flat surfaces covered in aeolian deposits (loess) that generate very fertile soils. The climate of both regions is oceanic.

South of the Alps, in Italy, Tuscany has a coastline on the Ligurian and the Tyrrhenian seas. The region is dominated by hilly landscapes, surrounded and intersected by high mountainous massifs, such as the Apennines (up to 2,912 m); plains are rare but very fertile. The coastal areas benefit from a mild climate, while the interior of the region is harsher and more rainy.

The northern part of the Iberian peninsula is mountainous: the Pyrenees and their foothills rise in the north-east; the Cantabrian mountains border the narrow strip of coastal land on the north – the Picos de Europa, part of this range, reach a height of 2,650 m; the León mountains rise in the north-west, separating Galicia from the Duero river basin. The *meseta*, a vast plateau 610 to 760 m in altitude, lies in the centre of the peninsula and the two main river basins are formed by the Duero in the west and centre and the Ebro in the east. This complex relief and the varying climatic influences from the Atlantic and the Mediterranean produce a high level of geographical diversity. Galicia, for example, with its high rainfall, tends to be wet and green; the *meseta* plain is dry, cold in winter and very hot in summer; while the lower reaches of the Ebro valley are semi-desert. The peninsula contains a large amount of arid land, except for that of Galicia and the north coast, but deep soils can be found in the river valleys that cut the arid or semi-arid plains.

---

[1] A hill or ridge with a steep slope on one side and a gentle slope on the other.

The island of Britain, north-west of the continental landmass, includes lowland areas in the south, east and midlands, from which most of the Anglo-Saxon evidence in this book originates. The combination of rolling hills and undulating lowland are a predominant landform, but landscapes vary greatly within this large area. The Fens, for example, in the east-central region, form an area of marshland, partly drained after the period considered here. Northern England offers a wider range of landscapes: while there are lowland areas of glacial deposits and very fertile soils, there are areas of moorland and the uplands are higher (up to 893 m in the Pennine chain). The climate of England is predominantly temperate, although colder in the north.

Political geography and political trends

Francia and Italy

The expansion of the influence of the Franks is a dominant political trend of the early Middle Ages. With origins in the north-east, the kingdom of the Franks (*regnum Francorum*) had rapidly extended to cover much of modern France in the sixth century and, at the same time, Frankish domination and influence grew east of the Rhine and in the Alpine regions.[2] From the 680s the 'mayors of the palace' became the rising power in the kingdom of the Franks, as the mayors Pippin II and his son Charles Martel (715–41), from the Pippinid/Carolingian family, gained control of Frankish territories and then extended beyond them.[3] Pippin III increased Frankish power in Hesse, Thuringia, Alsace and Alemannia (in modern Germany, Switzerland and Austria), which became integral parts of the Frankish kingdom, although retaining different degrees of regional identity (see figure 2.2).[4] Pippin became king in 751/754 and

---

2   I. N. Wood, *The Merovingian Kingdoms 450–751* (New York: Longman, 1994), esp. pp. 5–254; E. Ewig, *Die Merowinger und das Frankenreich* (Stuttgart: Kohlhammer, 6th edn, 2012), esp. pp. 9–112; G. Halsall, 'The barbarian invasions', in P. Fouracre (ed.), *The New Cambridge Medieval History, Volume I, c.500–c.700* (Cambridge: Cambridge University Press, 2005), pp. 35–55.

3   P. Fouracre, 'Frankish Gaul to 814', in R. McKitterick (ed.), *The New Cambridge Medieval History, Volume II, c.700–c.900* (Cambridge: Cambridge University Press, 1995), pp. 85–109; J. Jarnut, U. Nonn and M. Richter (eds), *Karl Martell in seiner Zeit* (Sigmaringen: Thorbecke, 1994).

4   H. K. Schulze, *Die Grafschaftsverfassung der Karolingerzeit in den Gebieten östlich des Rheins* (Berlin: Duncker & Humblot, 1973); U. Nonn, *Pagus und Comitatus in Niederlothringen. Untersuchungen zur politischen Raumgliederung*

SETTING THE SCENE

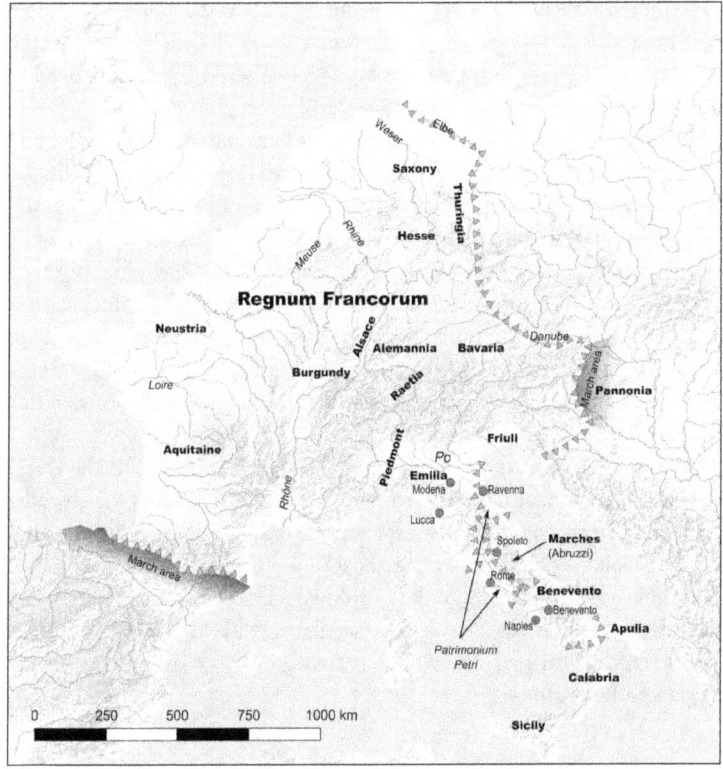

Figure 2.2   Later eighth-century Francia and Italy

his son, Charles (Charlemagne), led troops into Italy in 773/774, at the request of the pope.

There were several polities in Italy at this time. A Lombard kingdom stretched from Piedmont in the west to Friuli in the east (see figure 2.2).[5] There were two semi-autonomous Lombard duchies of Spoleto and Benevento in central and southern Italy. A Byzantine presence around Ravenna in the north-east of Italy matched another in the south, while

> *im frühen Mittelalter* (Bonn: Röhrscheid, 1983); M. Borgolte, *Geschichte der Grafschaften Alemanniens in fränkischer Zeit* (Sigmaringen: Thorbecke, 1984).
>
> 5   S. Gasparri, 'Il regno longobardo in Italia. Struttura e funzionamento di uno stato altomedievale', in S. Gasparri and P. Cammarosano (eds), *Langobardia* (Udine: Casamassima, 1990), pp. 237–305; S. Gasparri, *Italia longobarda. Il regno, i Franchi, il papato* (Rome/Bari: Laterza, 2012).

in central Italy there were possessions ruled by the pope (the duchy of Rome and the so-called *patrimonium Petri*).[6] Charlemagne routed the Lombard army, besieged Pavia and conquered the Lombard king, Desiderius.[7] Northern Italy became Carolingian, but it did not become Frankish, or at least not immediately. Charlemagne took the title of king of the Lombards, the Lombard kingdom surviving as a distinct polity. At the southern border, the authority of the duke of Lucca was increased, creating a substantial march of Tuscia (southern Tuscany and beyond). Secular and ecclesiastical office holders of the Lombard kingdom were gradually removed from their positions and the system of administration began to change as the office of count became the basis of organisation of the kingdom.[8] Meanwhile, the Lombard dukes of Benevento assumed the role of independent princes, while Byzantine control of southern Italy remained intact.

Carolingian expansion north of the Alps at first absorbed the duchy of Bavaria, in 788, and then proceeded to the destruction of the so-called Avar 'ring', a system of fortresses, and the conquest of the political centre of the Avars.[9] As a result, by 799 most of the former Roman province of Pannonia was integrated into the Carolingian march (border zone), where new Slavic polities also developed (see figure 2.2).[10] As is well known, a year later, on Christmas Day 800, Charlemagne was crowned emperor by Pope Leo III in Rome.

6   C. Wickham, *Early Medieval Italy: Central Power and Local Society, 400–1000* (London: Macmillan, 1981).
7   G. Tabacco, 'L'avvento dei Carolingi nel regno dei Longobardi', in Gasparri and Cammarosano (eds), *Langobardia*, pp. 375–403; P. Cammarosano, *Nobili e re. L'Italia politica nell'alto medioevo* (Rome/Bari: Laterza, 1998), pp. 74–96; M. Stoffella, 'In a periphery of the Empire: Tuscany between the Lombards and the Carolingians', in R. Große and M. Sot (eds), *Charlemagne. Les temps, les espaces, les hommes. Construction et déconstruction d'un règne* (Turnhout: Brepols, 2018), pp. 319–36.
8   On offices and office holders, see further below, Chapter 6. Cf. P. Delogu, 'Lombard and Carolingian Italy', in McKitterick (ed.), *The New Cambridge Medieval History, Volume II*, pp. 290–319.
9   H. Wolfram, *Salzburg, Bayern, Österreich. Die Conversio Bagoariorum et Carantanorum und die Quellen ihrer Zeit* (Vienna/Munich: Oldenbourg, 1995); Ch. Rohr (ed.), *Tassilo III. von Bayern* (Regensburg: Pustet, 2005).
10 W. Pohl, *Die Awaren. Ein Steppenvolk in Mitteleuropa 567–822 n. Chr.* (Munich: Beck, 3rd edn, 2015); F. Curta, *Southeastern Europe in the Middle Ages, 500–1250* (Cambridge: Cambridge University Press, 2006).

Carolingian rulers were associated with considerable governmental activity; consolidation of the empire was a central, though complicated, issue in which education and literacy were instrumental.[11] With Charlemagne's coronation the idea of a Christian empire, headed by a Christian emperor and united by a common Christian faith (and a common political as well as ecclesiastical structure), was promoted.[12] Already in 806, however, Charlemagne had envisaged the division of the vast *regnum Francorum* between his three sons, although at the end of his life, in 814, his son Louis was the only survivor and succeeded his father as ruler of the empire. Family conflict erupted in the rebellions of Louis's three older sons, particularly after the allocation of territory to Charles the Bald, Louis's six-year-old son by his second wife, Judith, in 829.[13] Following Louis's death, in 840, the Treaty of Verdun split the Frankish Empire into three major parts: in 843 Charles the Bald was allocated the west, Louis the German the territories east of the Rhine and Lothar a Middle Kingdom; in 855 this Middle Kingdom was split between Lothar's three sons, thereby creating Lothar II's realm of Lotharingia (*Lotharii regnum*) in the north, an Italian realm for Louis II and a realm for the minor, Charles, in Provence (see figure 2.3). Conflict over Lotharingia surfaced when Lothar II died without heir in 869 and this northern part of the Middle Kingdom was unstable in its political associations for the remainder of the ninth and tenth centuries.[14]

Meanwhile, Charles the Bald struggled with Viking raiders, whose attacks from the rivers Loire and Seine, and in Aquitaine, became frequent from 843.[15] From the island of Noirmoutier, at the mouth of the Loire,

---

11 R. McKitterick, *The Carolingians and the Written Word* (Cambridge: Cambridge University Press, 1989); R. Schieffer (ed.), *Schriftkultur und Reichsverwaltung unter den Karolingern* (Opladen: Springer, 1996).
12 M. de Jong, '"Ecclesia" and the early medieval polity', in S. Airlie, W. Pohl and H. Reimitz (eds), *Staat im frühen Mittelalter* (Vienna: Österreichische Akademie der Wissenschaften, 2006), pp. 113-26; M. de Jong, 'The state of the church: *ecclesia* and early medieval state formation', in W. Pohl and V. Wieser (eds), *Der frühmittelalterliche Staat – europäische Perspektiven* (Vienna: Österreichische Akademie der Wissenschaften, 2009), pp. 241-54.
13 M. de Jong, *The Penitential State. Authority and Atonement in the Age of Louis the Pious, 814-840* (Cambridge: Cambridge University Press, 2009).
14 J. Schneider, *Auf der Suche nach dem verlorenen Reich. Lotharingien im 9. und 10. Jahrhundert* (Cologne/Weimar/Vienna: Böhlau, 2010).
15 P. H. Sawyer, *Kings and Vikings: Scandinavia and Europe, AD 700-1100* (London: Methuen, 1982), pp. 78-99.

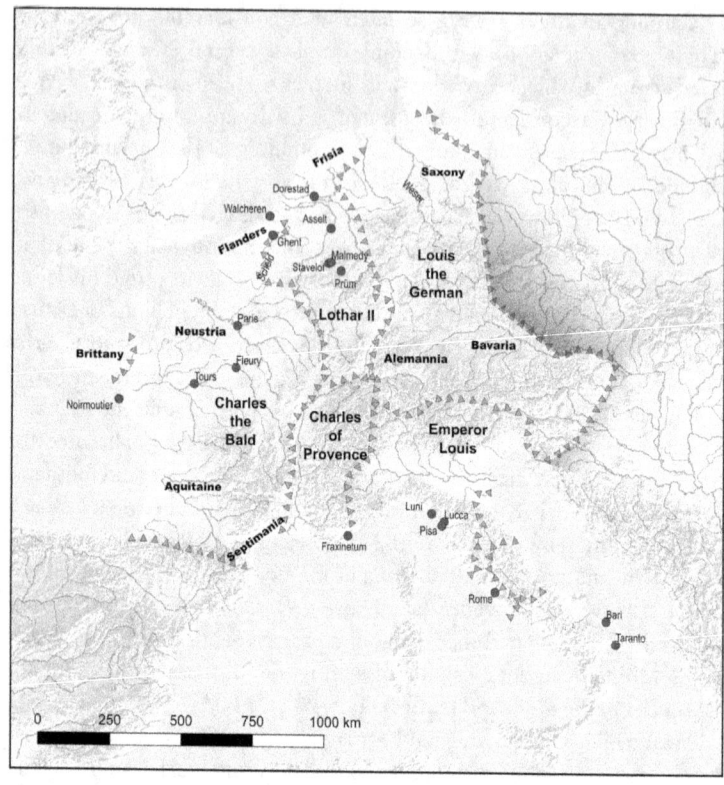

Figure 2.3   Mid-ninth-century Francia and Italy

Viking ships could penetrate far inland, so that Tours, Blois, Orléans, Poitiers and Fleury were repeatedly attacked in mid-century; they also turned north and west to Brittany from where Bretons periodically joined the Vikings raiding Neustria.[16] Other groups of Vikings travelled up the Seine to attack Paris.[17] Charles the Bald took defensive measures, which modified but did not stop the Viking threat, for in 885–86 Paris was again the object of attacks, this time defended by Odo, count of Paris; and, following a fresh wave of raids, Rouen and surrounding territory were ceded

16 J.-P. Brunterc'h, 'Le duché du Maine et la marche de Bretagne', in H. Atsma (ed.), *La Neustrie. Les pays au nord de la Loire de 650 à 850* (Sigmaringen: Thorbecke, 1989), vol. 1, pp. 29–127.
17 J. Nelson, 'The Frankish kingdoms, 814–898: the West', in McKitterick (ed.), *The New Cambridge Medieval History, Volume II*, pp. 110–41.

to the Viking leader Rollo, in 911, inaugurating what was to become the duchy of Normandy.[18] The north coast of the Middle Kingdom and inland territories accessible from the rivers Rhine, Meuse and Scheldt were also troubled by Viking raiders. The island of Walcheren and surrounding regions (in the modern Netherlands), at the mouth of the Scheldt, were given to Viking leaders in the mid-ninth century, but new Viking groups arrived and raids continued.[19] Using Ghent (in modern Belgium) as a base, from 879 the Viking Godfrid ranged widely in the Low Countries and northern Germany, attacking the important monasteries of Prüm and Stavelot-Malmedy. Peace terms were agreed with Godfrid in 882, but raids continued intermittently in this region throughout the tenth century;[20] so too did commercial activity, which developed in the context of an extensive Viking trading network, with new ports established at the mouth of the Rhine.[21]

The regions (*regna*) of Francia – such as Aquitaine, Septimania/ Gothia, Provence, Saxony, Alemannia and Bavaria – continued to function as sub-kingdoms for Carolingian princes, thereby sustaining an identity while the overarching kingdoms expanded or fragmented, a process that accelerated from 888 with the death of Emperor Charles the Fat. The ideology of royal authority nevertheless endured: an east and a west Frankish kingdom, and an increasingly fragmented Middle Kingdom, as well as an Italian kingdom, continued.[22] From 911 onwards, when the last

18 F. Neveux, 'La fondation de la Normandie et les Bretons (911–933)', in C. Laurent, B. Merdrignac and D. Pichot (eds), *Mondes de l'Ouest et villes du monde: Mélanges en l'honneur d'André Chédeville* (Rennes: Presses Universitaires de Rennes, 1998), pp. 297–309; P. Bauduin, *La première Normandie (Xe–XIe siècles): sur les frontières de la Haute Normandie, identité et construction d'une principauté* (Caen: Presses Universitaires de Caen, 2004).
19 M. Segschneider (ed.), *Ringwälle und verwandte Strukturen des ersten Jahrtausends n. Chr. an Nord- und Ostsee* (Neumünster: Wachholtz, 2009).
20 S. MacLean, *Kingship and Politics in the Late Ninth Century: Charles the Fat and the End of the Carolingian Empire* (Cambridge: Cambridge University Press, 2003), pp. 30–7.
21 C. Loveluck and D. Tys, 'Coastal societies, exchange and identity along the Channel and southern North Sea shores of Europe, AD 600–1000', *Journal of Maritime Archaeology*, 1 (2006), 140–69.
22 Nelson, 'The Frankish kingdoms', pp. 138–41; J. Nelson, 'Rulers and government', in T. Reuter (ed.), *The New Cambridge Medieval History, Volume III, c.900–c.1024* (Cambridge: Cambridge University Press, 1999), pp. 95–129. Cf. B. Schneidmüller, *Karolingische Tradition und frühes französisches Königtum*.

east Frankish line of Carolingians came to an end, Charles the Simple of west Francia called himself *rex Francorum*, firmly associating Frankish political identity with this western kingdom. Ultimately the dynasty was to change in the west too as Robert of Neustria, brother of Odo, defender of Paris, was chosen king in 922. Consequent conflicts were resolved by the coronation of the Robertian, Hugh Capet, in 987.[23]

In east Francia, influential magnates and important churchmen moulded the course of politics, while leading aristocrats struggled to establish a quasi-regal, ducal position in each of the east Frankish *regna*.[24] These pressures within the kingdom were intensified by Hungarian invasions, once Magyar groups had taken control of the Carpathian basin, as they did in the years on either side of 900.[25] They had raided east Francia intermittently in the later ninth century but became seriously disruptive during the first half of the tenth, attacking from Bavaria to Lotharingia. They were also disruptive in Italy, defeating Berengar in the north in 899, taking tribute from Tuscany and attacking Rome in 927 and 940; raids also penetrated to Burgundy and west Francia, reaching Reims in 937, and also exceptionally to Catalonia in north-east Iberia in 942.[26] The monastery of Fulda, an important source of early medieval evidence, was attacked in 915.[27] This was not a simple problem of hit-and-run raids: the Hungarians, of which (as with the Vikings) there were several groups,

---

Untersuchungen zur Herrschaftslegitimierung der westfränkisch-französischen Monarchie im 10. Jahrhundert (Wiesbaden: Steiner, 1979).

23   B. Schneidmüller, 'Karl III. ("der Einfältige"), 893/898–923/929', in J. Ehlers, H. Müller and B. Schneidmüller (eds), *Die französischen Könige des Mittelalters* (Munich: Beck, 2006), pp. 22–35; O. Guillot and R. Favreau (eds), *Pays de Loire et Aquitaine de Robert le Fort aux premiers Capétiens* (Poitiers: Société des antiquaires de l'Ouest, 1997).

24   On the danger of 'falling apart into constituent *regna*', E. Müller-Mertens, 'The Ottonians as kings and emperors', in Reuter (ed.), *The New Cambridge Medieval History, Volume III*, pp. 233–66, at p. 239.

25   M. G. Kellner, *Die Ungarneinfälle im Bild der Quellen bis 1150: von der 'Gens detestanda' zur 'Gens ad fidem Christi conversa'* (Munich: Ungarisches Institut, 1997); V. Spinei, *The Great Migrations in the East and South East of Europe from the Ninth to the Thirteenth Century*, trans. D. Bădulescu (Cluj-Napoca: Romanian Cultural Institute/Museum of Brăila Istros, 2003), pp. 13–91; Curta, *Southeastern Europe in the Middle Ages*, chs 3, 4.

26   K. Bakay, 'Hungary', in Reuter (ed.), *The New Cambridge Medieval History, Volume III*, pp. 536–52; T. Reuter, *Germany in the Early Middle Ages, c.800–1056* (London: Longman, 1991), pp. 127–31, 142–4.

27   For Fulda, see further below, p. 43.

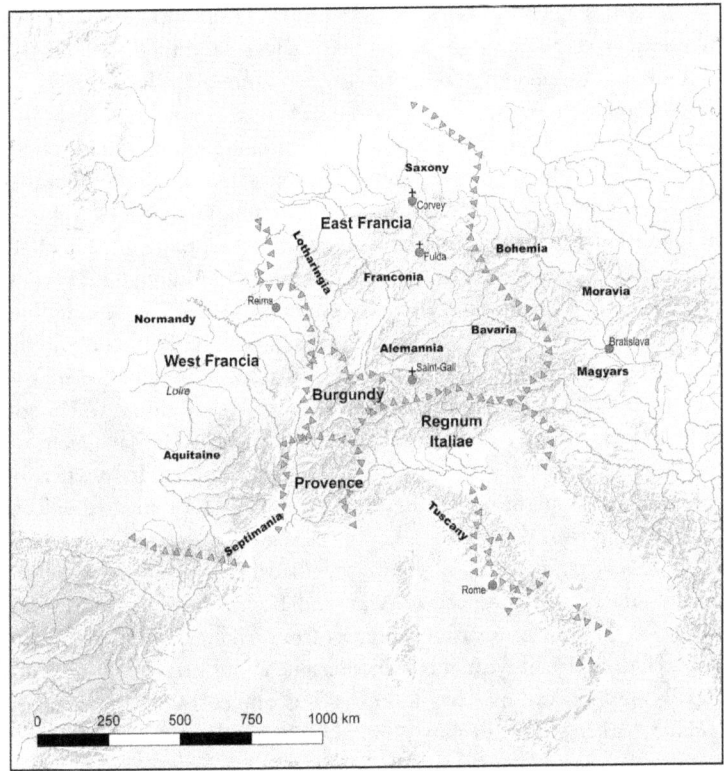

Figure 2.4 Early tenth-century Francia and Italy

were often present within the kingdoms of east Francia and of Italy; there were complex and shifting patterns of alliance with kings and dukes and more and less reliable negotiations over the payment of tribute.

Defence in east Francia was organised by the leaders of the *regna*: Saxons and Bavarians concluded separate peace treaties.[28] The unity of the east Frankish realm was stabilised by the Saxon duke Henry, initially elected by Frankish and Saxon magnates only, but later acknowledged by the dukes of Alemannia, Bavaria and Lotharingia, Lotharingia now finally within the orbit of the east Frankish kings, although west Frankish claims continued (see figure 2.4).

---

28 H. Wolfram, 'Bavaria in the tenth and early eleventh centuries', in Reuter (ed.), *The New Cambridge Medieval History, Volume III*, pp. 293–309, at p. 295.

Under Henry I and his successors Otto I, Otto II and Otto III, kings exercised direct royal rule in Franconia, the lands around the confluence of the rivers Rhine and Main, and also in Saxony, which bordered the pagan Slavs of the Elbe.[29] The last major rebellion of east Frankish noblemen collapsed in 955, in view of a decisive battle against a Hungarian army on the Lechfeld near Augsburg.[30] In the same year Otto I defeated the Slavs, paving the way for Christian missionary work among them, supported by new bishoprics in the eastern marches. Expeditions to Italy dominated Otto's final years, until his death in 973. Although his successor, Otto II, had at times to attend to relationships within the kingdom, his horizons were wider: he was married to a niece of the Byzantine emperor and campaigned against the Danes to the north and Bohemia to the east as well as in northern France and in Italy (see figure 2.5). His son Otto III (983–1002), a minor until 995, tried to deal with Slav revolts on the eastern border and also to establish Ottonian control of Italy, where he was crowned emperor in 996. Returning to Italy in 1001, he died of fever the following year.[31]

In Italy, existing political complexity had been further complicated by the attacks and presence of Arab and Berber Muslims from north Africa, as well as by occasional attacks from Vikings.[32] Already in 776 Pope Hadrian I had written to Charlemagne about the activity of Arabs and Byzantine slave merchants on the Tuscan coasts, where Lombard families had been forced into slavery.[33] The ninth and tenth centuries

29 G. Althoff, 'Saxony and the Elbe Slavs', in Reuter (ed.), *The New Cambridge Medieval History, Volume III*, pp. 267–92; H. Keller and G. Althoff, *Die Zeit der späten Karolinger und Ottonen: Krisen und Konsolidierungen, 888–1024* (Stuttgart: Klett-Cotta, 2008); Müller-Mertens, 'The Ottonians', p. 249.

30 L. Weinrich, 'Tradition und Individualität in den Quellen zur Lechfeldschlacht', *Deutsches Archiv für Erforschung des Mittelalters*, 27 (1971), 291–313; K. Leyser, 'The battle at the Lech, 955. A study in tenth-century warfare', in K. Leyser, *Medieval Germany and its Neighbours 900–1250* (London: Hambledon, 1982), pp. 43–67.

31 H. Seibert, 'Eines großen Vaters glückloser Sohn? Die neue Politik Ottos II.', in B. Schneidmüller, S. Weinfurter (eds), *Ottonische Neuanfänge. Symposium zur Ausstellung "Otto der Große, Magdeburg und Europa"* (Mainz: von Zabern, 2001), pp. 293–320; G. Althoff, *Otto III*. (Darmstadt: Wissenschaftliche Buchgesellschaft, 1997).

32 B. M. Kreutz, *Before the Normans: Southern Italy in the Ninth and Tenth Centuries* (Philadelphia, PA: University of Pennsylvania Press, 1992), pp. 18–35.

33 Gasparri, *Italia longobarda*, pp. 132–3; *Codex Carolinus*, in MGH Epp. 3, pp. 469–657, at pp. 584–5.

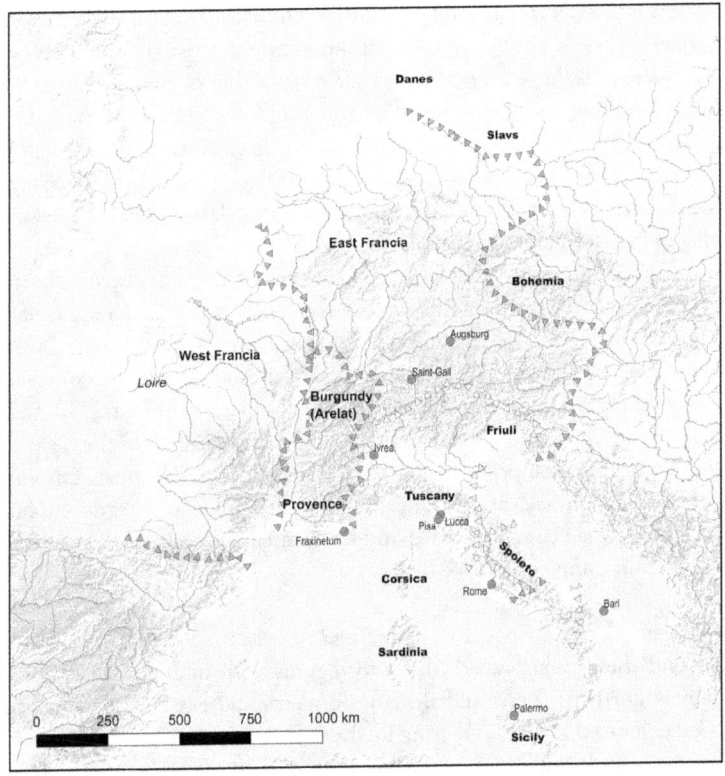

Figure 2.5   Late tenth-century Francia and Italy

saw repeated raids in northern, central and southern Italy, and there were also frequent raids on the south coast of France from the Arab fortified base at Fraxinetum, near Saint-Tropez, and some penetration into Alpine regions.[34] In Italy Lucca controlled the Tyrrhenian coast through a fleet harboured in Pisa and Luni. Lucca was the base of the Bavarian count Boniface I, whose son was appointed to manage the defence of Corsica against the Arabs in 825.[35] Rome was also hit several times in the 840s,

34 *Annales Regni Francorum,* s.a. 806, MGH SS rer. Germ., [6], p. 122.
35 See *Edictum de expeditione Corsicana*, in MGH Capit. 1, p. 325. For a new edition, see S. Esders, 'Die "Capitula de expeditione Corsicana" Lothars I. vom Februar 825. Überlieferung, historischer Kontext, Textrekonstruktion und Rechtsinhalt', *Quellen und Forschungen aus italienischen Archiven und Bibliotheken*, 98:1 (2018), pp. 91–144. See also *Annales Regni Francorum,* s.a. 828, MGH SS rer. Germ. [6], p. 176 for Boniface.

but it was the Lombard and Byzantine regions of the south that were most frequently assaulted.[36] A number of independent Muslim emirates were established on the southern mainland, such as that of Bari, captured by Louis II in 871, and Taranto, which ended in 880. The establishment of these small-scale emirates was essentially a ninth-century phenomenon and by 915 they had ended on the mainland. Not so the island of Sicily, which became an independent emirate from 965, lasting until the beginning of the Norman conquest in 1061.[37]

In the kingdom of Italy farther north there was progressive political fragmentation after 888.[38] Pressure on Adelaide, widow of King Lothar, who had died in 950, led members of the Italian aristocracy to invite Otto I to intervene in Italy and by 952 he had married Adelaide. In the course of a second Italian campaign he was crowned emperor in Rome, in 962. Thereafter, Otto spent the greater part of his remaining life in the *regnum Italiae*, in the attempt to integrate Italy fully into the Ottonian Empire. Both of his namesake successors continued this policy of integration, but with limited success, Otto II dying on campaign in southern Italy and Otto III on campaign to take Rome.

England

Beyond the Frankish world lay two regions with different trajectories, namely northern Iberia and Britain. Southern and eastern England had been colonised by migrants from the Low Countries, Denmark, northern Germany and southern Scandinavia in the fifth and sixth centuries. The number of settlers and their manner of integration with the existing population remain a matter of debate: even the highest estimates of numbers do not go beyond 100,000, a relatively small addition to the total population; and yet their long-lasting impact was to change the language of everyday speech from Brittonic (and late Latin) to English.[39] There was clearly a high degree of political fragmentation in these early post-Roman centuries. By 650, after at least two generations of Christian mission to the English, from Ireland and from Rome, more than ten very small kingdoms

---

36 Kreutz, *Before the Normans*, pp. 18–19, 48–54.
37 M. Amari, *Storia dei Musulmani di Sicilia*, 3 vols (Florence: Le Monnier, 1854).
38 See Cammarosano, *Nobili e re*.
39 H. Härke, '"Warrior graves"? The background of the Anglo-Saxon weapon burial rite', *Past and Present*, 126 (1990), 22–43; J. Hines, 'The becoming of the English: identity, material culture and language in early Anglo-Saxon England', *Anglo-Saxon Studies in Archaeology and History*, 7 (1994), 49–59.

are evidenced, in some cases replacing earlier British kingdoms;[40] hence, the English kingdoms of Kent in the south-east, of the East Angles in the east, of the West Saxons in the southern midlands and south, of Deira and Bernicia in the north.[41] In the succeeding hundred years the more forceful leaders conquered the lesser kingdoms to the extent that Northumbria became predominant in the north of the country, Mercia in the midlands and Wessex in the south, East Anglia retaining a distinctive political identity; the Mercian king, Offa (757–96), was ambitious to rule over all the English and was involved in continuing, if sometimes stormy, diplomatic relations with Charlemagne (see figure 2.6).[42]

Political trends of the eighth century, however, were interrupted from at least 793 by Viking attacks. These were initially coastal raids but the first record of Vikings spending the winter in England occurs in the Anglo-Saxon Chronicle for the year 851. The later ninth century saw permanent Viking settlements in the east, midlands and north of the country; the establishment of the Scandinavian kingdom of York, for a period ruled by the dynasty that also ruled Dublin in Ireland; and sustained Danish campaigns in the kingdom of Wessex in the south, where King Alfred of Wessex mounted a heroic defence, according to the vision of England's national story.[43] England was formally divided between English and Danes in 878, following peace made between Alfred and the Danish leader Guthrum, thereby creating the Danelaw and making Wessex in effect the sole surviving English kingdom.[44] The Viking impact brought traders and

40   The British kingdom of Dumnonia, in the south-west, continued in existence until the late ninth century; S. Pearce, *The Kingdom of Dumnonia. Studies in History and Tradition in South-Western Britain AD 350–1150* (Padstow: Lodenek Press, 1978).

41   S. Bassett (ed.), *The Origins of Anglo-Saxon Kingdoms* (London: Leicester University Press, 1989); K. R. Dark, *Civitas to Kingdom. British Political Continuity 300–800* (London: Leicester University Press, 1994).

42   P. Wormald, 'The age of Offa and Alcuin', in J. Campbell (ed.), *The Anglo-Saxons* (Oxford: Phaidon Press, 1982), pp. 101–28; B. Yorke, *Kings and Kingdoms of Early Anglo-Saxon England* (London: B. A. Seaby, 1990); M. P. Brown and C. A. Farr (eds), *Mercia: An Anglo-Saxon Kingdom in Europe* (London: Leicester University Press, 2001).

43   A. P. Smyth, *Scandinavian Kings in the British Isles, 850–880* (Oxford: Oxford University Press, 1977); T. Reuter (ed.), *Alfred the Great. Papers from the Eleventh-Centenary Conferences* (Aldershot: Ashgate, 2003). See below, pp. 112–13.

44   *Alfred the Great: Asser's Life of King Alfred and Other Contemporary Sources*, ed. and trans. S. Keynes and M. Lapidge (Harmondsworth: Penguin, 1983).

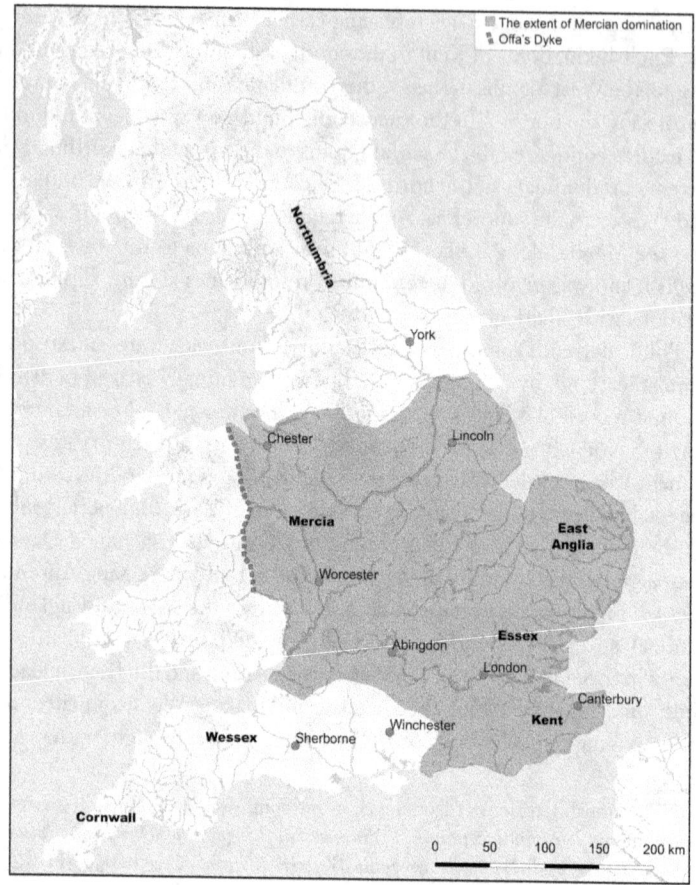

Figure 2.6   England c. 800

settlers too; while debates over the number of settlers have raged for decades, there can be no doubt about the strength of Viking cultural influence in northern England and its impact on the English language.[45]

---

[45] P. H. Sawyer, 'The density of the Danish settlement in England', *University of Birmingham Historical Journal*, 6 (1957–8), 1–17; K. Cameron, 'Scandinavian settlement in the territory of the five boroughs: the place-name evidence', in K. Cameron (ed.), *Place-Name Evidence for the Anglo-Saxon Invasions and Scandinavian Settlements* (Nottingham: English Place-Name Society, 1975), pp. 115–71; D. M. Hadley and J. D. Richards (eds), *Cultures in Contact: Scandinavian Settlement in England in the Ninth and Tenth Centuries* (Turnhout: Brepols, 2000).

SETTING THE SCENE

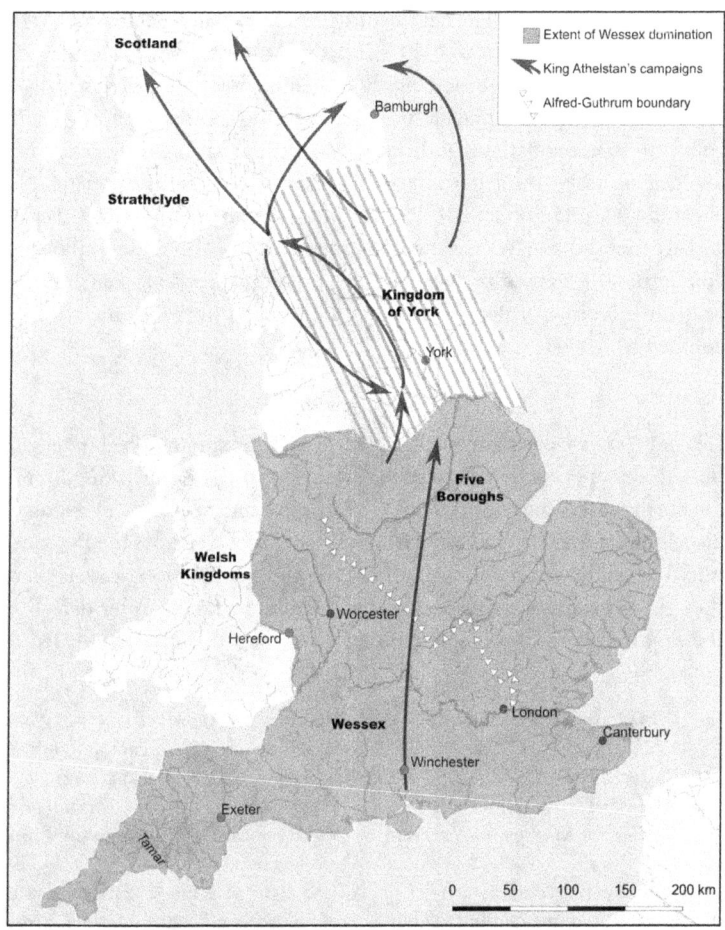

Figure 2.7   England in the reign of Athelstan

It was in the tenth century that the kingdom of England came into being: kings of Wessex campaigned against Scandinavian rulers in the midlands and north and sought to extend their influence over British and Gaelic rulers in Wales and Scotland, intermittently achieving the submission of some of them (see figure 2.7). After 954 the Scandinavian kingdom of York was absorbed by the English kingdom to the south. By 973 England had assumed a political shape comparable to that of the present, although more Scandinavian raids were to come at the end of the century and Danish and Norwegian rulers pursued an interest in the English

35

kingship until the later eleventh century, with England joining a Danish Empire under Cnut in 1016.[46] England also came into being in the tenth century in the sense that the kings and their advisors were active legislators, establishing an administrative system, taking control of minting coin, collecting tax, regularising judicial court sessions and making provision for local security; the latter aimed to make local groups responsible, in effect, for a kind of policing.[47] Tenth- and eleventh-century kings, clerics and aristocrats had a wide network of relationships with their continental counterparts – networks that were to be vastly extended from 1066 as England's Norman rulers established a structural link with the western continent.[48]

Iberia

Like much of western Europe, Iberia also saw migration in the immediate post-Roman period, resulting in the establishment of a Sueve kingdom in the north-west of the peninsula and – by the late fifth century – a Visigothic kingdom dominating the rest of it; the latter stretched across the Pyrenees into Aquitaine, with a political centre at Toulouse. In neither case is there thought to have been significant large-scale immigration. After defeat by the Frankish king Clovis at Vouillé in 507, Visigothic rulers retreated to

---

46 P. Stafford, *Unification and Conquest: A Political and Social History of England in the Tenth and Eleventh Centuries* (London: Edward Arnold, 1989); S. Baxter, *The Earls of Mercia. Lordship and Power in Late Anglo-Saxon England* (Oxford: Oxford University Press, 2007); G. Molyneaux, *The Formation of the English Kingdom in the Tenth Century* (Oxford: Oxford University Press, 2015).

47 Athelstan's second, Grately, Code of the 930s was much concerned with theft. In the undated but slightly later 'Hundred Ordinance', detailed provision was made for local people to join groups known as tithings which were charged with chasing and apprehending thieves; see Molyneaux, *Formation*, p. 144, and P. Wormald, *The Making of English Law. King Alfred to the Twelfth Century, Volume I: Legislation and its Limits* (Oxford: Blackwell, 1999), pp. 378–9 but *passim*; P. Wormald, *Papers Preparatory to the Making of English Law: King Alfred to the Twelfth Century, Volume II: From God's Law to Common Law*, ed. S. Baxter and J. Hudson (London: University of London, 2014), http://www.earlyenglishlaws.ac.uk/reference/wormald/ (accessed 3 September 2019).

48 Stafford, *Unification and Conquest*, pp. 101–28; M. Chibnall, *The Debate on the Norman Conquest* (Manchester: Manchester University Press, 1999); D. Crouch, *The Normans: The History of a Dynasty* (London: Hambledon, 2002).

Iberia, except for the narrow strip of Septimania on the southern French coast; in 585 the Sueve kingdom was absorbed by this Visigothic state, the records of which suggest a central kingship associated with considerable legislative activity and a strong episcopate.[49] Although the idea of Visigothic heritage remained strong throughout the early Middle Ages, the political reality of the Visigothic kingdom was destroyed in 711 by the invasion of Arabs and Berbers from north Africa, who campaigned across the peninsula and across the Pyrenees into southern Francia, from which they retreated after Charles Martel's victory of 732. Thereafter a Muslim emirate was established, encompassing the whole of the centre and south of Iberia until 929, when it was replaced by a Muslim caliphate, fragmenting into several *taifa* states from 1029.[50] While a Hispanic population remained in southern Iberia, al-Andalus, actively continuing their Christian culture at least until the tenth century, the new rulers, with their base in Córdoba, and new settlers, introduced the Arabic language and Muslim religion and initiated a long history of cultural contact with the eastern Mediterranean.[51]

In the north two Christian kingdoms were established from the fallout of the Visigothic state, although some powerful regional aristocracies added complexity to political trends (see figure 2.8).[52] A small kingdom of Pamplona or Navarre had its base in the mountains which are the western extension of the Pyrenees, although tenth-century kings had interests in the Ebro valley to the south and in effect incorporated the region of Aragón to the east.[53] We know relatively little of it until the tenth century,

49 R. Collins, *Visigothic Spain, 409–711* (Oxford: Blackwell, 2004); M. I. Loring, D. Pérez and P. Fuentes, *La Hispania tardorromana y visigoda, siglos V–VIII* (Madrid: Síntesis, 2007).

50 H. Kennedy, *Muslim Spain and Portugal: A Political History of al-Andalus* (London: Routledge, 1996); E. Manzano Moreno, *Conquistadores, emires y califas, Los omeyas y la formación de al-Andalus* (Barcelona: Crítica, 2006); for Berbers, P. Chalmeta Gendrón, *Invasión e islamización: la sumisión de Hispania y la formación de al-Andalus* (Madrid: Mapfre, 1994). See further below, pp. 110–11, 184–5.

51 A. Christys, *Christians in Al-Andalus (711–1000)* (Richmond: Curzon Press, 2002).

52 For broad general surveys, see R. Collins, 'The Spanish kingdoms', in Reuter (ed.), *The New Cambridge Medieval History, Volume III*, pp. 670–91; A. Isla Frez, *La alta edad media. Siglos VIII –XI* (Madrid: Síntesis, 2002).

53 See J. J. Larrea, *La Navarre du IVe au XIIe siècle* (Paris/Brussels: De Boeck Supérieur, 1998).

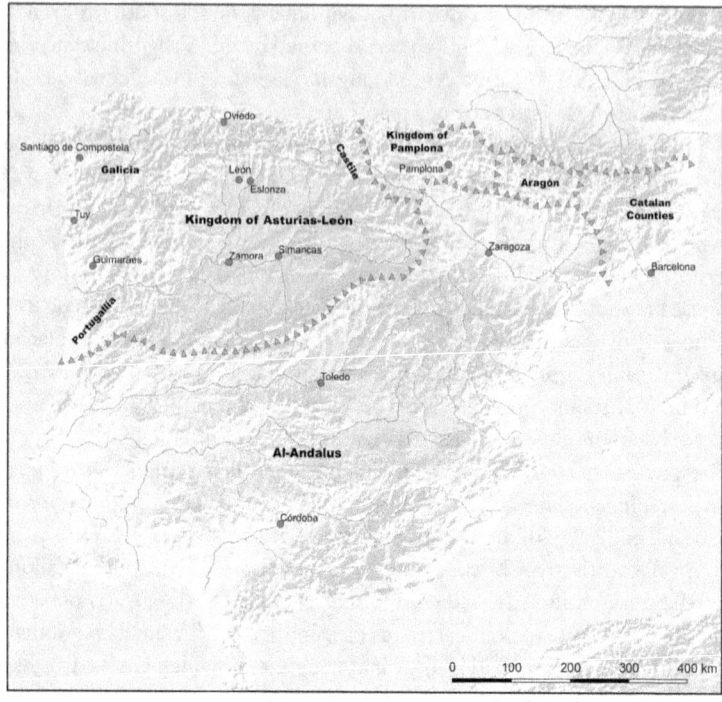

Figure 2.8   Iberia c. 950

although its kings had acquired considerable power by the end of the century and were to become very significant in the eleventh. We know much more about the kingdom of Asturias-León. Its origins lay in the very far north, with a royal base at Oviedo north of the Cantabrian mountains for most of the ninth century; the royal base moved south to the old Roman city of León round about 910. Rulership had a practical military dimension but government was extremely limited and administrative institutions did not begin to develop significantly until the eleventh century. Portugal did not acquire an independent political identity before the later eleventh century.

In the far north-east, in the Pyrenees and their southern and western hinterland, lay Catalonia, subject to Frankish expeditions in the late eighth century and established as a march of the Carolingian Empire in the early ninth. Initially comprising seven counties, more were added before the more prominent counts began to absorb the lesser counties; these counts continued to look to the north-east, towards the west Frankish kingdom, for over a century. In the later tenth century one count, the count of Barcelona, emerged predominant and the Frankish orientation began to weaken.[54] The ninth and tenth centuries have traditionally been associated with the beginning of the so-called *Reconquista*, by which kings of northern Spain began to recover control of territory from the Muslim state in the south. While the notion of ever-expanding reconquest is very questionable, it is certainly the case that kings of León were involved in campaigning in the south of al-Andalus in the early tenth century and in central Spain in mid-century; kings of Pamplona were campaigning in the Ebro valley in the early tenth century, probably taking Najera and Viguera in 923. Meanwhile Muslim expeditions continued to penetrate into the far north; Arab leaders raided intermittently throughout the tenth century but were especially effective in the 980s and 990s, besieging, sacking and capturing strong points, and in some cases establishing garrisons, as at Zamora in 999. Rural churches in the north were destroyed and prisoners were led to Córdoba in chains after the 986 Arab attack on Simancas.[55] This worked in both directions: the number of references to Moors transferred along with landed property in the north might suggest that more or as many captives were taken from the south as from the north.[56]

Iberia was also affected by Viking activity. There were two main phases of Viking attack, in the mid-ninth century and mid-tenth century, although disruption continued into the eleventh. Assaults came from the sea and affected coastal areas of Galicia and Portugal, rather than the inland plateau. Records focus on attacks on ecclesiastical centres, as they do in northern Europe. We hear of the abandonment of the see of Tuy in the 960s and of the death of Bishop Sisnando of Santiago at the hands of the Vikings in 968, as also of ecclesiastical fortification – Sisnando is held to have built the walls of Santiago, while the monastic community of Portuguese Guimarães had a *castellum* constructed against the

54 The classic study of Catalonia in this period is that of P. Bonnassie, *La Catalogne du milieu du Xe à la fin du XIe siècle: croissance et mutations d'une société*, 2 vols (Toulouse: Association des Publications de l'Université de Toulouse-Le Mirail, 1975–76); more recently, see J. Jarrett, *Rulers and Ruled in Frontier Catalonia, 880–1010: Pathways of Power* (Woodbridge: Boydell and Brewer, 2010); and, emphasising Frankish connections, J. M. Salrach, *Justícia i poder a Catalunya abans de l'any mil* (Vic: Eumo, 2013).
55 Li 17 (904); cf. Liii 706 (1012).
56 Cf. Li 109 (936), Li 220 (950); *Cartulario del Infantado de Covarrubias*, ed. L. Serrano (Valladolid: Cuesta, 1907), no. 7 (978).

'Gentiles'.[57] Occasionally there are references to captives taken from local communities by the Vikings, which serve to remind us of the extensive slave-trading of both Viking and Arab traders.[58]

Any overview of the political geography and political trends of western Europe in the early Middle Ages will strike the reader as extremely complex and suggest extreme political instability at the highest levels. Kingdoms and empires were established and destroyed, expanded and divided, and in some regions the pattern of political change was significantly complicated by the long-term impact of invaders from outside, as in Italy, England and Iberia. However, despite the instability, there were periods and places of exceptional governmental activity, as in Carolingian Francia and in tenth-century England and Germany. It was also a period when religious leaders, Christian and Muslim, influenced political decisions and developed the grammar of political discourse – leaders such as Hincmar of Reims or Wulfstan of York; and not only religious men: women such as Abbess Hild of English Whitby or the cloistered women of the tenth-century Saxon aristocracy influenced political directions too.[59] Further, despite high-level instability, many of the regions within kingdoms, such as Bavaria or Aquitaine or Galicia, sustained an identity over many centuries. In fact in many areas society was more stable at regional level, religious leaders and local aristocrats sharing the organisation of production and distribution, and peasant cultivators doing the farming. Life went on.

Written sources

Much of our information about aristocrats and peasants comes from charters, details of which can be found in the Appendix at the end of this book. Charters largely deal with localised landed property and are thereby inevitably about the local. Although those issued by emperors and kings in favour of their followers or religious institutions may reveal little about the people who lived on the lands transferred, there were also so-called 'private' charters. These were issued by all kinds of people: aristocrats and important clerics, but also peasant tenants and proprietors and local

---

57 See A. Christys, *Vikings in the South. Voyages to Iberia and the Mediterranean* (London: Bloomsbury, 2015), pp. 80–1, 75–6.
58 See below, p. 185.
59 K. J. Leyser, *Rule and Conflict in an Early Medieval Society: Ottonian Saxony* (London: Edward Arnold, 1979), pp. 49–73.

priests.[60] Most of these deal with the conveyance of property, that is, with gifts, leases, exchanges and sales of land; ecclesiastical institutions were often the beneficiaries of such property transfers but lay people could be beneficiaries too. Other private charters record the settlement of disputes – whether the outcome of a court session or some kind of negotiated settlement – and such settlements often depended on local relationships.[61] Charters that document exchange or sale, rather than gift, are scarce in areas such as Carolingian Francia. However, exchange of property increased from the second half of the ninth century, when ecclesiastical institutions and laymen tried to concentrate their often widely scattered lands.[62] Within some other regions, such as northern Iberia or Italy, records of sale are often more common than records of donation. In some areas charters record conditional gifts: the donor gave property to a church or a monastery asking for continuing lifelong use of the land transferred for him- or herself, and often also for children and their progeny. In the Frankish world this form of tenure was called precarial (from *precarium*) and the tenure might be referred to as a *beneficium*.[63] Many Italian charters of the later ninth century onwards are leases intended to last twenty-nine years (*contratti di livello*) and are thus a kind of formalised *beneficium*.

60 O. Redlich, *Die Privaturkunden des Mittelalters* (Munich/Berlin: Oldenbourg, 1911); A. de Boüard, *Manuel de diplomatique française et pontificale, Volume II: L'acte privé* (Paris: Picard, 1948); R. Härtel, *Notarielle und kirchliche Urkunden im frühen und hohen Mittelalter* (Vienna: Böhlau, 2011); M. Mersiowsky, *Die Urkunde in der Karolingerzeit. Originale, Urkundenpraxis und politische Kommunikation*, 2 vols (Wiesbaden: Harrassowitz, 2015). For reservations about the 'private' charter, see W. C. Brown, M. Costambeys, M. Innes and A. J. Kosto (eds), *Documentary Culture and the Laity in the Early Middle Ages* (Cambridge: Cambridge University Press, 2013), p. 11.

61 R. Hübner, 'Gerichtsurkunden der fränkischen Zeit', *Zeitschrift der Savigny-Stiftung für Rechtsgeschichte: germanistische Abteilung*, 12 (1891), 1–118, and 14 (1893), 1–152; S. Esders (ed.), *Rechtsverständnis und Konfliktbewältigung. Gerichtliche und außergerichtliche Strategien im Mittelalter* (Cologne: Böhlau, 2007); W. Davies, *Windows on Justice in Northern Iberia 800–1000* (Abingdon: Routledge, 2016), pp. 1–151; see further below, pp. 193–9.

62 I. Fees and Ph. Depreux (eds), *Tauschgeschäft und Tauschurkunde vom 8. bis zum 12. Jahrhundert / L'acte d'échange, du VIIIe au XIIe siècle* (Cologne: Böhlau, 2013).

63 B. Kasten, 'Beneficium zwischen Landleihe und Lehen – eine alte Frage, neu gestellt', in D. R. Bauer, R. Hiestand, B. Kasten and S. Lorenz (eds), *Mönchtum – Kirche – Herrschaft, 750–1000, Josef Semmler zum 65. Geburtstag* (Sigmaringen:

Thousands of private charters have survived from the early Middle Ages, from the late seventh century onwards. Many are preserved on a single sheet of parchment and originate from the time of the transaction recorded. However, in some regions most charters are only extant in later cartularies, that is to say in manuscript collections that contain transcriptions of earlier texts. Such books were compiled for the purpose of organising and managing estates, for creating dossiers of documents for juridical purposes, for the development of institutional identity and for the commemoration of donors.[64] Some cartularies were compiled already in the early Middle Ages but many date from the twelfth or thirteenth centuries or later. Where we can check later transcript against original, we can sometimes see a precise copy, but in other cases the original content of the charters was abbreviated or otherwise modified or even forged, although it is important to note that pseudo-original charters on single sheets could be forged too, and copies could be made on single sheets at the time of, as well as later than, the transaction.

Although there are many surviving documents, date ranges vary: some of the charters used in this book date from the eighth and ninth centuries, such as those from regions within the Carolingian Empire, but there are many from later ninth- and tenth-century Italy, both Frankish Italy and beyond, while two-thirds of pre-eleventh-century Anglo-Saxon charters focus on the tenth century and pre-eleventh-century Iberian collections focus on the late ninth and tenth centuries.[65]

There are inevitably limitations in the evidence provided by charters. In the early twelfth century the compiler of the Lorsch cartulary copied

Thorbecke, 1998), pp. 243–60; F. Bougard (ed.), *Les transferts patrimoniaux en Europe occidentale, VIIIe–Xe siècle* (1999), esp. pp. 607–73, 725–46; B. Kasten, 'Agrarische Innovationen durch Prekarien', in B. Kasten (ed.), *Tätigkeitsfelder und Erfahrungshorizonte des ländlichen Menschen in der frühmittelalterlichen Grundherrschaft (bis ca. 1000). Festschrift Dieter Hägermann zum 65. Geburtstag* (Stuttgart: Steiner, 2006), pp. 139–54; P. J. Fouracre, 'The use of the term *beneficium* in Frankish sources: a society based on favours', in W. Davies and P. Fouracre (eds), *The Languages of Gift in the Early Middle Ages* (Cambridge: Cambridge University Press, 2010), pp. 62–88.

64 O. Guyotjeannin, L. Morelle and M. Parisse (eds), *Les cartulaires* (Paris: Droz et H. Champion, 1993); P. Geary, *Phantoms of Remembrance: Memory and Oblivion at the End of the First Millennium* (Princeton, NJ: Princeton University Press, 1994); G. Declercq, 'Originals and cartularies: the organisation of archival memory (ninth-eleventh centuries)', in K. Heidecker (ed.), *Charters and the Use of the Written Word in Medieval Society* (Turnhout: Brepols, 2000), pp. 147–70.

65 For detail of charter collections, see Appendix, below.

about 3,000 acts in an abbreviated form, often only indicating the name of the donor, the donated property and its location. Losses of charters and cartularies are another problem: according to plausible estimates, more than 50 per cent of the Saint-Gall charters have been lost.[66] The cartularies of Fulda and Wissembourg only provide a small portion of the original monastic charter archive, and archives could be destroyed in particular circumstances such as the French Revolution. Further, much of our evidence comes from major ecclesiastical institutions which had an interest in preserving their archives. There is therefore an ecclesiastical bias in this corpus. However, as recent work has revealed, in almost all archives some charters record transactions in which no ecclesiastical institution was involved. Lay people also kept charters, which survived when the properties to which they related were absorbed by the archive of a long-lived ecclesiastical institution.[67] The Rankweil charters from Raetia, which appear to derive from the lay archive of a local official (*escultaizo*, *centenarius*) Folcwin, came to Saint-Gall as a group some time in the tenth century.[68] The famous eighth-century document list, once associated with the gastald Alahis, is an Italian example; now known as the archive of Ghittia (a relative of Alahis) or, more properly, as the *breve de moniminas* of the church of St Peter ai Sette Pini in Pisa, it refers to a private lay archive.[69]

Some charters were not drawn up by scribes from a receiving monastery or cathedral church but by local notaries, priests and clerics. Such texts can be found in almost all parts of Europe: within the sphere of the Frankish Empire, in Italy and also in northern Spain and Portugal. In

66 Wartmann, *Urkundenbuch*, vol. 1, p. v; W. Vogler, *Kostbarkeiten aus dem Stiftsarchiv St. Gallen in Abbildungen und Texten* (Saint-Gall: Verlagsgemeinschaft St. Gallen, 1987), p. 34; P. Erhart, '"… und mit alter briefen urkund (dorin gemischlet) bestäht". Der frühmittelalterliche Urkundenschatz des Klosters St. Gallen in den Händen Vadians', in R. Gamper (ed.), *Vadian als Geschichtsschreiber* (Saint-Gall: Sabon, 2006), pp. 69–98, at pp. 72, 76.
67 McKitterick, *The Carolingians and the Written Word*; W. Davies, *Small Worlds. The Village Community in Early Medieval Brittany* (London: Duckworth, 1988), p. 1; Brown et al. (eds), *Documentary Culture*.
68 K. Bullimore, 'Folcwin of Rankweil: the world of a Carolingian local official', *Early Medieval Europe*, 13:1 (2005), 43–77; Erhart and Kleindinst, *Urkundenlandschaft Rätien*, pp. 83–90.
69 CDL, vol. 2, no. 295, pp. 439–44; see P. S. Leicht, 'L'archivio di Alahis', in A. Giuffrè (ed.), *Studi di storia e diritto in onore di Enrico Besta*, vol. 2 (Milan: Giuffrè, 1937), pp. 29–36; A. Ghignoli, 'Su due famosi documenti pisani del secolo VIII', *Bullettino dell'Istituto Storico Italiano per il Medio Evo*, 106 (2004), 1–69, at 38–67.

Anglo-Saxon England, by contrast, it appears that the scribes of large ecclesiastical institutions were the sole writers of charters, at least until the ninth century: identifiable scribes of the community of Christ Church Canterbury prepared private charters in the ninth century as well as royal charters.[70] From the third decade of the tenth century, however, some royal charters were most likely prepared by a central agency, although other scriptoria continued to be used through the tenth and early eleventh centuries.[71]

Early medieval estate records complement charters. Often called polyptyques, they list the physical and human resources of great estates, including rents, labour services and other sources of income, and they provide information on demography, social and legal status, property and the organisation of lordship. These estate records usually originated in large ecclesiastical institutions, especially monasteries, although there are also a few royal examples. Roughly thirty survive from Carolingian times, many of them originating in the Frankish heartlands and dating from the ninth century.[72] Italy produced many polyptyques too, and twenty-five, dealing with ecclesiastical estates, survive.[73] A very special kind of survey comes from late eleventh-century England in the record of the taxable assets of the kingdom initiated by King William I. The considerable detail of landholding and associated resources preserved in the two late eleventh-century volumes known as Domesday Book is in fact an abbreviated version of primary records collected by the king's commissioners in 1086 in regional circuits.[74]

---

70 *Charters of Christ Church Canterbury*, ed. N. P. Brooks and S. E. Kelly, 2 vols (Oxford: Oxford University Press, 2013), e.g. vol. 2, nos 76, 85.

71 See 'Chancery, royal', in M. Lapidge, J. Blair, S. Keynes and D. Scragg (eds), *The Wiley Blackwell Encyclopedia of Anglo-Saxon England* (Chichester: John Wiley and Sons, 2nd edn, 2014), pp. 97–8.

72 See below, Appendix, for detailed examples.

73 See G. Pasquali, 'L'azienda curtense e l'economia rurale dei secoli VI–XI', in A. Cortonesi, G. Pasquali and G. Piccinni (eds), *Uomini e campagne nell'Italia medievale* (Rome/Bari: Laterza, 2002), pp. 5–71, at pp. 19–41; some are published in *Inventari altomedievali di terre, coloni e redditi*, ed. A. Castagnetti, M. Luzzati, G. Pasquali and A. Vasina (Rome: ISIME, 1979).

74 *Domesday book, seu Liber censualis Willelmi primi regis Angliæ*, ed. A. Farley, 2 vols (London: [Record Commission], 1783). There are a number of modern editions and translations, for example (by county) *Domesday Book*, 38 vols, ed. J. Morris (Chichester: Phillimore, 1975–92); or *Domesday Book: A Complete Translation*, ed. A. Williams and G. H. Martin (London: Penguin, 2002).

Polyptyques provide us with a considerable amount of information about non-elites in the countryside. Through them, we know the names of the inhabitants of hundreds of settlements.[75] More than that, we sometimes know to whom these inhabitants were married, how many children they had and the names given to those children. This information was mostly collected from the inhabitants themselves, using local enquiries: the Santa Giulia polyptyque from Italy appears to have been based on a standardised form, recorded locally, and the Domesday record was the outcome of systematic local enquiry, in some parts using pre-existing enquiry circuits.[76]

Narrative sources can also offer local detail, with hagiographical writing, in particular, providing information about life beyond royal courts and monasteries. Hagiography comes in several forms but is most often biographical, describing the lives (*vitae*) and/or the sufferings (*passiones*) of saints, their post-mortem miracles (*miracula*) and the translation of their relics from one locality to another (*translationes*). Many Saints' Lives are similar in structure and content, because they follow standard models; they had a strong didactic purpose and, written by members of influential ecclesiastical institutions, served as a means of moral instruction and religious edification. Nevertheless, they frequently included local detail in providing context for a moral tale or in elaborating the post-mortem miracles of a saint.[77] There are hundreds of surviving Lives and Miracle collections from the early Middle Ages, from virtually all regions covered in this book; the notable exception is northern Iberia, from which two extremely short Saints' Lives survive, offering negligible local information. The

75 See for example, J.-P. Devroey, 'La démographie du polyptyque de Saint-Remi de Reims', in P. Demouy and Ch. Vulliez (eds), *Compter les Champenois* (Reims: Université de Reims, 1998), pp. 81–94; J.-P. Devroey, 'Libres et non-libres sur les terres de Saint-Remi de Reims: la notice judiciaire de Courtisols (13 Mai 847) et le polyptyque d'Hincmar', *Journal des Savants* (2006/1), 65-103.
76 See Appendix for detailed references.
77 P. J. Geary, *Furta Sacra. Thefts of Relics in the Central Middle Ages* (Princeton, NJ: Princeton University Press, 1978, 2nd edn, 1990); P. Brown, *The Cult of the Saints, its Rise and Function in Latin Christianity* (Chicago: University of Chicago Press, 1981); W. Berschin, *Biographie und Epochenstil*, 5 vols (Stuttgart: Hiersemann, 1984-2004); A. Vauchez, *La Sainteté en Occident aux derniers siècles du moyen age. Après les procès de canonisation et les documents hagiographiques* (Rome: École française de Rome, 1988); M. Goullet and M. Heinzelmann (eds), *La réécriture hagiographique dans l'Occident médiéval: transformations formelles et idéologiques* (Ostfildern: Thorbecke, 2003).

45

earlier hagiographical texts from England, dating from the eighth century, tend to focus on ecclesiastics, hermits and royalty and rarely engage with lower strata of society, but texts from the tenth century onwards quite often do so.[78] Although the authors of many miracle accounts were monks, that does not prevent elements of local practice from being recorded. The first Book of the Miracles of Saint Remaclus (from Stavelot-Malmedy, written c. 850–c. 860), and the *Miracula Sancti Huberti* (from Saint-Hubert in the Ardennes, later ninth century), both illustrate social interactions in local societies in the Ardennes: the dependants of Stavelot, as well as working together, shared such rituals as drinking from the cup of Saint Remaclus.[79] Peasant visions are relatively commonplace in ninth-century miracle stories too. In many cases these visions are brief, undeveloped preludes to a marvellous cure; in others the peasant is primarily a conduit of communication: the saint appears and demands that the peasant tell someone what has been seen. The so-called *Apparitio Sancti Vedasti*, for example, written at some point in the ninth century, in recounting the warnings to individuals delivered through the visions of a sick carpenter, suggests the anatomy of a settlement group of considerable complexity: there are office holders, informal elites whose position was based on their relative prosperity, and subordinated and probably landless workers, as well as people less directly integrated into these circuits of power.[80]

History writing at its simplest level was based on an annalistic structure, with the historical record arranged year by year. Sometimes written in the circles surrounding a ruler or his followers, annals were often composed in ecclesiastical institutions associated with a ruling elite.[81] Although preoccupied with the deeds of rulers and aristocrats, annals and chronicles (a more expansive genre of history writing) do sometimes contain information about local events. History writing could also take

---

78 See D. Rollason, *Saints and Relics in Anglo-Saxon England* (Oxford: Blackwell, 1989), chs 4, 7 and pp. 98, 102.
79 *Miracula Sancti Remacli*, chs 30, 18, AASS, 3 sept, vol. 1, pp. 702–3, 700; *Miracula Sancti Huberti*, AASS, 3 nov; see N. Schroeder, *Les hommes et la terre de saint Remacle. Histoire économique et sociale de l'abbaye de Stavelot-Malmedy, VIIe–XIVe siècle* (Brussels: Université de Bruxelles, 2015), pp. 203, 245.
80 BHL 8512. C. West, 'Le saint, le charpentier et le prêtre: l'Apparitio Sancti Vedasti et les élites dans la Francie du IXe siècle', in L. Jégou, S. Joye, Th. Lienhard and J. Schneider (eds), *Faire lien. Aristocratie, réseaux et échanges compétitifs: Mélanges en l'honneur de Régine Le Jan* (Paris: Publication de la Sorbonne, 2015), pp. 237–48.
81 See below, p. 234.

the form of cartulary chronicles and *Gesta Abbatum*.[82] Long before the formulation of the Anglo-Saxon Chronicle in England, history writing of great sophistication was produced by the Englishman Bede, at the northern monastery of Jarrow. Of his many historical works, the *Ecclesiastical History of the English People*, completed in 731, dispenses with the annalistic framework and offers a compelling narrative; already circulating widely in continental Europe in the eighth century, it provides local detail in the anecdotes of books 3, 4 and 5.[83] The range of narrative sources from the north of the Iberian peninsula is much more limited than that from the Frankish or English worlds: there are, however, some short chronicles from the late ninth century as well as the early eleventh-century chronicle written by the royal notary Sampiro, and a brief set of tenth-century annals from Castile.[84]

The known corpus of Carolingian capitularies, texts recording governmental activity, runs from the mid-eighth to the late ninth century;[85] there are also some similar texts from Ottonian rulers in the tenth century, especially from Otto III in relation to Italy. These texts are divided into numerous *capitula*, short sections, and represent records of the decisions of kings and emperors in consultation with assemblies, dealing with juridical and administrative matters of the ecclesiastical as well as the secular sphere. They constitute a heterogeneous group of texts: several, such as the *Admonitio generalis* of 789, represent royal orders of general application; others were temporary instructions for particular office holders; and many offer a mix of permanent and temporary provisions, as they also offer a mix of practical and hortatory guidance. No single capitulary has survived in its original form, if there was a single original form, but already in the ninth century these texts were distributed from the palace, and copied and collected in different places; indeed, drafts

---

82 See below, p. 235.
83 *Venerabilis Baedae Opera Historica*, ed. C. Plummer, 2 vols (Oxford: Clarendon Press, 1896); *Bede's Ecclesiastical History of the English People*, ed. and trans. B. Colgrave and R. A. B. Mynors (Oxford: Clarendon Press, 1969).
84 J. Pérez de Urbel, *Sampiro. Su crónica y la monarquía leonesa en el siglo x* (Madrid: Consejo Superior de Investigaciones Científicas, 1952), at pp. 273–346. Ninth-century chronicles: *Crónicas Asturianas*, ed. and trans. J. Gil Fernández, J. L. Moralejo and J. I. Ruiz de la Peña (Oviedo: Universidad de Oviedo, 1985). Annals: J. C. Martín, 'Los *Annales Castellani Antiquiores* y *Annales Castellani Recentiores*: edición y traducción anotada', *Territorio, Sociedad y Poder*, 4 (2009), 203–26.
85 MGH Capit.

for discussion at assembly meetings could originate from places beyond the palace and many of the surviving texts are the remnants of communications between the political centre and regional office holders. The number and range of surviving capitularies is considerable: they survive in nearly 300 medieval manuscripts and recent work has suggested that more versions were produced.[86] Early medieval manuscripts recording capitularies often contain other juridical texts, such as selections of Roman law, canon law and the codifications of largely fifth- to eighth-century law relating to different regions of western Europe – Visigothic Spain, the Frankish kingdoms and Lombard Italy.[87] Hundreds of manuscripts of the eighth to tenth centuries survive and, while it remains debatable whether such collections were for practical or scholarly use, they include many provisions that bear upon relationships between local communities, and indeed neighbours.[88] How far knowledge of the content of any of these collections reached to ground level, and for how long, is difficult to assess, but provisions of *Lex Salica*, *Lex Alamannorum* and *Lex Baiuuariorum* are occasionally reflected in Carolingian and Saint-Gall charters, and it is quite clear that Visigothic law was widely known and widely cited in northern Iberia in the ninth and tenth centuries.[89]

86   F. L. Ganshof, *Recherches sur les capitulaires* (Paris: Sirey, 1958); R. McKitterick, 'Zur Herstellung von Kapitularien. Die Arbeit des Leges-Skriptoriums', *Mitteilungen des Instituts für Österreichische Geschichtsforschung*, 101 (1993), 3–16; H. Mordek, *Bibliotheca capitularium regum Francorum manuscripta. Überlieferung und Traditionszusammenhang der fränkischen Herrscherlasse* (Munich: MGH, 1995); H. Mordek, *Studien zur fränkischen Herrschergesetzgebung: Aufsätze über Kapitularien und Kapitulariensammlungen ausgewählt zum 60. Geburtstag* (Frankfurt am Main: Peter Lang, 2000); M. Innes, 'Charlemagne's government', in J. Story (ed.), *Charlemagne. Empire and Society* (Manchester: Manchester University Press, 2005), pp. 71–89; S. Patzold, 'Normen im Buch. Überlegungen zu Geltungsansprüchen so genannter "Kapitularien"', *Frühmittelalterliche Studien*, 41 (2007), 331–50; K. Ubl, 'Gab es das Leges-Skriptorium Ludwigs des Frommen?', *Deutsches Archiv für Erforschung des Mittelalters*, 70 (2014), 43–65; T. Tsuda, 'War die Zeit Karls des Großen "die eigentliche Ära der Kapitularien"?', *Frühmittelalterliche Studien*, 49 (2016), 21–48. See also http://capitularia.uni-koeln.de.
87   MGH LL; MGH LL nat. Germ.; *Leges Langobardorum, 643–866*, ed. F. Beyerle (Witzenhausen: Deutschrechtlicher Instituts-Verlag, 2nd edn, 1962).
88   For a useful survey, see McKitterick, *Carolingians and the Written Word*, pp. 37–75.
89   See C. I. Hammer, 'Land sales in eighth- and ninth-century Bavaria: legal, economic and social aspects', *Early Medieval Europe*, 6:1 (1997), 47–76; Davies,

English law codes, which run from the seventh century, have a separate chain of transmission and are distinctive in being written in the vernacular; in the tenth and eleventh centuries, especially, some of the new rule-making was clearly intended to impact on practice at ground level.[90] An important body of customary legal statements also survives, such as the tenth-century 'Dunsæte' ordinance, which deals with cattle theft. These suggest that a legal text could be written locally and apparently without official sponsorship, although it came to be included in higher-level legal collections.[91]

In Carolingian times, law texts were also issued by bishops. The first wave of episcopal statutes and conciliar acts dates from the first quarter of the ninth century. Addressed to priests and concerned with their operation within their local communities, these statutes were important for the implementation of Carolingian reforms on the ground. In contrast to the capitularies issued by emperors and kings, episcopal statutes contain more practical and detailed directions on how local priests should encourage the local Frankish population to become ideal Christians.[92]

There was also substantial production of liturgical manuscripts in western Europe in the early Middle Ages, especially from the eighth century onwards, with considerable innovation in the formulation of service books. Carolingian initiatives were influential, as indicated in the capitulary *Admonitio generalis*, which advocated the singing of Roman chant, *cantum Romanum*.[93] In practice, however, there remained great diversity within the Carolingian world throughout the ninth and tenth centuries, with elements of older Gallican practice adopted variously into the Roman rite in different parts of Francia and, in Italy, both Milanese and Beneventan liturgy retaining distinctive traits.[94] Practice

Windows on Justice, pp. 234–7; G. Barrett, 'The written and the world in early medieval Iberia', DPhil thesis, University of Oxford, 2015, esp. ch. 5.

90 See above, n. 47.
91 See Wormald, *The Making of English Law*, pp. 381–2.
92 MGH Capit. episc.; C. van Rhijn, *Shepherds of the Lord: Priests and Episcopal Statutes in the Carolingian Period* (Turnhout: Brepols, 2007). For more detail, see below, Chapter 5.
93 MGH Capit. I, pp. 52–62, at p. 61; R. McKitterick, *The Frankish Church and the Carolingian Reforms, 789–895* (London: Royal Historical Society, 1977), pp. 115–54.
94 R. McKitterick, 'Unity and diversity in the Carolingian church', in R. N. Swanson (ed.), *Unity and Diversity in the Church* (Oxford: Blackwell, 1996), pp. 59–82, at pp. 66–72; T. F. Kelly, *The Beneventan Chant* (Cambridge: Cambridge

was therefore highly localised, as is evident from the great variety of baptism and burial rites recorded.[95] In the Frankish world handbooks used by local priests in their day-to-day tasks contain liturgical material of this kind, as well as legal texts and homilies.[96] They were not, however, confined to the Frankish world: there is some evidence for local liturgical practice in Anglo-Saxon England. While there are indications of Roman influence on English practice already in the seventh century, precise evidence of local procedures dates from the late tenth and eleventh centuries.[97] Prescriptions for the books that priests should own survive in pastoral letters written by Ælfric of Eynsham.[98] There also survive some pocket books of homilies and *ordines* which, given the soiling and folding of some folios, must have been used in the field, as is in any case suggested by rubrics in the vernacular language giving instructions on how to perform the rituals.[99] These books provide material for the celebration of Mass, visitation of the sick, penance, baptism and burials, all of the rites a local priest would need. The extensive use of the vernacular in such manuscripts is especially striking and a pointer to local use.

University Press, 1989); M. Huglo, *Fonti e paleografia del canto ambrosiano* (Milan: Archivio Ambrosiano, 1956), pp. 127–37.

95 S. A. Keefe, *Water and the Word: Baptism and the Education of the Clergy in the Carolingian Empire*, 2 vols (Notre Dame, IN: University of Notre Dame Press, 2002).

96 Y. Hen, 'Priests and books in the Merovingian period', in S. Patzold and C. van Rhijn (eds), *Men in the Middle. Local Priests in Early Medieval Europe* (Berlin: De Gruyter, 2016), pp. 162–76; C. van Rhijn, 'Manuscripts for local priests and the Carolingian reforms', in Patzold and van Rhijn (eds), *Men in the Middle*, pp. 177–98; see further below, Chapter 5.

97 Y. Hen, 'Rome, Anglo-Saxon England and the formation of the Frankish liturgy', *Revue Bénédictine*, 112 (2002), 301–22; C. Cubitt, 'Unity and diversity in the early Anglo-Saxon liturgy', in Swanson (ed.), *Unity and Diversity*, pp. 45–57; F. Tinti, 'Looking for local priests in Anglo-Saxon England', in Patzold and van Rhijn (eds), *Men in the Middle*, pp. 145–61.

98 H. Gittos, 'Is there any evidence for the liturgy of parish churches in late Anglo-Saxon England? The Red Book of Darley and the status of Old English', in F. Tinti (ed.), *Pastoral Care in Late Anglo-Saxon England* (Woodbridge: Boydell Press, 2005), pp. 63–82, at p. 66.

99 Gittos, 'Is there any evidence?', pp. 68–70; V. Thompson, 'The pastoral contract in late Anglo-Saxon England: priest and parishioner in Oxford, Bodleian Library, MS Laud Miscellaneous 482', in Tinti (ed.), *Pastoral Care*, pp. 106–20; Tinti, 'Looking for local priests', pp. 155–61.

Evidence from northern Spain implies that comparable material was available in some parts of that territory, for there are references to a set of minor *ordines*, appropriate for use by local priests, in both charters and liturgical material. Charters are certainly explicit that many local churches had service books included in their endowment in the tenth century.[100] There is also a corpus of liturgical material from northern Iberia which is of relevance to local practice. The surviving liturgical manuscripts are from the eleventh century, but at least some elements of them were based on tenth-century models and they must have been known in northern parts of the peninsula in the ninth and tenth centuries. There are, for example, liturgical books (such as Silos MS 3, finished in 1039) that have a much more limited selection of *ordines* than those of episcopal collections and, rather like the Anglo-Saxon indicators, seem to have been compiled to include those things that were indispensable for local use: baptism, visitation of the sick, burial, marriage and blessings – again the rites a local priest would need.[101]

---

100 W. Davies, 'Local priests in northern Iberia', in Patzold and van Rhijn (eds), *Men in the Middle*, pp. 125–44, at pp. 139–42.
101 *Liber Ordinum Sacerdotal (Cod. Silos, Arch. Monástico, 3)*, ed. J. Janini (Silos: Abadía de Silos, 1981), sections I, II, III–VIII, XXVIII–XXXI, IX–X, XIII–XXVII respectively.

3

The fabric of local societies: people, land and settlement

This chapter discusses the basic constituents of early medieval rural societies. It focuses on material dimensions, such as settlement, topography and access to resources, as well as on fundamental factors that define the position of individuals within local societies and groups, such as legal status and socio-economic stratification. The first section therefore draws on recent settlement archaeology to discuss the shape, size and internal organisation of rural settlements. The second section deals with the socio-economic and legal stratification of local societies. The last section brings both of the former together to present an analysis of the organisation of landownership and the distribution of various resources at a local level. Examples of the topographic arrangement of landed property will provide concrete illustrations of 'neighbourhood'.

Houses and settlements: archaeological perspectives

In all regions considered in this book, the archaeology of early medieval rural settlements has made significant progress over the last decades.[1] The data and knowledge provided by archaeologists form a background of irreplaceable value to any interpretation of written evidence concerning early medieval local societies. Indeed, over the last thirty years or so, archaeology has revealed a lot more about the shape, size and organisation of early medieval rural households and settlements than any charter, hagiographic text or polyptyque will ever do.

Despite recent advances in the archaeology of early medieval rural settlement, there are difficulties and limitations inherent in this field of research. For example, early medieval buildings are not the most 'visible' to the archaeologist, for they were – with few exceptions – constructed of timber, earth, clay and a variety of perishable materials such as straw.[2] In most cases, early medieval settlements are discovered by chance, in so-called 'rescue excavations' that are intended to prevent the destruction of archaeological evidence during the construction of new buildings or infrastructures. This means that our knowledge is often limited to the regions that have seen important development projects over recent decades.[3] Usually the remains uncovered in such excavations are postholes, silos (underground storage pits), trenches or the faint traces that ground-level or sunken-featured buildings leave in the subsoil; contemporary ground surfaces are rarely conserved. Stone was occasionally used in some regions as a drystone base for superstructure or to build high-status buildings and rural churches.[4] In the village of Berslingen in northern

1 In general, see J. Klápště and A. Nissen-Jaubert, 'Rural settlement', in J. A. Graham-Campbell and M. Valor (eds), *The Archaeology of Medieval Europe*, 2 vols (Århus: Aarhus University Press, 2007), vol. 1, pp. 76–110, and H. Hamerow, *Early Medieval Settlements: The Archaeology of Rural Communities in North-West Europe 400–900* (Oxford: Oxford University Press, 2004). Northern France: E. Peytremann, *Archéologie de l'habitat rural dans le nord de la France du IVe au XIIe siècle*, 2 vols (Saint-Germain-en-Laye: AFAM, 2003); I. Catteddu, *Archéologie médiévale en France*, 2 vols (Paris: La Découverte, 2009), vol. 1. Southern Germany: R. Schreg, 'Farmsteads in early medieval Germany – architecture and organisation', in J. A. Quirós Castillo (ed.), *Arqueología de la arquitectura y arquitectura del espacio doméstico en la alta Edad Media Europea* (Madrid/Vitoria: CSIC, 2012), pp. 247–65. Italy: M. Valenti, 'Architecture and infrastructure in the early medieval village: the case of Tuscany', in L. Lavan, E. Zanini and A. Sarantis (eds), *Technology in Transition A.D. 300–650* (Leiden: Brill, 2007), pp. 451–90; P. Galetti (ed.), *Paesaggi, comunità, villaggi medievali. Atti del Convegno internazionale di studio, Bologna, 14–16 gennaio 2010*, 2 vols (Spoleto: Fondazione CISAM, 2012); A. Augenti, *Archeologia dell'Italia medievale* (Bari: Laterza, 2016), pp. 82–184. Northern Spain: J. A. Quirós Castillo, 'Early medieval landscapes in North-West Spain: local powers and communities, fifth–tenth centuries', *Early Medieval Europe*, 19:3 (2011), 285–311. Anglo-Saxon England: H. Hamerow, *Rural Settlements and Society in Anglo-Saxon England* (Oxford: Oxford University Press, 2012) and J. Blair, *Building Anglo-Saxon England* (Princeton, NJ: Princeton University Press, 2018).
2 Klápště and Nissen-Jaubert, 'Rural settlement', p. 82.
3 Hamerow, *Rural Settlements and Society*, pp. 2–3.
4 Klápště and Nissen-Jaubert, 'Rural settlement', pp. 86–7; G. Bianchi, 'Building, inhabiting and "perceiving" private houses in early medieval Italy', in Quirós Castillo (ed.), *Arqueología de la arquitectura*, pp. 195–212, at p. 198; Peytremann, *Archéologie de l'habitat rural*, vol. 1, pp. 289–90; Valenti, 'Architecture and infrastructure', p. 458; Hamerow, *Early Medieval Settlements*, p. 29; Hamerow, *Rural Settlements and Society*, p. 32.

Switzerland, for example, the only stone building was the church constructed in the Carolingian or Ottonian period.[5] This often leaves the archaeologist with evanescent traces that have to be combined, more or less satisfactorily, in order to identify houses, trackways, granaries, barns, silos or byres. Furthermore, the identification of a particular structure with a reasonable degree of certainty does not necessarily mean that it can be dated. Because of the inherent complexity of some sites and the difficulty of accurately dating structures, the reconstruction of an entire settlement, and its dynamic over time, can be difficult to achieve.

The excavation of Kirchheim in Bavaria, opening an area of about 45,000 sq m, gives us an idea of the potential and the difficulties of the archaeological interpretation of early medieval settlements.[6] The dots on the general excavation plan represent postholes (see figure 3.1a). Some of them form such obvious geometrical patterns that they can be grouped at first sight, even by an untrained eye, in order to reveal the structure of several post-built houses. This is particularly easy in the southern part of the settlement. Yet in the northern part, postholes are more abundant and patterns less obvious. In such cases, postholes might originate from several phases of rebuilding in the same area over a long period of time. Consequently, it is much more difficult to identify buildings and to provide a clear reading of this sector of the excavation.

The plan of Kirchheim is also testimony to another difficulty: some structures obviously extend beyond the limits of the excavated area; aerial photographs of the site suggest that only half of the entire settlement has been uncovered. This is a general problem: since many early medieval rural sites have not been excavated in their entirety, it is rarely possible to establish with certainty that the whole settlement has been encompassed.[7] Consequently, assessing the exact size of settlements is often impossible.

In spite of these problems, Kirchheim is an instructive example of a Bavarian settlement occupied in the seventh and eighth centuries: thirty post-built structures and forty sunken-featured buildings have been identified, forming about a dozen farmsteads aligned on each side of a north–south trackway (see figure 3.1b). A 'farmstead' is a cluster of various buildings and infrastructures that formed a unit within a settlement. Such

---

5 Schreg, 'Farmsteads in early medieval Germany', p. 253.
6 R. Christlein, 'Kirchheim bei München, Oberbayern', *Das Archäologische Jahr in Bayern*, 1980 (1981), 162–3.
7 Hamerow, *Early Medieval Settlements*, p. 53.

THE FABRIC OF LOCAL SOCIETIES

Figure 3.1a   General excavation plan of Kirchheim, Bavaria

units can be identified on many excavations in all the regions discussed, because they lie within some kind of enclosure or because they form a coherent cluster of buildings associated with their own storage facilities, hearths or wells.[8] In Kirchheim, some farmsteads were even associated with a small cemetery of between ten to thirty graves; they have been interpreted as familial graves associated with the households. The possibility of identifying these distinct units within a settlement is important from the point of view of social history, as written evidence suggests that the household – a nuclear family, occasionally with further family members or ancillaries, associated with a homestead, land and rights to use resources – was the basic building block of early medieval rural societies.

The units belonging to a single farmstead could be organised in many different ways. An early medieval rural settlement at Pacé, in Brittany, provides a nice example of the internal articulation of a farmstead.[9] The site was occupied over a period extending from the seventh to the tenth

8   Catteddu, *Archéologie médiévale*, vol. 1, pp. 28–9; Hamerow, *Early Medieval Settlements*, p. 53; Blair, *Building Anglo-Saxon England*, p. 294.
9   F. Le Boulanger, *Pacé (Ille-et-Vilaine) – ZAC Beausoleil. Une unité agricole du haut Moyen Âge dans un environnement mis en valeur anciennement* (Cesson-Sévigné: INRAP, 2011).

55

Figure 3.1b Interpretation of the excavation of Kirchheim, Bavaria

century. Figure 3.2 presents the excavators' interpretation of the later phase of occupation. It shows that ditches delimit two adjacent and approximately rectangular areas: one of about 2,800 sq m to the south, and another of about 1,100 sq m to the north. The smaller area had access from the north; the larger parcel had openings at both western corners. Finds and soil analyses shed light on the use of these sectors: the rectangular areas were probably surrounded by arable land and it is likely that the smaller enclosure was also used as a field or garden. Almost three-quarters of the larger enclosed area apparently served for keeping livestock or more intensive agrarian use, such as manured cultivation. The north-western quarter of this enclosure was occupied by at least three post-built structures, surrounding a courtyard of approximately 180 sq m (part of the area was damaged in modern times, preventing excavation). The largest building, interpreted as a house, has a ground plan of about 36 sq m. Traces of silos and hearths have been identified directly to the north of this area,

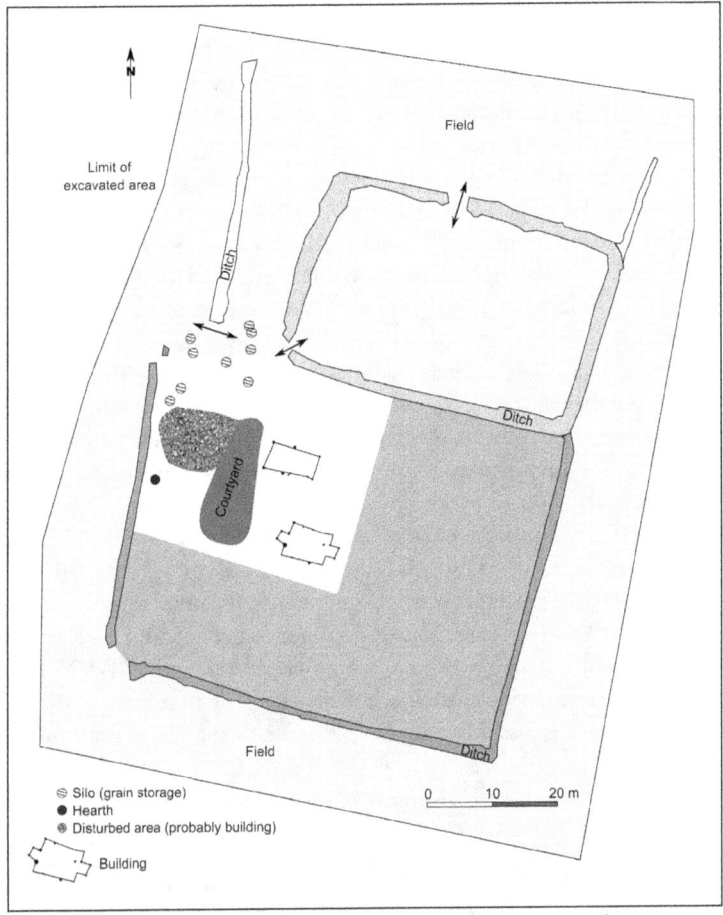

Figure 3.2   Farmstead at Pacé, Brittany: the last phase of occupation

but as the excavation has not been extended farther, it is unclear if this farmstead was isolated or was part of a larger settlement.[10]

Some historians and archaeologists have interpreted a dispersed pattern of settlement as a sign of the 'underdevelopment' of early medieval societies and economies.[11] This approach is now largely dismissed, as single farmsteads and dispersed settlement patterns are recognised as efficient

10   Le Boulanger, *Pacé (Ille-et-Vilaine)*, p. 121.
11   See, for example, G. Duby, *Guerriers et paysans, VIIe–XIIe siècle. Premier essor de l'économie européenne* (Paris: Gallimard, 1973), p. 31.

adaptations to particular socio-economic or environmental conditions.[12] The incidence of single farmsteads varied within different regions and sub-regions. In the Duero basin, it has been suggested that the settlement pattern of the seventh and eighth centuries consisted of a network of single farmsteads spread between more concentrated settlements.[13] In Tuscany – certainly the area with the best archaeological survey – it has been argued that dispersed settlement 'played a very marginal role, or even none'.[14] Settlements in Bavaria were partly dispersed, even after a phase of settlement concentration that started in the tenth/eleventh centuries.[15] In northern France, dispersed settlement appears 'dominant' in the sixth–seventh centuries, but gradual settlement nucleation can be observed from the second half of the seventh century; in the ninth to twelfth centuries, dispersed settlements were a minority.[16] It has been argued that in England settlements tended to be 'fairly dispersed' until the seventh century.[17] Yet other scholars support the idea that more substantial settlements already existed by then, at least in some regions.[18] Be that as it may, in the mid-seventh century a process of relative settlement nucleation was initiated. Settlements emerged that are characterised by the regular collocation of enclosures 'on a format that was coherent, but on the other hand was quite spaced out'. This type of settlement remained dominant until the eleventh century, in combination with genuinely isolated farmsteads.[19] While these trends have some obvious parallels, notably a tendency towards nucleation, it is important to stress that these processes are neither linear nor general:

12   A. Nissen-Jaubert, 'Habitats ruraux et communautés rurales', in J. Fridrich, J. Klápště, Z. Smetánka and P. Sommer (eds), *Ruralia II. Conference, Spa, 1st–7th September 1997* (Prague: Archeologický ústav, 1998), pp. 213–25; B. Cursente (ed.), *L'Habitat dispersé dans l'Europe médiévale et moderne. Actes des XVIIIes Journées Internationales d'Histoire de l'Abbaye de Flaran 15–17 Septembre 1996* (Toulouse: Presses Universitaires Le Mirail-Toulouse, 1999).
13   C. Tejerizo García, 'Settlement patterns and social inequality: the Duero basin in early Middle Ages (4th–8th centuries)', in J. A. Quirós Castillo (ed.), *Social Complexity in Early Medieval Rural Communities. The North-Western Iberia Archaeological Record* (Oxford: Archaeopress, 2016), pp. 17–34, at pp. 24–5.
14   Valenti, 'Architecture and infrastructure', p. 482.
15   Schreg, 'Farmsteads in early medieval Germany', p. 261.
16   Peytremann, *Archéologie de l'habitat rural*, pp. 354–8.
17   Hamerow, *Rural Settlements and Society*, p. 165.
18   See the nuanced discussion in Blair, *Building Anglo-Saxon England*, pp. 139–41.
19   Blair, *Building Anglo-Saxon England*, pp. 288–301. John Blair talks about 'semi-nucleation' to describe the process that led to the formation of settlements which are 'not tightly nucleated, but also not dispersed' (ibid., p. 139).

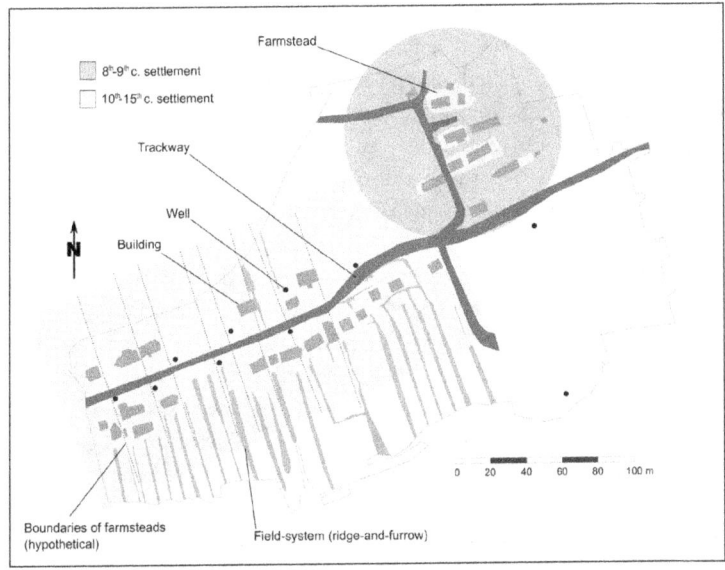

Figure 3.3   Excavation plan of Vallange, Lorraine

in southern Germany, for example, row settlements are frequent before the Carolingian period but tend to be replaced by less regular and more spaced-out arrangements from then onwards.[20] The number of farmsteads forming a settlement varied significantly, of course: an estimation for north-west Europe suggests that they generally ranged between five and twenty.[21] For central Europe, Peter Donat has calculated that up to 150 people could live in a single settlement.[22] The farmsteads that formed a settlement could be articulated in many different ways. The excavation of Vallange, in Lorraine, has revealed two settlement phases belonging respectively to the eighth–ninth and tenth–fifteenth centuries (see figure 3.3).[23] The earliest settlement combines six

20   Schreg, 'Farmsteads in early medieval Germany', p. 261.
21   Hamerow, *Early Medieval Settlements*, p. 53; Peytremann, *Archéologie de l'habitat rural*, vol. 1, p. 355.
22   P. Donat, *Haus, Hof und Dorf in Mitteleuropa vom siebten bis zwölften Jahrhundert: Archäologische Beiträge zur Entwicklung und Struktur der bäuerlichen Siedlung* (Berlin: Akademie Verlag, 1980), pp. 133–6.
23   F. Gérard, 'La structuration du village pour une économie agraire planifiée à la fin du IXe siècle en Lorraine. Les sites de Vitry-sur-Orne et de Demange-aux-Eaux', *Archéopages*, 34 (2012), 38–47.

59

farmsteads that are roughly aligned within a network of perpendicular trackways. Around 900 this settlement was abandoned and a more regular settlement was established, of a type often referred to as 'perpendicular', the excavators identifying seven farmsteads. The farmsteads are aligned perpendicular to a main trackway and each of them has access to a well situated beside the trackway. Fields expand behind each farmstead, forming a regular field-system with ridge-and-furrow perpendicular to the trackway.

Kirchheim can be characterised as a 'row settlement', its farmsteads loosely aligned with a trackway.[24] Farmsteads could also lie together in clusters, without a clear articulating structure, forming 'polyfocal settlements'. A further type is the so-called 'grouped settlement' that is organised around a central space or feature. The second phase of occupation of the hilltop village of Poggibonsi in Tuscany illustrates this form (see figure 8.4): a group had settled on the hilltop in the sixth century (see figure 3.4a), but in the ninth, the settlement was reorganised around a large and oblong central building, interpreted as a seigneurial hall (see figure 3.4b).

The case of Gózquez, a settlement situated about 20 km to the southeast of Madrid and occupied from the first quarter of the sixth century to the middle of the eighth century, offers yet another type.[25] Here the arrangement is irregular but is notable for the cultivation plot that lies beside each of the twelve to fifteen farmsteads, separating them from each other. A cemetery, forming a square of approximately 3,200 sq m, was located in the centre of the settlement.

Most excavations of rural settlements produce objects, areas and structures devoted to farming and animal husbandry; these include tools, barns, granaries, silos, mills, kilns, ovens and corn dryers, which testify that their inhabitants engaged in the production, transformation and storage of agrarian produce.[26] Craft activities, such as the production of textiles or pottery, tanning, iron and metalworking, or the carving of bone, antler and horn could also take place within settlements or in their

---

24 We use the typology suggested by Hamerow, *Early Medieval Settlements*, p. 54.
25 A. Vigil-Escalera Guirado, M. Moreno-García, L. Peña-Chocarro, A. Morales Muñiz, L. Llorente Rodríguez, D. Sabato and M. Ucchesu, 'Productive strategies and consumption patterns in the early medieval village of Gózquez (Madrid, Spain)', *Quaternary International*, 346 (2014), 7–19.
26 Peytremann, *Archéologie rurale*, vol. 1, pp. 334–52; Catteddu, *Archéologie médiévale*, vol. 1, pp. 50–66; Hamerow, *Rural Settlements and Society*, pp. 144–62.

Figure 3.4 The hilltop village of Poggibonsi in (a) sixth and (b) ninth centuries

surroundings.[27] These activities could be organised on a small scale in order to cover the needs of a single household or settlement, following strategies of self-sufficiency, but they could also be organised on a larger scale in order to answer aristocratic demand within estates or to supply

27 R. Córdoba, 'Technology, craft, and industry', in Graham-Campbell and Valor (eds), *The Archaeology of Medieval Europe*, pp. 208–30; Catteddu, *Archéologie médiévale*, vol. 1, pp. 68–87.

commercial networks of exchange via markets and fairs.[28] Overall, the importance of the latter forms of economic organisation tended to increase during the period under consideration.[29]

Settlement change has been variously related to these trends, although it is often unclear how, precisely, they were related. In Anglo-Saxon England, enclosures increasingly became a crucial component of settlements from the mid-seventh century onwards. This shift has been interpreted as evidence of the reorganisation (in all likelihood the intensification) of agro-pastoral activities.[30] In the tenth century, new trends started to transform rural settlements in England: churches were built in some villages, as well as 'architecturally impressive houses, which dominated the village scene and were obviously different from their neighbours'.[31] In northern France, from the mid-seventh century, parcels, buildings, farmsteads and settlements tended to become larger; settlements were increasingly nucleated and structured around features such as trackways or a church.[32] In comparison with Anglo-Saxon England, some of the settlements established in central Frankish areas in the eighth century were much denser and had a more regular layout; forms like this only emerged during the high Middle Ages in England.[33] In Bavaria, a process of partial settlement concentration is attested from the tenth/eleventh century.[34] Some sites in northern Iberia were reorganised in a more hierarchical form during the considered period: at Aistra (Zalduondo, Álava), a longhouse was erected and a new cemetery established during the eighth century; in Zaballa (Iruña de Oca, Álava), a church associated with large grain silos and a granary was erected around 950 (see figure 8.5).[35]

28 R. Hodges, *Dark Age Economics. A New Audit* (London: Bloomsbury, 2012), pp. 57–64.
29 C. Wickham, 'Rethinking the structure of the early medieval economy', in J. R. Davis and M. McCormick (eds), *The Long Morning of Medieval Europe. New Directions in Early Medieval Studies* (Aldershot: Ashgate, 2008), pp. 19–31; Hodges, *Dark Age Economics*.
30 Hamerow, *Rural Settlements and Society*, pp. 88–90; Blair, *Building Anglo-Saxon England*, pp. 282–301.
31 Blair, *Building Anglo-Saxon England*, p. 378.
32 Peytremann, *Archéologie de l'habitat rural*, p. 335; Catteddu, *Archéologie médiévale*, vol. 1, pp. 29–31.
33 Hamerow, *Rural Settlements and Society*, p. 88.
34 Schreg, 'Farmsteads in early medieval Germany', p. 261.
35 J. A. Quirós Castillo, 'Archaeology of power and hierarchies in early medieval villages in Northern Spain', in J. Klápště (ed.), *Hierarchies in Rural Settlements*.

These transformations have been interpreted as evidence of increasing social hierarchisation and of 'seigneurialisation' or 'manorialisation'.[36] The excavation of Tuscan sites such as Scarlino and Montarrenti has revealed that *incastellamento* – elite-driven nucleation of dispersed and agglomerated settlements from the plain to hilltops – already took place in the seventh/eighth centuries.[37] It is important to stress, however, that the emergence of these upland sites was not a single process: various actors, such as monasteries, public authorities and peasants themselves, contributed to shaping quite diversified settlement patterns in the Tuscan plains and uplands until the eleventh century.[38] This remark can be extended for all regions: early medieval settlement patterns did not invariably follow a standard tendency towards nucleation and increasing regularity. On a regional and even local level, continuity and change coexisted; models based on generalisation from a few sites usually turn out to be overly simplistic.[39]

These notes of caution are important. The brief survey of forms and evolution of settlements presented here barely scratches the surface of an extremely complex and heterogeneous subject. For many regions, the evidence remains too patchy to develop sound synthetic perspectives and, as soon as data are more abundant, archaeologists point to the heterogeneity of settlement patterns and trends.[40] Therefore, syntheses remain provisional and tentative. It is only in very broad terms that the following general observations might hold some validity: over the three and a half centuries considered in this book, settlements tended to become larger and more structured; specialised agrarian structures, such as barns and granaries,

---

Ruralia IX. 26th September–2nd October 2011. Götzis, Austria (Turnhout: Brepols, 2013), pp. 199–212.

36 For Spain, see Quirós Castillo, 'Archaeology of power and hierarchies'; for Anglo-Saxon England, see Blair, *Building Anglo-Saxon England*, pp. 354–80.

37 R. Francovich and R. Hodges, *Villa to Village. The Transformation of the Roman Countryside in Italy, c. 400–1000* (London: Duckworth, 2003); see further above, pp. 12–13.

38 G. Bianchi, 'Analyzing fragmentation in the early Middle Ages: the Tuscan model and the countryside in central-northern Italy', in S. Gelichi and R. Hodges (eds), *New Directions in Early Medieval Archaeology: Spain and Italy Compared* (Turnhout: Brepols, 2015), pp. 301–33.

39 The point is made by Hamerow, *Rural Settlements and Society*, p. 83; Catteddu, *Archéologie médiévale*, vol. 1, pp. 48–9; Bianchi, 'Analyzing fragmentation'.

40 J. A. Quirós Castillo and A. Vigil-Escalera, 'Networks of peasant villages between Toledo and Uelegia Alabense', *Archeologia Medievale*, 33 (2006), 79–128, at 1.

appeared or increased in size and number;[41] hierarchies emerged with farmsteads that distinguished themselves from others by their size and marks of conspicuous consumption, with seigneurial courts, halls and churches built in settlements. These changes are often related to a reorganisation of work within the settlement.[42] Such developments can reasonably be interpreted as signs of demographic growth, a general increase in wealth (which does not, of course, exclude the existence of inequalities), agrarian expansion and intensification, increasing economic complexity, social stratification and the emergence or consolidation of elites.[43]

Legal status and socio-economic stratification

Local societies were internally stratified and structured by legal status and socio-economic differences. In legal terms, the opposition between free and unfree was a fundamental categorisation.[44] While the notion of 'unfree' implies the deprivation of liberty, its social reality in the early Middle Ages was much more complex and nuanced.[45] Significant variations in the restriction of liberties can be observed from one region to another and, sometimes, from one settlement, or estate, to another. Although fully fledged slavery certainly existed, terms such as *servus* or *ancilla* cannot simply be interpreted as absolute terms for slavery in every

---

41 See A. Vigil-Escalera Guirado, G. Bianchi and J. A. Quirós [Castillo] (eds), *Horrea, Barns and Silos. Storage and Incomes in Early Medieval Europe* (Bilbao: Universidad del País Vasco, 2013).

42 Valenti, 'Architecture and infrastructure', p. 456; Augenti, *Archeologia*, pp. 114-22.

43 See Peytremann, *Archéologie de l'habitat rural*, pp. 355-7; C. Wickham, *Framing the Early Middle Ages: Europe and the Mediterranean, 400-800* (Oxford: Oxford University Press, 2005); Hamerow, *Rural Settlements and Society*, pp. 163-8; Hodges, *Dark Age Economics*.

44 T. Kohl, *Lokale Gesellschaften: Formen der Gemeinschaft in Bayern vom 8. bis zum 10. Jahrhundert* (Ostfildern: Thorbecke, 2010), pp. 46-51; J.-P. Devroey, *Puissants et misérables. Système social et monde paysan dans l'Europe des Francs (VIe-IXe siècles)* (Brussels: Académie Royale de Belgique, 2006), pp. 265-315; M. J. Innes, *State and Society in the Early Middle Ages. The Middle Rhine Valley, 400-1000* (Cambridge: Cambridge University Press, 2000), p. 83.

45 See A. Rio, *Slavery after Rome, 500-1100* (Oxford: Oxford University Press, 2017); Kohl, *Lokale Gesellschaften*, pp. 46-51, 189-200; C. West, *Reframing the Feudal Revolution: Political and Social Transformation Between Marne and Moselle, c. 800-c. 1100* (Cambridge: Cambridge University Press, 2013), pp. 66-7.

context.[46] Already in the late Roman period, socio-economic change and the diffusion of Christianity had led to the establishment of unfree people on tenures and to increasing enfranchisement. While some unfree had to return most of the product of their labour to their owners, others only had to pay annual rent.[47] And individuals who had been freed could still be submitted to reduced forms of subordination such as the annual payment of a relatively small amount of money.[48]

In the Carolingian period, connubial restrictions for the unfree were moderated.[49] In parallel, many legally free stepped into de facto subordinate positions, entering the clientele of a powerful person, becoming tenants or accepting the burden of a *servitium* ('service', that is, giving rent or performing labour services).[50] As some of the charters of Saint-Gall suggest, there were many different paths leading from full freedom into some sort of dependence or patronage. Round about 868, for example, Cotefrida and her daughter Hungund transferred property to the monastery of Saint-Gall, but obtained it back as a tenure. In the future, they would benefit from the advantages and protection given by the monastic community to its tenants (*familiaritas et mundiburdium*); as members of the group of monastic dependants (*familia*), they obtained the right to use particular resources belonging to the monastery.[51] One year later, in 869, a certain Oterihc and his wife transferred property to the same monastery, obtained it back in tenure and were granted rights to use the pastures, paths, woodlands and other locations belonging to the monastery.[52] Between 812 and 826, a certain Gisalrich and his wife Udalrat made

46 See below, p. 66.
47 W. Davies, *Small Worlds: The Village Community in Early Medieval Brittany* (London: Duckworth, 1988), p. 88.
48 See the examples of Carolingian *censarii* and *tributarii* discussed by S. Esders, *Die Formierung der Zensualität. Zur kirchlichen Transformation des spätrömischen Patronatswesens im früheren Mittelalter* (Ostfildern: Thorbecke, 2010), pp. 20–1.
49 H.-W. Goetz, 'Serfdom and the beginnings of a "seigneurial system" in the Carolingian period: a survey of the evidence', *Early Medieval Europe*, 2:1 (1993), 29–51, at 37; P. Toubert, *L'Europe dans sa première croissance: de Charlemagne à l'an mil* (Paris: Fayard, 2004).
50 Goetz, 'Serfdom and the beginnings of a "seigneurial system"', 42; W. Davies, *Acts of Giving: Individual, Community, and Church in Tenth-Century Christian Spain* (Oxford: Oxford University Press, 2007), pp. 19–20.
51 W 537: 'et illorum res ... inter eos fruendi facultatem habeamus'.
52 W 550: 'ut familiaritatem et communionem in ceteris sancti Galli locis in pascuis, in viis, silvis aliisque utilitatibus ... habere possimus'.

several donations to the monastery of Wissembourg.⁵³ First, they gave away parts of an allod (land possessed in full ownership, as opposed to a tenure) inherited from their parents, except a part the wife had inherited from her mother. Later on, Gisalrich gave ten *iurnales* (a unit of land measurement: the surface ploughed in one day) of land for the salvation of the soul of a certain Wolfolt. Both donations were then given back to them, for a yearly payment of ten pence. Such transactions, which were made by free landowners, but implied the establishment of tenurial arrangements, are common in all regions of the Frankish realm discussed in this book. They potentially blurred the line that separates freedom and dependence. Similar texts feature in early Carolingian Italy, where the situation may have been particularly harsh immediately after 774, given that Charlemagne intervened with a capitulary to limit such transactions: all documents through which personal dependences were established (*cartulae obligationis*) and which transformed free families (*liberi*) into personal dependants (*in servitio*) were to be destroyed.⁵⁴ Charles also cancelled all sales of estates sold on account of hunger (*necessitas famis*) or given to churches and monasteries without a true estimate of their value.⁵⁵

On a conceptual level, the linguistic proximity between *servus* and *servitium* was often interpreted as a sign of a connection between particular tasks and personal status.⁵⁶ Accordingly, the performance of a *servitium* was itself frequently interpreted as a marker of dependence, in practice blurring the boundaries between free and unfree.⁵⁷ Further complexity in personal status developed with the contraction of mixed marriages.⁵⁸ To put it in other words, legal categories did matter in early medieval societies, but their apparent straightforwardness does not reflect the complexity and dynamism of social practices. The charters of Saint-Gall, for example, show that the same term *mancipia* could designate

---

53 TW 239.
54 Traditionally dated to 776 but more probably 781; H. Mordek, 'Die Anfänge der fränkischen Gesetzgebung für Italien', *Quellen und Forschungen aus italienischen Archiven und Bibliotheken*, 85 (2005), 1–35, at 33.
55 *I capitolari italici*, ed. C. Azzara and P. Moro (Rome: Viella, 1998), no. 1 (88), pp. 50–3.
56 Goetz, 'Serfdom and the beginnings of a "seigneurial system"', 36; Devroey, *Puissants et misérables*, p. 268.
57 See the case of Mitry, below, pp. 68–9.
58 See E. R. Coleman, 'Medieval marriage characteristics: a neglected factor in the history of medieval serfdom', *The Journal of Interdisciplinary History*, 2:2 (1980), 205–19, at 210; Kohl, *Lokale Gesellschaften*, pp. 195–200.

dependants living at an estate centre or on tenures (*mancipia sive intra curtis sive in hobis*).[59] While the word is the same, the actual social situations and experiences of individuals were profoundly different. Legally unfree are attested in all the regions discussed here, although their proportion and socio-economic situation could vary significantly. Within the estates of the Seine basin and the Champagne region, estimates of the servile population oscillate between 5 and 15 per cent.[60] As a comparison, in ninth-century Brittany, the unfree who were owned by aristocrats and the most affluent members of the *plebs* (the primary local unit of association) are estimated at about 25 per cent of the population, with high sub-regional and local variations in density.[61] The individuals referred to as *theowas* and *wealas* in Anglo-Saxon texts are identified as slaves.[62] Conjectural estimations based on the Domesday record suggest that nearly 12 per cent of the population were slaves.[63] The charters of tenth-century northern Iberia attest slaves, who were bought and given away.[64] Slaves were exchanged in Tuscany.[65] The same observations apply to Bavaria, where the evidence shows that unfree people with different socio-economic positions certainly existed in this region, although proportions cannot be estimated.[66]

In all regions discussed here, a stratum of 'lesser free' can be identified: in Anglo-Saxon England the words *gebur*, *colliberti* and *lisingar* were used to refer to various types of tenant who were legally free but still dependent.[67] In Bavarian texts, lesser free appear as *tributales*, *barscalci*, *accolae* or *aldiones* before c. 850. These terms disappear in the middle of the ninth century and, from then on, only the expressions *servi* and *mancipia* are used. This change in terminology might suggest that the 'lesser free' were increasingly assimilated to servile populations.[68] Similar

59 Goetz, 'Serfdom and the beginnings of a "seigneurial system"', 41.
60 Devroey, *Puissants et misérables*, p. 275.
61 Davies, *Small Worlds*, pp. 87–9.
62 R. Faith, *The English Peasantry and the Growth of Lordship* (London: Leicester University Press, 1997), pp. 59–70. See also D. A. E. Pelteret, *Slavery in Early Mediaeval England: From the Reign of Alfred until the Twelfth Century* (Woodbridge: Boydell Press, 1995).
63 Faith, *The English Peasantry*, p. 60.
64 Davies, *Acts of Giving*, pp. 18–19; W. Davies, 'Free peasants and large landowners in the West', *Revue belge de philologie et d'histoire*, 90 (2012), 361–80, at 372–3.
65 For example, ChLA 34, no. 992 (766); MDL V/3, no. 1468 (975).
66 See Kohl, *Lokale Gesellschaften*, p. 50.
67 Faith, *The English Peasantry*, pp. 64, 76–84.
68 See Kohl, *Lokale Gesellschaften*, pp. 43–6, 380.

patterns can be observed elsewhere, although there are significant divergences in chronology and mechanisms.

In some localities of the Rhineland, monastic communities were already transforming the collection of dues from free men and women into tenurial relationships in the late eighth century.[69] In Schwanheim, for example, the monastery of Lorsch had received several donations of land from peasant proprietors in the 760s and 770s.[70] In 782, however, the monks were involved in a court case in order to establish that Schwanheim had always been part of the villa of Hurfeld, which had been donated to Lorsch by Charlemagne (see figure 8.3).[71] The monks won their case, thereby establishing that an entire settlement that once belonged – at least partly – to peasant proprietors was one of their properties. As observed by Matthew Innes, the implicit consequence for the inhabitants was that they were now tenants holding their land from Lorsch, rather than owner-cultivators.

In the Frankish heartland of the Île-de-France and Champagne, the abundant ninth-century evidence suggests that tenants with an intermediate status, such as free rent-paying or labour-service-fulfilling tenants (they often appear in the evidence as *coloni* or *accolae*), were increasingly pressured by estate owners and assimilated to unfree tenants.[72] Two well-known examples illustrate the tensions relating to legal status in this period. On 13 May 847, two *missi* sent out by the archbishop of Reims, a priest of the church of Reims and one of the archbishop's vassals, held a public *placitum* in Courtisols (see figure 8.2).[73] They had heard that some male and female *mancipia* (tenants) were hereditarily servile (*servi/ancillae*) but that they were pretending to be free (*ingenui*). Seven witnesses testified that these *mancipia* were servile by birth, as their ancestors had been bought by Saint-Remi. More men and women were then assessed as servile at the same *placitum*. A few years later, in July 861, twenty-three men and eighteen women, some of whom had brought

---

69 Innes, *State and Society*, pp. 74–5.
70 CL 226, 227.
71 CL 228.
72 The trends are described by Devroey, *Puissants et misérables*, pp. 282–6, and West, *Reframing the Feudal Revolution*, pp. 72–6.
73 This case is discussed by J. Barbier, '*De minimis curat praetor*: Hincmar, le polyptyque de Saint-Remi de Reims et les esclaves de Courtisols', in G. Constable and M. Rouche (eds), *Auctoritas: Mélanges offerts à Olivier Guillot* (Paris: PUPS, 2006), pp. 267–79; see further below, pp. 116–17, 206–7, for further detail of this case and more references.

their children with them, came before the royal tribunal of Charles the Bald at Compiègne.[74] They were from Saint-Denis's estate of Mitry. They argued that they were free *coloni* by birth but that Deodadus, the monk responsible for the management of the estate, was unjustly trying to force them to perform an inferior service — that is, paying rent or doing labour services due from servile tenants. Deodadus and the *maior* answered that several *coloni* from Mitry were willing to witness that the claimants were already performing inferior service (*inferiorem servicium*) in the time of Louis the Pious. They did so and the claimants lost their case. Several ninth-century *placita* reveal that some Italian monasteries also tried to transform their landholdings into 'coercive power over men [and women]', following quite similar strategies.[75]

In northern Iberia, decline in status through the extension of lordship seems much less frequent before the year 1000 than later and than in the previously discussed regions.[76] With the exception of some royal estates and those of very powerful monasteries such as Celanova, aristocrats were usually receiving rent from numerous small working units, rather than developing large estates. However, tenth-century charter material does appear to attest hereditary or tenurial obligations and their gradual extension.[77] It is important to stress that the numbers of such cases are extremely small, and several are fabrications of the eleventh century. An example of the extension of seigneurial control is provided by a charter from 959 that reveals that five heads of household were taken to court by the monastery of Celanova, because they had built houses,

---

[74] *Recueil des actes de Charles II le Chauve, roi de France*, ed. G. Tessier, 3 vols (Paris: L'imprimerie nationale, 1943), vol. 2, no. 228. Case discussed by J. L. Nelson, 'Dispute settlement in Carolingian West Francia', in W. Davies and P. Fouracre (eds), *The Settlement of Disputes in Early Medieval Europe* (Cambridge: Cambridge University Press, 1986), pp. 45-64, at p. 51.

[75] See the nuanced discussion in G. Albertoni, 'Law and the peasant: rural society and justice in Carolingian Italy', *Early Medieval Europe*, 18:4 (2010), 417-45, at 444-5.

[76] Davies, *Acts of Giving*, pp. 19-21; Davies, 'Free peasants and large landowners', pp. 369-71.

[77] See, for example, SJP 31, s.d.: 'illum terminum de Saues qui erat de Cella laborassent illi uicini de Capannas'; SM 88 (971) = BG 42 (false): 'itaque obedientes sint ad honorem Sancti Emiliani ... ut per omni anno in ebdomada duobus dies seruire precipimus'; Cel 92 (968): 'ut faceremus hanc seriem testamenti de homines qui habitant in uilla quam dicunt Gallecos in Lamprelana cum omuntiolos qui sedent in angulbus quod dicunt Recasio ubi sunt saline'.

planted vines and cultivated fields in the monks' villa of Santa Eulalia.[78] They were finally allowed to stay and work the land, but would have to give a quarter of their produce in chestnuts and grapes to the monastery every year. In 944 the monastery of Pardomino made a complaint against the inhabitants (*omnibus habitatoribus*) of seven nearby settlements over rights to use the Pardomino mountain. The people, it was claimed, had crossed the bounds, cut down trees, ploughed the land and pastured their animals.[79] The immediate outcome was that the mountain was divided between the monastery and the people, a boundary being fixed by a panel of ten, on the king's order, and each of the seven settlements then nominated a guarantor that they would not intrude across the boundary in future (*qui sumus uigarii de parte plebium et fideiussores*). In fact, only eleven years later, 'all of the inhabitants' of three of those settlements agreed, before a judge, to pay the monastery an annual rent of a quarter of their produce – twenty-one people were named.[80] The establishment of rents and tenurial agreements based on such claims of inhabitants' 'intrusion' into monastic land was a common pattern in the extension of seigneurial control in northern Iberia. A less clear case is recorded in a charter of 976.[81] Two named people, their unnamed relations and *omnes habitantes* of Villa Castellana gave their whole village to León cathedral, and promised thereafter to serve the bishop. No pious reasons are expressed in the document and it might be that unrecorded pressures lay behind this transaction.

In all regions analysed, the free section of the population was extremely diverse in socio-economic terms – a large spectrum extended from small owner-cultivators to top aristocrats. In Tuscany before the Carolingian period, small and medium landowners involved in local affairs could form a clearly defined and homogeneous group, the *arimanni*.[82] They were bound together by common interests and intervened in social life at a local level.[83] However, this is exceptional. In general, there were no institutionalised

78 Cel 446.
79 Li 184.
80 Lii 290; the agreement survives as an 'original'.
81 Lii 443.
82 G. Tabacco, *I liberi del re nell'Italia carolingia e postcarolingia* (Spoleto: Fondazione CISAM, 1966); S. Gasparri, 'La questione degli arimanni', *Bullettino dell'Istituto Storico Italiano per il Medio Evo e Archivio Muratoriano*, 87 (1978), 121–153; Albertoni, 'Law and the peasant', 417–21.
83 The existence of more structured rural communities has recently been hypothesised by T. Lazzari, 'Comunità rurali nell'alto medioevo: pratiche di descrizione

groups of local owners. Just as with the unfree, it is virtually impossible to establish the exact proportion of each stratum of free landowners at a regional or local level.[84] The aristocracy was not legally defined, nor did it form a clearly delimited social group. Small owner-cultivators appear more rarely in the evidence and, with some notable exceptions, not much information is provided about them. The intraregional complexity of social stratification and patterns of landowning, as well as the lack of statistically exploitable material, make systematic comparisons very difficult and only impressionistic overviews can be provided.

As one would expect, the most visible strata are the regional or micro-regional elite. They appear in the written evidence as they gave land to the church, had military obligations, or were active as witnesses in transactions and court cases.[85] As a result, this upper stratum is visible in all regions. In 755, for example, a donation charter was written in the name of a certain Gaiprand in favour of St Fridianus of *Griciano*, an ecclesiastical institution in the territory west of Lucca. Gaiprand defined himself as a *vir devotus*, a man devoted to his lord, and he justified the endowment of his estates by stating that he was supposed to join the army in Francia as a warrior (*exercitalis*). The estates were given to the church, funding a priest (*presbiter*) who was obliged to perform rituals to commemorate the donor's deeds and to save his soul.[86] Families with a similar status are attested in the Middle Rhine, Bavaria and Francia.[87] In Anglo-Saxon England, the term thegn refers to free landowners of varying status,

e spie lessicali nella documentazione scritta', in Galetti (ed.), *Paesaggi, comunità, villaggi medievali*, vol. 2, pp. 405–23.

84 The figures suggested for six *plebes* in Brittany are as close as we can get to such questions; they suggest that, varying from one *plebs* to another, between 30% and 56% of proprietors had significant accumulation of properties, while between 6% and 33% of proprietors owned properties in more than one *plebs*; Davies, *Small Worlds*, pp. 92–5.
85 See further below, pp. 167–72.
86 Cf. CDL, vol. 2, no. 117, pp. 353–5.
87 For the middle Rhine, see the cases of Siggo and Starcrat discussed by T. Kohl, 'Ländliche Gesellschaft, lokale Eliten und das Reich – der Wormsgau in der Karolingerzeit', in T. Kohl, S. Patzold and B. Zeller (eds), *Kleine Welten. Ländliche Gesellschaften im Karolingerreich* (Ostfildern: Thorbecke, 2019), pp. 309–36; or the family of Liutwin, Stahal, Ripwin and Giselhelm in Innes, *State and Society*, pp. 148–50, and G. Halsall, *Warfare and Society in the Barbarian West, 450–900* (London: Routledge, 2003), pp. 80–1. We would, however, follow Franz Staab who sees this family as small aristocrats, rather than Innes, who identifies them as owner-cultivators: F. Staab, *Untersuchungen zur*

although usage changed over time. By the late Saxon period many were important and wealthy individuals who served the king.[88]

The abundant evidence from northern Iberia that records small-scale property deals and disputes indicates that free peasant proprietors were quite numerous there.[89] Their properties coexisted with those of larger owners and aristocrats, who controlled slaves and tenants. In Bavaria, the term *nobilis* was used from the eighth to the tenth century to designate free owners, distributed on a large spectrum, reaching from the highest aristocracy to small owner-cultivators.[90] The preferential use of *nobilis* rather than *liber* or *ingenuus* may reflect the increasing social depreciation of the 'lesser free' discussed above.[91] Small Bavarian owner-cultivators were under threat of incorporation into the estates of the most powerful and probably did not constitute a significant part of the population. While the proportions of each legal and socio-economic group cannot be assessed with any precision, it is nevertheless likely that, unlike northern Iberia, the majority of the population here was either unfree or 'lesser free'.[92]

The Middle Rhenish evidence suggests a similar social spectrum among the free population, reaching from high aristocrats to small owner-cultivators, who might hold a few parcels in tenure or have to pay rent and perform labour service.[93] Between these groups, a medium stratum of owner-cultivators occasionally appears in charters, witnessing in local court cases.[94] Estimates of proportions remain elusive, but the situation was probably closer to Bavarian standards than Iberian.

In the heartland of Francia – loosely defined as the region between the Seine and the Rhine – the evidence originating from monastic or royal estates (in polyptyques) suggests that a greater proportion of land was integrated into estates belonging to the king, the church or major aristocrats, and that, consequently, independent landowners forming

Gesellschaft am Mittelrhein in der Karolingerzeit (Wiesbaden: Steiner, 1975), pp. 260–2. For Bavaria, see Kohl, *Lokale Gesellschaften*.
88 Faith, *The English Peasantry*, pp. 94–5.
89 Davies, 'Free peasants and large landowners', pp. 369–70.
90 Kohl, *Lokale Gesellschaften*, pp. 39–43.
91 See above, pp. 67–8.
92 Kohl, *Lokale Gesellschaften*, p. 50.
93 Innes, *State and Society*, pp. 82–5. See also S. Freudenberg, *Trado atque dono. Die frühmittelalterliche private Grundherrschaft in Ostfranken im Spiegel der Traditionsurkunden der Klöster Lorsch und Fulda (750 bis 900)* (Stuttgart: Franz Steiner, 2013).
94 Kohl, 'Ländliche Gesellschaft'.

local elites or small-scale owner-cultivators were rare.[95] Recent regional surveys, however, suggest that such actors could nevertheless be found in regions as diverse as the Île-de-France, the middle Meuse valley, Champagne and the Ardennes.[96] They were certainly less numerous than in any other area under discussion, but they could be found.

Socio-economic stratification, land and resources

Among the social and legal factors that had an impact on access to land and resources, gender is the most easily discernible. Charters and estate records reveal that female landowners and tenants were far from nonexistent, but their proportion was always significantly lower than that of male owners and tenants.[97] The influence of legal status and ties of dependence on access to resources is much more complex.[98] Servile individuals could be attached to estates or farmsteads in which they had little freedom of movement, power of negotiation or control over land and produce.[99] On the opposite side of the social spectrum, high-level aristocrats could own

95 West, *Reframing the Feudal Revolution*, pp. 64–5; Wickham, *Framing the Early Middle Ages*, pp. 398–406.
96 For for the Île-de-France: Wickham, *Framing the Early Middle Ages*, pp. 400–4; for the Middle Meuse valley: A. Wilkin, 'Le patrimoine foncier des élites dans la région de la Meuse moyenne jusqu'au XIe siècle', in R. Le Jan, J.-P. Devroey and L. Feller (eds), *Les élites et la richesse au haut Moyen Âge* (Turnhout: Brepols, 2010), pp. 327–43; for the estates of Saint-Remi of Reims in the Champagne region: J.-P. Devroey, 'Perception de la nature productive et aspects des paysages ruraux à Saint-Remi de Reims au IXe siècle', *Revue belge de philologie et d'histoire*, 89:1/2 (2011), 267–94, at 272–5; for the Ardennes: J.-P. Devroey and N. Schroeder, 'Beyond royal estates and monasteries: landownership in the early medieval Ardennes', *Early Medieval Europe*, 20:1 (2012), 39–69.
97 For tenth-century northern Spain, see Davies, *Acts of Giving*, p. 165; five female for twenty-three male attested landowners in Lembach, between *c*. 750 and *c*. 850, G. Caro, 'Zwei Elsässer Dörfer zur Zeit Karls des Großen. Ein Beitrag zur wirtschaftsgeschichtlichen Verwertung der *Traditiones Wizenburgenses*', *Zeitschrift für die Geschichte des Oberrheins*, 56, n.s. 17 (1902), 450–79, 563–87. In Courtisols, the *ingenua* Benimmia was co-tenant of a free *mansus* with a certain Adelhardus; the *ingenua* Gerouuagdis held an entire free *mansus*: *Le polyptyque et les listes de cens de l'abbaye Saint-Remi de Reims (IXe–XIe s.). Edition critique*, ed. J.-P. Devroey (Reims: Académie nationale de Reims, 1984), p. 17.
98 See West, *Reframing the Feudal Revolution*, p. 66.
99 For example, Davies, *Small Worlds*, p. 47.

land in several settlements, spread over one or several regions.[100] Between these extreme cases, the connection between social status and landowning is less direct. The social dynamics of early medieval societies were such that legally unfree people could hold well-equipped farmsteads in tenure and be relatively wealthy. Conversely, being a free landowner did not prevent economic struggle. Therefore, the connection between legal status and socio-economic position was not necessarily direct and the lowest free strata and the upper unfree strata of peasant societies might often overlap.

Land was a resource that drew distinctions between people. It was usually owned or held in tenancy by individuals or nuclear families, and hence records of transfer or records listing tenures usually specify a single individual or a couple as owner/tenant. However, there are also cases of co-ownership and co-tenancy, although they appear less numerous. In northern Iberia, it is explicitly recorded that some family members co-owned property; there are frequent references to co-ownership with siblings, cousins and the offspring of cousins.[101] In a charter of 777, land transferred to the monastery of Wissembourg is said to be adjoining a plot owned by Frodulf and his *consortes*.[102] Co-tenancy was frequent in the large estates of Francia. In the aforementioned estate of Courtisols, but also in Prüm's estate of Villance, in the Ardennes, up to four individuals could be co-tenants of a single tenure.[103] This probably reflects a situation in which several families lived in separate homesteads, but shared the resources, rights and dues attached to a single tenure.

How can we picture the distribution of properties and land at the local level? A useful reflection on the topographic distribution of land is

---

100 For Tuscany, see C. Wickham, 'Aristocratic wealth in Tuscany and Lazio, 700–1050: elements for a comparison', in Le Jan, Feller and Devroey (eds), *Les élites et la richesse au Haut Moyen Âge*, pp. 251–63.

101 'ut donaremus uobis Fraterno et Uistregotoni pomare in Argonaues quod abemus comune con Monesto'; 'damus uobis iiii portione, quam abeo comune cum mea socra et mea mulier'; 'ut uinderem tiui mea uinea quem abeo tecum comune in Pauualias'; 'medietate tibi conzedimus, extra illas ii terras quem abeo comunes con illos meos congermanos'; T 13 (875), Lii 304 (957), V 37 (966), Liii 585 (999). See Davies, *Acts of Giving*, ch. 3.

102 TW 230; and, for *consortes*, see further below, p. 154.

103 For Villance, see J.-P. Devroey and N. Schroeder, 'Land, oxen, and brooches. Local societies, inequality, and large estates in the early medieval Ardennes (c. 850–c. 900)', in J. A. Quirós Castillo (ed.), *Social Inequality in Early Medieval Europe: Local Societies and Beyond* (Turnhout: Brepols, 2019), pp. 187–92. For Courtisols, *Le polyptyque et les listes de cens*, ed. Devroey, pp. 16–19.

provided by Chris Wickham's characterisation of rural societies and landowning in Tuscany.[104] He described the distribution of land as

a complex network of landowning, with greater and lesser estateowners (who formed an as yet ill-defined 'aristocratic' stratum), larger and smaller ecclesiastical establishments, and rich and poor peasant owners, all owning side by side – often, thanks to a high level of fragmentation of property, all in the same village.

On a structural level, similar conditions of intermingled and variable landownership are observed in all regions discussed here. Charters from Bavaria, the Rhineland, northern Iberia and the Ardennes transmit statements of boundaries which show that, at least in certain areas of these regions, worked properties belonging to different owners were packed close together, side by side.[105] For example, there were at least twenty-three men and five women owning land in Lembach between c. 750 and c. 850, and there were twenty-one different landowners in Preuschdorf in Alsace between c. 720 and c. 820.[106] In the villages along the Rhine – which can be studied through particularly rich collections of charters – more than a hundred landowners are sometimes attested within a single

104 C. Wickham, 'Problems of comparing rural societies in early medieval Western Europe', *Transactions of the Royal Historical Society*, 2 (1992), 221–46, at 228–9; Wickham, *Framing the Early Middle Ages*, pp. 387–93.
105 For Bavaria, see Kohl, *Lokale Gesellschaften*, pp. 154–5; for the Rhineland, Kohl, 'Ländliche Gesellschaft', and Freudenberg, *Trado atque dono*. For Northern Iberia, Davies, *Acts of Giving*, pp. 8–9; a comparison between Brittany and northern Iberia is presented in Davies, 'Free Peasants and Large Landowners'.
106 For Alsace, Caro, 'Zwei Elsässer Dörfer'; see also F. Schwind, 'Beobachtungen zur inneren Struktur des Dorfes in karolingischer Zeit', in H. Jankuhn, R. Schützeichel and F. Schwind (eds), *Das Dorf der Eisenzeit und des frühen Mittelalters – wirtschaftliche Funktion – soziale Struktur. Bericht über die Kolloquien der Kommission für die Altertumskunde Mittel- und Nordeuropas in den Jahren 1973 und 1974* (Göttingen: Vandenhoeck & Ruprecht, 1977), pp. 444–93; C. Wickham, *The Inheritance of Rome: A History of Europe from 400 to 1000* (London: Allen Lane, 2009), pp. 207–8; Wickham, 'Problems of comparing rural societies', 234. For the Ardennes, see Devroey and Schroeder, 'Beyond royal estates and monasteries', 54; P. Mignot and N. Schroeder, 'Agrarian practices and landscape in the estate of Wellin (Belgium) from the early Middle Ages to the modern period: archaeology and history', in J. Klápště (ed.), *Agrarian Technology in the Medieval Landscape. Ruralia X. 9th–15th September 2013, Smolenice, Slovakia* (Turnhout: Brepols, 2016), pp. 267–78, at pp. 273–4.

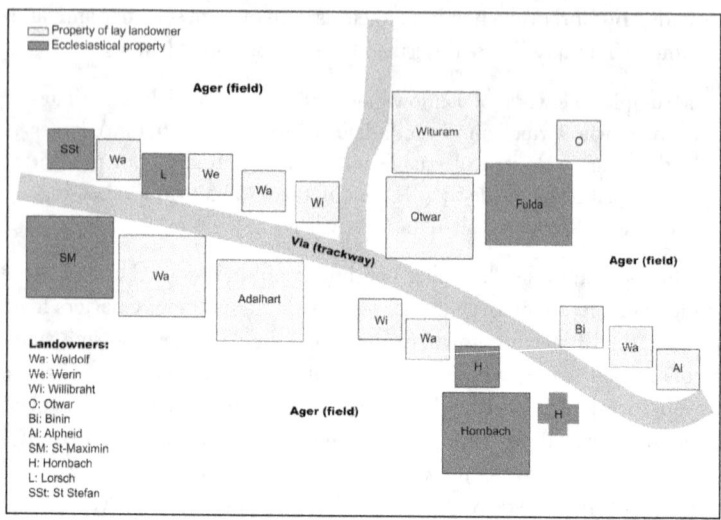

Figure 3.5 Property in Eimsheim

settlement, albeit across quite a long period. In Dienheim, at least 216 are named for the period between 754 and 841.[107]

While it is reasonable to generalise the pattern of land distribution of Tuscany and the Middle Rhine, important variations in the quantity of fragmentation of land and in the proportions of landowners and tenants of different types have to be expected both within a region and in different regional ensembles.[108] Multiple environmental, economic, demographic and social factors affect this balance. Particular agricultural activities, such as the growing of vines, often generated highly fragmented landscapes of property.[109] In the Frankish heartlands (Île-de-France, Champagne, Ardennes), the coexistence of different types of demesne land and land belonging to peasants created complex patterns of fields of different sizes, worked more or less intensively.[110] Importantly, patterns of landowning

107 Kohl, 'Ländliche Gesellschaft'.
108 Local variation within a region is discussed by Davies, *Small Worlds*, pp. 91–104.
109 Kohl, 'Ländliche Gesellschaft'.
110 J.-P. Devroey, 'Mise en valeur du sol et cycles de culture dans le système domanial (VIIIe–Xe siècle) entre Seine et Rhin', in R. Viader and C. Rendu (eds), *Cultures temporaires et féodalité. Les rotations culturales et l'appropriation du sol dans l'Europe médiévale et moderne* (Toulouse: Presses Universitaires du Mirail, 2014), pp. 33–57.

could change quite significantly over time, as recent discussions of the relationship between settlement, landscapes and farming in England exemplify.[111] In England, the long-term agrarian expansion and intensification between the seventh and eleventh centuries was associated with the emergence of new forms of management of land and resources. At the beginning of the period, arable farming was predominantly carried out in relatively small enclosed fields of permanent arable (the infield) surrounded by extensive pasture that could be partly cultivated for short periods of time when needed (the outfield). With growing population and increasing exchange, the balance between arable and pastoral production gradually shifted and farmers had to find new ways to manage local resources. Several charters reveal that in the second half of the tenth century, in regions of England such as Wiltshire and Berkshire, fields of arable land consisted of intermingled strips.[112] A charter of 956 concerning five hides of land at Charlton in Berkshire, for example, states that this land 'is not divided up by fixed boundaries, but the acres adjoin other acres' (see figure 8.6).[113] Farmers who owned shares in such a field probably engaged in *some* form of cooperation that made this arrangement beneficial, such as common pasturing after harvest. Yet it would be excessive to conclude from this evidence that the extensive open fields known from high and late medieval evidence already existed in tenth-century England. It is likely that at that time only part of the arable land of a settlement was organised in strip fields; shareholders could be relatively small groups of farmers rather than entire village communities; in all likelihood, cooperation was voluntary and flexible rather than enforced by compulsory regulations.[114] More extensive open fields that covered entire townships and whose rules were binding on entire village communities are only known from later times, both in England and on the continent.[115]

111 The following discussion is based on D. Banham and R. Faith, *Anglo-Saxon Farms and Farming* (Oxford: Oxford University Press, 2014), pp. 269–92; Blair, *Building Anglo-Saxon England*, pp. 294–301.
112 E.g. Sawyer 691, 730.
113 Sawyer 634: 'Nam prefatum rus nullis certis terminis dirimitur sed iugera adiacent iugeribus'.
114 This is discussed further below, pp. 88–91.
115 See above, pp. 8–9. For the continent, see H. Renes, 'Grainlands. The landscape of open fields in a European perspective', *Landscape History*, 31:2 (2010), 37–70, at 38–40; S. Moorhouse and J. Bond, 'An approach to understanding medieval field systems', in Klápště (ed.), *Agrarian Technology in the Medieval Landscape*, pp. 1–48; N. Schroeder, 'Medieval and modern open fields in

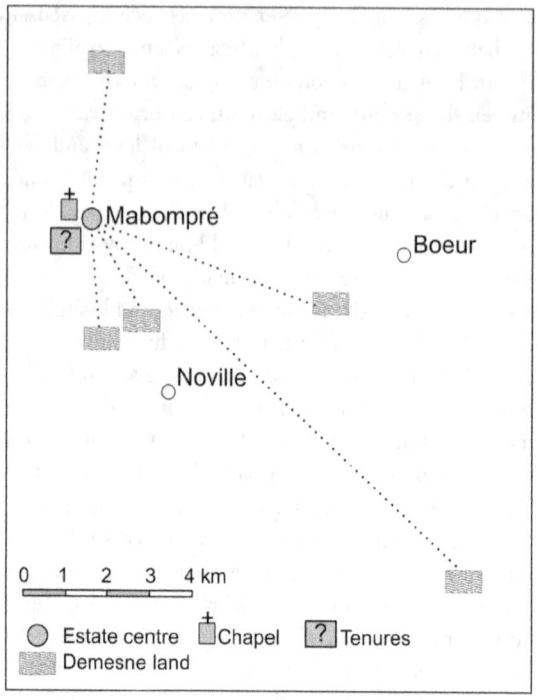

Figure 3.6   Prüm's estate of Mabompré (893)

For the most part, we know more about the estates of high aristocrats, kings and churches than about the property of small owner-cultivators. Aristocratic property could be scattered or concentrated. Regions with a strong aristocratic implantation, such as the Île-de-France, the Rhineland or the Ardennes, are more likely to present important local concentrations of land, which put a single landowner in a hegemonic position. In Courtisols, Saint-Remi of Reims owned a seigneurial *mansum*, 92.5 free *mansa*, 35 unfree *mansa* and a church.[116] Even if other actors owned land in the settlement, the monks' position must have been hegemonic in the local context. It is important, however, to stress that while exclusive aristocratic dominance over compact block-estates is attested locally, it

   Southern Belgium: a summary review and new perspectives', in C. Dyer, E. Thoen and T. Williamson (eds), *Peasants and their Fields. The Rationale of Open-Field Agriculture* (Turnhout: Brepols, 2018), pp. 183–206, at p. 189. For the earliest Bavarian evidence, Kohl, *Lokale Gesellschaften*, p. 343.
116   *Le polyptyque et les listes de cens*, ed. Devroey, pp. 16–28.

often coexisted with more scattered forms of landowning and estate organisation.[117] One of Prüm's monastic estates in the Ardennes, for example, consisted of several seigneurial buildings in a locality named Mabompré, an aggregate of tenures that are not located with any precision, and fifteen fields of demesne land that are partly located in Mabompré, but also spread in surrounding settlements (see figure 3.6).[118]

The charters of Saint-Gall suggest that power and wealth could be manifest through the use of place-names that display a link between a settlement and an individual or his family. Around 800 the cleric Hadubert held property in *Haddinuuilare* (modern Hatzenweiler), a place-name that probably refers to his father Haddo.[119] In 816 a certain Werinpertus transferred property in a place named Werinpertivilare to Saint-Gall. This place seems to have been founded by a homonymous ancestor of Werinpert, as the charter states that the latter gave 'everything that my ancestors left me there through the right of inheritance' (*omne quicquid ibidem antecessores mei iure hereditario supersti reliquerunt*).[120] At roughly the same time, a certain Wisrih donated the so-called *Wisirihiscella* and the *presbiter* Maio transferred his *cella Maionis* to the monastery.[121]

If we focus on the property and tenures of less wealthy individuals and families, an important distinction in terms of structures can be made between northern Iberia and the other regions.[122] In Bavaria, Brittany, England, Francia, the Middle Rhine and Tuscany there were standard farming units with distinctive names: hide in England, *ran* in Brittany, *mansus*, *casa et res* or *casa massaricia* in Tuscany, *mansus* (Romance) or *hoba* (Germanic) in Francia and east of the Rhine.[123] In Bavaria, the

117 Devroey, *Puissants et misérables*, pp. 443–74.
118 J.-P. Devroey, 'La hiérarchisation des pôles habités et l'espace rural. Autour des possessions de l'abbaye de Prüm (893) en Ardenne belge', in M. Gaillard et al. (eds), *De la mer du Nord à la Méditerranée. Francia Media. Une région au coeur de l'Europe (c. 840–c. 1050)* (Luxembourg: CLUDEM, 2011), pp. 175–206; Devroey and Schroeder, 'Beyond royal estates and monasteries', 52–3.
119 W 58, 215. For Hadubert, see B. Zeller, 'Local priests in early medieval Alamannia: the charter evidence', in S. Patzold and C. van Rhijn (eds), *Men in the Middle: Local Priests in Early Medieval Europe* (Berlin: De Gruyter, 2016), pp. 32–49, at pp. 44–5.
120 W 219.
121 W 222, 216, 219.
122 See Devroey, *Puissants et misérables*, pp. 413–15.
123 Compare Faith, *The English Peasantry*, pp. 128–43; Davies, *Small Worlds*, pp. 39–47; C. Wickham, *The Mountains and the City. The Tuscan Appennines in the Early Middle Ages* (Oxford: Clarendon Press, 1988), p. 27.

homestead was called *curtifer* (*area* in the charters from Regensburg after *c.* 840), while *mansus* (*hoba*/*hobonia* from the middle of the ninth century onwards) was used to refer to the entire living and farming unit within the context of estate organisation.[124] In northern Iberia, however, there was no equivalent concept referring to farming and property units.[125] In the latter region, the property of a typical peasant household appears to have consisted of a mixture of different plots scattered within the territory of a residential group: for example, an exchange of one property on the *meseta* in 965 involved a house, parcels of arable, half a mill, water rights, half a meadow and half a bramble patch.[126] This set of properties was not fundamentally different from a Bavarian *hoba*, or a *mansus* in the Ardennes or Champagne. However, it was not perceived as an organic unit designated by a specific label, but as separate pieces of property, whose single common characteristic was to be owned by the same landowner at a particular moment in time.

The size of properties varied significantly at regional and local levels. Based on the work of Pallares on Rabal, in southern Galicia, one might note an average size of about 15 hectares for a peasant property in that region and 2 hectares (maximum) for a constituent parcel.[127] In Saint-Germain-des-Prés's estates of Épinay, Thiais, Verrières and Palaiseau, tenants held respectively 9.65 (free tenures) and 5.5 hectares (unfree tenures); 8 (free) and 5.7 (unfree) hectares; 4.85 (free) and 1.85 (unfree) hectares; and 6.1 (free) and 1.6 (unfree) hectares of arable land.[128] In the Middle Rhine, the average size of peasant properties can be estimated between 15 to 25 *iurnales* of arable land, a few vineyards and grassland.[129] For households with no vineyards, the arable part was larger: somewhere between 25 and 50 *iurnales*. The average size of a *hoba* as it appears in the *Liber possessionum* of Wissembourg was 30 *iurnales*.[130] In Bavaria, the average size of an exploitation is estimated between 20 and 60 *iurnales*.[131] This

---

124 Kohl, *Lokale Gesellschaften*, pp. 324–6.
125 Davies, 'Free peasants and large landowners', p. 369. *Villa* is often used but it has a very wide range of reference.
126 Lii 388 (965).
127 M. del C. Pallares Méndez, *Ilduara, una aristócrata del siglo X* (La Coruña: Ediciós Do Castro, 1998); see Davies, *Acts of Giving*, pp. 189–90.
128 Toubert, *L'Europe dans sa première croissance*, pp. 59–60.
129 Kohl, 'Ländliche Gesellschaft'; Freudenberg, *Trado atque dono*, pp. 94–8.
130 LPW, pp. 51–2.
131 Kohl, *Lokale Gesellschaften*, pp. 329–31; Kohl, 'Ländliche Gesellschaft'.

slightly higher figure might reflect the general imbalance in soil quality between the fertile Rhine valley and Bavaria. In all these regions, properties could be more or less scattered.

It has often been assumed that within monastic or royal estates of the Frankish heartlands, holdings such as *mansi* and *hobae* were standardised in size and composition.[132] However, on closer examination, it appears that the size of holdings within an estate often varied; evidence attesting the direct intervention of large landowners in local contexts to impose standard farming units or smooth over socio-economic disparities remains elusive.[133] As already noticed by Charles-Edmond Perrin, the very detailed polyptyques of the Île-de-France suggest that the size of *mansi* varied, even in a single estate.[134] In 893 in Prüm's estate of Villance, individual tenants or co-tenants could occupy a full *mansus*, half a *mansus*, a quarter *mansus*, one-eighth of a *mansus*, or a full *mansus* and a quarter; this observation points to an unequal distribution of land and doubtless socio-economic disparities among the tenants.[135] In particular monastic estates, a tendency to standardisation can be observed, but it is never absolute: the polyptyque of Saint-Bertin, for example, suggests that 58 per cent of all *mansi* belonging to the monastery held 12 *bonnarii* of arable;[136] while this number reveals an element of homogenisation, it also shows that it was limited, as 42 per cent of the *mansi* had less or more arable. Variations in size might reveal socio-economic disparities,

---

132   See, for example, H.-J. Nitz, 'The Church as colonist: the Benedictine abbey of Lorsch and planned *Waldhufen* colonization in the Odenwald', *Journal of Historical Geography*, 9 (1983), 105–26; H.-J. Nitz, 'Settlement structures and settlement systems of the Frankish central state in Carolingian and Ottonian times', in D. Hooke (ed.), *Anglo-Saxon Settlements* (Oxford: Blackwell, 1988), pp. 249–73; C. Sonnlechner, 'The establishment of new units of production in Carolingian times: making early medieval sources relevant for environmental history', *Viator*, 35 (2004), 21–48.

133   See the observations in Kohl, *Lokale Gesellschaften*, p. 326; N. Schroeder, 'Der Odenwald in Früh- und Hochmittelalter. Siedlung, Landschaft und Grundherrschaft in einem Mittelgebirge', *Siedlungsforschung. Archäologie, Geschichte, Geographie*, 33 (2016), 355–87, at 373–7.

134   C. E. Perrin, *Recherches sur la seigneurie rurale en Lorraine d'après les plus anciens censiers (IXe–XIIe siècle)* (Paris: Les Belles Lettres, 1935), p. 64.

135   Devroey, Schroeder, 'Land, oxen, and brooches'.

136   J.-P. Devroey, *Économie rurale et société dans l'Europe franque (VIe–IXe siècles)*. 1. *Fondements matériels, échanges et lien social* (Paris: Belin, 2003), p. 302; Devroey, *Puissants et misérables*, pp. 434–5.

but also forms of economic specialisation and adaptation to particular environments.[137]

The repeated attempts of tenants to obtain more land to add to their normal share suggest that the composition of tenures could fluctuate, something that is not to be expected from highly standardised units. At some point between 902 and 922, Madelgerus, Officia and Hildebertus, three members of the *familia* of Gorze at Vanault, were accused of treating the monastery's land (*terra indominicata*) as if it was part of their tenures (*hereditas*).[138] In 977 several men belonging to the same monastery and living in the estate of Flomersheim near Worms bribed the monastery's local estate managers in order to obtain demesne land (*indominicatis terris*) and work it as if it were part of their tenures.[139] When the abbot and the community found out about this, they first decided to reclaim this unjustly alienated land. However, 'taking into account the labour of poor people', they finally agreed to transform this demesne land into tenures. The very fact that some tenants tried to extend the amount of land they controlled suggests that a certain degree of fluctuation in the composition of tenures was normal.

As observed above, farming units were very often composed of a homestead associated with different pieces of land that could be more or less scattered. Some resources, however, such as woodland or water, were not 'owned', either as private or collective property. Individuals or groups had the right to access them and withdraw resources, yet this did not imply any formal claim over the 'property' or any 'ownership' of land. It is likely, for example, that the *terrae indomitae* and *montes* into which peasant groups intruded in northern Iberia did not designate land that was appropriated directly and managed intensively by a proprietor, but areas in the neighbourhood of settlements that were used occasionally for pasture, collecting wood and so on.[140] Given the nature of the northern Iberian texts that survive, we only hear about such circumstances

---

137 Devroey, *Économie rurale et société*, pp. 300–7; Devroey and Schroeder, 'Land, oxen, and brooches'.
138 *Cartulaire de l'abbaye de Gorze. Ms. 826 de la bibliothèque de Metz*, ed. A. D'Herbomez (Paris: Klincksieck, 1898), no. 78, pp. 141–3.
139 *Cartulaire de l'abbaye de Gorze*, ed. D'Herbomez, no. 114, pp. 207–9. See J.-P. Devroey, 'Du grand domaine carolingien à la "seigneurie monastique". Saint-Remi de Reims, Gorze, Saint-Vanne de Verdun (880–1050)', in D. Iogna-Prat et al. (eds), *Cluny. Les moines et la société au premier âge féodal* (Rennes: Presses Universitaires de Rennes, 2013), pp. 279–98.
140 For the 'intrusion' of peasants into monastic land, see above, pp. 69–70.

if rights to use the land were challenged; on the whole, that did not happen until monasteries started claiming exclusive rights to pasture in the eleventh century, which they partly did by massaging tenth-century charters.[141] Several charters also refer to tensions about the use of water to power mills. In these cases, monasteries argued that the mills of locals would deprive them of water. In 932 the abbot of San Torcuato took legal action in the count's court against the *heretarios* in five successive settlements along the river Arlanzón in order to get access to the watercourse (see figure 8.5 for locations).[142] In this record twenty-three people are named from the settlements. The abbot was successful in securing access, though only limited – the rights of the locals were in effect confirmed, for the abbot was awarded only a little water. In another case, in 938, the abbot of Valdevimbre took action in the king's court against the people of San Juan en Vega in order to access water, again to power the abbey's mills.[143] He made a series of complaints that the locals were drawing off so much water that there was none left for the monastery; after several sessions the judges pronounced against the abbot, saying that there was clearly enough water for everyone. However, in the spirit of harmony, the text ends by laying an obligation on the locals to let the monastery have water as necessary.

References to shared resources from the northern regions discussed here also refer to shared use of woodland and water. In 827 the abbot of Stavelot in the Ardennes complained to Louis the Pious because the manager (*actor fisci*) of the royal estate of Theux had authorised his people to use woodlands that belonged to the monastery.[144] The emperor sent out two *missi*. After investigating the case, they declared that both the members of the monastic *familia* and the people belonging to the royal estate had the right to access these woodlands and withdraw resources. In the Rhineland, a priest named Lantfried gave to the monastery of

141 For example, V 2; BG 27, BG 340, BG 318 – all false.
142 C 22; see further below, pp. 106, 197.
143 Li 128; see further below, p. 194.
144 See HR 29 and C. Wickham, 'European forests in the early Middle Ages: landscape and land clearance', in *L'ambiente vegetale nell'alto medioevo* (Spoleto: Fondazione CISAM, 1990), pp. 479–548, at p. 512; N. Schroeder, *Les hommes et la terre de saint Remacle. Histoire sociale et économique de l'abbaye de Stavelot-Malmedy, VIIe–XIVe siècle* (Brussels: Université de Bruxelles, 2015), p. 27. Cf. *actor regis* in Italy, below, p. 176.

Wissembourg a 'common wood' that could feed 200 pigs.[145] The phrasing of the charter suggests that while Lantfried owned the ground, the resources supported by it were open to shared use – probably for a fee. In another case, c. 868, Heripreht and Alpcoz exchanged property with the monastery of Saint-Gall; they gave 105 *hobae* of land situated next to Lake Zurich as well as their share in the local common wood.[146] Shared resources are also attested in Bavarian charters. An exchange between Bishop Anno of Freising and Reginfrid in Jakobsbaiern and in Glonn notes that Reginfrid received usage rights with others in a piece of woodland (*in silva communem usum cum aliis*);[147] Isanperht gave some land and 'a share with others in the common wood' in Wang (*de silva communem partem cum aliis*).[148] In tenth-century Bavaria, the word *cives* was used to designate a group of landowners who had access to a particular tract of common woodland.[149]

Contemporary cases of shared rights in woodlands are also known in England. In 825 a council was held at a location known as *Clofesho*; it involved on one side Bishop Heahberht of Worcester and, on the other, an unspecified number of *swangerefan*.[150] This word refers to an officer (*gerefa*, reeve) in charge of the pasturing of swine in woods. The record, obviously presenting Worcester's view of the matter, says that the reeves in charge of the swineherds at Sinton, in Leigh, had tried to extend the pasture farther, and take in more of the wood than the ancient rights permitted. The bishop and his men argued that since the time of Æthelbald, the reeve only had the right to feed 300 pigs in these woods, as two-thirds of the wood and the mast belonged to the bishop and the cathedral community. The dispute was settled through an oath taken by the bishop thirty days later at Worcester. Hama, the reeve in charge of the swineherds, rode to Worcester, watched the oath, but did not challenge the bishop. As a result, the case was resolved in favour of Worcester.

145 TW 200: 'Ego igitur in dei nomen Lantfridus corepiscopus dono ad ipso loco sancto pro anime mee remedium [...] silua in communiis que possunt porci saginari numero CC, si fructus euenerit'.
146 W 531: 'de communi silva quantum ad portionem nostram pertinet'.
147 TF 817 (859/64), a similar clause in 805 (857/64).
148 TF 951 (876/83).
149 TF 1180 (957/72), 1305 (981/94): 'communio in silva sicut mos est illorum civium'.
150 Sawyer 1437.

Fishing rights could also be managed as a form of shared access to resources. With permission of King Louis the German, c. 874, the royal vassal Witpert transferred two *hobae* of land in Feldbach, next to Lake Zurich, including fishing rights in the lake.[151]

Conclusion: uniformity and diversity

Farmsteads mostly made out of perishable materials; settlement networks that combine isolated and more or less regularly grouped farmsteads; farmers who are busy cultivating their fields or taking care of their animals; individuals who engage in crafts, either for their household or in order to produce surplus for the lord or the market; woodland, rivers and wastelands that are used as shared resources; a church, a hall or a few larger buildings that stand out in the landscape and signal the presence of God or an overlord: these observations could characterise any of the local societies discussed in this book.

Yet, beyond this apparent uniformity, diversity prevails: the environment gave regional and local characteristics to settlements and farming; the socio-economic status of individuals and ties of dependency could vary significantly from region to region, from settlement to settlement and even from farmstead to farmstead. Over time, demographic and economic processes as well as the accumulation of wealth and power transformed local societies and the material world that surrounded them. These changes were rarely linear and are characterised by temporal and spatial variability. The rural societies discussed in this book were dynamic and contrasted; they were neither as primitive nor as stagnant as has sometimes been affirmed in the dismissive 'Dark Age' historiography.

---

151 W 576: 'necnon et piscationis usum illius laci, qui supradicto loco contiguus fore videtur'.

4

Making groups: collective action in rural settlements

As Chapter 3 has shown, clustered settlements of different kinds were common across early medieval western Europe. As a consequence, interacting with neighbours was for most people a fact of life. So when the ninth-century Carolingian monk Ratramnus of Corbie offered advice in a famous letter to a Frankish missionary in the field in Scandinavia, he advised that cohabitation in villages (*villarum cohabitatio*) implied that the residents followed laws of society (*societas*). The learned monk therefore considered that Late Antique ideas about the rule-bound life of cities also applied to communal living (*contubernia*) in the countryside: for Ratramnus, village life was in that sense a mark of civilisation.[1]

Yet although in the same text Ratramnus also discussed agricultural activity – ploughing, sowing, harvesting – he said nothing about the collective aspects of this work. And his assumption that rural cohabitation was necessarily associative or communal was perhaps based on the intensely rule-bound monastic life he himself took part in as much as on any real experience of rural communities, whether in Scandinavia or closer to home in northern Francia – unless he was thinking of groups

---

1 Ratramnus of Corbie, *Epistolae*, MGH Epp. 6, p. 155. See S. Bruce, 'Hagiography as monstrous ethnography: a note on Ratramnus of Corbie's letter concerning the conversion of the Cynocephali', in G. Wieland, C. Ruff and R. G. Arthur (eds), *Insignis Sophiae Arcator: Medieval Latin Studies in Honour of Michael Herren on his 65th Birthday* (Turnhout: Brepols, 2006), pp. 45–56. Bavarian charters also sometimes described residents of settlements as *cives*: see T. Kohl, *Lokale Gesellschaften. Formen der Gemeinschaft in Bayern vom 8. bis zum 10. Jahrhundert* (Ostfildern: Thorbecke, 2010), p. 126; the term is also used in hagiography (see p. 108), and appears also in a formulary from Saint-Gall, *Formulae Sangallenses Miscellanae*, no. 9, in MGH Formulae, p. 383.

of people who farmed the monastery's lands and perhaps came there for communal prayer and the liturgy from time to time.² Simple proximity of residence is not in itself proof of joint organisation, activity or a sense of community, and we should be careful not to project modern or indeed medieval preconceptions on to it. After all, we know that rural settlements were socially heterogeneous, fractured by variations in wealth, property tenure and legal status.³ Quite apart from the unfree population, there were differences between wealthier and less wealthy peasants: Dienheim on the Middle Rhine, for instance, had many free residents who never witnessed any charters.⁴ Such disparities in the social makeup of settlements are particularly evident in the ninth-century polyptyque of Prüm. It distinguishes between men and women who belong to the monastery and live in Villance as tenants, those who belong to the monastery and live in Villance without being tenants, those who belong to the monastery but have moved away from Villance, and those who do not belong to the monastery but live in Villance. On the ground, individuals were distinguished by where they lived and to whom they did or did not belong.⁵

This chapter therefore focuses on specific evidence for local collective activity, defined narrowly here as a residential group working together in pursuit of some shared goal or objective, in this way side-stepping more abstract (and essentially unanswerable) questions about the nature of the collective that such activity may have generated.⁶ Even if collective

---

2   This is suggested by Angilbert's order of the liturgy of the monastery of Saint-Riquier: Angilbert, *Institutio sancti Angilberti abbatis de diversitate officiorum (800–811)*, ed. K. Hallinger, D. M. Wegener and D. H. Frank, in K. Hallinger (ed.), *Initia consuetudinis benedictinae. Consuetudines saeculi octavi et noni* (Siegburg: Schmitt, 1963), pp. 283–303, detailing the involvement of neighbouring settlements in processions at Easter and Pentecost. See S. Rabe, *Faith, Art and Politics at Saint-Riquier* (Philadelphia, PA: University of Pennsylvania Press, 1995), pp. 122–32 (labelling the nearby settlements 'towns' despite their rural character).
3   See above, pp. 64–85.
4   T. Kohl, 'Gemeinde vor der Gemeinde? Dienheim in karolingischer Zeit', in A. Greule (ed.), *Die ländliche Gemeinde im Spätmittelalter* (Berlin: Weidler, 2005), pp. 185–204.
5   For Villance, see above, pp. 74, 81.
6   For relevant problems and perspectives, see J. Morsel (coord.), *Communautés d'habitants au moyen âge (XIe–XVe siècles)* (Paris: Editions de la Sorbonne, 2018), pp. 5–39.

activities were only undertaken by a section of a residential group, they will still be considered here.

Our focus is resolutely local, concentrating on collective action within residential groups rather than between them. What follows concentrates on three dimensions: the role of collective action as a matter of routine, the extent to which it could take on legal definition and its relationship to a variety of locally present outsiders: foreigners, strangers and the excluded.

Routine collective activity

Farming

For most of the population in early medieval Europe, the bulk of their time was taken up with agricultural work and with processing its products. There is good reason to suppose that neighbours loomed large in this. We may imagine that it would have been necessary from time to time to borrow items of equipment such as carts from neighbours – as the ninth-century peasant Dagobert did in the *Apparitio Sancti Vedasti*, to fetch timber from the nearby wood.[7] And we can presume too that farmers might have relied on help from their neighbours when required by imbalances of labour within the household, at moments of crisis, or at pinch points throughout the year, while the active land market visible in much of the Latin West helped negotiate longer-term changes in household capacities and needs, as families grew and shrank.[8]

---

7 Hupertus, *Apparitio sancti Vedasti*, AASS, 6 feb, vol. 1, pp. 803–5: 'vicini sui carpentum mutuans, perrexit siluam'; see C. West, 'Visions in a ninth-century village: an early medieval microhistory', *History Workshop Journal*, 81 (2016), 1–16.

8 P. Fowler, *Farming in the First Millennium* (Cambridge: Cambridge University Press, 2002). For the peasant life-cycle, see J.-P. Devroey, *Économie rurale et société dans l'Europe franque (VIe–IXe siècles) 1. Fondements matériels, échanges et lien social* (Paris: Belin, 2003) and J.-P. Devroey and N. Schroeder, 'Land, oxen, and brooches. Local societies, inequality, and large estates in the early medieval Ardennes (c. 850–c. 900)', in J. A. Quirós Castillo (ed.), *Social Inequality in Early Medieval Europe: Local Societies and Beyond* (Turnhout: Brepols, 2019), pp. 177–202. For the land market, R. Portass, *The Village World of Early Medieval Northern Spain: Local Community and the Land Market* (Woodbridge: Boydell Press, 2017); L. Feller, A. Gramain and F. Weber, *La fortune de Karol: Marché de la terre et liens personnels dans les Abruzzes au haut Moyen Âge* (Rome: École française de Rome, 2005); O. Bruand, *Les origines de la société féodale: l'exemple de l'Autunois* (Dijon: Editions Universitaires de Dijon, 2009). For Bavaria, Kohl, *Lokale Gesellschaften*, pp. 117–19.

It seems nevertheless that most agricultural work between the North Sea and the Mediterranean was carried out by households, sometimes acting in concert but seldom working collectively.[9] There is no clear evidence before the tenth century for collective farming comparable to that of the open field system of the later Middle Ages, in which individuals owned patches of a large field that was managed as a single unit. Rather, we have a picture of individually owned, demarcated fields, whose boundaries could be delineated by listing neighbours' equally demarcated fields.[10] Those boundaries could also be infringed by these neighbours, as many charters and miracle stories attest: a man named Joseph, in the ninth-century *Miracula Remacli* from Stavelot, blamed the curvature of his spine on divine wrath for grazing his horse in his neighbour's field.[11]

Of course, not all land was owned by individual households, for co-ownership of agricultural assets is well evidenced.[12] However, the existence of shared assets does not in itself indicate collective action in their exploitation or management. When collective agricultural work does appear in the evidence – such as the 'multitude of ploughmen' (*aratorum multitudo*) featuring in a tenth-century miracle near Trier in Germany – it is usually in the context of obligations owed to landlords, in this case the monastery of St-Maximin of Trier.[13] There are occasional documented examples of *collaboratores* outside a seigneurial context, such as the ten co-workers at Papi in northern Italy who leased half a *fundus* there in 963, who were clearly peasants. These were probably cooperating entrepreneurs rather than representatives of a locality, but were still working together outside a household context.[14] Yet such examples are isolated.

9   See the still exemplary study of L. Kuchenbuch, *Bäuerliche Gesellschaft und Klosterherrschaft im 9. Jahrhundert. Studien zur Sozialstruktur der Familia der Abtei Prüm* (Wiesbaden: Steiner, 1978); cf. N. Schroeder, *Les hommes et la terre de saint Remacle. Histoire sociale et économique de l'abbaye de Stavelot-Malmedy, VIIe–XIVe siècle* (Brussels: Université de Bruxelles, 2015).
10 See above, pp. 59–60, 74–7, 80–2.
11 *Miracula Sancti Remacli*, AASS, 3 sept, vol. 1, pp. 696–721, at p. 697. Cf. *Miracula Sancti Huberti*, AASS, 3 nov, vol. 1, p. 807; Heiric of Auxerre, *Miracula Sancti Germani*, AASS, 31 jul, vol. 7, p. 268.
12 See above, pp. 83–4.
13 *Miracula Sancti Maximini*, AASS, 29 may, vol. 7, pp. 25–34; see K. Krönert, 'Les "Miracula Sancti Maximini" (BHL 5826): entre hagiographie et historiographie', *Revue Bénédictine*, 115 (2005), 112–50.
14 See C. Wickham, 'The Tivoli *breve* of 945', in A. Dierkens, N. Schroeder and A. Wilkin (eds), *Penser la paysannerie médiévale, un défi impossible?* (Paris: Editions de la Sorbonne, 2017), pp. 161–76.

Arguments that the adoption of new technologies, such as the heavy plough, required or promoted routine collective action by the residents of any given locality are based on surprisingly thin evidence.[15] Even medieval naming patterns suggest that strong collective bonds within settlements emerged only in the central Middle Ages; before this point, names were coined to mark out individuals, as opposed to the later practice in which names tended to indicate belonging to a group.[16]

When written sources describe peasants at work, they primarily portray the labouring individual – whether the individual farmers described in Wandalbert of Prüm's *On the Twelve Months*, the ploughmen depicted in iconographic representations from Carolingian Francia, or the lone tenth-century woman (*rusticana mulier*) ploughing the fields in southern France to whom Count Gerald of Aurillac gave money so that she could hire a man for this evidently gendered labour (*virile opus*).[17] Miracle stories imply that agricultural work was done within household units – for instance, a story in the *Miracula Remacli* about a certain Amulger, who was struck by divine wrath for gathering in his harvest on a Sunday with his spouse.[18]

These are of course elite images of work and labour.[19] Medieval (literary) elites were often suspicious of local collective action, which could bring to mind images of the lawless crowd (*turba*).[20] Frankish rulers and

---

15 R. Viader, 'Les grandes charrues. Cultures temporaires, communautés rurales et corvées de labour', in Dierkens, Schroeder and Wilkin (eds), *Penser la paysannerie médiévale*, pp. 363–85.

16 J. Chetwood, 'Re-evaluating English personal naming on the eve of the Conquest', *Early Medieval Europe*, 26:4 (2018), 518–47.

17 Wandalbert of Prüm, *De mensium duodecim*, in MGH poetae Latini aevi carolini 2, pp. 604–33 - translated in C. Hammer, *Charlemagne's Months and their Bavarian Labors: The Politics of the Seasons in the Carolingian Empire* (Oxford: British Archaeological Reports, 1997), pp. 53–70; *Vita sancti Geraldi Auriliacensis*, ed. A.-M. Bultot-Verleysen (Brussels: Société des Bollandistes, 2009), p. 168.

18 *Miracula Sancti Remacli*, p. 697.

19 See M. Lauwers, 'Le "travail" sans la domination?', in Dierkens, Schroeder and Wilkin (eds), *Penser la paysannerie médiévale*, pp. 303–32; cf. P. Freedman, *Images of the Medieval Peasant* (Stanford, CA: Stanford University Press, 1999), for a full study of elite representations (with a post-1000 focus), especially pp. 15–39.

20 S. Bobrycki, 'The flailing women of Dijon: crowds in ninth-century Europe', *Past and Present*, 240 (2018), 2–44. See further below, pp. 198–9.

their circle of advisors were keen to keep a close eye on guilds and confraternities, which gave a quasi-institutional setting to collective action. In a set of instructions to parish priests issued in 852, Archbishop Hincmar of Reims permitted guilds (*geldonia*) to meet for the purposes of prayer, but forbade feasting and joint dinners, where 'shameful and stupid mirth and disorder often take place, leading, as we have seen, to murder and hatred and dissension'.[21] Here Hincmar was taking his cue from an older tradition: in 779 Charlemagne had prohibited guild members from taking oaths to one another, which he associated with drunkenness. Whether guilds such as these were organised on a local basis, or as part of a trade or professional network, is not clarified.[22] But the prohibitions raise the possibility that there was more informal collective action than is now recorded.

Yet the unremittingly individual focus of the written evidence is also matched by the story of One Ox, or the *Versus de Unibove*. A folktale about a cunning peasant that was popular in later medieval and early modern Europe, the tale first appears in an eleventh-century manuscript from northern Francia, preserved in the monastery of Gembloux.[23] Despite its monastic transmission, this story is perhaps the closest that we can come to an early medieval peasant's own view of the world. The eponymous hero's bad luck means that he does not have enough oxen for a full plough team, hence his name. He nevertheless proudly runs his own affairs and household, relying on his cunning to see him through bad times, rather than teaming up on routine business with a neighbour. His social superiors in the settlement, all office holders, jealous of his independence and feigned luck, conspire against him, but in the end he outwits them. In this slightly ambivalent celebration of the quick-witted peasant householder, there is very little of collective action.

---

21 Hincmar of Reims, Capitulare 1, ch. 16, in MGH Capit. episc. 2, pp. 34–45, at p. 43: 'quas geldonias vel confratrias vulgo vocant'.
22 J.-P. Devroey, *Puissants et misérables. Système social et monde paysan dans l'Europe des Francs (VIe–IXe siècles)* (Brussels: Académie royale de Belgique, 2006), pp. 146–54.
23 Various editions of *Versus de Unibove* are available, of which the most recent is *La Beffa di Unibos*, ed. F. Bertini and F. Mosetti Casaretto (Alessandria: Edizione dell'Orso, 2000); see C. West, 'Exclusion et la paysannerie au XIe siècle au miroir des Versus de Unibove', in S. Joye, S. Gioanni and R. Le Jan (eds), *Richesse, pauvreté et exclusion dans les sociétés du haut Moyen Âge* (Turnhout: Brepols, forthcoming).

Collective obligations

The chief force in generating routine, local, collective obligations was that of landowners wherever they were powerful, especially in the Frankish heartlands. Charters frequently record transfer of land with all the people resident upon it (*commanentes*). Some obligations to landowners were carried out individually – for instance, the messenger service that is prominent in the polyptyque of Prüm. But demands for corvée labour, such as helping with the harvest, imply collaborative agricultural work on the lord's lands, as mentioned already in the context of Trier, and as documented in the estate records of Wissembourg.[24] One of the few legal texts to concern itself directly with labour services owed to lords, a ninth-century Frankish edict known as the Capitulary of Le Mans, even specified that farmers who were too poor to carry out ploughing obligations alone had to associate themselves with others to carry it out.[25] A comparable text is provided by Adalhard's directions about the management of the abbey of Corbie and its lands at the beginning of the ninth century, in which the abbot associated whole estates in arrangements through which the one nearer the monastery had to pay a double tithe in order not to burden one farther away with the task.[26] Monasteries such as Prüm might even demand that people travel to other estates to assist at harvest time.[27]

Female labour, such as weaving and spinning, was for the most part carried out within the household, but when coordinated as part of obligations to landlords, it was sometimes represented as collective work, as a drawing in the Utrecht Psalter depicts; in these circumstances, it may have taken place in a dedicated building.[28] These female spaces appear

---

24 LPW, pp. 60–71.
25 *Capitulare in pago cenomannico datum*, in MGH Capit. 1, pp. 81–2. See C. West, 'Carolingian kingship and the peasants of Le Mans: the *Capitulum in cenomannico pago datum*', in R. Große and M. Sot (eds), *Charlemagne: les temps, les espaces, les hommes. Construction et déconstruction d'un règne* (Turnhout: Brepols, 2018), pp. 227–44.
26 Adalhard of Corbie, *Consuetudines Corbeienses*, ed. J. Semmler, in *Initia consuetudinis benedictinae*, ed. Hallinger, pp. 355–418, at pp. 390–4. Adalhard of Corbie: 'Customs of Corbie', trans. C. W. Jones, in W. Horn and E. Born (eds), *The Plan of St. Gall* (Berkeley, CA: University of California Press, 1979), pp. 91–131.
27 *Das Prümer Urbar*, ch. 116, ed. I. Schwab (Düsseldorf: Droste, 1986), pp. 254–5.
28 For the gendering of labour and the places of work, see L. Kuchenbuch, 'Opus feminile. Das Geschlechterverhältnis im Spiegel von Frauenarbeiten im früheren Mittelalter', in H.-W. Goetz (ed.), *Weibliche Lebensgestaltung im frühen Mittelalter* (Cologne/Weimar/Vienna: Böhlau, 1991), pp. 139–75.

elsewhere too, for instance in the *Capitulare de Villis* and the Staffelsee Urbar. Unfortunately the sources do not really allow us to know whether it was only unfree women who had to work at these centralised sites, or whether those free tenants obliged to do textile work did so too.[29]

Not only did working together for the lords clearly involve group activity on the lord's behalf, but paying these lords their dues was most likely a collective action. Ninth-century monasteries such as Saint-Remi of Reims organised choreographed events in which the whole estate would collectively demonstrate its loyalty and subordination to the monks as they toured their lands.[30] On other occasions, dependants would bring their dues to the monastery in person. Those who became dependent on a monastery (*censuales*) had to give their dues on the same specific day (usually a saint's feast day), and it seems likely that they did this together, even though the dues themselves were individual obligations. These *censuales* might be scattered across a region, but it is likely that in areas where (church) lands were extensive, the payment of dues was organised by locality. Clear evidence is provided by the *Miracula* of Saint Remaclus, with a story about a dependant who stole the cup of Remaclus, a relic that was used by tenants who brought their rent (*annona*) to the monastery.[31] The same set of miracles also records how these tenants as a group also brought the *stipendia* for the brothers.[32] It seems to have been common for the monks to give a counter-gift of food and drink in exchange for labour service, as attested by the polyptyques; we might imagine a feast or at least some celebratory meal.[33]

These events were organised for the *familia* or dependants of monasteries rather than for the residents of a particular locality, but in northern France and the Low Countries, churches in particular could own entire settlements, making it difficult to draw a distinction between residential groups and church tenants. Though landlords seem to have weighed

29 M. Obermeier, *"Ancilla"*. *Beiträge zur Geschichte der unfreien Frauen im Frühmittelalter* (Pfaffenweiler: Centaurus, 1996), pp. 217–30.
30 J.-P Devroey, 'Communiquer et signifier entre seigneurs et paysans', in *Comunicare e significare nell'alto medioevo* (Spoleto: Fondazione CISAM, 2005), pp. 121–53.
31 *Miracula Sancti Remacli*, p. 703, 'singulis cum ipso vasculo bibentibus'.
32 *Miracula Sancti Remacli*, p. 699, each according to the *mensuram sibi indictam*.
33 L. Kuchenbuch, 'Porcus donativus: language use and gifting in seigniorial records between the eighth and the twelfth centuries', in G. Algazi et al. (eds), *Negotiating the Gift. Pre-modern Figurations of Exchange* (Göttingen: Vandenhoeck & Ruprecht, 2003), pp. 193–246.

most heavily on localities in Francia, there is evidence elsewhere too that the pressure placed on settlements by landlords could provide incentives for people living in those settlements to collaborate. For instance, the residents of Fuentes together apparently agreed to pay rent to the monastery of Sahagún in 977, an example of collective action that has parallels elsewhere in northern Iberia.[34]

Yet in much of Europe – notably in the south and east – this kind of pressure was sporadic, at least before 900. Even in northern Francia, where landlords had perhaps the greatest influence and power, it seems that the nature and value of the rent they could demand was as dependent on custom as on the landlord's wishes.[35] This custom was probably regional, rather than strictly local, but the English treatise known as *Gerefa* (*c.* 1000) stressed that these customs could vary from one estate (*onland*) to another.[36] In any case, none of these English customs referred to collective work; and it is striking that all the Frankish and Italian polyptyques organise their information primarily around individual households, whose duties could and often did vary within particular estates and settlements.

In England, the remarkable evidence of Domesday Book (1086) shows that peasants (*villani*) sometimes managed ('farmed') the demesne on the lord's behalf.[37] This was the case at an estate in Oare in Kent,[38] and at Willesden in Middlesex, where 'the villeins held this manor at farm from the canons [of St Paul's of London]' (*hoc manerium tenent villani ad firmam canonicorum*) – though in the latter case it seems likely that it was a group of the residents, not the whole settlement.[39] However,

---

34 W. Davies, *Windows on Justice in Northern Iberia 800–1000* (Abingdon: Routledge, 2016), pp. 219–26.

35 For a judicious discussion of the so-called *Rentenlandschaften*, see H.-W. Goetz, 'Herrschaft und Recht in der frühmittelalterlichen Grundherrschaft', *Historisches Jahrbuch*, 104 (1984), 392–410.

36 *Gerefa*, ed. and trans. T. Gobbitt, *Early English Laws*, online edition www.earlyenglishlaws.ac.uk/laws/texts/rect (accessed 29 July 2018): 'Geneat riht is mistlic be ðam ðe onlande stænt'.

37 S. Hoyt, 'Farm of the manor and community of the vill in Domesday Book', *Speculum*, 30 (1955), 147–69.

38 *Domesday Book: Kent*, ed. P. Morgan (Chichester: Phillimore, 1983), fol. 10b: 'Hanc tenent iii villani modo ad firmam'.

39 *Domesday Book: Middlesex*, ed. S. Wood (Chichester: Phillimore, 1975), fol. 127d. The text states there were 25 *villani* and 5 *bordarii* resident in Willesden, but only mentions the *villani* as holding the 'firma'.

these are exceptions in the enormous body of material provided by Domesday, and these arrangements may not have antedated the Norman Conquest of 1066, still less inform us about practice before the eleventh century.

Religion

Although the pace of change varied according to time and geography, local settlements in early medieval Europe were in general increasingly furnished with church buildings.[40] The role that the priests of these churches and chapels played within those residential groups is discussed below; here, however, the evidence for the collective action that developed around these buildings is briefly discussed.

In Francia, the deep involvement of the laity in the divine cult is a recurring theme in the normative sources that sprang up with the Carolingian reform, and this involvement was supposed to be localised. Carolingian bishops insisted that everyone was to be baptised at the local church and go there to hear Mass.[41] As Archbishop Amolo of Lyons wrote in the 840s,

> each parish community (*plebs*) should remain quietly in the parishes and churches to which it is allocated. And let them take their offerings and gifts to the churches where they take holy baptism, where they receive the body and blood of Christ, where they are accustomed to hear the solemnity of Mass, where penance for guilt, visitation of the sick, and burial of the dead is arranged by the priest, where they are commanded to bring their tithes and first-fruits, where they rejoice in having their sons baptised, and where they listen attentively to the word of the Lord, and recognise what is and what is not to be done.[42]

Amolo was writing in the context of a large group of women who had congregated in the crypt of a Burgundian monastery to venerate newly arrived relics; he was clear that they should return at once to their local

---

40 M. Lauwers, 'De l'incastellamento à l'inecclesiamento. Monachisme et logiques spatiales du féodalisme', in D. Iogna-Prat, M. Lauwers, F. Mazel and I. Rosé (eds), *Cluny, les moines et la société au premier âge féodal* (Rennes: Presses universitaires de Rennes, 2013), pp. 315–38.

41 For the centrality of the local church, see Hincmar of Reims's *Collectio de ecclesiis et capellis*, MGH Font iur. Germ. 14; see below, pp. 122–32.

42 For a new edition and French translation of Amolo's letter, see appendix in Agobard of Lyon, *Œuvres*, trans. M. Rubellin (Paris: Cerf, 2016), pp. 428–57. On the letter, see Bobrycki, 'The flailing women'.

churches, which was the proper framework for communal worship. Amolo was here giving voice to an established Carolingian ideology that put a premium on stability and rootedness, and, by implication, locality, as documented by earlier texts such as the Council of Chalon-sur-Saône in 813.[43]

This emphasis on the local church as the best setting for collective religious practice is attested in other sources too. For instance, according to the church dedication *ordo* of the so-called Romano-German Pontifical, the bishop, after consecrating a church and before performing the first Mass, was to remind the people of their duties to that church.[44] As well as requesting them to pay their tithes and other dues, he also urged the assembled parishioners to commemorate the consecration every year.[45] Similarly, the capitulary of Archbishop Herard of Tours asked the congregation coming to church to pray together on their way there.[46] Whether they actually did so is not recorded, but there are suggestions in the documentary evidence that local people were sufficiently committed to their churches to be able to remember (and to be prepared to attest to) their territorial boundaries.[47] Bishop Gerbald of Liège required priests to keep lists of local tithe payers, and it is possible that some such lists survive.[48] The archives of the rural church of Varsi in northern Italy even

---

43 *Concilium Cabillonense*, ch. 19, in MGH Conc. 2, 1, no. 37, p. 277. The term used is *familiae*, who had to pay tithes to the churches where their children were baptised.

44 PRG XL, 128, p. 169. See H. Parkes, *The Making of Liturgy in the Ottonian Church. Books, Music and Ritual in Mainz, 950–1050* (Cambridge: Cambridge University Press, 2015).

45 PRG XL, 128, p. 169: 'habeat pontifex verbum ad plebem de honore ecclesiastico et de pace venientium ac redeuntium et decimis vel oblationibus ecclesiarum, ac de anniversaria ipsius aecclesiae dedicatione, et annuntiet tam clero quam populo, in cuius honore constructa et dedicata sit aecclesia vel etiam nomina sanctorum ibi quiescentium'.

46 Herard of Tours, *Capitulare*, ch. 114, in MGH Capit. episc. 2, p. 152.

47 L. Pellegrini, 'Plebs e populus in ambito rurale nell'Italia altomedievale', in *Società, istituzioni, spiritualità. Studi in onore di Cinzio Violante*, 2 vols (Spoleto: Fondazione CISAM, 1994), vol. 1, pp. 599–632.

48 Gerbald of Liège, *Capitula*, ch. 5, in MGH Capit. episc. 1, p. 17. The last folio of München BSB clm 14508, a handbook for a priest, contains a list of dues that might be a list of tithes owed, though this is not the only possible interpretation: http://daten.digitale-sammlungen.de/~db/0004/bsb00046287/images/index.html (accessed 29 July 2018).

document how, in 857, eighteen male residents from Spióla collectively committed to pay an annual tithe to the church, newly integrated into the control of the bishop of Piacenza.[49] Much better attested than active participation in the cult are the property dealings with which local churches were involved, and that were to some extent undertaken communally. Although churches in private hands seem mostly to have belonged to individuals or to have been divided or shared among family members, there is scattered evidence that local churches were sometimes owned by locally resident groups.[50] Indeed there is some evidence that they were occasionally built by these groups, at Marche-en-Famennes; possibly in Bavaria; possibly at Villabáscones in northern Iberia in the 940s, when twenty-four men with their families – apparently the entire population of the settlement (*omnes de Uilla Uascones*) – endowed the church; and in Campania in southern Italy in 965.[51]

There is moreover a celebrated series of ninth- and tenth-century Catalan charters which claim that local groups (*nos homines commantes*) had constructed and then donated churches to bishops, in particular that of Urgell.[52] These charters are increasingly viewed by historians with caution, since on closer inspection it seems that they were written by episcopal rather than local scribes, and it is further apparent that not all of a locality had been involved in building these churches; but at the very least they point to how collective local involvement could generate legitimacy.[53]

---

49 F. Bougard, 'L'église de Varsi', in D. Chamboduc de Saint Pulgent and M. Dejoux (eds), *La fabrique des sociétés médiévales méditerranéenes. Le Moyen Âge de François Menant* (Paris: Editions de la Sorbonne, 2018), pp. 421–31; ChLA 69, no. 4.

50 S. Wood, *The Proprietary Church in the Medieval West* (Oxford: Oxford University Press, 2006), pp. 601–27.

51 Marche-en-Famennes: *Miracula Sancti Remacli*, ch. 18, p. 700; see Schroeder, *Les hommes et la terre*, p. 203. Bavaria: Kohl, *Lokale Gesellschaften*, p. 235. Villabáscones: C 45; cf. Davies, *Windows on Justice*, pp. 215, 219. Campania: *Codex diplomaticus Cavensis*, ed. Morcaldi et al., no. 231; Wood, *Proprietary Church*, describes the fourteen men of the latter as 'two possibly unrelated families and four other individuals', p. 606.

52 *Les actes de consagracions d'esglésies de l'antic bisbat d'Urgell (segles IX–XII)*, ed. C. Baraut (Urgell: Societat Cultural Urgel·litana, 1986). For influential discussion, P. Bonnassie, *La Catalogne du milieu du Xe à la fin du XIe siècle*, 2 vols (Toulouse: Université de Toulouse-Le-Mirail, 1975–6), pp. 308–9.

53 For criticism, see forthcoming work by Lluís To Figueras.

For the most part, donations to churches were the result of individual rather than collective piety, but there are rare hints of collective grants too, such as a record in the Wissembourg cartulary which lists twelve smaller gifts made to the parish church in Dauendorf, all for the salvation of the soul.[54] While we can only speculate about the collectivity of these donations, a Catalan charter of 890 from the Urgell archives, relating to the settlement of Ardòvol, unambiguously described the endowment of the local church as a collective act of the residents: 'we, all the people living in the above-mentioned village, give ...'.[55] Perhaps this was simply how the episcopal scribe wanted it to appear, but the Catalan material is supplemented by evidence from elsewhere in northern Iberia. Further to the west, in 932 ten named people and *omni collacio de* Melgar gave a meadow to the abbot of the local monastery of San Juan.[56] Another joint gift named seventeen people – seemingly their family representatives – giving away mixed plots from all the inhabitants of Caldelas and Quiroga to the monastery of San Xoán de Lamas in 934.[57] On another occasion, neighbours joined together to provide for the proper burial of a poor monk. These Iberian examples can be paralleled by occasional instances in Italy, too, such as when the villagers of Musciano near Lucca in 746 consented as a *plebs* to the appointment of a priest.[58]

In southern Europe, then, the local church could serve as a focus for community action. The priest and gastald at Varsi in 915 even collected oaths of loyalty from a group of eight people who promised to support the church in legal matters.[59] Yet there is no reason to suppose that the local church always served this function; and of course, many settlements in the Latin West did not have a church, even if they were seldom very distant from one. In general, the evidence for collective local action undertaken on a routine basis between neighbours, beyond that required by landowners, is surprisingly thin.

---

54 TW 181, pp. 384–5. For hints in Lorsch charters of giving as collective action, see E. Goosmann, 'Aristocratic exploitation of eccesiastical property in the ninth century. The case of the villa Gendt', *Francia*, 45 (2018), 27–59.
55 *Les actes*, ed. Baraut, no. 7, pp. 63–4.
56 S 44; Davies, *Windows on Justice*, pp. 215, 219.
57 Cel 224 (934).
58 C. Wickham, *Framing the Early Middle Ages. Europe and the Mediterranean 400–800* (Oxford: Oxford University Press, 2005), p. 390.
59 Bougard, 'Varsi', p. 429. The charter is not yet edited.

Collective legal action

Francia

Around 664 the monastery of Saint-Bénigne of Dijon brought a complaint to the Frankish king Chlothar III about the residents of Larrey-sur-Ouche in Burgundy (see figure 8.2). A previous king, Guntramn (d. 592), had granted the territory to the monastery, but the 'people living within the boundary' (*homines infra ipsum terminum commanentes*) were refusing to pay their dues to the monastery. These people were also present at the hearing, and counter-claimed that King Guntramn had also guaranteed the rights of their ancestors as property owners. The group brought out Guntramn's charter (*praeceptio*) to prove their claim to King Chlotar; and they presented another charter (*pactio*) about the boundaries of this territory, recording how their ancestors, together with Saint-Bénigne's abbot of the time, had walked around the boundaries and placed markers (*signa*). King Chlothar and his court decided that these documents, while perfectly genuine, did not affect the monastery's control over the territory, which the king duly confirmed.[60]

If we can trust the monks' record of the Larrey episode, it suggests that people in early medieval Francia could act in a legal setting as a local group, and even preserve legal documentation for several generations. As Chris Wickham has noted, however, the Larrey dispute is relatively isolated in Europe north of the Alps and Pyrenees. A late ninth-century formulary from the Alemannian monastery of Saint-Gall records a dispute between the monastery and 'countrymen' (*pagenses*) over woodlands of unknown size and location; the fact that the *pagenses*, also called *cives*, were interested in these woods for timber and for pasture suggests that we may be dealing with a small-scale local dispute.[61] But we cannot be sure; and the complaint of *pagenses* to the king which is recorded in an earlier Frankish formulary suggests that this label could be used for a supra-local elite.[62]

---

60 *Die Urkunden der Merowinger*, MGH DD Mer. 1, no. 103, pp. 264-8. See C. Wickham, 'Space and society in early medieval peasant conflicts', in *Uomo e spazio nell'alto Medioevo* (Spoleto: Fondazione CISAM, 2003), pp. 551-86, esp. pp. 552-4.
61 *Formulae Sangellenses miscellanea*, no. 9, in MGH Formulae, pp. 383-4.
62 *Formulae Marculfi* I, no. 34, in MGH Formulae, pp. 64-5; see A. Rio, *The Formularies of Angers and Marculf. Two Merovingian Legal Handbooks* (Liverpool: Liverpool University Press, 2008), p. 168.

In general, most recorded Frankish peasant disputes involved individuals or groups constituted not on co-residence alone but on their connections with an institution – in other words, on their individual members' status in the *familia*, not as neighbours. For example, the complaint brought in 861 by forty-one men and women from Mitry to King Charles the Bald against the abbey of Saint-Denis is undoubtedly a very clear case of collective action, but the basis of the action was these people's ties to the monastery rather than to one another. Moreover, Saint-Denis's agents presented twenty-two free witnesses from the same place, who swore that the plaintiffs were in reality of servile status. These disputes display not so much collective solidarity but rather, to borrow Alice Rio's phrase, 'odious backstabbing by neighbours'.[63]

The discourse of collaboration within *familia* continued to dominate in Francia even in the tenth century, when monasteries began to produce their own written records of negotiations with their *familia* in particular places. For example, in 932 the monks of Stavelot negotiated with the inhabitants of the settlement of Xhoris, much as the monks of Gorze negotiated with the inhabitants of Bruoch in 984.[64] These texts seem to prefigure later franchise and Weistümer agreements that recorded negotiations between groups of residents and their lords.[65] But unlike those later franchise agreements, these tenth-century agreements did not necessarily extend to all residents of the places concerned, but only to those living there who were dependent on the institution in question. They are not evidence for what Peter Blickle and Beat Kümin have influentially termed, in a later medieval context, 'communalism'.[66]

63 See above, pp. 68–9; A. Rio, *Slavery after Rome, 500–1100* (Oxford: Oxford University Press, 2017), p. 198.

64 Schroeder, *Les hommes et la terre*, pp. 248–9; J.-P. Devroey, 'Confronter la coutume domaniale entre seigneurs et paysans en Lorraine au Xe siècle', in L. Jégou, S. Joye, T. Lienhard and J. Schneider (eds), *Faire lien. Aristocratie, réseaux et échanges compétitifs: Mélanges en l'honneur de Régine Le Jan* (Paris: Editions de la Sorbonne, 2015), pp. 155–78.

65 On Weistümer, see J. Demade, 'The medieval countryside in German-language historiography since the 1930s', in I. Afonso (ed.), *The Rural History of Medieval European Societies* (Turnhout: Brepols, 2007), pp. 173–252; S. Teuscher, *Lords' Rights and Peasant Stories. Writing and the Formation of Tradition in the Later Middle Ages* (Philadelphia, PA: University of Philadelphia Press, 2012).

66 P. Blickle, *Kommunalismus. Skizzen einer gesellschaftlichen Organisationsform*, 2 vols (Munich: Oldenburg, 2000); B. Kümin, *The Communal Age in Western Europe c. 1100–1800. Towns, Villages and Parishes in Pre-Modern Society* (Basingstoke: Palgrave Macmillan, 2013).

Lists of witnesses to local charters, which are abundant in the surviving evidence, may seem a source of evidence for collective legal action. Surviving witness lists, especially from the Middle Rhine and Bavaria, may preserve traces of a locality's sense of itself as a legal community: the fact that all witnesses had property in a settlement, or that all the men from one settlement turned up to witness a procedure, suggests that this was relevant to judicial process.[67] According to the seventh- or eighth-century *Lex Baiuuariorum*, for certain transactions, only *commarcani* – people living in the same *marca* – could act as witnesses.[68] Formularies, such as the formulary of Angers (probably sixth-century but copied by eighth- and ninth-century scribes), occasionally state that witnesses for particular actions had to be neighbours, for instance declaring that a man had to swear with three 'neighbours living close to this place (*condita*)'.[69] In principle, according to the Frankish archbishop Hincmar of Reims, the best early medieval witnesses were local men with a good knowledge of local affairs.[70]

However, despite the prescriptions of these early legal texts, some witnesses were probably supra-local figures. In the Middle Rhine, for instance, witness leaders were often *centenarii*, who might be active on a micro-regional scale, beyond the purely local: only further down the lists are there people who may have stood for the settlement in some capacity. The same seems also to have been true in Alemannia.[71] Moreover, a capitulary of Emperor Louis the Pious defines 'neighbours' (*vicini*) as people living in the same county (*comitatus*), which is not exactly local.[72] When formularies require all the people living in a particular place (*ibidem conmanentes*) to come together before a judge, it was because these people had information relating to an incident, not because they formed a pre-existing legal community.[73] Most of these occasions could

---

67 For example, CL 730; UBF, no. 246 (*c.* 796): 'isti habent hereditatem in Dienheim'; cf. Wickham, *Framing*, pp. 396–7.
68 *Lex Baiwariorum*, ch. 17, 2, MGH LL nat. Germ. 5, 2, p. 447. Kohl, *Lokale Gesellschaften*, p. 123.
69 *Formulae Andecavenses*, no. 28, in MGH Formulae, p. 13, *vicinis circa manentis de ipsa condita*, trans. Rio, *Formularies*, pp. 71–2. Cf. nos 29, 50, and more *vicini circa manentes* in so-called *appenis* documents, nos 31–3.
70 Hincmar, *De presbiteris criminosis*, MGH Studien und Texte 34, pp. 94–5.
71 Cf. Rolf Sprandel, *Das Kloster Sankt Gallen in der Verfassung des karolingischen Reiches* (Freiburg im Breisgau: Eberhard Albert, 1958), pp. 98–133.
72 MGH Capit. 1, p. 268.
73 *Formulae Turonenses*, no. 30, in MGH Formulae, p. 153.

be considered meetings of individuals rather than gatherings of legally defined groups.

It is especially striking that early medieval Frankish law did not recognise the village as a legal category, though we should not expect every rural resident to have lived in a village. Here, the most interesting evidence comes from the *Lex Salica*, a pre-Carolingian work that was nevertheless keenly studied, edited and copied in our period. Its only substantial discussion of a village concerns incomers; in fact the text's most important spatial marker is the house and the household, and the key actors are, unequivocally, individuals, with occasional references to 'armed bands'.[74] Only in a late addition to the *Lex Salica* text were neighbours (*vicini*) legally compelled to act, in a section on what happens if a body is found in the fields between two settlements (the neighbours were to build a scaffold to display the body, and to take an oath to exonerate themselves).[75] The Salian law also talks of a court called the *mallus*, but although it is sometimes described as a 'local judicial assembly', it was probably not local as understood in this book.[76] In fact it seems similar to English hundred courts.[77]

Beyond Francia

Beyond the Frankish heartlands, the evidence for collective legal activity based squarely on locality is a little richer. In England, Domesday Book provides a few instances of the people from a particular settlement (*villa*) bearing collective witness, for instance at Mendlesham and Bramford, both in Suffolk.[78] These examples are, however, dwarfed by Domesday's much more plentiful evidence for legal organisation at the level of the hundred, a rather larger area which, nominally encompassing a hundred

---

74 *Pactus legis Salicae*, ch. 11, 1, ch. 58, 2, ch. 42, 1–3, ch. 43, 1–3, in MGH LL nat. Germ. 4, 1, pp. 55, 218, 162–3, 165–7; see further below.
75 *Decretio Childeberti*, ch. 102, 1–3, MGH LL nat. Germ. 4, 1, pp. 258–9.
76 T. Barnwell, 'The early Frankish mallus: its nature, participants and practices', in A. Pantos and S. Semple (eds), *Assembly Places and Practices in Medieval Europe* (Dublin: Four Courts Press, 2004), pp. 233–46.
77 A. Pantos, 'The location and form of Anglo-Saxon assembly-places: some "moot points"', in Pantos and Semple (eds), *Assembly Places and Practices*, pp. 155–80.
78 R. Fleming, *Domesday Book and the Law: Society and Legal Custom in Early Medieval England* (Cambridge: Cambridge University Press, 1998), nos 2762, 3011. Mendlesham: *Domesday Book: Suffolk*, ed. A. Rumble (Chichester: Phillimore, 1986), vol. 1, fol. 285b: *homines illius ville testantur*; Bramford: ibid., vol. 2, fol. 393a: *v villani de eodem manerio testantur*.

hides, often included a number of settlements. Perhaps the hundred court replaced earlier, even more local, courts, but it is more likely that the new system formalised older assemblies of a similar scale. In any case, it was the hundred not the settlement to which tenth-century Anglo-Saxon law entrusted formal obligations for maintaining peace and carrying out basic policing duties, including pursuing and detaining thieves, and it was the hundred that was most active in the scores of disputes that Domesday Book records.[79] There was a requirement for people to join groups of ten to chase thieves and to stand surety for one another, which implies something more local, but we do not have any evidence of the system in operation before the twelfth century.[80]

In the kingdom of Italy, a number of disputes show inhabitants of a particular locality appearing in court, whether to answer legal charges or to press them. In a famous dispute of 824, the inhabitants (*habitatores*) of Flexo, in the *plebs* of Saint Lawrence, complained that the monks of Nonantola had stopped them from accessing common lands that had been guaranteed to them by royal diploma. The monks countered by presenting older charters supporting their case; the peasant *consortes* argued that these charters had been issued without knowledge of their diploma. The judges interrogated neighbours (*circummanentes*), decided in favour of the monastery and had the three ringleaders beaten.[81]

Here we can see people, identified as living in a particular place, acting collectively, and it seems likely that these people represented the whole residential group. The instance of Flexo is perhaps 'an extraordinary case' (Lazzari), but the residents of the Valle di Trita ran long-term campaigns over several years against San Vincenzo al Volturno, as did the residents of Oulx against Novalesa and the residents of Limonta against San Ambrogio of Milan (see figure 8.4).[82] In all these cases, what

---

79 Fleming, *Domesday*; G. Molyneaux, *Formation of the English Kingdom in the Tenth Century* (Oxford: Oxford University Press, 2015), pp. 141–55; T. Lambert, *Law and Order in Anglo-Saxon England* (Oxford: Oxford University Press, 2017), pp. 243–50; on older assembly traditions, ibid., pp. 136–47.
80 Lambert, *Law and Order*, pp. 280–1.
81 ChLA 88, no. 32. For a wider discussion of this important case, see T. Lazzari, 'Comunità rurali nell alto'medioevo: pratiche di descrizione e spie lessiciali nella documentazione scritta', in P. Galetti (ed.), *Paesaggi, comunità, villaggi medievali* (Spoleto: Fondazione CISAM, 2012), pp. 405–22, esp. pp. 415–22.
82 G. Albertoni, 'Law and the peasant: rural society and justice in Carolingian Italy', *Early Medieval Europe*, 18 (2010), 417–45; C. Wickham, 'Land disputes and

was at dispute was whether these settlements were properly subject to the (distant) monasteries at all; these seem to be more about the legal action of local groups than contemporary Frankish examples such as Mitry, Courtisols or Cormery. These were not, however, representative of the wider situation in northern Italy. In other cases, we can see disputes concerning legal status within a *familia* that are more comparable to the Frankish material – for instance, the dispute over legal status that pitted twenty-one residents of Bedonia against the church of Piacenza *c*. 880.[83] Farther to the south, settlement patterns could be so dispersed that, far from living in a close-knit community, peasants did not always know in which village they lived.[84]

Brittany is in many respects a special case. The cartulary of the monastery of Redon reveals a region divided into small territories labelled as *plebes*, whose foci were usually less than 10 km apart from one another (see figure 8.1). In some ways these territories resembled English hundreds, but whereas hundreds appear as units of royal government, the *plebes* seem more bottom-up. Each *plebs* had regular meetings that dealt with routine legal business – land transfers in particular, though this focus may simply reflect the nature of the archive, and these courts were perfectly capable of settling disputes too. For the most part, residents in each *plebs* attended their local meetings, with only a minority travelling further afield. Similarly, those who stood as sureties for particular legal transactions were local residents too, suggesting that for small-scale Breton farmers in the ninth century, 'the people they relied on to support them – and who were prepared to support them – were neighbours'.[85] Here, then, we have unambiguous evidence for local societies equipped with an institutional framework.

The early medieval evidence from Iberia – including north-western Spain, until quite recently relatively neglected, as well as the better-known Catalan material – shows very clear cases of people from local settlements acting collectively in a legal context, and being identified as doing so too (for locations, see figure 8.5). This was not manifested through

their social framework in Lombard-Carolingian Italy, 700–900', in W. Davies and P. Fouracre (eds), *The Settlement of Disputes in Early Medieval Europe* (Cambridge: Cambridge University Press, 1986), pp. 105–24.
83 ChLA 71, no. 33.
84 Wickham, *Framing*, p. 390.
85 W. Davies, *Small Worlds: The Village Community in Early Medieval Brittany* (London: Duckworth, 1988), p. 128.

judgements, since the people acting on legal panels in northern Iberia were not usually from the locality. An exception is a dispute at Baroncelli in 950, where the assessors seem to have come from the local community.[86] In general these meetings of people to make decisions were ad hoc, not institutionalised.[87] And unlike in Brittany, these local groups did not apparently run their own courts.

Nevertheless we can see some pointers, through the northern Iberian charters, that there was a sense of shared responsibilities. In some cases, the charters are written in the first person plural, 'we'. This is ostensibly the voice of named members of groups who took action together, to make rent agreements or boundary agreements or water management agreements with landlords, or with other groups: in the words of one charter, 'Nos omnes ... Galuarra, Galindo Soliz, Gazo, Laztago, Fortuni Appatiz, Ferro Sangiz, Galindo, Garcia ...', listing a group of locals who agreed to endow a church.[88] The mode of reference is usually initially a listing of individuals (often as many as twenty or thirty), and thereafter 'we'. Often these people were defined residentially too, as coming from Place X, such as the people of Melgar who made a donation to the local church, and the 'homines de collacione Sancti Ihoannis in Uega', against whom the monastery of Valdevimbre took legal action in 938.[89] There are a handful of Iberian charters that group witnesses by (neighbouring) settlements; we might infer that these people had travelled to witness a transaction that was relevant to their own settlement. The grouping could also have been the scribe's decision, but these charters mostly come from the *meseta*, where group identities perhaps crystallised more than elsewhere in Iberia.[90]

On occasion, closer inspection suggests that larger-scale forces were at work behind what appears at first glance to be collective legal action undertaken by residential groups. For instance, a dispute is reported to have arisen between the inhabitants (*habitantes*) of Santa María and those

---

86 Davies, *Windows on Justice*, p. 211.
87 Davies, *Windows on Justice*, p. 217.
88 C 45 (944–50); Davies, *Windows on Justice*, p. 219.
89 Li 128; see further below, p. 194. For full discussion of the terms *collatio* and *concilium*, see W. Davies, *Acts of Giving. Individual, Community, and Church in Tenth-Century Christian Spain* (Oxford: Oxford University Press, 2007), pp. 201–07; cf. Davies, *Windows on Justice*, pp. 213–15. Melgar: see above p. 98.
90 Davies, *Windows on Justice*, p. 218.

of Abedes, Regaulfus and Saquetina, in the neighbourhood of modern Verín, southern Galicia, close to the modern Portuguese border, around 950.[91] When the judgement was confirmed the following year, it emerged that the successful protagonist was not in reality a group of local people who lived in Santa María but the aristocrat, Countess Trudildi. Trudildi and her husband, it appears, had acquired Santa María by exchange twenty years before the Santa María case.[92] In other words, the dispute was not between groups of locals at all but between an aristocrat, who won, and groups of locals, something that also holds true for the other Iberian cases.

Nevertheless, there are cases in which it is clear that people of different settlements had combined for some legal purpose, most obviously to resist the accusations of a monastery, for example over the cultivation of 'monastic' land or over access to water, especially to power mills. The seven settlements of the Pardomino mountain entered in a joint conflict with the monastery of Pardomino in 944, three of them agreeing to pay regular rent in 955;[93] five settlements along the river Arlanzón similarly resisted the monastery of San Torcuato.[94] There also survives a severely damaged original in which a Count Gonzalo was asked by the people (*omines*) of Saidres and those of Villamayor to settle a boundary dispute between them; the count took his surveyors, walked the bounds and settled the line of the boundary.[95] Despite the monastic colouring of most of these texts, it looks as if there really were a few groups of local residents who took collective action against each other in defence of what they believed to be their territorial rights. In doing this they used a standard procedure of asking a count to send surveyors.

Even in northern Iberia, then, the evidence for collective legal action is inconsistent. In a region as diverse as the early medieval Latin West, one should be wary of pointing out exceptions: yet it does seem as if Brittany was unusual in its villages that possessed autonomous legal structures.

91 Cel 95 (950, 951); Davies, *Windows on Justice*, p. 221; see further M. del Carmen Pallares and E. Portela Silva, 'El lugar de los campesinos. De repobladores a repoblados', in A. Rodríguez (ed.), *El lugar del campesino. En torno a la obra de Reyna Pastor* (València: Consejo Superior de Investigaciones Científicas, 2007), pp. 61–87, at pp. 65–7, including a useful map of the places concerned.
92 Cel 460 (931).
93 Li 184, Lii 290.
94 C 22 (932).
95 LaC 65 (before 962).

Parallels are hard to find from Bavaria, Tuscany, west and east Francia and England.

Resistance

Everyday activities provide one possible context for collaboration between neighbours; conflict represents another. While starting a court case was one means of settling grievances, open resistance was in theory another option. However, there are notoriously few documented peasant uprisings in the early Middle Ages. The two most famous episodes – the Saxon Stellinga in 841 and the revolt of the Norman peasants in *c.* 996 – are not well recorded, so it is impossible to determine how far they were coalitions of local communities with grievances, as some later medieval peasant revolts seem to have been, or were based on wider, trans-local solidarities.[96] According to the chronicler William of Jumièges, writing some two generations after the event, the Norman peasants (*rustici*) formed 'many assemblies' (*plurima conventicula*), each of which sent two representatives (*legati*) to a central meeting in a movement to establish free access to woodlands and fisheries, but William, who is our only source, does not give a sense of the scale of these groups.[97]

For the most part, we may presume that grievances against lords were held and acted upon primarily by individual households rather than entire local groups. Yet there are occasional hints of local groups taking a stand, for instance in the shape of the armed 'guilds' that Frankish peasants (*villani*) were forming 'against those who were stealing from them'. These guilds seem altogether more active than their dimly visible earlier forms; King Carloman II responded in 884 by simply prohibiting them, advising the peasants to turn instead to their village priest.[98]

Equally dramatic action was taken by the residents of Sault-Saint-Remi in the sixth century, according to the ninth-century *Vita Remigii*. When Saint Remigius ordered grain to be stored against the food shortage that he predicted would come, the people of this settlement (*villa*) – *seditiosi*

---

96 C. Wickham, 'Looking forward: peasant revolts in Europe, 600–1200', in J. Firnhaber-Baker (ed.), *The Routledge History Handbook of Medieval Revolt* (London: Routledge, 2016), pp. 155–67; on the Stellinga, see I. Rembold, *Conquest and Christianization. Saxony and the Carolingian World, 772–888* (Cambridge: Cambridge University Press, 2018), pp. 85–140.

97 William of Jumièges, *Gesta Normannorum Ducum*, ed. and trans. E. van Houts, 2 vols (Oxford: Oxford University Press, 1992–5), vol. 2, V, ch. 2, p. 8.

98 *Karolomanni capitulare Vernense (a. 884)*, ch. 14, in MGH Capit. 2, p. 375.

et rebelles – mocked him for wanting to construct a city and 'urging each other on' they burned down the heaps of stored grain.[99] This strange story may simply have provided a context for a more recent event, since the *Vita Remigii* goes on to explain that several centuries later, the men of this same settlement murdered an official (*vicedominus*) from Reims. In reprisal, Charlemagne had the leaders executed and those who consented exiled, while the place was 'resettled' by people from other settlements in the area (though some of the original inhabitants' descendants later returned).

Relations with outsiders

Around the seventh century, or so the story has it, a pilgrim named Arnulf who had been seriously injured by thieves staggered into the village of Gruyères (Ardennes) and collapsed. The people of the village watched him for a while, thinking that he was just resting. Then, fearing that he might be a scout for bandits, they approached him to ask who he was. Happily for Arnulf, the village was made up of honest men, and so when they discovered this stranger (*peregrinus*) to be badly wounded, they felt pity for him. News spread. Everyone from the greatest to the least gathered together, including the married women (*matronae villae*), who wanted to take the stranger into their homes and care for him. When, after a short but moving speech, Arnulf died of his injuries, the 'citizens' (*cives*) of Gruyères arranged a decent burial, though he was not buried among the villagers themselves but at the roadside. It is a good illustration of how burial could exclude as well as include.

This account of how an early medieval Frankish village treated an outsider – with wariness, balanced by a fundamental humanity – is unfortunately apocryphal, written around the year 1000 as part of the promotion of the cult of the mysterious pilgrim, whose relics had by this time been removed from Gruyères to the nearby church of Mouzon.[100] It nevertheless raises important questions: how far did local residential groups interact with outsiders of various kinds and how far did those interactions shape their self-understanding? For Jean-Pierre Devroey,

---

99 Hincmar of Reims, *Vita Remigii*, MGH SS rer. Merov. 3, pp. 239–349, at p. 315. See M.-C. Isaïa, *Remi de Reims: mémoire d'un saint, histoire d'une église* (Paris: Cerf, 2010), pp. 465–546.

100 *Chronicon Mosomense*, ed. and trans. M. Bur (Paris: CNRS, 1989), pp. 148–50. For the literary aims of the depiction of this idyllic village, see ibid., pp. 33–4.

drawing on the sociologist Henri Mendras, the outsider/insider distinction is central to understanding the small worlds of early medieval Europe.[101] A key element of this relationship was its mediation through office holders, who connected the locality to a wider overarching society ('société englobante'). Since these figures will be discussed below, here we shall concentrate on local interactions with outsiders more generally.

Labelling
One approach to interaction with outsiders is through terminology and practices of labelling. Labels can be self-identifiers, or can be given by someone else as an act of identification. While in the first instance labels could be used as an affirmation of ties, in the second instance labels may be part of a discourse of differentiation. Although there are instances in our material where labels were used to identify groups, our sources often leave us short of detail, making it impossible to demonstrate modes of labelling as tools of identity building. Moreover, we can seldom be sure whether classifications were used by local residents themselves or were projected on to them by outsiders, since all names are recorded by a scribe, who was not necessarily part of the group (although some scribes may have been, for instance in the case of local priests). There seems to be no evidence that names of residential settlements were used in ways that tied local identity to those places.

More common is evidence for exclusionary attitudes linked to labelling practices. Some of the best evidence here comes from northern Iberia. Northern Iberian scribes sometimes labelled people as Jewish: for instance Habaz, 'once a Jew, later a Christian and a monk', who passed land on to Lazarus the priest some time before 905; *Abzecri iudeo*, whose land bounded a vineyard confirmed to Sahagún in 977; and *Abozaque ebreo et uxor sua* ('Abozaque the Hebrew and his wife') who bought land near León in 997. A charter of 1015 refers back to the 990s and a complicated story of two Jews who had bought land, thereby depriving two young men of their inheritance, as a result of which King Alfonso V confiscated the land *de manibus ebreis* ('from the hands of the Hebrews').[102] However, although separately identified by their religion, Jews appear to have been agriculturally and economically integrated into local society, despite the

101 Devroey, *Puissants et misérables*; Devroey, 'Communiquer'.
102 Li 19, S 290, Liii 579, Liii 737.

background of very hostile Visigothic legislation against them.[103] There is nothing different about their behaviour as the holders of small plots of land – apart from the labels, they are indistinguishable from other peasant farmers.

Northern Iberian scribes also refer often to *Mauri* or Moors. These *Mauri* are almost invariably referred to as servile dependants, and they feature in the lists of stock appurtenant to farms: for example '8 yokes of oxen, 60 cows, 200 sheep, 2 Moors, a fifth of two mills on the river Cea'; or '10 horses, 15 yokes of oxen, 2 Moors and 200 *solidi* for redeeming a third, 40 horses with stallion, ass and 6 colts'.[104] While it is likely that some Moors were of North African origin, there is nothing in any of the personal names cited that positively supports this. For instance the Moor Salvador Rodesindiz, who was a dependent worker in the Celanova kitchens, had five children, called Pedro, Pelayo, Ero, Audesinda and Usorio, none of whose names indicates an Arabic background.[105]

Some residents of northern Iberia certainly did use personal names that pointed to an Arabic tradition. There are in the order of 3,000 citations of names of Arabic form in the northern charters of this period, mostly of individuals occurring in agricultural contexts. Scholars nowadays have reservations about interpreting these as the names of Arabised Christian immigrants from al-Andalus, given that naming practice can be influenced by fashion, whim, honour or gratitude, but some of those members of northern farming residential groups with Arabic names may actually have come from the south, or have been descended from people who had.[106] If so, these people appear to have been fully integrated both

---

103 W. Drews, *The Unknown Neighbor: The Jew in the Thought of Isidore of Seville* (Leiden: Brill, 2006); R. Stocking, 'Forced converts, "Crypto-Judaism", and children: religious identification in Visigothic Spain', in J. V. Tolan, N. de Lange, L. Foschia and C. Nemo-Pekelman (eds), *Jews in Early Christian Law: Byzantium and the Latin West, 6th–11th centuries* (Turnhout: Brepols, 2014), pp. 243–65.

104 S 114 (949), a gift from an aristocrat to the monastery of Valdávida; Li 220 (950), a gift from Bishop Oveco to the monastery of San Juan en Vega.

105 Cel 158 (s.d. but probably early eleventh century, referring back to the mid-tenth century).

106 F. J. F. Conde, 'Poblaciones foráneas: mozárabe, musulmana y judía en el reino de León', in *Monarquía y sociedad en el reino de León. De Alfonso III a Alfonso VII* (León: Centro de Estudios e Investigación San Isidoro, 2007), pp. 763–891; see also C. Aillet, *Les mozarabes. Christianisme, islamisation et arabisation en péninsule ibérique (IXe–XIIe siècle)* (Madrid: Casa de Velázquez,

into court circles (such as the royal judge Abaiub) and into farming communities, and there is no evidence in the charters that they were labelled as foreigners.[107] We see them taking part in property exchanges without any apparent difficulty: for instance, Nonniti, Placenti, Egero and Todeia sold Abozuleiman their vines for three oxen in 912, while Mudarrafe sold Menicio and his wife Avola a parcel of land in León territory for a goat and its kid in 914.[108] They all seem to have been farmers, just like the indigenous (or descendants of Visigothic) peasant proprietors around them – and they behaved in exactly the same ways.

Not only that, but there are plenty of people, and families, with names of mixed types. Abzuleiman Fredenandi and Sesgute Maruaniz were witnesses of transactions, in 915 and 998, respectively; Abolkaceme was married to Jimena and Habuhab to Uistrildi; Dominico, Mahomet and Salvator gave the layman Fruela a parcel of land they got from parents, and the brothers Abdelmelic and Abuhabe acted as executor for Siseguto.[109] And there was the deacon Mahomet, the priests Abolbalite and Abdimelke – both purchasers – and the monk Abolfeta, who gave land to the monastery of San Salvador de Matallana.[110] Although bearing Arabic names, these farmers and clerics are not associated with the enemy Arabs, the Ishmaelites and the Saracens. This is in contrast to the Moors, who were certainly differentiated, of servile status, and who do not appear to have been integrated into local communities in any way.

Although northern Iberia has unusually good documentary evidence, the sometimes troubled integration of incomers into existing population groups took place in northern Europe too. While the group movements of the fifth and sixth centuries remain contentious in scale and in nature despite recent technical advances, meaning that their impact on the locality remains very difficult to discern, by the ninth and tenth centuries the interaction of local residents with incomers is better documented,

2010), pp. 247–79; L. Becker, *Hispano-romanisches Namenbuch. Untersuchung der Personennamen vorrömischer, griechischer und lateinisch-romanischer Etymologie auf der Iberischen Halbinsel im Mittelalter (6.–12. Jahrhundert)* (Berlin: de Gruyter, 2009).
107 E.g. Li 128 (938); cf. Lii 291 (955), Liii 573 (996): 'de una parte termino de Gomez, de secunda termino de fratres de Zellanoua, de III parte termino de Abdella, de IIII parte karrale publica'.
108 Li 29, Li 32.
109 Li 34, Liii 580; Lii 376 (964), Lii 266 (954), Lii 315 (959), Lii 273 (954).
110 Li 40 (916), Lii 418 (972), Lii 422 (973), Liii 529 (989).

especially in the case of Scandinavian settlers.[111] The establishment of a diasporic polity led by pagan warriors in Normandy from 911 raised difficult questions for contemporary churchmen, as correspondence of Archbishop Heriveus of Reims makes clear, offering advice to the archbishop of Rouen on pagans who did not change their behaviour after baptism.[112] Material traces of these settlers are very scarce, yet there are hundreds of place-names in Normandy with Old Norse elements, including some that combine Romance and Old Norse and thus suggest a degree of bilingualism. Dozens of settlements were named after now obscure Scandinavian individuals.[113]

People of Scandinavian origin also settled in northern and eastern Anglo-Saxon England, and here traces of Scandinavian culture are even stronger. Despite attempts to draw on modern genetics, it seems unlikely that we shall ever be sure of the numbers involved, but recent assessments have cautiously suggested that we should be thinking of tens of thousands of people arriving over a period of several decades – numbers that we know travelled to Iceland around the same time. More than a third of Yorkshire's place-names recorded in Domesday Book attest to Scandinavian influence.[114] Excavations of individuals who had migrated from Scandinavia to England, such as the ninth-century woman found at Adwick-le-Street (South Yorkshire) in 2001, buried in relatively humble Scandinavian-style dress and who – isotopic analysis suggested – had come from Norway, remain rare (see figure 8.6). However, archaeological

---

[111] For a recent discussion of the Anglo-Saxon *adventus*, perhaps the most studied of the various group migrations, see H. Härke, 'Anglo-Saxon immigration and ethnogenesis', *Medieval Archaeology*, 55 (2011), 1–28. For a preliminary study drawing on ancient DNA, with a focus on the Lombards, see C. E. G. Amorim et al., 'Understanding 6th-century barbarian social organization and migration through paleogenomics', *Nature Communications*, 9 (2018), doi: 10.1038/s41467-018-06024-4. Cf. above, p. 32.

[112] Heriveus of Reims, Letter to Archbishop Wido of Rouen, in PL 132, pp. 661–74, explaining 'qualiter consulendum vobis foret his qui rebaptizati sunt, aeque ut ante baptismum juxta paganismi morem ... ludicras voluptates nefando paganorum ritu exercuere', p. 663. The text survives in Paris BnF lat. 4280A, fols 102–03v. See M.-C. Isaïa, 'Hagiographie et pastorale: la collection canonique d'Hervé, archevêque de Reims († 922)', *Mélanges de Science Religieuse*, 67:3 (2010), 27–48; Lesley Abrams has forthcoming work on this.

[113] L. Abrams, 'Early Normandy', *Anglo-Norman Studies*, 35 (2013), 45–64.

[114] M. Townend, *Viking Age Yorkshire* (Pickering: Blackthorn Press, 2014), p. 228; see above, pp. 33–5.

evidence for Scandinavian settlements on the ground is growing, whether as direct settlement evidence, as at Cottam in the Yorkshire Wold, or in the form of large amounts of Scandinavian-style jewellery, including hundreds of brooches that have recently been registered by metal detectorists.[115]

Although incomers and existing residents could probably have communicated with one another, since Old Norse and Old English were not so very far apart, cultural and linguistic differences would nevertheless have been apparent. Yorkshire place-name evidence confirms this assumption – indeed, places such as Danby, Normanby and Ferrensby suggest that people were able to differentiate in their labelling between particular kinds of Scandinavian immigrants, in these cases Danes, Norwegians and Faroe Islanders, groups from whom these settlements took their names.[116] Clothing styles, especially for women, to judge from the archaeological evidence, would have been visually distinct too, and remained so into the tenth century. Moreover, we should remember that the settlement process took place as the direct consequence of considerable violence and disruption, though for the most part this is documented only through annals and later histories, in the absence of much charter material from the region.

The only unambiguous evidence for ethnically based tensions with Scandinavians in England, the St Brice's Day massacre of 1002, comes from Oxford, an urban context far from the centres of Scandinavian settlement.[117] And there is considerable evidence for cultural assimilation at the lower levels of society. For instance, Jane Kershaw has argued that with the emergence of Anglo-Scandinavian brooches in Norfolk – essentially Scandinavian motifs applied to Anglo-Saxon dress practices – we can see evidence that the settled residents of humble status were not slow to copy the newcomers' appearance, much as they may have copied their personal names (45 per cent of the county's landowners bore Scandinavian names in Domesday).[118] There is much less archaeological evidence of this kind from northern England, but place-names again suggest that in practice

---

115 For the jewellery, J. Kershaw, *Viking Identities. Scandinavian Jewellery in England* (Oxford: Oxford University Press, 2013).
116 Townend, *Viking Age Yorkshire*, pp. 114–15. Such ethnic place-names can be paralleled elsewhere: for instance Villabáscones in northern Iberia, which literally means 'settlement of the Basques': Davies, *Windows on Justice*, p. 219.
117 See L. Roach, *Æthelred the Unready* (New Haven, CT: Yale University Press, 2016), pp. 186–216.
118 Kershaw, *Viking Identities*, pp. 228–35, 210.

there was a great deal of collaboration – for instance in the form of the so-called 'Grimston' place-names, in which the English *-tun* suffix (meaning a settlement) is matched with an Old Norse personal name prefix (such as Grímr), or other kinds of Old Norse vocabulary. Forty-two of these kinds of settlement name are recorded in Domesday for Yorkshire alone. The names are primarily evidence of landowners, but loanwords from Old Norse into Northumbrian English suggest a more demotic level of interaction too.[119]

Strangers

As we saw, the village of Gruyères treated the stranger Arnulf with some caution. Although this is a literary text, the wariness of the village is reflected in a famous though problematic section of the *Lex Salica*, dealing with newcomers in a settlement.[120] Its premise is that residents might object to the arrival of the newcomer, and it sets out the procedure for making that objection.[121]

The text begins by declaring that

> If someone wishes to move into another *villa* in place of someone else, and one or more of those who live in the *villa* wish to receive him but there is one of them who objects, he may not have the right to move.[122]

If the stranger settles anyway, the objector had to protest formally against him. And if the stranger is still not willing to leave, then the objector had to make a speech before an unnamed number of witnesses: 'I declare to you, as the Salic law provides, that on the next day after you took up residence I have made declaration to you that you should depart from this village within ten days'. Ten days later, the objector had to repeat his declaration

---

119 Townend, *Viking Age Yorkshire*, pp. 101–8, 121, for Old Norse loanwords as part of 'a heavily Scandinavianized English'.

120 F. Staab, *Untersuchungen zur Gesellschaft am Mittelrhein in der Karolingerzeit* (Wiesbaden: Steiner, 1975), pp. 254–62; K. Ubl, *Lex Salica. Sinnstiftungen eines Rechtsbuchs. Die Lex Salica im Frankenreich* (Ostfildern: Thorbecke, 2017).

121 *Pactus legis Salicae*, ch. 45, 1–4 'De migrantibus', MGH LL nat. Germ. 4, 1, pp. 173–6. See K. Fischer-Drew, *The Laws of the Salian Franks (Pactus legis Salicae)* (Philadelphia, PA: University of Pennsylvania Press, 1991), p. 109.

122 *Pactus legis Salicae*, ch. 45, p. 173: 'Si quis <homo> super alterum in villa migrare voluerit et unus vel aliqui de ipsis qui in villa consistunt <tunc> eum suscipere uoluerit, si uel unus <ex ipsis> extiterit, qui contradicat, migrandi ibidem licentiam non habeat'.

and, if the stranger would not leave, do so again after a further ten days. Only after this period of thirty days could the complainant summon the newcomer to court, in the presence of the witnesses that had been present at each declaration. If the newcomer refused to come to court, the complainant could lay hands on the property of his opponent and ask the count (*grafio*) to expel the newcomer.

The wider residential group (*vicini*) has a role here as witnesses, as is also implied by the *Lex Baiuuariorum*.[123] Yet despite the section's centrality for the historiography of rural communities, if read closely it is clear that the expulsion of an unwanted stranger is not a concerted effort of a larger group, much less of the whole settlement. It is rather a resident individual who is central to the legal action, in making his objections felt and in pursuing the matter. The court is clearly located beyond the settlement. In other words, the residential group did not accept a newcomer; rather, a single individual could reject him, but had to appeal to the regional legal official to do so.

The local suspicion of the outsider so evident in this text appears in other contexts too. In pagan parts of Europe, Christian missionaries faced potential violence not just from political leaders but also from local communities who were suspicious of their intentions, such as those residents of a *vicus* who were collectively responsible in the late seventh century for the deaths of the 'two Hewalds' in Saxony (the Saxon *satraps* was angered by the murders, and had the whole *vicus* burned down in retaliation).[124]

But converted Europe could be dangerous for strangers, too. In a treatise written in the early ninth century, Archbishop Agobard of Lyon described how one woman and three men had been brought to him in chains, on the grounds that they had fallen from sky ships, on which they sailed with the intention of stealing crops. Instead of having them stoned to death as seems to have been expected, Agobard released them.[125] Agobard does not say who had captured these people, but it is implied

123 *Lex Baiwariorum* ch. 17, 2, in MGH LL nat. Germ. 5, 2, p. 447: 'Ille homo qui hoc testificare voluerit, commarcanus eius debet esse et debet habere VI solidorum pecuniam et similem agrum'.
124 Bede, *Historia Ecclesiastica Gentis Anglorum*, V.10, ed. B. Colgrave and R. A. B. Mynors (Oxford: Clarendon Press, 1969), p. 482.
125 Agobard, *De grandine et tonitruis*, ed. L. van Acker, in *Agobardi Lugdunensis opera omnia* (Turnhout: Brepols, 1981), pp. 3–15; Agobard, *Œuvres*, trans. Rubellin, pp. 131–77.

that they were farmers, worried about crop failure. He went on to lament that other strangers had been killed because it was feared that they were carrying magic powder to poison cattle on behalf of foreign kings. Such suspicion of strangers found its way into early Anglo-Saxon law too: in the decades around 700, King Ine of Wessex decreed that if a foreign man or a stranger (*feorcund mon oðe fremde*) left the path through the woods and did not make his presence known by shouting or blowing a horn, he could be treated as a thief, and killed.[126]

Yet not all strangers met such hostility. In 864 King Charles the Bald of west Francia decreed that migrants (*adventitii*) fleeing from recent Viking attacks in the west should be enabled, but also compelled, to return home, at least once the wine harvest had been gathered.[127] Charles moreover dissolved any marriages that these migrants, both men and women, might have entered into, and clarified that any children were to stay with their mother. The king was probably here responding to aristocratic pressure, unhappy that they had not been consulted in these marriages and worried about losing labour; in any case, the decree shows that the migrants had integrated very well into local society.[128] Peasant migrants of this kind are often to be found in polyptyques, although these texts unfortunately do not tell us how far the migrants had travelled.[129]

The excluded

If village communities sometimes welcomed newcomers, there is also some evidence for social exclusion of long-term residents, itself a form of collective action. In the case of Courtisols, we can see a community in northern Francia apparently willingly denouncing some of its unfree residents who had attempted to cloak their status and to advance into free status. In this text, we find the elders and a large number of witnesses from Courtisols testifying that several of their fellow residents were in fact *servi*

---

126 Ine 20, *Die Gesetze der Angelsachsen*, ed. F. Liebermann, 3 vols (Halle: Niemeyer, 1903–16), vol. 1, p. 98. King Wihtred of Kent's law code made a similar pronouncement at the same time.
127 *Edictum Pistense (a. 864)*, ch. 31, in MGH Capit. 2, no. 273, pp. 323–4.
128 J. L. Nelson, 'England and the continent in the ninth century III: rights and rituals', *Transactions of the Royal Historical Society*, 14 (2004), 1–24, at 11.
129 J.-P. Devroey, 'Peasant mobility and settlement', in B. Kasten (ed.), *Tätigkeitsfelder und Erfahrungshorizonte des ländlichen Menschen in der frühmittelalterlichen Grundherrschaft (bis ca. 1000)* (Stuttgart: Steiner, 2006), pp. 37–48.

and *ancillae*. It is noticeable that none of these allegedly unfree tenants' co-tenants testified against them.[130] These forms of social exclusion – the withdrawal of support in court – were relatively indirect. However, there is scattered evidence for more direct forms of exclusion in early medieval localities. When a thief named Dierbert in the villa of *Dulcorio* near Saint-Riquier was put in the stocks, he could not be released because no one was prepared to be his guarantor; his custodian eventually took him on the road, with his neck and hands chained, in order to make a living from him.[131] A comparable ninth-century account from Saint-Germain-des-Prés near Paris relates a story of a baby abandoned by his impoverished mother outside the door of a church (a course of action recorded in various sources).[132] One of the congregation, 'moved by pity', adopted him but threw him out at the age of seven, when it became apparent that he was deaf and mute and thus of little use as a servant. The unlucky child was then taken up by a travelling pedlar, partly from pity but partly too as a beast of burden, to carry smaller wares; eventually the child ran away to a church in Paris, where he was cured (and later became a cleric).[133]

An anecdote from the Annals of Fulda's entry for 858 provides another snapshot of collective exclusion at work. In Kempten, not far from Mainz, a man and his entire family was forced to live outside the settlement, in the fields, because he had been possessed by a demon that caused buildings into which he had walked to combust (see figure 8.3).[134] The Annals remind us of kinship ties, by noting that not even this man's kin (*propinqui*) would offer him lodging. But they also demonstrate a clear, and very hostile, sense of group feeling in specifying that all his neighbours (*vicini*) 'wished to kill him'.[135]

---

130 See further below, pp. 206–8; J. Barbier, 'The praetor *does* concern himself with trifles: Hincmar, the polyptych of St-Remi and the slaves of Courtisols', in R. Stone and C. West (eds), *Hincmar of Rheims: Life and Work* (Manchester: Manchester University Press, 2015), pp. 211–27.
131 *Miracula Sancti Riquarii*, AASS, 26 apr, vol. 3, p. 451 'nullum suae relaxationis fide jussorem haberet'.
132 Cf. *Formulae Andecavenses*, no. 49, in MGH Formulae, pp. 21–2; see also Regino of Prüm, *Libri duo* II, 68–9, *Das Sendhandbuch des Regino von Prüm*, ed. W. Hartmann (Darmstadt: Wissenschaftliche Buchgesellschaft, 2004), pp. 284–5.
133 *Miracula Sancti Germani Parisiensis*, ch. 2, AASS, 28 may, vol. 6, p. 792.
134 *Annales Fuldenses*, s.a. 858, MGH SS rer. Germ. [7], pp. 51–3.
135 *Annales Fuldenses*, s.a. 858, p. 52.

Finally, we should remember that exclusion from local communities could happen after death as well as before it, as the case of the stranger Arnulf shows. Everywhere in the Latin West, burial became increasingly close to the church, as indeed was requested by church councils such as Tribur in 895.[136] This was, however, a long-term process, which did not become a norm until the eleventh century. Before that, community burial was only one of a range of burial practices that can often be found together in a single settlement.[137] Burial practice might again point to a heterogeneous local society. Moreover, archaeologists frequently discover isolated burials in yards, ditches and fields, as well as the notorious 'execution burials' of Anglo-Saxon England.[138] In some cases, these people may have been victims of violence, authorised or otherwise; in other cases, these burials may have been a matter of family choice; but it has recently been argued that such deliberate exclusion from group practice might also represent traces of rural slavery.[139]

Collective activity on the part of residential local groups in the Latin West from 700 to 1000 is surprisingly elusive, outside of the specific context of labour services owed to landowners. Perhaps this is to some extent determined by the nature of our primary form of evidence, charters recording private land transactions: these are texts that are intrinsically less likely to record instances of group activity. Yet the pattern seems to be

136 Council of Tribur, ch. 15, in MGH Capit. 2, pp. 206–49, at pp. 221-2.
137 A. Dierkens and C. Treffort, 'Le cimetière au village dans l'Europe médiévale et moderne: rapport introductif', in C. Treffort (ed.), *Le cimetière au village dans l'Europe médiévale et moderne: actes des XXXVes journées internationales d'histoire de l'abbaye de Flaran 11 et 12 octobre 2013* (Toulouse: Presses Universitaires du Midi, 2015), pp. 8–19; I. Cartron, 'Avant le cimetière au village: la diversité des espaces funéraires. Historiographie et perspectives', in ibid., pp. 23–39; M. Lauwers, 'Le cimetière au village ou le village au cimetière? Spatialisation et communauturisation des rapports sociaux dans l'occident médiéval', in ibid., pp. 41–60.
138 A. Reynolds, *Anglo-Saxon Deviant Burial Customs* (Oxford: Oxford University Press, 2009).
139 For example, A. Vigil-Escalera Guirado, 'Invisible social inequalities in early medieval communities: the bare bones of household slavery', in J. A. Quirós Castillo (ed.), *Social Complexity in Early Medieval Rural Communities. The North-Western Iberia Archaeological Record* (Oxford: Oxbow Books, 2016), pp. 113–24; M. Vivas, 'La privation de sépulture au Moyen Âge. L'exemple de la province ecclésiastique de Bordeaux (Xe–début du XIVe siècles)', *Revue historique de Bordeaux et du département de la Gironde*, 19 (2013), 238–41.

confirmed by all other forms of evidence too. It seems that beyond what was determined by outside forces, farming was something generally done within households rather than undertaken by groups, though doubtless there was occasional ad hoc mutual assistance. It seems too that in most of the regions under scrutiny, local settlements did not have a collective identity as such. Only in Brittany do rural communities appear to have had an exceptionally strong sense of identity. And while there is good evidence for an informal sense of local 'Wirgefühl', which we can see playing out in relation to outsiders of different kinds, this seldom amounted to local 'collective action' of all inhabitants of one locality. This perhaps reflects the reality that local societies in many cases were socially, legally and economically heterogeneous.

5

Shepherds, uncles, owners, scribes: priests as neighbours in early medieval local societies

A priest ordained to a local church had a series of duties that served two main purposes. For one, he looked after a community of baptised Christians who went to the same church; for another, he was responsible for the spiritual well-being of all individual members of his flock. Who exactly belonged to a local priest's flock is, however, not always easy to tell. Even by the end of the period covered in this book, we cannot simply assume that a priest's flock equated to the inhabitants of a settlement, or at least not in the way of later medieval parishes. A local church's community in more recently converted regions, such as the north and east of Europe, would be drawn from a larger area than in, say, northern and central Italy or southern France, characterised by an older and denser network of churches. Moreover, settlement structures also varied widely in this period, with the nucleated village being just one of several possibilities.[1] Whatever the spatial organisation of settlements and the density of church infrastructure, however, by the early medieval period people did have access to churches in most parts of western Europe. Texts about pastoral care that started to appear in the Frankish realms in the eighth century assume the availability of priests and Christian rituals to the laity, even if some people had to travel to get to a church.[2] What is more, such texts

---

1 C. Wickham, *The Inheritance of Rome: A History of Europe from 400 to 1000* (London: Penguin, 2009), ch. 9, esp. pp. 211–14. See above, pp. 52–64.
2 Frankish conciliar texts and capitularies assume that everybody could go to Mass on Sundays: *Admonitio generalis*, ch. 81, ed. H. Mordek, K. Zechiel-Eckes and M. Glatthaar (Hanover: Hahn, 2012); cf., also, eighth-century sources dealing with Saxony, even though only recently conquered and converted: *Capitulatio de partibus Saxoniae (a. 775–790)*, ch. 18, in MGH Capit. 1, p. 69. The Council of Tribur (895), ch.14, in MGH Capit. 2, at p. 221, states that new churches could

often assume that those who went to hear Mass, or celebrate a saint's day, would always go to the same church, which was the one to which they also paid their tithes.[3] With ecclesiastical councils, royal decrees and episcopal instructions trying to regulate nearly all spheres of the laity's life in Carolingian realms and, somewhat later, in England, local priests had several means at their disposal to influence people's sense of individual and collective identity. Recent publications have emphasised the unique position priests held in early medieval communities and it has become clear that priests had much greater agency than previously thought. Traditional studies, often relying on the *Eigenkirche* model as their starting point, tended to reduce many priests to passive, dependent, almost powerless puppets at the mercy of lay lords.[4] The local priests who emerge from new analyses of large corpora of primary sources, however, were active people, often fully integrated into local society. At the same time, they were also part of social groups that were not strictly local, such as the clergy of the diocese or, in some cases, the regional wealthy. In this sense, they were 'men in the middle', or 'hinge persons', to borrow a term recently coined by John Howe, that is, men who connected the local laity to the church and its hierarchy, to the world of writing and knowledge, and, on occasion, to the supra-local level of landowners.[5]

   be founded no less than four or five miles from an existing one, with episcopal permission, so that the new church would not divert tithes from the earlier.
3 This combination of pastoral care and payment of tithes tied people to a specific church and thereby in principle shaped a local Christian community. On tithes in Frankish Europe, see J.-P. Devroey, 'L'introduction de la dîme en Occident: entre espaces ecclésiaux et territoires seigneuriaux à l'époque Carolingienne', in M. Lauwers (ed.), *La dîme, l'église et la société féodale* (Turnhout: Brepols, 2012), pp. 87–106; S. Wood, *The Proprietary Church in the Medieval West* (Oxford: Oxford University Press, 2006), ch. 15. On the relationship between church dues and pastoral care in England, see F. Tinti, 'The "costs" of pastoral care: church dues in Anglo-Saxon England', in F. Tinti (ed.), *Pastoral Care in Late Anglo-Saxon England* (Woodbridge: Boydell Press, 2005), pp. 27–51. For regulations forbidding priests to attract the faithful normally attending other churches, see Theodulf of Orléans' episcopal statute, ch. 14, in MGH Capit. episc. 1, p. 112.
4 C. van Rhijn and S. Patzold, 'Introduction', in S. Patzold and C. van Rhijn (eds), *Men in the Middle: Local Priests in Early Medieval Europe* (Berlin: De Gruyter, 2016), pp. 1–10.
5 J. Howe, *Before the Gregorian Reform: The Latin Church at the Turn of the First Millennium* (Ithaca, NY: Cornell University Press, 2016), pp. 253–5; Patzold and van Rhijn (eds), *Men in the Middle*.

In what follows, we shall assess the extent to which local priests promoted group cohesion within the Christian communities they served, but also how, by contrast, they purposely or inadvertently disrupted life within those same communities, paying attention to the tensions that their position as clerics living in the secular world could cause. We shall examine four main areas of activity in which local priests were involved, starting with those most closely related to their pastoral role, before moving on to more secular activities in which they took part, in spite of the many prohibitions in episcopal statutes and other normative sources. We shall first consider priests as shepherds, who, through their teaching, preaching and interventions in potentially disruptive situations, had several tools with which they could foster collective Christian community awareness. Secondly, priests as members of local families will be considered, bearing in mind the potential conflicts between their interests and those of the church. Thirdly, there is the evidence for priests as local landowners active in buying, selling, giving and obtaining land in ways that would not have met with episcopal or canonical approval. Fourthly, we shall consider the charter-writing activities that, thanks to their education, priests often also carried out within local rural societies.

The challenge is to provide a framework built on different types of evidence from various regions of the early medieval Christian West: from northern Iberia to Anglo-Saxon England through the Frankish realms to northern and central Italy. There were important differences between these areas in terms of settlement and ecclesiastical structures, as well as in their development over time. For Carolingian and post-Carolingian Europe, with its relative wealth of sources, this task is easier than for areas such as northern Iberia, where most types of primary source (with the exception of charters) are scarce before the tenth century.[6] Inevitably, then, there is more to say about some themes and regions than about others.

Priests, pastoral care and local communities

Most of what we know about the pastoral duties of early medieval priests is based on the many prescriptions for, and admonishments of, priests of the period, especially those surviving from the Carolingian realms. However, these ideas can be supplemented with texts that were probably used by the priests themselves for pastoral purposes. It goes without saying that

---

6 See above, Chapter 2, and below, Appendix.

prescriptive texts represent ideals rather than lived realities, and that variation was great through time and space; texts with more practical purposes, such as sermons and homilies, tracts and expositions, may reveal a glimpse of what they actually did with the instructions they received.[7] The richest and earliest body of evidence comes from the Frankish kingdoms and from Italy, while relevant Anglo-Saxon sources, and especially those from early medieval Christian Iberia (beyond Catalonia), are scattered, more fragmented and at least a century later. All the same, there seem to have been shared ideas, and indeed ideals, throughout early medieval Europe on the role that priests could or should play in the formation of and care for Christian communities. In what follows, the focus will be on preaching, baptism and the education of catechumens, as three central areas of close interaction between priests and their flocks. Confession and penance will also be considered as areas of priestly activity that could have important consequences for the social cohesion of local communities.

Sermons preached throughout Christian Europe were the regular occasions for teaching lay people about the main precepts of their religion, but also for communicating ideals of Christian behaviour. From the sixth century onwards, conciliar, papal and episcopal instructions prescribed preaching by priests for every Sunday and feast day, and lay people were expected to go to church on those days, behave well during the service and not leave before the entire Mass was over.[8] Sermons provided positive and negative role models for their audiences, as Max Diesenberger has recently shown, specifying how they were supposed to live, think and believe in order to gain eternal life in the heavenly kingdom after death.[9] According to a recent estimate, about one thousand sermons survive from all over early medieval Europe, in collections that may well have formed the main resource for weekly preaching by local priests. According to James McCune, sermons were not necessarily read out from these books,

---

7 See C. van Rhijn, 'The local church, priests' handbooks, and pastoral care in the Carolingian period', in *Chiese locali e chiese regionali nell'alto medioevo* (Spoleto: Fondazione CISAM, 2014), pp. 689–706.
8 Preaching was originally an episcopal prerogative, but in the course of the sixth century it was delegated to priests. See Y. Hen, *Culture and Religion in Merovingian Gaul, AD 481–751* (Leiden: Brill, 1995), pp. 33-4; R. Godding, *Prêtres en Gaule Mérovingienne* (Brussels: Société des Bollandistes, 2001), pp. 375–81.
9 M. Diesenberger, *Predigt und Politik im frühmittelalterlichen Bayern: Karl der Große, Arn von Salzburg und die Salzburger Sermones-Sammlung* (Berlin: De Gruyter, 2015), pp. 18–19.

but priests could use them as a source of inspiration for their preaching.[10] This would imply that priests may well have preached without the aid of a collection of homilies and sermons, which are thin on the ground in Tuscany, totally absent in northern Iberia, and appear later in England than in the Frankish world, which is where the bulk of the evidence for preaching priests comes from. Sermons and homilies that deal with matters well suited to a lay audience, and that are contained in many Carolingian pastoral compendia, tend to be short and relatively easy. The famous decree of the Council of Tours of 813 required homilies to be translated (*transferre*) 'in the rustic Roman language or in Germanic' (*in rusticam Romanam linguam aut Theotiscam*).[11] However, written evidence for vernacular preaching is notably scant from the Carolingian world, especially if compared with the Anglo-Saxon organised programmes of vernacular homilies in the tenth and early eleventh centuries.[12] What does survive shows some glimpses of how preaching in the vernacular may have worked. Within this limited evidence, a small group of early ninth-century

10   J. McCune, 'The sermon collection in the Carolingian clerical handbook, Paris, Bibliothèque nationale de France, lat 1012', *Mediaeval Studies*, 75 (2013), 35–91, at 36–7; J. McCune, 'The preacher's audience, c.800–c.950', in M. Diesenberger, Y. Hen and M. Pollheimer (eds), *Sermo doctorum: Compilers, Preachers and their Audiences in the Early Middle Ages* (Turnhout: Brepols, 2013), pp. 283–338, at pp. 288–92. Still fundamental is R. McKitterick, *The Frankish Church and the Carolingian Reforms, 789–895* (London: Royal Historical Society, 1977), ch. 5. See also M. Swan, 'Memorialised readings: manuscript evidence for Old English homily composition', in P. Pulsiano and E. M. Treharne (eds), *Anglo-Saxon Manuscripts and their Heritage* (Aldershot: Ashgate, 1998), pp. 205–17.

11   On *transferre* in this context cf. R. Wright, *Late Latin and Early Romance in Spain and Carolingian France* (Liverpool: Francis Cairns, 1982), pp. 118–22; M. van Uytfanghe, 'The consciousness of a linguistic dichotomy (Latin-Romance) in Carolingian Gaul: the contradictions of the sources and their interpretation', in R. Wright (ed.), *Latin and the Romance Languages in the Early Middle Ages* (London: Routledge, 1991), pp. 114–29, at p. 120; M. Banniard, *Viva voce: communication orale du IVe au IXe siècle en occident latin* (Paris: Institut des études augustiniennes, 1992), pp. 411–13. A decree of the council of Mainz, of 813, ch. 25, required the word of God to be preached so that the *vulgus* could understand: MGH Conc. 2, 1, p. 268. Cf. other Carolingian conciliar canons (Reims, 813; Mainz, 847). For the view that preaching in the vernacular was more an ideal than reality, C. Edwards, 'German vernacular literature: a survey', in R. McKitterick (ed.), *Carolingian Culture: Emulation and Innovation* (Cambridge: Cambridge University Press, 1993), pp. 141–70, at p. 146.

12   Homiletic materials are the most numerous vernacular items to survive from Anglo-Saxon England. Almost half (about 130) were composed by Ælfric

fragments, known as the Mondsee-Vienna fragments, is especially important, for it consists of a mixture of texts in the vernacular, including a translation of St Augustine's homily on Matthew 14.24ff.[13] Further evidence is provided by two other early ninth-century manuscripts containing an Old High German translation of a sermon known as *Exhortatio ad plebem christianam*,[14] which addresses some of the most basic requirements for all Christians, such as the duty to learn the Lord's Prayer by heart, since it contained the central precepts of the Christian religion.[15] The fairly free translation suggests that its main aim was audience comprehension rather than strict adherence to the original Latin.[16]

In spite of encouraging preaching in the vernacular, the leaders of the Carolingian church do not appear to have done much to assist those in charge of 'transferring' the Latin of homilies into the languages of local communities, possibly indicating that priests could do so on their own initiative.[17] A clearer example of the effort required to convey the meaning of Latin homilies to the laity survives from a Romance-speaking region, thanks to the preservation of a manuscript fragment from Saint-Amand, dating to the first half of the tenth century and containing a sermon on Jonah.[18] By this time, Medieval Latin and Gallo-Romance had become

of Eynsham, a little more than twenty by Archbishop Wulfstan, and the rest survive as anonymous texts. For a short introduction, see D. Scragg, 'Homilies', in M. Lapidge, J. Blair, S. Keynes and D. Scragg (eds), *The Wiley Blackwell Encyclopaedia of Anglo-Saxon England* (Chichester: John Wiley and Sons, 2nd edn, 2014), pp. 247-8. Don Scragg has identified a palimpsest in Oxford, Bodleian Library, Digby 63, containing vernacular homiletic material dated palaeographically to the ninth century, whose dialect features indicate Northumbria as its region of origin: D. Scragg, 'A ninth-century Old English homily from Northumbria', *Anglo-Saxon England*, 45 (2016), 39-49.

13 Hanover, Niedersächsische Landesbibl., MS I 20b and Vienna, ÖNB, MS 3093. On their linguistic features, see J. West, 'Into German: the language of the earliest German literature', in B. Murdoch (ed.), *German Literature of the Early Middle Ages* (Woodbridge: Boydell Press, 2004), pp. 35-56, at pp. 46-7.
14 Kassel, Cod. Kassell theol. quart. 24, fos 13v-17v; Munich clm 6244, fos 144v-6r.
15 On the importance of this duty for the Carolingian *populus christianus*, see S. Patzold, '*Pater noster*: priests and the religious instruction of the laity in the Carolingian *populus christianus*', in Patzold and van Rhijn (eds), *Men in the Middle*, pp. 199-228.
16 Edwards, 'German vernacular literature', p. 146.
17 Even though texts insist on intelligibility and appropriateness of style according to the audience addressed: McCune, 'The preacher's audience', pp. 288-90.
18 Valenciennes, Bibliothèque municipale, MS 521.

more clearly separated and the latter could be represented on parchment as a distinct written language. The main interest of this sermon lies in the fact that it demonstrates the kind of process that a tenth-century preacher would have had to use in order to deliver a sermon in the Romance vernacular based on a Latin biblical text.[19] The sermon presents a peculiar combination of Latin, Romance and tironian notes (a system of shorthand inherited from the Roman world) for both languages. Scholars disagree as to whether this unusual linguistic mixture should be interpreted as a preacher's working notes or the record of an actual sermon which could be repeated throughout the liturgical year on Rogation days;[20] either case would provide unique evidence of the ways in which a preacher could move from the Latin scriptures to a vernacular explanation of the biblical text.[21]

Many surviving sermons address topics that are related to local life. Relevant first and foremost are those sermons about the ways in which good Christians ought to deal with their *proximi* and *vicini*. The biblical theme of loving one's *proximi*, a conveniently broad term that could embrace relatives, friends, neighbours and other near and dear, turns up frequently in homiletic materials.[22] One sermon collection, included in a handbook for a Bavarian priest (now München, Bayerische Staatsbibliothek clm 28135), contains a set of twenty sermons and homilies, six of which address the ways in which one should and should not treat *proximi*.[23] The starting point for most of these is the biblical precept

19 D. Ganz, 'The Old French sermon on Jonah: the nature of the text', in Diesenberger, Hen and Pollheimer (eds), *Sermo doctorum*, pp. 427-39: 'the text retells the story of the prophet Jonah's journey to the city of Nineveh and urges the audience to trust in God's mercy granted to penitent sinners, urging them to give alms and to pray to be saved from pagans and bad Christians, and to pray for the forgiveness of their sins' (p. 427).

20 Cf. McCune, 'The preacher's audience', p. 291; Ganz, 'The Old French sermon', pp. 434-7.

21 On the importance of language for early medieval priests, see R. Meens, 'Conclusions: early medieval priests – some further thoughts', in Patzold and van Rhijn (eds), *Men in the Middle*, pp. 222-8, at p. 227.

22 Blaise, *Dictionnaire latin-français des auteurs chrétiens* (Turnhout: Brepols, 1954-67), consulted online via Brepolis database of Latin dictionaries, lemma *proximus*. The lemma *vicinus* similarly gives a range of meanings: neighbours, near and dear, people close to oneself.

23 The manuscript is available online at http://daten.digitale-sammlungen. de/~db/0004/bsb00047308/images/index.html?id=00047308&groesser=&fip= 193.174.98.30&no=&seite=1, for which see R. Étaix, 'Un manuel de pastorale

according to which one should love one's *proximi* as much as oneself.[24] According to one sermon in the collection, those who failed to do so were considered sinners and should do penance.[25] An anonymous Mass commentary from the late eighth century, which had reached Italy and England by the tenth century, even states that those at loggerheads with their near and dear were not allowed to take Communion until they had been reconciled.[26] Explanations of vices and virtues in sermons elaborate on this theme, for good works were mostly done through love of one's fellow men, while many sins were committed against *proximi* as a result of not loving them enough. Unchristian acts such as bearing false witness, adultery, stealing, committing murder or practising avarice took place almost by definition against one's *proximi* or *vicini*. The local community, on the other hand, provided ample opportunities for individuals to perform good works, for instance by carrying out acts of charity and compassion or by offering forgiveness and generosity. One sermon in the above-mentioned Bavarian collection admonishes all to be examples to the people around them by living lives of chastity and sobriety, and by admonishing their children and *vicini* to do the same.[27] Another sermon

de l'époque carolingienne (Clm 27152)', *Revue Bénédictine*, 91 (1981), 105–30; C. D. Wright and R. Wright, 'Additions to the Bobbio Missal: *De dies malus* and *Joca monachorum* (fos 6r–8v)', in Y. Hen and R. Meens (eds), *The Bobbio Missal: Liturgy and Religious Culture in Merovingian Gaul* (Cambridge: Cambridge University Press, 2004), pp. 79–139, esp. pp. 89–91.

24 Attested many times in both the Old and, especially, the New Testament: e.g. Eccl. 23.19; Matthew 5.43; Mark 12.33; Luke 10.27.

25 München BSB clm 28135, fos 95r–97v. After a long list of sins, at fo. 97v the text reads: 'Diligat deum plus quam se ipsum, amat proximum suum sicut seipsum, quicumque de his supradictis commisit cito emendet confessionem donec ueram paenitentiam agat et ut remittuntur ei peccata sua'. This is in fact Caesarius of Arles' sermo 10, in *Sancti Caesarii Arelatensis sermones, nunc primum in unum collecti et ad leges artis criticae ex innumeris mss recogniti*, ed. G. Morin (Turnhout: Brepols, 2nd edn, 1953), p. 51.

26 See Amalarius, *Opera liturgica omnia*, ed. J. M. Hanssens, vol. 1 (Vatican City: Biblioteca Apostolica Vaticana, 1950), pp. 284–339. A new edition of this text, based on more than fifty manuscripts, is being prepared by Els Rose and Carine van Rhijn. An Italian example of the late ninth or tenth century is Monza, Biblioteca Capitolare MS e-14/127; an English example of the late tenth century is London, British Library, Royal MS 8 C III.

27 München BSB clm 28135, fos 47v–50v, at fo. 49v: 'Qui non solum lites concitat sed etiam discordes ad concordiam reuocat [reuat]. Qui et ipse caste uiuit et filios suos uel uicinos suos, ut caste et subrie uiuant et uerbis admonet et exemplis docet ille bonus est'. This is Augustine's sermo 266, in PL 36, cols 2240–2.

offers a boiled-down summary of how one's everyday behaviour towards others contributed to salvation: 'Therefore, by fear of God and love of your *proximi*, you will gain eternal life.'[28]

Being a Christian, then, implied forms of behaviour towards *vicini* and *proximi* which should be virtuous and motivated by love. This was the message preached in many forms throughout many regions of early medieval Europe, emphasising that, through their membership of the church, lay people belonged to communities in which they should live in peace and harmony and deal with each other in virtuous ways. This not only demanded hard work and effort from each individual, but it would in theory be beneficial for everybody, who would not only give but also receive charity, patience, generosity and forgiveness. All who had become members of the Christian *ecclesia* through their baptism should in this way know how to live in harmony at the level of their community. Social cohesion within such a Christian framework was therefore an integral part of the message that, as far as we can tell from the surviving manuscripts, preachers shared with their Sunday audience.

The foundation for each individual's membership of the *ecclesia* in general, and of the community in which he or she happened to live, was laid out during the catechumenate. This period of learning about Christianity was crowned by the ritual of baptism, when candidates underwent an elaborate *rite de passage* that changed them from pagan outsiders into members of the Christian community. By their baptism, catechumens were symbolically reborn and became full members of the Christian church and, hence, of local Christian society.[29] The ritual was a public event: the priest executed and, as it were, stage-managed the rite, and the members of the local church were expected to be present to witness and remember it. Social cohesion may have been strengthened

---

28 München BSB clm 28135, 'Predicatio de timore domini ad diviti', fos 69r–75r, at fo. 69v: 'Ergo per timorem domini et amorem proximi adqueritur vitam aeternam'. See Wright and Wright, 'Additions', pp. 88–9. This sermon is most similar to Ps-Augustine, Sermo 62 *Ad fratres in eremo*, in PL 40, cols 1345–7.

29 For the political and social implications of baptism, see A. Angenendt, 'Taufe und Politik im frühen Mittelalter', *Frühmittelalterliche Studien*, 7 (1973), 143–68; McKitterick, *The Frankish Church*; O. M. Phelan, *The Formation of Christian Europe: The Carolingians, Baptism, and the Imperium Christianum* (Oxford: Oxford University Press, 2014); J. M. H. Smith, 'Religion and lay society', in R. McKitterick (ed.), *The New Cambridge Medieval History, Volume II, c.700–c.900* (Cambridge: Cambridge University Press, 1995), pp. 654–78, at pp. 656–60.

by godparenthood, which created bonds between families that were considered equivalent to blood ties.[30] From 'followers of the devil', candidates became 'followers of Christ' through the ritual, and from outsiders they became full participants in local Christian life with access to all sacraments and rituals for laymen. Susan Keefe has called baptism 'the cornerstone of Christian society'; priests held the keys that opened the door to membership of Christian communities.[31]

Baptism was no uniform ritual in early medieval Europe and the catechumenate could likewise take many forms depending on local conditions and traditions: there were lived variations on these themes, ranging from baptism preceded by barely any instruction at all to a long and elaborate process of teaching, while the ritual itself could follow a wide range of *ordines*.[32] The age at which people were baptised varied too. There is much evidence for child baptism throughout Europe, but extant explanations of the ritual also allow for baptism at a more mature age.[33] A common feature is that each candidate for baptism (or, in the case of a child too young to be able to talk and understand, its godparents) should know by heart, and understand, the Lord's Prayer and the Creed, on which, so one bishop asserted, 'the foundations of the Christian faith rest'.[34] From Late Antiquity onwards, numerous explanations of the two prayers were produced, mostly in Latin but also in vernacular languages, showing that education about these prayers was considered of utmost importance and may well have taken place in languages that illiterate people could

30 See J. H. Lynch, *Godparents and Kinship in Early Medieval Europe* (Princeton, NJ: Princeton University Press, 1986), esp. Part IV.
31 S. A. Keefe, 'Carolingian baptismal expositions: a handlist of tracts and manuscripts', in U.-R. Blumenthal (ed.), *Carolingian Essays: Andrew W. Mellon Lectures in Early Christian Studies* (Washington DC: Catholic University of America Press, 1983), pp. 169–237, at p. 174.
32 As recorded by S. Keefe, *Water and the Word. Baptism and the Education of the Clergy in the Carolingian Empire*, 2 vols (Notre Dame, IN: University of Notre Dame Press, 2002), vol. 2.
33 See Keefe, *Water and the Word*, vol. 1, p. 3; ibid., vol. 2, Text 14, at p. 262, for an example of child baptism as a norm, but see Text 9, at p. 240, for an example where the candidate for baptism is called 'paganus', without any indication of age. Iberian baptismal liturgy left the possibility of child and adult baptism open; see the 'Ordo baptismi', in *Liber ordinum sacerdotal (Cod.Silos, Arch. Monástico 3)*, ed. J. Janini (Silos: Abadía de Silos, 1981), pp. 54–8.
34 This requirement continued to be repeated throughout the period. The quotation is from Theodulf of Orléans' first episcopal statute [c. 800], ch. 22, ed. P. Brommer, MGH Capit. episc. 1, p. 119.

understand.[35] A significant quantity of vernacular material survives from Germanic-speaking regions, including an explanation of the Lord's Prayer in a Bavarian dialect,[36] and several Old English versions of the same prayer, both in prose and in verse. Old English translations of the Lord's Prayer and the Creed are occasionally said to have been provided for the uneducated faithful who could not learn them in Latin.[37]

From the moment catechumens were baptised, they could join their neighbours and relatives in taking Communion during Mass, they were welcome to celebrate Christian feast days and pray to saints to ask for intercession, they could get forgiveness for their sins when confessed to a priest and, in some regions, especially towards the end of the period here investigated, they would be buried in consecrated ground after death.[38] On the other hand, membership of the community of Christians also meant subscribing to a code of behaviour that extended far beyond things that happened in church, and covered, for instance, rules about what one could and could not eat, one's sexual life and medical practices.[39] While

35 Looking at Carolingian manuscripts, Susan Keefe identified nearly 400 different explanations of the Creed, dating from the fifth to the late ninth centuries, which survive in hundreds of different manuscripts: S. Keefe, *A Catalogue of Works Pertaining to the Explanation of the Creed in Carolingian Manuscripts* (Turnhout: Brepols, 2012).

36 München, BSB clm 6330, fos 70v–71r.

37 Some vernacular versions of the Lord's Prayer occur in homilies by Ælfric of Eynsham and Archbishop Wulfstan, dating to the late tenth or early eleventh century. For detailed though somewhat dated discussion of Old English materials, see R. A. Banks, 'A study of the Old English versions of the Lord's Prayer, the Creeds, the Gloria and some prayers found in British Museum MS. Cotton Galba A. xiv, together with a new examination of the place of liturgy in the literature of Anglo-Saxon magic and medicine', PhD thesis, Queen Mary College, University of London, 1968. Already in the eighth century, Bede had advocated the use of English translations: H. Gittos, 'The audience for Old English texts: Ælfric, rhetoric and the edification of the simple', *Anglo-Saxon England*, 43 (2014), pp. 231–66.

38 See above, pp. 95–8. In many parts of Europe evidence for churchyards becoming the necessary burial places for parish communities only begins to appear between the tenth and the twelfth centuries; see E. Zadora-Rio, 'The making of churchyards and parish territories in the early medieval landscape of France and England in the 7th–12th centuries: a reconsideration', *Medieval Archaeology*, 47 (2003), 1–19.

39 These subjects are covered in the penitentials. See, for example, the ninth-century elaborate *Paenitentiale pseudo-Theodori*, ed. C. van Rhijn (Turnhout: Brepols, 2009), book XXV (*De discretione ciborum mundum et inmundum*),

sermons mostly focused on fundamental Christian items of belief (for instance the Trinity, the Resurrection of the Dead, the Virginity of Mary) and morals, the nitty-gritty of ideal Christian behaviour can be found in other texts, such as handbooks of penance, episcopal statutes and collections of canon law.[40]

This brings us to a third aspect of pastoral care. Penance and confession could cast priests in the role of marriage counsellors, intermediaries, dispensers of advice and, when needed, judges of lay behaviour. Many manuscripts for priests contain texts that reflect such concerns; especially interesting for our purposes are two categories of texts that often occur in these same manuscripts: handbooks of penance and collections of canon law. While such prescriptive texts are often interpreted as reflections of norms, values and ideal behaviour with the aid of which contrite sinners could make amends, Rob Meens has suggested a second, more social way in which these texts can be understood.[41] Many sins and transgressions described in penitentials did not just touch the sinner but also one or more of his *proximi* and *vicini*. While the consumption of milk in which a mouse had drowned might only worry the consumer him- or herself, issues such as violence, adultery, theft or even hating a neighbour would easily cause local conflict and scandal. An adulterous husband, for instance, could be the source of bad rumours and problems (or even revenge) between families or groups of neighbours. If the culprit decided to go to the priest, confess and do penance for sins, this would not only take away the sin in due course but also remove the culprit from society for a while. Penitents were not allowed to enter church or even

books X (*De fornicatione*) to XIII (*De incestis*) about matters sexual, and book XXI, chs 14–16 (*De idolatria et sacrilegio* ...) about forbidden medical practices; see also chs 3, 4 of this penitential.

40 See R. Meens, *Penance in Medieval Europe* (Cambridge: Cambridge University Press, 2015). The many surviving (but largely unedited) early medieval collections of canon law have been catalogued by L. Kéry, *Canonical Collections of the Early Middle Ages (ca. 400–1140). A Bibliographical Guide to the Manuscripts and Literature* (Washington DC: Catholic University of America Press, 1999). Both works attest to the wide distribution of these types of texts. However, such material is remarkably rare in Iberian contexts, which did have a rich tradition of canon law, but apparently did not produce penitentials, episcopal statutes or collections of sermons and homilies.

41 The following paragraph draws on Rob Meens's paper entitled 'Confession and marriage counselling', delivered on 2 July 2013 at the International Medieval Congress, Leeds.

talk or eat with other people until they had been reconciled.[42] Penance for sins such as violence or adultery often took years, which would probably give potentially explosive situations the chance to die down – in this way, confession to a priest could well be a first step towards defusing conflicts by removing one of the parties from the scene, and making this person suffer visibly for his or her deeds. It does not take a great leap of imagination to picture a priest suggesting confession and penance to those who caused unrest – pastoral care was meant to be active, with the priest giving advice when he saw fit. If priests were active in restoring peace in their communities through the mechanisms of pastoral care that they were trained to use, it is also possible that they functioned as advisers or intermediaries in conflicts. What is more, there is evidence that priests were also familiar with secular procedures of conflict resolution, even though it was, according to the *canones*, utterly forbidden to them to have anything to do with such trials. A few Carolingian manuscripts for priests contain texts needed for such procedures, such as blessings for boiling water or red-hot ploughshares, both elements of trial by ordeal,[43] while tenth-century charters from northern Iberia show that priests were often involved in court cases as litigating parties, as providers of evidence, as sureties, as members of inquest panels and occasionally as *saiones*.[44]

Priests as members of local families

As shepherds of local lay flocks, priests were not necessarily clerical outsiders to the people who came to their churches to hear Mass, witness baptisms and celebrate saints' days. There is evidence from all over early medieval Europe that priests were often themselves from local stock.[45]

---

42 As described by Theodulf of Orléans, first episcopal statute ch. 26, in MGH Capit. episc. 1, p. 123.

43 For instance, München, Bayerische Staatsbibliothek clm 14508: blessings for boiling water and red-hot ploughshares, fos 146v–147v.

44 W. Davies, 'Local priests in northern Iberia', in Patzold and van Rhijn (eds), *Men in the Middle*, pp. 125–44, esp. pp. 142–3.

45 W. Davies, 'Priests and rural communities in east Brittany in the ninth century', *Études Celtiques*, 20 (1983), 177–93. In Tuscany the well-known *breve inquisitionis* of 715, dealing with a dispute between the bishop of Siena and Arezzo for control of some *plebes*, attests to the local origin of the clergy as well as to frequent cases of kinship between such clerics: CDL, vol. 1, no. 19; see L. Pellegrini, '*Plebs* e *populus* in ambito rurale nell'Italia altomedievale', in *Società, istituzioni,*

This led to situations in which priests were related to people who lived in the same settlement as they did, or just a few kilometres away. That bishops appointed men with local roots as priests of local churches makes sense in more ways than one: such candidates would have no problem speaking and understanding the local vernacular, while a priest from a family known and respected locally may have been more easily accepted by the community than a total stranger.[46] Priests and their lay relatives often moved in the same lay worlds, while the priest at the same time had one foot in the ecclesiastical hierarchy. This could have a huge impact on local rural societies, as local families became tied to the church via their clerical members, who were, in turn, directly connected to the bishop, to their diocesan colleagues and to monasteries in the area. Some priests, for instance in Tuscany and northern Spain, owned their churches as well as land and other goods, which they regularly left to their heirs, thus making the well-being of the church family business.[47] The other side of the coin was that, if priests caused trouble, this could easily spill over to their relatives and to the wider lay community of neighbours and acquaintances.

spiritualità. Studi in onore di Cinzio Violante, 2 vols (Spoleto: Fondazione CISAM, 1994), vol. 1, pp. 599–632, at pp. 608–9. For many parts of Europe, see J. Barrow, *The Clergy in the Medieval World: Secular Clerics, their Families and Careers in North-Western Europe, c.800–c.1200* (Cambridge: Cambridge University Press, 2015), esp. ch. 4.

46 In Bavaria, and elsewhere, episcopal appointment was not the only way to assign a priest to a local church: the local *plebs* could choose; see T. Kohl, '*Presbyter in parochia sua*: local priests and their churches in early medieval Bavaria', in Patzold and van Rhijn (eds), *Men in the Middle*, pp. 50–77, at p. 66. An anonymous ninth-century priests' exam, probably from France, enquired if the candidate 'electus a populo sit'; see W. Hartmann, 'Neue Texte zur bischöflichen Reformgesetzgebung aus den Jahren 829/31: Vier Diözesansynoden Halitgars von Cambrai', *Deutsches Archiv für Erforschung des Mittelalters*, 35 (1979), 368–94, at 392–4. In northern Iberia, priests may have inherited their function, since there were not enough bishops to teach, select and/or ordain them; this impression seems to be corroborated by the references to *quasi-presbiteri* that can be found in charters from various collections; see Davies, 'Local priests in northern Iberia', pp. 131–2.

47 M. Stoffella, 'Local priests in early medieval rural Tuscany', in Patzold and van Rhijn (eds), *Men in the Middle*, pp. 98–124, at p. 119. Clerics in Tuscany may have deliberately chosen to stay in the lower clerical orders in order to have children and facilitate strategies of church inheritance: R. Stone, 'Exploring minor clerics in early medieval Tuscany', *Reti medievali*, 18:1 (2017), doi: 10.6092/1593-2214/5076.

The few recorded cases of priests causing disruption suggest that under such circumstances pastoral care could be endangered.

Around the year 800, Bishop Theodulf of Orléans included the following instruction in his widely copied first episcopal statute:

> If any of the presbyters wishes to send his nephew or other relative to school, in the church of the Holy Cross, or in the monastery of Saint Aignan, or of Saint Benedict, or of Saint Lifard, or in others of those monasteries which it has been granted us to rule, we grant him permission to do so.[48]

In the course of the ninth century, Theodulf's instructions were distributed all over the Carolingian Empire, while in the tenth and eleventh centuries the text reached Italy, Spain and England. In many manuscripts copied outside Theodulf's diocese, the names of the monasteries were adapted or omitted altogether, showing that this invitation was understood and used widely.[49] Of course, not every early medieval priest was in a position to use such episcopal permission to have a young relative educated, but there is enough evidence to believe that Theodulf was not referring to exceptions but to living practice. As Julia Barrow has recently stated and as several in-depth regional studies have confirmed in more detail,[50] priests often played the role of mentor for nephews or other relatives (sometimes even sons) who were destined for a career in the church.[51] Such a relationship probably started at an early age, and

---

48 Theodulf I, ch. 19, in MGH Capit. episc. 1, pp. 115–16; trans. P. E. Dutton, *Carolingian Civilization: A Reader* (Peterborough, Ont.: Broadview Press, 1993), p. 93.

49 For the extant manuscripts, see MGH Capit. episc. 1, pp. 76–99, with additions in MGH Capit. episc. 4, pp. 76–80; variants to monasteries' names: MGH Capit. episc. 1, p. 115. Manuscripts showing that the text was distributed: Cambridge, Corpus Christi College 201 (s.XI, Exeter) and 265 (s.XI, Worcester); Monza, Biblioteca Capitolare b 23/141 (s.X, northern Italy); Barcelona, Biblioteca Universitaria 228 (s.X, S-France or N-Italy, but probably arriving at Girona at an early date).

50 Barrow, *The Clergy*, ch. 4, which only deals with clergy in north-western Europe; T. Kohl, *Lokale Gesellschaften. Formen der Gemeinschaft in Bayern vom 8. bis zum 10. Jahrhundert* (Ostfildern: Thorbecke, 2010), pp. 258–63; see also Patzold and van Rhijn (eds), *Men in the Middle*, chapters on Alemannia, Bavaria, northern Francia, Tuscany and northern Iberia.

51 See C. Mériaux, 'Ideal and reality: Carolingian priests in northern Francia', in Patzold and van Rhijn (eds), *Men in the Middle*, pp. 78–97, at p. 87; Stoffella, 'Local priests', p. 121.

since priests were required by their bishops to provide basic education for intelligent local boys, their nephews may well have been among those they taught to read and sing.[52]

In many, though not all, regions of early medieval Europe, these nephews, once they had become priests themselves, succeeded their priestly uncles, a pattern that can sometimes be followed through several generations.[53] Keeping the priesthood of specific churches within the family, then, was clearly important enough for these families to develop strategies to that end.[54] Churches were sought since they came with property and were always a source of income and status; on the other hand, a family had to invest to produce acceptable candidates for these functions, which needed planning and the cooperation of its members. Uncles and nephews were the ideal way of organising priestly succession, since their ties were close but not problematic in times when clerical celibacy was becoming increasingly important.[55] The families that did develop such strategies would have become central players in their respective small worlds. If one family managed to produce several generations of priests, it had clearly risen to a position that was too strong for the competition. In other words, the priests who held such churches were not only their bishops' local representatives, but also the living results of successful family strategies.[56]

Some bishops show awareness of the way in which such families manoeuvred themselves into a position of local power through the priesthood. While the connections between lay communities and their churches may well have become stronger in this way, especially in settlements where more or less everybody was related, very close bonds between priest and lay flock could raise questions about ecclesiastical discipline and canon law. There is some evidence that priests used their positions to help their relatives, as emerges from the mid-ninth-century episcopal statutes of Hincmar of Reims. In his first statute, the archbishop forbids priests to give sinners who happened to be their relatives (or their friends)

---

52 See C. van Rhijn, *Shepherds of the Lord. Priests and Episcopal Statutes in the Carolingian Period* (Turnhout: Brepols, 2007), pp. 175-9.
53 Barrow, *The Clergy*, p. 129, calls this 'a dog-legged clerical succession'. She notes that such succession can only be observed from the eleventh century in England.
54 As observed by Wendy Davies in 1983; see her 'Priests and rural communities'.
55 Barrow, *The Clergy*, especially pp. 125-9.
56 This function of 'episcopal representative' is one a priest held everywhere according to canon law, but practice could look quite different. See Davies, 'Local priests in northern Iberia', pp. 131-2, 136-7, for northern Iberia before the year 1000, with many local priests but few bishops.

a lighter penance than they deserved, or no penance at all.[57] Hincmar was also worried that relatives could profit from financial favouritism by the priest and be unnecessarily included among those local poor who deserved alms.[58] It seems that priests kept relationships with their lay relatives warm after ordination and stayed active as members of free, wealthy families. This is especially clear when wealthier members of the priesthood traded, received, gave, sold and bought land, sometimes together with one or more relatives.

While the appointment of a priest in his native region may have had its advantages for many of those involved, this was not necessarily always the case. Competition between families over the appointment of a priest to a local church, or over the resources a church generated, could turn nasty. For instance, an unnamed priest mentioned in a letter of 852/3 from Pope Leo IV to the bishops of Senlis and Beauvais, was forcefully removed from his church by another priest, upon which his relatives took revenge by blinding the perpetrator.[59] Another scandal, recorded in a letter that the victim wrote to Emperor Louis the Pious, features the priest Atto, who read Mass for the cleric Frothwin in exchange for part of the tithes; but when Atto asked for his money, Frothwin and his relatives turned up in the middle of the night to beat him up.[60] Such violent competition over a church and its wealth had long-term repercussions on the relations between the families involved, and it is easy to imagine how this may have divided local society.

In what is perhaps the best-known early medieval case of a misbehaving priest, the priest Trisingus was suspected of having an affair with his stepniece, over which he came to blows with his brother-in-law after a bout of drinking at a local *castellum* (they all lived in the same village near Reims).

---

57   Hincmar of Reims I, ch. 13, in MGH Capit. episc. 2, pp. 40-1. Rephrased, this admonishment occurs in Regino of Prüm's *Libro duo de synodalibus causis et disciplinis ecclesiasticis* I, chs 38, 215, ed. W. Hartmann (Darmstadt: Wissenschaftliche Buchgesellschaft, 2004), pp. 30-1, 120-1.

58   See below, n. 85.

59   For detail, see Mériaux, 'Ideal and reality', p. 88. Another case, which involved a *domina* having a priest castrated, is mentioned in the Council of Metz (893), ch. 10, in MGH Conc. 5, p. 312.

60   See MGH Epp. 5, no. 25, pp. 339-40, and S. Patzold, 'Bildung und Wissen einer lokalen Elite des Frühmittelalters: das Beispiel der Landpfarrer im Frankenreich des 9. Jahrhunderts', in F. Bougard, R. Le Jan and R. McKitterick (eds), *La culture du Haut Moyen Âge, une question d'élites?* (Turnhout: Brepols, 2009), pp. 377-91.

In the process Trisingus chopped off some of his brother-in-law's fingers while attempting to kill him with his own sword. He subsequently went off to Rome to solicit papal support against his bishop, instead of appearing at several local synods to explain himself. What triggered the case was not in the first instance the alleged – and completely forbidden – sexual relationship, the drinking or even the amputated fingers of the brother-in-law, but rather the complaints of the local community, who told their bishop that they had been left without pastoral care since their priest had disappeared.[61] One can only wonder what might have happened had the villagers not complained; would the bishop have ever heard about the case? It took them a year and a half to report the missing priest to their bishop, and it is interesting to speculate what took them so long:[62] did they think their priest would be back? Did they refrain from informing the bishop out of a sense of loyalty? Were they simply not interested in the whereabouts of their priest? In another case, the local people seem to have been very happy to lose their shepherd: the priest Gerelandus was so unpopular with local lay people that they falsely accused him of a crime, whereupon his bishop relieved him of his office without following the canonical procedure of inquiry.[63] There were, in other words, ways in which a community could protect its priest, but it could also get rid of him if need be.

Priests as local owners

A priest's main source of sustenance was in most cases the land attached to the church in which he carried out his ministry. A well-known capitulary

---

61 See *De presbiteris criminosis*: *Ein Memorandum Erzbischof Hinkmars von Reims über straffällige Kleriker*, ed. G. Schmitz (Hanover: Hahn, 2004), pp. 7–9; M. de Jong, 'Hincmar, priests and Pseudo-Isidore: the case of Trising in context', in R. Stone and C. West (eds), *Hincmar of Rheims: Life and Work* (Manchester: Manchester University Press, 2015), pp. 268–88; C. Mériaux, '*Boni agricolae in agro Domini*: Prêtres et société à l'époque carolingienne (VIIIe–Xe siècle)', Dossier d'Habilitation à diriger des Recherches II, Université Charles de Gaulle, Lille 3, 2014, pp. 85–7. Description in Hincmar of Reims, 'Ad Adrianum papam', in PL 126, cols 641–8, trans. de Jong, 'Hincmar', pp. 281–3.
62 See de Jong, 'Hincmar', p. 282. Cf. a letter from Bishop Mancio of Châlons-en-Champagne to Bishop Fulk of Reims mentioning a priest Angelricus who, wishing to marry the woman Grimma, had obtained the approval of her relatives (*consentientibus propinquis eius*). See the digital pre-edition of MGH Epistolae 9 at http://www.mgh.de/datenbanken/epp/results?id=BEb20.
63 A letter of appeal to the pope records the case: MGH Epp. 6, no. 144, pp. 661–2.

of Louis the Pious issued at Aachen in 818/819 laid down that every church should be assigned one whole *mansus* and that the priest established in it did not owe any service from that land.[64] Carolingian sources appear to show an increased interest in provision for the clergy as opposed to the focus on churches' endowment that had characterised earlier legislation on these matters.[65] Charter collections, however, make it clear that local priests could also rely on other resources: Saint-Gall charters, for instance, depict several cases of clerics (mainly priests) directly involved in granting, transferring and exchanging properties.[66] Similar actions characterise other areas of the Carolingian world and well beyond. The numerous surviving ninth-century wills of local priests in the diocese of Lucca in Italy show how such clerics accumulated landed properties in areas which could lie as far as 40 kilometres from the church assigned to them.[67] In northern Iberia tenth-century local priests also acquired lands thanks to the gifts they received and by buying property.[68] An illuminating ninth-century case from Brittany shows that local priests also managed to alienate property that they had received as *elemosina* in favour of a specific church. Having heard that the priest Maenuueten had given away the land he had granted for the benefit of the church at Ruffiac, the original donor, Uuordoetal, wanted to make a complaint, but when he saw Maenuueten collecting evidence (or so the text says), he reached out to the priest in order to settle the issue amicably; he suggested that if Maenuueten were to pay four silver shillings, he would confirm the grant and allow him to alienate the property as he wished ('ita ut faceret exinde quicquid illi placeret ... sive tribuendo, sive vendendo, seu transferendo').[69]

In several regions of early medieval Europe, local priests appear to have been directly involved in the local land-market, as they can be seen inheriting, buying, selling and giving lands themselves and not just mediating between different parties in the property market. The priests who were most likely to participate in such activities were naturally those coming

---

64 'neque de prescripto manso aliquod servitium faciant', *Capitulare ecclesiasticum*, ch. 10, in MGH Capit. 1, no. 138, p. 277.
65 Wood, *The Proprietary Church*, pp. 438–9.
66 B. Zeller, 'Local priests in early medieval Alemannia', in Patzold and van Rhijn (eds), *Men in the Middle*, pp. 32–49, at pp. 34–7.
67 Stoffella, 'Local priests', pp. 115–18.
68 Davies, 'Local priests in northern Iberia', pp. 133–5.
69 CR 144 (851/57), pp. 110–11. See W. Davies, *Small Worlds: The Village Community in Early Medieval Brittany* (London: Duckworth, 1988), pp. 151, 191–2.

from relatively well-to-do backgrounds, whose assets were comparable to those of rich peasants.[70] The Saint-Gall charters clearly show that the priests' possessions were often based on family property, as emerges from those tenurial transactions in which clerics acted together with a relative. Evidence for a late eighth-century dispute in the Italian diocese of Lucca presents a group of clerics belonging to the same family who claimed for themselves the property of the church of Saint Quiricus in *Monticello*. In the end the dispute was won by the bishop of Lucca, who presented a document purporting to demonstrate that the late father of the principal two claimants – a priest himself – had already recognised that the church and all its properties belonged to the cathedral. In northern Iberia local priests can also be seen relying on family properties and transacting lands with their close relatives.[71] Even the sparser and later evidence available for England offers similarities. In a vernacular will preserved in the archive of the monastery at Bury St Edmund's, probably dating to the late tenth or early eleventh centuries, a woman named Siflæd bequeathed land in Norfolk to the monastery, specifying that her church had to remain free and that her priest was 'to sing at it, he and his issue, so long as they [were] in holy orders'.[72] Later on in the eleventh century, Domesday Book provides several examples of priests inheriting property within their families.[73] In ninth-century Brittany priests were often in control of inherited properties, either on their own or jointly with other members of their families.[74]

Even in those cases in which priests did not come from a particularly wealthy background, their ministry, their role within local communities

70 For evidence of priests in Bavaria possessing inherited property and slaves, see S. Esders and H. J. Mierau, *Der althochdeutsche Klerikereid: Bischöfliche Diözesangewalt, kirchliches Benefizialwesen und volkssprachliche Rechtspraxis im frühmittelalterlichen Baiern* (Hanover: Hahn, 2000), p. 87, n. 28, p. 120; also Kohl, 'Presbyter in parochia sua', pp. 69–71. In Brittany some priests had servile dependants: Davies, *Small Worlds*, pp. 99–102.

71 W. Davies, *Acts of Giving: Individual, Community, and Church in Tenth-Century Christian Spain* (Oxford: Oxford University Press, 2007), ch. 2.

72 *Anglo-Saxon Wills*, ed. and trans. D. Whitelock (Cambridge: Cambridge University Press, 1930, repr. 2011), no. 37.

73 J. Barrow, 'The clergy in English dioceses, c. 900–c. 1066', in Tinti (ed.), *Pastoral Care*, pp. 17–26, at p. 20; see also F. Tinti, 'Looking for local priests in Anglo-Saxon England', in Patzold and van Rhijn (eds), *Men in the Middle*, pp. 145–61, at pp. 150–3.

74 Davies, *Small Worlds*, pp. 100–1.

and their access to a number of resources would have set them apart from the rest of local society.[75] Wendy Davies has discussed the range of financial activities that local priests in ninth-century Brittany would have carried out thanks to their special position: more often than any other members of the community they seem to have been able to provide, through loans, the cash needed by peasants.[76] In other words, priests were able to rely on a surplus that allowed them to lend money.[77] The existence of such a surplus can also be inferred from Carolingian texts aiming to protect local priests from abuses by their respective bishops. A council held at Toulouse in 844 in the presence of Charles the Bald established that bishops should not ask too much of their priests' resources.[78] Very specific instructions for payments in kind, detailing legitimate quantities of wheat, barley, wine and so on, are provided, together with guidelines on how episcopal visitations should be conducted so as to avoid an excessive burden on local priests; as Carine van Rhijn has observed, these regulations are especially interesting: they not only provided protection for local churches' incumbents but they also suggest there was some awareness of the existence of a surplus on which local priests could rely to pay or feed the bishops and their entourage.[79]

As well as landed properties, early medieval priests would also have access to financial resources that were directly related to their office. The payment of tithes and other pastoral revenues was beginning to be regulated in many areas of Latin western Christendom in the early Middle Ages, and these represented an important source of income for many local priests as well as another possible cause of tension, disputes and abuses. These were formative times, for the pastoral system was becoming increasingly localised, taking with it the payment of church dues. When new churches were founded, especially when the initiative came from a local lay landlord, the latter was clearly interested in ensuring that the tithes owed by local inhabitants were used to support the local church rather than the clergy of the mother church to which those same revenues

---

75 On poor priests in the Carolingian world, see J. L. Nelson, 'Making ends meet: wealth and poverty in the Carolingian church', *Studies in Church History*, 24 (1987), 25-36; but cf. van Rhijn, *Shepherds of the Lord*, pp. 182-200.
76 Davies, *Small Worlds*, p. 101.
77 See also Mériaux, 'Ideal and reality', p. 87.
78 MGH Conc. 3, no. 4, chs 1-4, pp. 20-1.
79 Van Rhijn, *Shepherds of the Lord*, pp. 189-91; against this: J. Nelson, 'Making ends meet'.

had hitherto been paid. In Francia we see several concessions being made in the ninth century in favour of new lesser churches, with previous episcopal approval.[80] Competition for the control of such an important source of income was often high. An interesting example is provided by a dispute in the diocese of Nîmes in 921; this involved a priest named Ansemirus who claimed that some tithes traditionally assigned to the two churches he controlled (Saint-André-de-Costebalen and Notre-Dame-de-l'Agarne) had more recently been paid to another church (Saint-Martin-de-Quart) whose incumbent was a priest called Geusaldus.[81] This was the result of a property transaction between local landowners. In the ensuing investigation launched by the bishop of Nîmes, local inhabitants appear to have played a major role in providing crucial evidence in favour of Ansemirus. The document lists the names of the people summoned as well as those who supported the oath that Ansemirus took to support his claim. This case shows that priests' control of ecclesiastical dues was a potential source of social disruption.

In Anglo-Saxon England a system of tithe payment made its appearance in tenth-century law codes. King Edgar's legislation of the 960s established that all tithes were to be paid to the old minster, while allowing those thegns who had a church with a graveyard on their bookland to pay one-third of the due tithe to their own estate church, instead of the minster; if there was no graveyard he was to pay all the tithe to the minster and 'pay to his priest from the [remaining] nine parts what he chooses'.[82] Concessions for new churches were being made more slowly in England, because the process of local church foundation started later than in Carolingian Francia. No significant evidence on the payment of tithes survives from northern Iberia in this period.[83]

---

80 Wood, *The Proprietary Church*, p. 464.
81 *Cartulaire du chapitre de l'église cathédrale Notre-Dame de Nîmes (834–1156)*, ed. E. Germer-Durand (Nîmes: Catélan, 1874), no. 20, pp. 33–7.
82 On Anglo-Saxon minsters and the lively historiographical debate on these institutions, see F. Tinti, 'Introduction', in Tinti (ed.), *Pastoral Care*, pp. 1–16. Edgar's code: *Councils and Synods with other Documents Relating to the English Church, Volume 1 A.D. 871–1204, Part 1 871–1066*, ed. D. Whitelock, M. Brett and C. N. L. Brooke (Oxford: Clarendon Press, 1981), pp. 97–8.
83 J. Blair, *The Church in Anglo-Saxon Society* (Oxford: Oxford University Press, 2005), pp. 368–425; Tinti, 'Looking for local priests'; Barrow, *The Clergy*, pp. 318–19; W. Davies, 'Where are the parishes? Where are the minsters? The organization of the Spanish church in the tenth century', in D. Rollason, C. Leyser and H. Williams (eds), *England and the Continent in the Tenth Century:*

Although relevant sources often originated from the top, that is, from episcopal or royal normative actions, local priests were directly affected by these pronouncements, even though there was notable variation across the territories and the period here considered. In many cases priests themselves were responsible for dividing the tithes into the traditional three or four parts, that is for the poor, the fabric, the local clergy and the bishop, presumably with room for manoeuvre in one or other direction.[84] Hincmar of Reims was worried about the way in which such partitioning took place and required two or three faithful to be present when the division was made.[85] Here we see lay representatives of the locality taking part in an important annual event to ensure the correct allocation of the tributes that had been paid by the entire community. In Jinty Nelson's words: 'with the lay witnesses to the priest's accounting, we feel the world coming in at the window, paradoxically to keep the priest from worldly temptation'.[86] From what Hincmar has to say, it would seem that lay witnesses were also there to avoid possible favouritism towards members of the priest's family: he was allowed to include indigent and sick relatives among those entitled to a portion of the tithes, but if he wanted to have other members of his family with him, he had to use his own portion of the tithes to feed them.[87] As has been observed by Charles Mériaux, however, abuse by clerics should not be interpreted as the norm, for it was in everybody's interest that rural priests should have access to resources that would guarantee adequate sustenance. Hincmar himself, notwithstanding all his preoccupations, wanted to make sure that his priests could rely on proper financial support.[88] On the other hand, the involvement of local priests' families in the control of churches and their resources could, as we have seen, lead to tensions, disputes and, in extreme cases, physical violence.[89]

In sum, the evidence of early medieval priests' access to resources allows us to see local clergy actively involved with their neighbours. In spite of repeated prohibitions, especially in Carolingian normative

---

Studies in Honour of Wilhelm Levison (1876-1947) (Turnhout: Brepols, 2010), pp. 379-97, at p. 392.

84 Wood, *The Proprietary Church*, pp. 476-8.
85 Hincmar of Reims II, ch. 16, in MGH Capit. episc. 2, p. 49.
86 Nelson, 'Making ends meet', 151.
87 Hincmar of Reims II, ch. 17, in MGH Capit. episc. 2, p. 50.
88 Mériaux, 'Ideal and reality', p. 87.
89 For examples, see ibid., pp. 88-90; van Rhijn, *Shepherds of the Lord*, pp. 186-7.

sources, they can often be seen selling, buying and transferring properties. In many cases the neighbours with whom they transacted were relatives who had a lot to gain by having one of their kin in this position. However, a degree of control on priests as tenants or owners of properties and recipients of revenues could also be exercised by members of the local community, even though priests had an obvious advantage; they could be perceived as neighbours in many respects, but always as special ones.

Priests as local scribes

Thanks to their education, priests also performed a specific significant function in early medieval local societies, namely, that of scribes. Literacy in the early Middle Ages has received a great deal of attention in recent decades; while positions vary noticeably between those who emphasise the very limited role of the written word in early medieval societies and those who, by contrast, stress its centrality,[90] most scholars would agree that the overall control and exercise of literacy, whatever its effective extent, fell within the remit of educated clerics. In early medieval Italy it is also possible to observe 'functional' lay literacy in collections of documents from Lucca, Pisa, Piacenza, Bergamo, Milan, Salerno and so on, through the analysis of autograph subscriptions of many laymen. Professional lay charter scribes played an increasingly significant role, especially in the northern and central regions. It should be noted, however, that the evidence points primarily towards urban, rather than rural, documentary production, which is clearly reflected in the focus adopted in the principal studies of early medieval Italian literacy.[91]

90 Cf. R. McKitterick, *The Carolingians and the Written Word* (Cambridge: Cambridge University Press, 1989); M. Richter, '"... quisquis scit scribere, nullum potat abere labore". Zur Laienschriftlichkeit im 8. Jahrhundert', in J. Jarnut, U. Nonn and M. Richter (eds), *Karl Martell in seiner Zeit* (Sigmaringen: Thorbecke, 1994), pp. 393–404.
91 A. Petrucci and C. Romeo, '*Scriptores in urbibus*': *Alfabetismo e cultura scritta nell'Italia altomedievale* (Bologna: Il Mulino, 1992); see also H. Keller, 'Der Gerichtsort in oberitalienischen und toskanischen Städten', *Quellen und Forschungen aus italienischen Archiven und Bibliotheken*, 49 (1969), 1–72; N. Everett, *Literacy in Lombard Italy, c. 568–774* (Cambridge: Cambridge University Press, 2003), chs 3, 5; M. Costambeys, 'The laity, the clergy, the scribes and their archives: the documentary record of eighth- and ninth-century Italy', in W. Brown, M. Costambeys, M. Innes and A. Kosto (eds),

Within most rural communities, access to reading and writing would have had to be mediated through local priests. Bodies of documentary materials such as those surviving from early medieval Alemannia or ninth- and tenth-century northern Iberia testify most vividly to the scribal role of secular clerics.[92] As Bernhard Zeller has observed, elaborating on the steps taken by Rosamond McKitterick, local priests in Alemannia seem to have taken their role of charter scribes seriously, with transactions taking place in many cases in the *atrium* of a church.[93] The remarkable body of single-sheet original charters from the Carolingian period preserved in the Saint-Gall archive allows for the identification of features that set charters written by secular priests apart from those drafted by the monastery's scribes. Both the extrinsic and intrinsic features of these charters, including their often more crude scripts, their graphic symbols, their peculiar ligatures and abbreviations, as well as the character of their sometimes fairly rustic Latin, point towards decentralised training, probably reflecting local writing traditions sustained through successive generations of local clerics. They would thus have contributed to an infrastructure of local scribes serving local landowners and peasant proprietors and facilitating their access to documentary culture.[94]

Similar patterns can be identified in other eastern Frankish regions where remarkable early medieval collections of charters do not normally survive in the single-sheet original format. By focusing on the Middle

---

Documentary Culture and the Laity in the Early Middle Ages (Cambridge: Cambridge University Press, 2013), pp. 231–58.

92 W. Davies, 'Local priests and the writing of charters in northern Iberia in the tenth century', in J. Escalona and H. Sirantoine (eds), *Chartes et cartulaires comme instruments de pouvoir: Espagne et Occident chrétien (VIIIe–XIIe siècles)* (Toulouse: Université de Toulouse-Le-Mirail, 2013), pp. 29–43.

93 Zeller, 'Local priests', p. 41; B. Zeller, 'Writing charters as a public activity: the example of the Carolingian charters of St Gall', in M. Mostert and P. S. Barnwell (eds), *Medieval Legal Process: Physical, Spoken and Written Performance in the Middle Ages* (Turnhout: Brepols, 2011), pp. 27–37, at p. 35. Local churches often appear as a venue for peasant transactions in other areas of western Europe; see, for instance, Davies, *Small Worlds*, pp. 81, 101, 137.

94 McKitterick, *The Carolingians*, pp. 115–26; K. Heidecker, 'Urkunden schreiben im alemannischen Umfeld des Klosters St. Gallen', in P. Erhart, K. Heidecker and B. Zeller (eds), *Die Privaturkunden der Karolingerzeit* (Dietikon-Zürich: Urs Graf, 2009), pp. 183–91; M. Innes, 'Archives, documents and landowners in Carolingian Francia', in Brown et al. (eds), *Documentary Culture*, pp. 152–88, at pp. 165–73.

Rhine region, Matthew Innes has emphasised the role of local scribes, mainly churchmen, who shared a common regional tradition before the monastic foundations of the eighth century.[95] After the foundation of Fulda and Lorsch, the evidence points towards the predominant activities of monastic scribes who recorded the gifts that donors made to their respective monasteries. This is not to say that local priests stopped acting as scribes within their local communities; the evidence for the Dienheim area, as Innes points out, shows that a variety of different scribes, including local priests, wrote charters dealing with lands in this area in the early ninth century (see figure 8.3).[96] Local priests can also be found acting as scribes of charters in Bavaria, as emerges from the extensive collection of Carolingian charters from the cathedral see of Freising.[97] Although it is not always possible to establish whether the priests who were participants in transactions, witnesses or scribes were clerics in charge of local pastoral care or priests belonging to higher social echelons, it is clear that in some cases they were priests who recorded transactions in their local areas.[98]

How exactly local priests would have acquired the necessary knowledge and skills to record such transactions is an interesting question, though not easy to answer. The possibility that they would have used formularies is certainly worth considering, particularly in light of the preservation of a late ninth-century manuscript, perhaps from northern Francia: Biblioteca Apostolica Vaticana, Reg. Lat. 612.[99] Its combination of material points strongly towards priestly use;[100] the book includes several episcopal statutes, texts on calculating time, a description of the proper way to conduct a Roman Mass and a set of formulas uniquely preserved in this manuscript, known as *Formulae Salicae Merkelianae*.[101] These open with the heading 'Incipiunt cartae pagensis', and the formulas include templates for sales, donations, precaria and manumission of slaves; the second section of this set of formulas, by contrast, contains letter templates, which

---

95 M. Innes, *State and Society in the Early Middle Ages* (Cambridge: Cambridge University Press, 2000), pp. 112–13.
96 Ibid., p. 117.
97 Kohl, '*Presbyter in parochia sua*', pp. 54–8.
98 For example, Fastheri, in 828, ibid., p. 55.
99 Available at http://digi.vatlib.it/view/MSS_Reg.lat.612.
100 See A. Borst, *Schriften zur Komputistik im Frankenreich von 721 bis 818*, vol. 1 (Hanover: Hahn, 2006), p. 304, who calls it a 'Vademecum für Weltpriester'.
101 MGH Formulae, pp. 241–63. For manuscript contents, see A. Rio, *Legal Practice and the Written Word in the Early Middle Ages: Frankish Formulae, c. 500–1000* (Cambridge: Cambridge University Press, 2009), pp. 266–7.

appear less local, as they include letters from a bishop to a count, a bishop to an archbishop, an abbot to an archdeacon, a bishop to another bishop and so on. The combination of templates for charters and letters makes this collection especially interesting, bearing in mind the requirement of an interesting short text for the examination of priests known as *Capitula Frisigensia prima*, likely to date from the end of Charlemagne's reign, that priests should learn to write charters and letters. It lists the things that all ecclesiastics must learn and, as well as the Creed and the Lord's Prayer, it also mentions 'to write charters and letters' (*scribere cartas et epistolas*).[102] This is clearly at odds with other Carolingian normative sources in which such activities are explicitly forbidden.[103] The presence of such a requirement in these *Capitula* testifies to the important role that clerics played in the documentary culture of early medieval societies by recording transactions as well as writing letters. The fact that other contemporary sources forbade the same activities is also highly interesting, as it indicates that those activities were clearly taking place and testifies to the tensions that characterised the position of secular priests: they lived and interacted with local communities and were effectively part of them, while at the same time they were expected to behave differently and not engage in worldly affairs.

Further evidence pointing in the same direction comes from other areas of the early medieval Latin West. The pre-910 collection of charters from Cluny, that is, the documents preceding the foundation of the abbey, provides many examples of records written by priests. Some of the transactions are also said to have taken place at local churches.[104] Northern Iberian charters dating to the ninth and tenth centuries clearly attest to the writing activities of priests, who, in Wendy Davies's words, 'acted as *de facto* notaries for peasant transactions'.[105] Priests recording

---

102 *Capitula Frisingensia prima*, in MGH Capit. episc. 3, pp. 204–5.
103 For instance, the roughly contemporary Ansegis, *Collectio capitularium*, MGH Capit. n.s. 1, p. 513, 'ut nullus presbiter cartas scribat'; Radulf of Bourges' episcopal statute, ch. 19, in MGH Capit. episc. 1, p. 248.
104 M. Innes, 'On the material culture of legal documents: charters and their preservation in the Cluny archive, ninth to eleventh centuries', in Brown et al. (eds), *Documentary Culture*, pp. 283–320, at pp. 290, 302–4.
105 Davies, 'Local priests in northern Iberia', p. 142. See also J. A. Fernández Flórez, 'Los documentos y sus *scriptores*', in J. M. Fernández Catón (co-ord.), *Monarquía y sociedad en el Reino de León. De Alfonso III a Alfonso VII* (León: Centro de Estudios e Investigación 'San Isidoro', 2007), pp. 97–139. For local priests and writing in ninth-century Brittany, see Davies, 'Priests and rural communities'.

local transactions can be found throughout northern Iberia, from Galicia to Catalonia. Such local records tend to make use of a Latin that reflected local speech and was more distant from classical Latin than the language used in documents produced at the same time in important monasteries.[106] Recurrent features include variant orthography for consonants and a tendency to lose or modify case endings. We are obviously dealing with a Romance-speaking region in which Latin writing practices were noticeably influenced by the local vernacular. In such areas, participants in and witnesses to transactions would have been able to understand the Latin documents that recorded them when these were read out, as has been demonstrated by the socio-philological work of Roger Wright and others.[107] This is especially significant, because it means that the priests could participate in the negotiations that preceded the transactions they recorded: the words and formulas they then chose to describe the results of those negotiations would be heard by all participants and would thus constitute powerful tools with which to influence local relationships. In non-Romance-speaking regions, such as the eastern Frankish areas, the relationship between literacy and orality was obviously more complex, and it would seem that the rustic Latin of charters from Alemannia, for instance, was more the result of the scribes' limited knowledge than of any attempt to make the language accessible to the Germanic-speaking population. By contrast, in the Saint-Gall documents which deal with lands in the Romance-speaking areas of Raetia, it is possible to see some evidence of local vernacular influence, especially in the written production of the local scribes who were active *c.* 815.[108]

Though often taken for granted, the differences in access to and experience of the written word between early medieval Romance-speaking and non-Romance-speaking societies should be kept in mind. In this respect, local priests clearly had a crucial function both as shepherds and as local scribes. Their mediating role within local society would have involved a strong linguistic component, especially in those regions in which the gulf between the spoken vernaculars and the written Latin of the charters was

---

106 Davies, 'Local priests and the writing of charters', p. 35.
107 R. Wright, *A Sociophilological Study of Late Latin* (Turnhout: Brepols, 2002); Banniard, *Viva voce*.
108 B. Zeller, 'Language, formulae, and Carolingian reforms: the case of the Alemannic charters from St Gall', in R. Gallagher, E. Roberts and F. Tinti, *The Languages of Early Medieval Charters: Latin, Germanic Vernaculars, and the Written Word* (Leiden: Brill, forthcoming).

wider than in Romance-speaking areas such as Italy and northern Iberia. An awareness of the difficulties that such linguistic mediation entailed occasionally emerges from the formularies; this is evident in the Germanic vernacular glossing of key Latin words in a fragmentary ninth-century formulary from Regensburg, where, for instance, the vernacular word *ferkepan* (a variant of *firgeban*, from which comes the modern German *vergeben*, meaning 'to allow', 'to grant' or 'to concede') is used to gloss Latin *concessum*, and *ferlazzan* (meaning 'to leave' or 'to allow') glosses Latin *indultum*.[109]

Conclusion

Local priests were unlike other members of the communities in which they lived for several reasons. First of all, they were educated and skilled in ways important for their religious duties, which also enabled them to fulfil other kinds of service than the strictly pastoral, such as writing charters and letters for third parties. Secondly, they were often rooted in the region in which they operated through family connections, but at the same time they belonged to the ecclesiastical hierarchy and were thus directly answerable to the bishop.[110] In this sense, they bridged the gap between small farmers and the (powerful, often aristocratic, and educated) episcopal court, but also between their own families and the bishop himself. Their hinge position could potentially benefit all: bishops could rely on well-placed informants on local affairs, while priests could use this connection to further family interests, facilitating the education of young male relatives and, possibly, succession to 'their' churches. Thirdly, most priests were free landowners but, unlike their lay peers, they were not supposed to be married and were not allowed to enjoy a wealthy lifestyle. All the same, some belonged to the social circles that bought and sold land, exercised rights over land and managed real estate.

The pastoral duties exercised by priests underlined community, neighbourliness, Christian charity and the merits of living together peacefully. These messages were woven into sermons but also into the cycle of

---

109 *Formularum codicis S. Emmerami fragmenta*, in MGH Formulae, pp. 461–8, at p. 465, with further examples at pp. 466–7. We are grateful to Warren Brown, Edward Roberts and Annina Seiler for this reference and useful discussion.

110 In northern Iberia there were so few bishops before the year 1000 that priests were left more to their own devices than elsewhere; Davies, 'Local priests in northern Iberia', p. 125.

confession-penance-reconciliation, the public ritual of baptism and the catechumenate that preceded it. If anything, Christian pastoral care was intended to enhance social cohesion through the ideals it communicated. However, the person of the priest and the way in which he dealt with his many different roles could undermine that message. His priesthood gave him access to resources with which he ought to support the poor and this offered the possibility of diverting funds from the authentically destitute to relatives who did not, strictly speaking, qualify. In other words, favouritism was a risk factor, and there is no reason to think that priests did not use such possibilities to make life easier for their friends and relatives. At the same time, it is clear that successful priests managed to balance their many roles by trying not to push anything too far – as we have seen, lay people were perfectly capable of chasing an unwanted priest away or of complaining about his misbehaviour to the bishop. On the other hand, a community content with its pastor would give a priest room for manoeuvre. In a favourable scenario, then, a priest was as much a member of his family and of the local flock as set apart from them.

A priest could be useful to the wealthier people in his community in ways that did not necessarily lead to heaven, but had to do with their literacy and education. Neighbours who wanted to sell or donate goods did not have to look far if they needed a trusted person to write or witness a charter for them, or to compose a letter on their behalf. In cases of (impending) conflict, priests could help to calm things down through the penitential system, or through their knowledge of legal procedure. Their familiarity with both Latin and the local vernacular meant, moreover, that they could make written knowledge available to local audiences, and thereby communicate episcopal instructions or royal demands in a language understood by all. Successful priests must have been versatile people, capable of managing their multiple roles and positions within different circles. What they learned before their ordination to a church went further than theology and liturgy and enabled them to fulfil important functions. However, because of their central role within communities, when their activities and behaviour did not match expectations – either of their lay neighbours or of the higher echelons of the ecclesiastical hierarchy – social cohesion would be seriously affected. In other words, priests all over western Europe, notwithstanding the many differences in settlement structures and church organisation, were key players within the wide variety of activities that characterised the lives of their respective flocks.

6

Interventions in local societies: lower office holders

Local societies were not independent of their surroundings in most parts of western Europe in the early Middle Ages, perhaps with the exception of some very localised regions in northern Iberia. Most 'small worlds' belonged to regional or supra-regional networks and structures. Office holders and agents – ranging from mayors and priests to bishops, counts, viscounts and *centenarii* (hundredmen) – intervened in local affairs for landowners, kings and other lords they represented. Since kings, powerful lay aristocrats and religious institutions had large scattered land holdings in many regions, even those lords who were involved in macro-politics might be neighbours in small settlements, allowing us to see them both as outsiders to local society and as insiders.

The following two chapters treat the question of how outside interventions influenced local practices. In this chapter we will discuss the ways in which secular office holders, especially lower office holders, were present and how they acted within local society. Chapter 7 will change the perspective: in it, we will focus on other kinds of outside intervention. We will leave divine interventions aside – an accepted part of life in the early Middle Ages, but in quite a different way from those of that chapter.

Here, we will understand as office holders persons charged with certain tasks and given a certain authority, conferred on them – at least in theory – by a higher authority, marked with a title and held for a certain period of time. Lower-level secular office holders of this type are found in all the regions treated in this book, with the possible exception of northern Iberia. We will begin with a survey of cases from the regions treated here to illustrate the scope of office holders' titles, activities and interventions. After this, we will discuss the social background of the office holders and the question of access to office. Since intervention in local societies necessarily involved outside authorities, we will then turn to the ways in which kings used norms to influence lower-level office holders.

In what follows, we will treat both office holders from the 'public' and 'private' sphere. This modern distinction between public and private is entrenched in scholarship but was much more blurred in the perception of contemporaries; it is therefore not especially helpful as an analytical distinction in the study of power structures (especially in those regions in which there were either no or weak central powers). We have to take all types of intervener in local society into account, such as those acting as administrators of large-scale land holdings or advocates serving as legal representatives for clergymen and women. Some, but by no means all, of these 'non-public' interveners were probably much more local in their spheres of action than those who held an office that was controlled by a king.

Distinguishing between 'secular' and 'clerical' office holders – the subject of Chapter 5 – is in some ways easier, because the distinction was clearly perceived by contemporaries, but this is not clear-cut either. As Chapter 5 has shown, ecclesiastical office holders were hinge persons connecting the local to higher levels. Clerics often acted very much like many of the 'secular' office holders: they took part in assemblies, in which conflicts were carried out and resolved, they were involved in land transactions, they acted as witnesses in legal acts of all kinds, they wrote charters, especially in Italy where they sometimes also described themselves as notaries, and in Iberia they sometimes fulfilled the function of a *saio*. Quite a few Carolingian normative texts explicitly prohibit priests from acting as *villici* or other office holders in a manor – an indication that this, in fact, happened often enough to merit these rulings.[1] Nevertheless, the distinction between 'secular' and 'clerical' local office holders remains valid in early medieval western Europe. The latter were expected to follow different sets of norms, such as those set out in the Carolingian episcopal normative texts issued by bishops, exclusively meant for the clergy, and they were subject to different courts. There were also marked differences between lay office holders and priests regarding marriage and inheritance.

---

1 For example, Radulf of Bourges, *Capitula*, ch. 19, in MGH Capit. episc. 1, p. 248; Riculf of Soissons, *Capitula*, ch. 17, in MGH Capit. episc. 2, p. 108 (= Hincmar of Reims, *Collectio de ecclesiis et capellis*, MGH Fontes iuris 14, p. 103); *Concilium Parisiense (a. 829)*, ch. 28, in MGH Conc. 2, 2, p. 630; *Episcoporum ad Hludowicum imperatorem relatio (a. 829)*, ch. 13, in MGH Capit. 2, no. 196, p. 33.

The sources mention a bewildering range of titles for subordinate office holders: in the Carolingian Empire alone we find *gastaldi, centuriones, centenarii, sculdhaizi, tribuni, vicarii, vicecomites, decani, actores* and more. The use of these terms varies through time, by region and sometimes by scribe. There are marked differences not only between the Anglo-Saxon world and the Frankish Empire but also on a smaller scale between Alemannia and Bavaria, and even between northern and southern Tuscany. However, the duties of these office holders in the Carolingian world often seem comparable and the titles interchangeable, at times even synonymous. This is evident also in the capitularies, in which office holders are listed as *centenarii, vicecomites, vicedomini, locopositi* and so on, without any reference to differences between these groups. Other office titles implied more specific duties, however. This is the case for *scabini*, that is, jurors and sometimes judges (*iudices*), whose office pertained specifically to courts of law. *Iudices*, however, could also be applied as a collective term for office holders of all kinds.[2] Outside the Frankish Empire, we find men charged with organising proceedings in court and enforcing court decisions called *saiones* (or *sagiones*) in northern Iberia. In Anglo-Saxon England, reeve (*gerefa* in Old English, translated into Latin as *prepositus* or *prefectus*) was the word most commonly used for office holders of a lower status;[3] royal reeves were clearly important for the local administration of the realm.

And to make matters even more complicated, in the Carolingian Empire outside Italy, holders of lower offices were only rarely named with their titles in the sources – this is a marked contrast to counts, and also to holders of ecclesiastical offices, who were almost always named with their ranks and titles. So even for well-documented *centenarii* we might find only one or two mentions of their office, although they – as individuals – appear in the sources dozens of times.[4] Only very few *centenarii* are

---

2 For example, in the *Capitulare de villis*, for which see *Cod. Guelf. 254 Helmst.*, in *Herzog August Bibliothek Wolfenbüttel*, ed. C. Brühl (Stuttgart: Müller and Schindler, 1971).

3 The title of *prepositus* is also attested in the regions of Alemannia and Raetia. Cf. R. Sprandel, *Das Kloster Sankt Gallen in der Verfassung des karolingischen Reiches* (Freiburg: Eberhard Albert, 1958), pp. 110–27; K. Bullimore, 'Folcwin of Rankweil: the world of a Carolingian local official', *Early Medieval Europe*, 13:1 (2005), 43–77, at 52–7.

4 An early example is Hardoin, documented in several charters of the monastery of Wissembourg between 699 and 721, sometimes as *centenarius*, once as *centurio*,

known in western and northern Francia, and several of the major charter collections from the east, such as the cartularies of Lorsch and Fulda, contain virtually no titled lower office holders at all. They do, however, document men who acted just like them and whom we might assume were office holders as well.[5]

Office holders and local society - surveying the evidence

The survey begins in Lombard and Carolingian Italy, the region for which we have the most substantial evidence for lower-level office holders, then continues with the Frankish world north of the Alps, represented mostly by Bavaria and Alemannia, then Anglo-Saxon England, and finally northern Iberia.

In northern and central Italy, we find more local office holders than elsewhere, and over a longer period. Even within Italy, however, there are great differences: in southern Tuscan charters preserved at the monastery of San Salvatore al Monte Amiata, many rural office holders are mentioned, while in the north, in the episcopal archives of Pisa and Lucca, only a few can be found in rural locations and they are not mentioned in, or around, the two episcopal cities.[6] The following examples come from southern rural Tuscany (see figure 8.4).

In the village of *Romiliano* (Rovigliano, Viterbo), cited in charters once belonging to Monte Amiata, Anso, a witness, is named as *decano de Romiliano* in 765 and presumably lived in the village of Rovigliano itself.[7] The settlement is also mentioned in other Monte Amiata charters,

---

sometimes without title: texts accessible at www.neg.uni-tuebingen.de (NeG-ID P14941); cf. also n. 19.

5 T. Kohl, 'Ländliche Gesellschaft, lokale Eliten und das Reich - der Wormsgau in der Karolingerzeit', in T. Kohl, S. Patzold and B. Zeller (eds), *Kleine Welten. Ländliche Gesellschaften im Karolingerreich* (Ostfildern: Thorbecke, 2019), pp. 309-36.

6 F. Bougard, *La justice dans le royaume d'Italie: de la fin du VIIIe siècle au début du XIe* (Rome: École française de Rome, 1995), pp. 100-01; CDMA; W. Kurze, 'I momenti principali della storia di San Salvatore al Monte Amiata', in M. Ascheri and W. Kurze (eds), *L'Amiata nel medioevo* (Rome: Viella, 1989), pp. 33-48; C. Wickham, 'Paesaggi sepolti: insediamento e incastellamento sull'Amiata 750-1250', in Ascheri and Kurze (eds), *L'Amiata nel medioevo*, pp. 101-37; M. Marrocchi, *Monaci scrittori. San Salvatore al monte Amiata tra Impero e Papato (secoli VIII-XIII)* (Florence: Florence University Press, 2014).

7 CDMA 12 (765) = ChLA 23, no. 740.

for example in a short notice from 823 reporting settlement of a dispute between the abbey of San Salvatore and the *sculdais* Silvestrus, son of the deceased Lupone.[8] Silvestrus is described as belonging to the village of Rovigliano ('from the village (*vico*) of Rovigliano in the territory of Marta'). The contested estates were said to have belonged to the community that lived in Rovigliano. Other estates that belonged to some *consortes* closely related to a local office holder were mentioned, too: the estates of Autari, 'who was *sculdais* and of his *consortes*'.[9] Since two or three different office holders were said to belong to this village within a span of sixty years, this might indicate that two or more lower-ranking office holders lived in some villages of southern Tuscany at the same time. This was certainly true in the same period in the Po valley, where communities such as the *homines Solariensis* ('men of Solara') or the *homines Flexiciani* ('men of Flexo'), who lived in the area of Mirandola not far from Carpi and Modena, could be represented in an early Carolingian court by more than one local office holder (the *homines Flexiciani* were represented by a *scabinus*, a *decanus* and by six other freemen).[10] Unfortunately, we do not have much further detailed evidence of this kind, but the impression is that larger settlements in Italy had more than one local office holder resident, while *centenarii* and *decani* are often said to have lived in smaller villages.

Accordingly, in 777 the witness Teudilari was described as *decano de Cosuna*; like Rovigliano, Cosona was called a *vicus* (village) in the same document and by the same writer.[11] There are many more examples of

8 CDMA 92 (823) = ChLA 61, no. 38. Cf. Bougard, *La justice*, p. 373.
9 Witnessed by Vincentio *sculdais* among others. The *breve* was subscribed by Immo *scabino* and by Occhino; cf. Bougard, *La justice*, p. 161, n. 81, p. 373.
10 *I placiti*, vol. 1, no. 30, pp. 92–5 (818); G. Tabacco, *I liberi del re nell'Italia carolingia e postcarolingia* (Spoleto: Fondazione CISAM, 1966), pp. 134–7; A. Castagnetti, *L'organizzazione del territorio rurale nel Medioevo. Circoscrizioni ecclesiastiche e civili nella 'Langobardia' e nella 'Romania'* (Bologna: Pàtron, 2nd edn, 1982), pp. 71–87; A. Castagnetti, 'Flexo e Carpi nell'alto medioevo. La storia dei territori come verifica di teorie e ricerca di radici delle autonomie', in *Mirandola e le terre del Basso Secchia* (Modena: Aedes Muratoriana, 1984), pp. 13–27; A. Castagnetti, 'Il conte Anselmo I: l'invenzione di un conte carolingio', *Studi storici Luigi Simeoni*, 56 (2006), 9–60; T. Lazzari, 'Comunità rurali nell'alto medioevo: pratiche di descrizione e spie lessicali nella documentazione scritta', in P. Galetti (ed.), *Paesaggi, comunità, villaggi medievali. Atti del Convegno internazionale di studio, Bologna, 14–16 gennaio 2010*, 2 vols (Spoleto: Fondazione CISAM, 2012), vol. 2, pp. 405–23.
11 Teudilari witnessed, without subscribing, a division of estates made by Walderano; CDMA 29 (777) = ChLA 24, no. 756. For the meaning and

this kind among the Monte Amiata charters: an interesting one dates to 793, when a charter was witnessed by Brancato, son of a certain Branculano, who was called *centenarius de Stauno* and *vir devotus*, that is, a free man, and *exercitalis* of the king;[12] *exercitales*, whose name derived from the army service they had to perform because of their freedom and wealth, were found in villages as well as cities in late Lombard and early Carolingian Italy.[13] This example is even more interesting if we also take into account a document issued in 805, in a place to which the *centenarius* Branculano seems to have been attached, since the document was written in *Stauno/Stagnu*, within the *curtis* of the same *centenarius* Branculano.[14] We may assume that Branculano's *curtis* was his core estate and that it may have coincided with the political centre in which he exercised his office. This seems likely, since two other lower-ranking local office holders were summoned as witnesses: Burrone *decano de vicum Sausani vir devotus* and Pertulo *decano de vico Clogiano vir devotus*.[15] Another witness, Leoperto *de Stagnu vir devotus*, did not carry any further title but was defined as *exercitalis*. He was said to be living in the same village as the *centenarius*; as a free man he had to join the army and was also supposed to contribute to the exercise of justice locally.

Although an older historiographical tradition assumed that *centenarii* in Lombard Italy had the same status and were synonyms of *sculdhais*, this is not the case here (although north of the Alps these titles were used interchangeably).[16] The difference between *sculdhais* and *centenarius* emerges clearly in sources from southern Tuscany, although it is difficult

> dimensions of a *vicus* in the early Middle Ages, see C. Wickham, 'Bounding the city: concepts of urban–rural difference in the West in the early Middle Ages', in *Città e campagna nei secoli altomedievali*, 2 vols (Spoleto: Fondazione CISAM, 2009), vol. 1, pp. 61–80.

12 Brancato witnessed, without subscribing, the donation made by Vualcari, son of Gregorio, of half the church of S. Stefano to the abbey of San Salvatore; CDMA 42 (793) = ChLA 24, no. 769.
13 Tabacco, *I liberi del re*, pp. 89–112.
14 CDMA 55 (805) = ChLA 61, no. 4.
15 They did not subscribe the document, perhaps because they were unable to do so.
16 F. Schupfer, *Le istituzioni politiche longobardiche* (Florence: Le Monnier, 1863), pp. 327–8, 331, stated that both *centenarii* and *decani* had specific military duties in the army; he also supposed that *centenarii* had the same competences as the *sculdhais*. See Bougard, *La justice*, pp. 158–66, for an overview on the *sculdhais* in early medieval Italy.

to describe the functions of *centenarii* precisely: they were mostly attached to a single locality, in which they lived, and for which they could have been responsible. They may have worked in collaboration with other *centenarii* in territories as wide as those controlled by *presbiteri*, rectors of baptismal churches to which several settlements (and sometimes several churches) were attached. This seems to have been the case with S. Peter of Musciano, in the Tuscan Valdarno, where two *centenarii* were involved in 746 at baptismal church level, perhaps indicating their radius of action.[17] Later examples from northern Italy are laconic with regard to an office holder's range of activity: Petrus *de Niviano*, one of the best-documented late Carolingian *sculdassii*, is always described as a resident of the village of Niviano, in the Apennines south of Piacenza in the *fines Castellanas* (one of three Lombard subdivisions of Piacenza territory still functioning in the Carolingian period), but he was never described with respect to the district of his duties of *sculdhais*.[18] It seems that the citation of place of residence was important, for local office holders as well as others.

We also need to note that the role of minor local office holders might be explicitly indicated in a charter or might not, for reasons which are unclear, as is also true in other parts of the Carolingian Empire, as the following surveys show. For instance, the *clericus* and *notarius* Cristiano wrote two documents, in 825 and in 834, in the baptismal church of San Quirico d'Orcia and in the nearby city of Chiusi respectively:[19] in the first, he called himself *centenarius*, while in the second he did not mention this role. We might suppose that within ten years he had lost the office of

---

17   CDL 1, no. 86: *centenarii* Ratperto and Barbula, together with all the free inhabitants of the baptismal church district of S. Peter of Musciano, confirmed *presbiter* Luceri, with Bishop Vualprand of Lucca, in the baptismal church. Cf. Bougard, *La justice*, p. 167; C. Wickham, 'Social structures in Lombard Italy', in G. Ausenda and P. Delogu (eds), *The Langobards before the Frankish Conquest: An Ethnographic Perspective* (Woodbridge: Boydell Press, 2009), pp. 118-48, at p. 130.

18   F. Bougard, 'Pierre de Niviano, dit le Spolétin, et le gouvernement du comté de Plaisance à l'époque carolingienne', *Journal des Savants*, 2 (1996), 291-337, at 293-4; see also N. Mancassola, *Società e istituzioni pubbliche locali. Gli ufficiali minori del comitato di Piacenza in età carolingia* (Spoleto: Fondazione CISAM, 2017). The dossier of Petrus of Niviano is nearly completely published in ChLA: 65, nos 26, 29, 30, 32, 37; 66, nos 3, 5, 11, 15, 16, 24, 29, 30, 32, 33, 34, 40, 42; 67, nos 1, 4, 9, 10, 15.

19   CDMA 96 (825) = ChLA 62, no. 2; CDMA 111 (834) = ChLA 62, no. 17.

centenarius or, alternatively, that he simply did not mention his office in 834. It is possible that people held different public roles at the same time, or that minor public offices were held temporarily, or that public officials had no interest in spelling out their multiple roles within a local society.[20]

Removal from office was also possible in Carolingian and post-Carolingian Italy, especially in times of political turmoil: Petrus *de Niviano* probably gained his office of *sculdassio* through the favour of the Alemann *gastaldus* Teupertus and the count of Piacenza, Adelgis II, in 881. He lost it in 891 after the defeat of King Berengar by Guy of Spoleto and the appointment of a new count and a new *gastaldus* in Piacenza. The absence of links with these new men apparently caused Petrus to lose office, although his connections probably allowed him to regain his property after it was confiscated.[21]

In post-Carolingian Italy, political instability therefore made positions available for the followers of new leaders, and the same is true for Ottonian northern Italy, in particular for the territory of Verona, which became the capital of the newly instituted Marca Veronese under Otto I.[22] Here, in the last decades of the tenth century, the Gandolfingi family of counts ruled, with the support of their vassals.[23] One of these vassals, Wincardo, was appointed *vicecomes* in the last decade of the tenth century by Count Riprando. He moved to the city centre of Verona because of his office, but the bases of his family property remained in the countryside, especially around the villages of Lonigo and Sabbion, situated in a strategic area between the districts of Verona and Vicenza; several of his family members were defined in documents as *de Lonigo*. Even if Wincardo

20 Cf., in Monte Amiata charters, the *notarius* Donnulino, who wrote nos 737, 741, 754, 767 of ChLA 23 and 24, and who subscribed no. 743 (765) of ChLA 23, without mentioning his title; also the *notarius* Firmo, who wrote nos 743, 745, 746 of ChLA 23, and subscribed no. 741 (765) of ChLA 23, without mentioning his office.
21 Cf. Bougard, 'Pierre de Niviano', p. 294; see below, p. 169.
22 A. Castagnetti, *Il Veneto nell'alto medioevo* (Verona: Libreria Universitaria, 1990), pp. 119–20; for political change, see above, pp. 30–2.
23 See V. Fumagalli, *Terra e società nell'Italia padana. I secoli IX e X* (Bologna: Università degli studi, Istituti di storia medioevale e moderna e di paleografia e diplomatica, 1974), pp. 94–5; R. Pauler, *Das Regnum Italiae in ottonischer Zeit. Markgrafen, Grafen und Bischöfe als politische Kräfte* (Tübingen: Niemeyer, 1982), pp. 174–80; F. Bougard, 'Entre Gandolfingi et Obertenghi: les comtes de Plaisance aux Xe et XIe siècles', *Mélanges de l'École française de Rome. Moyen Âge*, 101 (1989), 11–66.

and his heirs eventually lost the office of *vicecomes*, their proximity to the counts' family and the patrimonial base, which in the eleventh century included two castles in the countryside in addition to the urban property, made it possible for a family member named Cadalo to enter the cathedral clergy as a deacon, to rule the estates of the Verona bishopric as *vicedominus*, to be appointed bishop of Parma in 1046 and to be promoted antipope with the name of Honorius II in 1061.[24] Public office remained important in Italy in the tenth and eleventh centuries, although there were changes: *decani*, *centenarii* and *scabini* disappeared from the record, and the number of *sculdassi* declined, while more and more *iudices* and *notarii* are recorded.

Beyond the Alps, we find far less evidence for public office holders than in Italy, and for a shorter period only, mainly in the late eighth and ninth centuries. We know from capitularies and other normative texts that they were expected to exist throughout the Frankish Empire, but conclusive evidence of their activities is mainly found in Bavaria and Alemannia – that is, in those regions bordering on Italy, which may have influenced the practice of recording an office holder's title in charters. In the tenth century, it becomes very hard to follow their activities, if in fact they still existed. At the same time, men titled bishops' or abbots' advocates (*advocati*) became more prominent in the sources, indicating their increasing role in conducting the secular affairs of churches.

In Bavaria, in the region around the episcopal see of Freising, an office holder named Engilperht was active in several disputes and transactions around the turn of the eighth to ninth centuries. Variously titled as *sculdhaizus*, *vicarius* and *centenarius*, he first appears in a charter of 798, in which he was involved in resolving a dispute between the bishop of Freising and a man named Selprih, who had claimed some property that belonged to the church of Freising.[25] In the agreement, in which Selprih

---

24 A. Castagnetti, *Preistoria di Onorio II antipapa. Cadalo diacono nella società italica della prima metà del secolo XI* (Spoleto: Fondazione CISAM, 2014), pp. 1–37.

25 TF 176 (798). See S. Esders, 'Amt und Bann: Weltliche Funktionsträger (*centenarii*, *vicarii*) als Teil ländlicher Gesellschaften im Karolingerreich', in Kohl, Patzold and Zeller (eds), *Kleine Welten*, pp. 255–307; H. Dannenbauer, 'Hundertschaft, Centena und Huntari', *Historisches Jahrbuch*, 62/69 (1942/49), 155–219. After the Carolingian conquest of Italy in 774, there was some interchange in the use of names of offices between Italy and north of the Alps. On the use of Lombard terms in early ninth-century Raetia in the well-known

finally dropped his claim in return for a sum of money, Engilperht *sculdhaizus* is listed as second witness directly after the count. About ten years later, we find him mentioned with the same title in a charter that was probably also the result of a court held in Freising; once again, he is named in second place behind a higher-ranking office holder, the judge Ellanbert.[26] In a document about a public court session from 807 or 808, Engilperht is called *vicarius* and is once again listed directly after the count.[27] By 814 he had been replaced by his son Deothard, who is now referred to as *centenarius* and *vicarius dominicus* in several documents, acting in the same area and doing the same things as his father: he was involved in judicial proceedings with counts and judges, although it is unclear in what way. He took part in property transactions, conveying property from the old to the new owner, and he witnessed several other transactions; usually, he is named as one of the first witnesses in the witness lists, indicating his high social standing.[28] While all these documents are vague as to what exactly Engilperht and Deothard did in these transactions, it is clear that it was important, although not indispensable, that *centenarii* were present.[29]

Only rarely can we see more of the power relations between these office holders and the local population. One charter shows a clear abuse of power that was corrected by Deothard in 819.[30] It reports that the predecessors of two brothers named Erchanhart and Cartfrid had given a field in Freising to the church of Freising during the reign of Duke Tassilo III – deposed in 788, that is, at least thirty years before the creation of the charter. Because of the brothers' 'negligence and stupidity', and most of all because of Engilperht's anger towards the church of Freising,

case of Folcwin of Rankweil, and in late Carolingian Piacenza, see Bougard, 'Pierre de Niviano', p. 301; Bullimore, 'Folcwin of Rankweil'; P. Erhart and J. Kleindinst, *Urkundenlandschaft Rätien* (Vienna: Österreichische Akademie der Wissenschaften, 2004), pp. 83–219.

26   TF 244 (806/11).
27   TF 268a (807/8). For Engilperht and Deothard, see H. Krug, 'Untersuchungen zum Amt des 'Centenarius'-Schultheiß. Teil I und II', *Zeitschrift der Savigny-Stiftung für Rechtsgeschichte. Germanistische Abteilung*, 87 (1970), 1–31, and 88 (1971), 29–109, at 50, 76–8. See also Dannenbauer, 'Hundertschaft', at 214, with TF 430 (819).
28   In the Frankish world, social standing was reflected in the ranking of witnesses in the witness lists (see Sprandel, *Das Kloster Sankt Gallen*, pp. 110–18, one of the seminal studies).
29   See below, pp. 203–8, on property transactions.
30   TF 430 (819).

the field had never actually passed into the church's ownership. In 819 the *centenarius* Deothard, Engilperht's son and successor, wanted to rectify his father's mistake and called on the brothers Erchanhart and Cartfrid to renew the donation, which they did, with the permission and even at the admonition of Deothard, who is styled as the brothers' master (*magister*).

Both office holders, Engilperht and Deothard, clearly exercised some authority over the brothers Erchanhart and Cartfrid and their predecessors – one preventing the donation, the other effectively ordering it to take place decades later. We do not know the nature of that authority: Deothard is called Erchanhart's master, but that word is not common in the sources. There is no indication that the brothers were unfree – Erchanhart is attested as a witness in several charters, indicating that he must have been free, if of lower status.[31] We must therefore assume that there was some kind of patron–client relationship between the *centenarii* and the brothers, and that this was connected in some way to Engilperht's and Deothard's status, because otherwise their titles would probably not have been mentioned in the charter.

The Freising charters give us some evidence for relations between office holders – variously titled as *sculdhaizi*, *vicarii* and *centenarii* – and local societies: they were involved in land transactions in some way, giving them the potential to block transfers if they wished. It is important to note another aspect: Engilperht blocked the transfer of the brothers' land to the bishop because of his anger towards the Freising church, the episcopal church being the biggest landowner in the city and its surroundings. We do not know the reason for his anger but this was a period in which the relationship between secular and ecclesiastical authority was defined in a new way, causing some unrest.[32]

A similar range of titles for office holders can be found in the neighbouring regions of Alemannia and Raetia: here, they were usually called *centenarii* or *vicarii* in the ninth century; in the eighth century, however, *iudex* and *tribunus* were more common. Here, as elsewhere, scribes seem to have been very flexible in attributing titles to holders of a single office.

---

31 TF 401a (819), 497 (824), 592a (830?), 626 (837) and perhaps 715a (849); he is always named towards the end of witness lists, indicating his mediocre social standing.

32 Cf. M. de Jong, *The Penitential State: Authority and Atonement in the Age of Louis the Pious, 814–840* (Cambridge: Cambridge University Press, 2009); S. Patzold, *Episcopus: Wissen über Bischöfe im Frankenreich des späten 8. bis frühen 10. Jahrhunderts* (Ostfildern: Thorbecke, 2008), pp. 105–84.

INTERVENTIONS IN LOCAL SOCIETIES

In one isolated example, an office holder named Perahtger is called *castaldus* in a charter that was drawn up in a public court assembly in 826.[33] Perahtger is probably the only bearer north of the Alps of this Lombard title, still in use in Carolingian Italy.[34]

Perahtger is also unique among lower-level office holders for being mentioned in a narrative source, Rudolf of Fulda's *Miracula sanctorum in Fuldenses ecclesias translatorum*.[35] Some time between 842 and 847, when Rudolf wrote his account, Perahtger, introduced as the son of Theodald, was passing through Kempraten, a small settlement on Lake Zurich, when a boy stopped him near a church, where the relics of Saint Alexander were kept at this time (see figure 8.3). The boy invited him to worship the holy relics of the saint, but Perahtger refused, having to complete a mission for his lord, but he promised to return another time to pray. When he tried to ride on, his horse did not move; only after praying in the nearby church, and giving it a small piece of land that bordered on the property of the church, was he able to continue his journey.

Apart from this miracle and the unusual title used for him in the 826 charter, Perahtger behaved like other public office holders: he is mentioned in the witness lists of some fifteen Saint-Gall charters from the region around Lake Zurich, all of which can be dated to the years 826-37. In these charters, drawn up in several places at a maximum distance of 20 km from each other, Perahtger is always the first person mentioned in the witness list.[36] We know that he was not a count: the count in this area was Gerold, also mentioned in Rudolf of Fulda's narrative, and it seems likely that he was Perahtger's *dominus*, for whom the mission had to be completed.[37]

A remarkable dossier of charters relating to the *sculdhaizus* Folcwin was created between 817 and 828 farther to the east, near the present-day border of Austria and Switzerland.[38] These twenty-seven charters,

---

33   W 297 (826).
34   On gastalds in the Lombard period, see S. Gasparri, *I duchi longobardi* (Rome: ISIME, 1978), pp. 20-32.
35   Rudolf of Fulda, *Miracula sanctorum in Fuldenses ecclesias translatorum*, in MGH SS 15, 1, p. 331.
36   Cf. Sprandel, *Das Kloster Sankt Gallen*, pp. 124-6.
37   Perahtgar is not called count (*comes*) in any Saint-Gall charter. Counts are mentioned in the *sub-comite* formula of the dating clause in the charters in which he appears as top witness, indicating that his position was below the level of a count.
38   Bullimore, 'Folcwin of Rankweil'.

all recording donations or sales of land to Folcwin, provide a unique perspective as the private collection of a local office holder. Presumably, Folcwin's position allowed him – or at least made it easier for him – to become an important landowner in the area around Rankweil, although the charters do not give reasons for the transactions. Nevertheless, it is hard to avoid the conclusion that locals selling or giving their land to him were probably reacting to pressure from Folcwin or at least attempting to gain his favour in this way.[39]

In the second half of the ninth century, public office holders are mentioned less and less frequently in the charters; in the tenth century they have all but disappeared from Bavaria and Alemannia. At the same time, advocates became more and more prominent in the ecclesiastical charters. The reasons for both of these developments are not entirely clear, but they apparently reflect the loss of the authority that public office holders exercised in ecclesiastical property, from which almost all of the documentation originates. An important factor in this change was the presence of immunities, privileges granted mainly to monasteries and episcopal churches, exempting them from public dues and prohibiting the entry of public office holders, specifically judges. However, this did not mean that the king's influence over these churches and their property was diminished since, from the early ninth century, kings only granted immunity in association with the king's protection (*tuitio* or *defensio*), which in effect gave the kings direct control over the churches.[40]

This special status led, over time, to the greater importance of those men charged with the exercise of juridical functions for bishops and abbots: the advocates (*advocati*).[41] In 802 Charlemagne had ordered all clergy, abbots and abbesses to use advocates to represent them in court, and from this point onward advocates increasingly appear in the charters from Bavaria, Alemannia, Italy and elsewhere in the Frankish Empire.[42] At first only representing their abbots and bishops in court, they feature in more and more legal acts until they are mentioned in nearly every charter

---

39 See below, pp. 176–7, for abuses of power by local officials and attempts to stop them by legal means.
40 B. H. Rosenwein, *Negotiating Space: Power, Restraint, and Privileges of Immunity in Early Medieval Europe* (Manchester: Manchester University Press, 1999), pp. 99–114.
41 C. West, 'The significance of the Carolingian advocate', *Early Medieval Europe*, 17:2 (2009), 186–206.
42 W. Dohrmann, *Die Vögte des Klosters St. Gallen in der Karolingerzeit* (Bochum: Brockmeyer, 1985).

in the tenth century. They were also necessarily involved in local matters – they were important for transactions of property, they represented the church in disputes of all kinds and they exercised justice for the *familia* of a church.

Much more local in scope were those charged with the day-to-day administration of property belonging to large institutional landowners. Both royal and ecclesiastical landowners, but also lay landowners, entrusted the administration of their property centres (mostly called *villae* in the sources) to mayors, men called variously *villicus* or *maior*, *actor*, *missus* and *procurator*, sometimes also *vicedominus*.[43] References to such men are rare in Bavaria and Alemannia but quite common in Italy and in the polyptyques from northern Francia, which document the enormous land holdings of monasteries such as Saint-Germain-des-Prés or Prüm. In these, mayors appear as agents of the landowners, organising work on the demesne, collecting rents and dues from the peasants and conducting their transfer to the landowners. They were thus an important interface between local society and the supra-local, sometimes empire-wide, level of great landowners. This placed them in a unique position of power, especially in those places in which one landowner dominated. Their local power may be seen in several narrative sources, especially in miracle narratives. One such example occurs in the ninth-century text from northern Francia known as the *Epistola Huberti* or *Apparitio Sancti Vedasti*. It tells of the vision of a carpenter named Dagobert, in which the evil doings of the village elite are recounted.[44] Here, the mayor of the village, Oric, 'the head of this wickedness', supported a local landowner in successfully laying claim to ownership of a dozen unfree peasants, and was punished for this deed. The fact that he was clearly acting in respect of more than the property he administered shows his local standing (and the potential for abuse).

Power relations between mayors and their often distant landowners were variable, oscillating between greater control from above and de

---

43 See above, pp. 78–9 [ch. 3], for *villae*; J.-P. Devroey, 'Le petit monde des seigneuries domaniales: seigneurs, notables et officiers dans les seigneuries royales et ecclésiastiques à l'époque carolingienne', in Kohl, Patzold and Zeller (eds), *Kleine Welten*, pp. 165–203.

44 Hupertus, *Apparitio Sancti Vedasti*, AASS, 6 feb, vol. 1, pp. 803–5; see C. West, 'Visions in a ninth-century village: an early medieval microhistory', *History Workshop Journal*, 81:1 (2016), 1–16, https://doi.org/10.1093/hwj/dbv040. English translation at http://history.dept.shef.ac.uk/translations/medieval/saint-vaast/ (accessed 4 September 2019).

facto independence. There is evidence of both: Charlemagne's biographer Einhard complained bitterly in a letter to a *vicedominus* about the amount and quality of pigs and vegetables he had been sent and ordered another to send provisions to his house in Aachen in a further letter.[45] The king himself in his famous *Capitulare de villis* was eager to retain control over the office holders in his domains; he tried to prohibit them from abusing their powers to extract dues and services from members of the *familia* and tried to force his office holders to perform manual labour personally (although he allowed some to have the services performed by deputies).[46] This was probably one way to demonstrate that they remained part of the *familia*, in spite of their office. From the tenth century onwards, we find increasing evidence of mayors attempting to distance themselves from their peasant surroundings and attempting to live as noblemen – a development that monastic authors such as Ekkehard of Saint-Gall in the early eleventh century strongly criticised for fear for their monasteries' properties.[47]

However, their intermediary status between local society and higher levels also meant that mayors might sometimes act as representatives of their local community in confrontations with the landowners. This happened in 932 when the *villicus* Remigius was one of the men asking the monastery of Stavelot to 'alleviate the yoke of servitude' for its people in Xhoris.[48]

Beyond the Carolingian world, in Anglo-Saxon England, lower-level office holders were usually called reeves, the modern English rendering of Old English *gerefa*. The problem with this label is that it is generic and was used for a series of office holders operating at different levels. When looking for a common denominator, we can say that the term simply denotes a man with administrative responsibilities; in fact, we encounter different types of reeve throughout the Anglo-Saxon period: royal reeves, bishops' reeves, nobles' reeves, port-reeves in towns, as well as

---

45 *Einhards Briefe. Mobilität und Kommunikation im Frühmittelalter*, ed. A. Grabowsky, C. Haack, T. Kohl and S. Patzold (Seligenstadt: Einhard-Gesellschaft e.V., 2018), nos 37, 23, pp. 162, 118.
46 *Capitulare de villis*, chs 3, 10, 26, in MGH Capit. 1, pp. 82–91.
47 Ekkehard IV, *Casus sancti Galli*, ed. H. F. Haefele (Darmstadt: Wissenschaftliche Buchgesellschaft, 3rd edn, 1991), chs 48–9, pp. 108–10.
48 See above, p. 100, and N. Schroeder, *Les hommes et la terre de saint Remacle. Histoire sociale et économique de l'abbaye de Stavelot-Malmedy, VIIe–XIVe siècle* (Brussels: Université de Bruxelles, 2015), p. 179.

shire reeves and even swine reeves.[49] Reeves – in the service of kings and bishops – are mentioned in the late seventh-century laws issued by Wihtred of Kent, indicating that they had been part of the administrative structure of the Anglo-Saxon kingdoms from the earliest times. The reeves' duties included the management of estates, collection of food renders due to the king as well as the supervision of labour services owed by dependants. Importantly, they were also in charge of a variety of legal tasks, scheduling assemblies, pronouncing sentences, collecting legal fines and provisioning prisoners without kin. They also presented appeals on the rulings of local assemblies to kings.[50] However, the law codes do not envision reeves as enforcers of rulings if there was resistance – armed action was apparently not part of their duties.[51]

When kings granted their estates to other lords, reeves passed into the service of these bishops, abbots or lay aristocrats, such as ealdormen, and they seem to have continued to fulfil the same duties, including, at least in the early tenth century, the legal tasks. With the emergence of the hundred system in the second half of the tenth century, reeves seem to have lost much of their influence.[52]

In spite of all we know about the tasks of reeves according to the law codes, we know very little about individual reeves, how they were chosen and how they understood their duties. Among the few reeves known by name is a Kentish royal reeve named Æthelnoth, who lived in the ninth century and whose vernacular will has survived as a single sheet.[53] We have some more information about his office because Æthelnoth describes himself as 'the reeve at Eastry'. On the parchment on which his will has survived, this is preceded by a royal charter of Cuthred, king of Kent, in favour of Æthelnoth himself, who is described as *prefecto meo fidelissimo in prouincia Cantiæ* ('my very faithful prefect in the province of Kent').[54]

---

49 P. Stafford, 'Reeve', in M. Lapidge, J. Blair, S. Keynes and D. Scragg (eds), *The Wiley Blackwell Encyclopaedia of Anglo-Saxon England* (Chichester: John Wiley and Sons, 2nd edn, 2014), pp. 397–8; T. Lambert, *Law and Order in Anglo-Saxon England* (Oxford: Oxford University Press, 2017), pp. 121–5. For swine reeves, see above, p. 84.
50 Lambert, *Law and Order*, pp. 127–9, 143.
51 Lambert, *Law and Order*, pp. 154–5.
52 Lambert, *Law and Order*, p. 133.
53 Sawyer 1500 (805/32); *Charters of Christ Church Canterbury*, ed. N. P. Brooks and S. E. Kelly, 2 vols (Oxford: Oxford University Press, 2013), vol. 1, no. 39A.
54 Sawyer 41 (805/7); *Charters of Christ Church Canterbury*, ed. Brooks and Kelly, vol. 1, no. 39.

Through this charter, Æthelnoth acquired three *aratra* of land (corresponding roughly to six *mansi*) at Eythorne, also in Kent, in return for the substantial sum of 3,000 *denarii*. The land was to be free from every secular service and Æthelnoth could dispose of it as he wished. Moreover, the will, which follows the grant on the same single sheet, deals specifically with the arrangements made by the reeve and his wife for the disposition of this very land. The church of Canterbury was an interested party, since in case Æthelnoth and his wife died childless, the archbishop of Canterbury was to inherit this estate at Eythorne.

The reference to Eastry is what makes this will especially interesting, as it helps us get a sense of the development of administrative districts assigned to such local officers as royal reeves. Archaeological evidence shows that Eastry had been an important place since the earliest times of Anglo-Saxon settlement.[55] The presence of a royal reeve in the first half of the ninth century makes perfect sense, as does the fact that he had acquired *bocland* (that is, land he could freely dispose of) from the king in the same area, less than five miles away from the district centre at Eastry, the main site of his activity as reeve (see figure 8.6). It is also worth underlining that by 1066 Eastry had consolidated its role as the district centre, as it was the main site of the hundred that took its name from this very place; moreover Eythorne, which had indeed passed on to the archbishop of Canterbury, lay within this hundred as well.

In spite of the different history and organisation, it seems clear that royal reeves such as Æthelnoth occupied a position not unlike those of their continental counterparts – they were wealthy members of the elites of the areas in which they were tasked with fulfilling their duties.

In northern Iberia, the least centralised region studied in this book, evidence for office holders is sparse. Some charters, do, however, mention the *saio* (or *sagio*). *Saiones* are already named in the Visigothic laws, and reappear when the northern Iberian charter documentation begins in the late ninth century. Like Frankish *centenarii* and English reeves, *saiones* were active in the administration of justice.[56] However, unlike

55 T. Dickinson, C. Fern and A. Richardson, 'Early Anglo-Saxon Eastry: archaeological evidence and the development of a district centre in the kingdom of Kent', *Anglo-Saxon Studies in Archaeology and History*, 17 (2011), 1–86; T. Dickinson, 'The formation of a folk district in the kingdom of Kent: Eastry and its early Anglo-Saxon archaeology', in R. Jones and S. Semple (eds), *Sense of Place in Anglo-Saxon England* (Donington: Shaun Tyas, 2012), pp. 147–67.

56 W. Davies, *Windows on Justice in Northern Iberia 800–1000* (Abingdon: Routledge, 2016), pp. 164–8.

their counterparts from beyond the Pyrenees, they apparently had no functions beyond this. Also, since only very few *saiones* appear with their titles in the sources more than once – indeed, most of them never appear in charters again, even where there is adequate documentation – it is doubtful if we should understand *saio* as an office at all in this period; rather it may have been a function assigned to an individual for a specific court case or for a limited time period. *Saiones* appear to have been named by the court holders – kings, counts, monasteries, but also by local communities, and their function was tied to them. Hence, charters sometimes mention 'my' or 'our' *saio*. *Saiones* fulfilled executive duties in judicial matters. They invited the parties to court, ordered them to present witnesses, and took oaths, supervised ordeals, transmitted the judges' orders, executed the court's ruling by transferring property and enforced other court decisions. For their services, *saiones* received a fee called the *saionicum*.[57]

Access to office, social background and local ties of lower-level public office holders

Our case studies from present-day Switzerland, Germany, Italy and England already show that we rarely know enough about local office holders to see how they acquired their offices. But one important factor is visible in several of the case studies: as ever in the early medieval world, being related mattered. It was generally accepted that sons of office holders (or nephews in the case of ecclesiastical offices) could become their ancestors' successors, even if succession was by no means immediate or necessary.

Let us take a closer look. Perahtger, the *castaldus* from Alemannia, was possibly the son of a count: in his *Miracula*, Rudolf of Fulda mentions the name of Perahtger's father, Theodald, who is attested as a count and witness in a Saint-Gall charter of the same area some thirty years earlier.[58] The scribe of this charter from 810 or 811, the priest Peringer, was possibly also a relative. The priest appears in numerous charters across a 20-km area around Lake Zurich between 797 and 811 and, as his own and his family's donations to Saint-Gall indicate, he seems to have belonged to a wealthy family of the same region. Even if we can neither prove that the Count Theodald mentioned in this charter was in fact Perahtger's father,

---

57 OD 4 (946): *sagoniciu*.
58 Sprandel, *Das Kloster Sankt Gallen*, pp. 113–14.

nor that the priest and charter-scribe Peringer was actually a relative of 'our' Perahtger, a kinship or affinity (also indicated by the names Perin-ger and Peraht-ger) seems quite likely.

In the Argengau and Linzgau on the northern shore of Lake Constance, in the 830s, a contemporary of Perahtger, the *vicarius* Sigibert, seems to have been the head or one of the heads of a family that held extensive property in this region, which can be traced in the charter material from the 770s up to the 880s. We find the *vicarius* Sigibert in ten charters from the late 820s to the 860s. Two of these charters were issued by him; in three charters he is the first witness; and in the five remaining charters he appears as a witness in a prominent position.[59] In the late 860s he was succeeded by another, namesake, member of his family, who is attested as a leading witness until the 880s – although not as an office holder – in several charters from the very same region. The clerics of the area seemed to have belonged to the same familial context, which demonstrates how tightly secular and ecclesiastical representatives were interwoven through family networks. One member of this family, Bernhard, became a monk in Saint-Gall, and can probably be identified with the namesake charter-scribe in the monastic scriptorium; he might even have become abbot of the monastery in 883. His family is just one of several indications that these influential local family groups, which produced local office holders and local priests, usually kept close contact with the larger ecclesiastical communities of the region.

A similar picture of the background of lower-level office holders emerges in other areas of the Frankish Empire – most of them seem to have come from the (micro-) regional elites, and from families that had produced other office holders. The latter point is especially obvious in the case of the Freising *centenarii* Engilperht and Deothard, who were father and son, but whose family connections are otherwise unknown.[60] We know more about the family ties of Liutprant, a *centenarius* who was active in and around the Isen and Inn rivers east of Freising in the early ninth century. His sons gave some of the family goods – a piece of land, located right in the middle of Liutprant's area of activity in Burgrain, and four *mancipia* – to the episcopal church of Freising. Liutprant's son Podalunc was a subdeacon who was probably in the service of either Freising or its dependent monastery

---

59 Cf. Sprandel, *Das Kloster Sankt Gallen*, pp. 111–12, 129–30.
60 There have been attempts to tie them to the Bavarian noble clan of the *Huosi* and to Bishop Hitto (Krug, *Untersuchungen*, pp. 76–9), which is possible, but supported by very little evidence.

of Isen.⁶¹ Neither of his other sons, who were named Meginrat and Ascrih, followed in Liutprant's footsteps. Meginrat appears as a regular witness around the river Isen, sometimes with his father, but he remained at the lower end of the witness lists, ruling out that he held an office. Ascrih also acted as a witness a few times with his father and/or his brother.⁶² In this instance, the sons did not inherit their fathers' office, though one of them did receive an ecclesiastical office. The same was true for Perahtger in Alemannia, who obviously was not able to inherit his father's office as a count, but who obtained a less prestigious office instead.

In the rural area of Piacenza, the example of Petrus *de Niviano* shows that in late Carolingian Italy, and in the subsequent period, the appointment and removal of a local officer were both closely related to the fortunes of the political leader of the county and to changes of regime. When Guy of Spoleto defeated King Berengar in 889 and replaced the men and the clientele of the former king in the key positions of the realm, a new count named Sigefredus was appointed in Piacenza, and the *sculdassio* Petrus lost his position because of his fidelity to the former count Adelgis II, supporter of Berengar. Not only this: after holding his office for ten years, which had evidently made him a richer man, he was accused in court in 891 and in 893, and his estates were temporarily confiscated.⁶³ They were returned to him in 893 by a court headed by a new *gastaldus* who acted for the new local count, flanked by a new *sculdassio* and some *scabini*.⁶⁴ The proximity of Petrus to the former *gastaldus* of this territory, the Alemann Teupertus, seems to have made his rise, and his appointment as *sculdassio*, possible; the closeness and the patronage system that bound Petrus to the lower-ranking local officers who judged him in 893 seem to have made it possible for him to receive his confiscated estates back. While we have evidence that his property interests concentrated around the village where he lived (*Niviano*), we do not know if they were part of the area in which Petrus exercised his office of *sculdassio*.⁶⁵

61 TF 517 (825), 619 (836); cf. M. Neumann, 'Die bairische Volksordnung zur Karolingerzeit auf Grund genealogischer Untersuchungen', PhD dissertation, University of Erlangen, 1947, pp. 212–19, and T. Kohl, *Lokale Gesellschaften. Formen der Gemeinschaft in Bayern vom 8. bis zum 10. Jahrhundert* (Ostfildern: Thorbecke, 2010), pp. 294-7.
62 Their family ties are known from TF 517 (825).
63 Bougard, 'Pierre de Niviano', p. 297; Mancassola, *Società e istituzioni*, pp. 55–67.
64 ChLA 66, no. 40.
65 Bougard, 'Pierre de Niviano', pp. 294–6; Mancassola, *Società e istituzioni*, pp. 65–9.

When we move from an area close to the capital city of Pavia to early Carolingian rural Tuscany, we find a comparable picture. Tuscan documents indicate similar backgrounds and careers, but they also suggest links between the office holder's place of origin, his property and the place in which he acted as an office holder:[66] was the place in which local officers carried out their duties also the village where they lived and where they had their own estates? The formulas used by notaries and other scribes sometimes explicitly describe a witness as living in a village or in a locality (*habitator in vico Cosuna*) but sometimes, even within the same document, they simply describe someone as being from Casule, from Cosuna (*de Casule, de Cosuna*) and so on, as in the case of the *sculdassio* Petrus *de Niviano*. Given that notaries seem to have changed formulas in order not to repeat themselves within the same document, we should probably assume that lower local officers were explicitly associated with one locality or another in order to state where they resided, but not necessarily where they also carried out their duties.[67]

Another case provides more detail: in 806 a certain Cunipert, son of the deceased Teodelari – possibly the same Teudilari who was the *decano de Cosuna* mentioned in 777 – living in *Hoile*, next to Montepulciano and a few kilometres from Cosona, father of the cleric Agiprand, gave to his son a piece of land on which an oratory dedicated to San Stefano was under construction.[68] The property bordered on the king's lands, indicating that this family may have had ties to the royal court. None of the family

---

66 See, for instance, Allerad, *centenario de vico Pantano*, between Siena and Arezzo, who in 714 declared that his *avus et besavus* held the baptismal church of Santa Restituta; CDL 1, no. 19 (715). Cf. Castagnetti, *L'organizzazione del territorio rurale*, p. 39; S. Campana, C. Felici and L. Marasco, 'Progetto valle dell'Asso: Resoconto di otto anni di indagini', in S. Campana, C. Felici, R. Francovich and F. Gabbrielli (eds), *Chiese e insediamenti nei secoli di formazione dei paesaggi medievali della Toscana (V–X secolo): Atti del seminario San Giovanni d'Asso-Montisi, 10–11 novembre 2006* (Florence: All'Insegna del Giglio, 2008), pp. 7–35, at pp. 13–14.

67 In the *breve de inquisitione* of 20 June 715 on the dispute between Siena and Arezzo, *exercitales, centenarii* and even *decani* were identified as belonging to a *vicus* or to a baptismal district. However, qualified people (such as clerics, freemen, *exercitales* and low-ranking office holders) were asked to give sworn evidence according to the baptismal church to which they belonged; CDL 1, no. 19.

68 For possible identification of Cosona near Pienza, see Campana, Felici and Marasco, 'Progetto valle dell'Asso', pp. 11–13.

members subscribed to the document, since they were unable to write, and only Cunipert left his *signum manus*.[69] Cunipert, however, had two more sons, Iohannis and Petrone, who feature in other documents from the same area: in 819 the *centinarius* Iohannis with his brother Petrone witnessed a lease from the abbot of San Salvatore of Monte Amiata to a free man of estates near the church of San Stefano of Oile, the same oratory founded by their father.[70] Iohannis can also be identified with Iohannis *de Oile* who, together with the *centenarius* Pipino, witnessed a sale in 803 in the presence of Irchempaldo *gastaldo*.[71]

This case shows a locally influential family, whose first known member was perhaps a local office holder who probably had access to fiscal goods. His son Cunipert apparently had no public functions, but founded an oratory; he probably had contacts with other local officers, such as the *aurifex* Petronius *de Hoile*, whose *signum manus* is recorded in 806 and in 807.[72] Under the control of Cunipert's son Agiprand, first attested as *clericus*, then as *presbiter* in 812 and 819, the oratory was soon given to the abbey of Monte Amiata.[73] The oratory attracted donations from other members of the local community, who explicitly asked to be buried there.[74] Cunipert's son Iohannis became a local public office holder and his associates included another *centenarius* and a *gastaldo*. It seems, therefore, that in this part of Tuscany – as in regions north of the Alps – public functions could be retained within the same family over time. The Carolingian conquest of 774 does not seem to have changed this. Public office holders who controlled fiscal land could keep royal estates and transform them into sacred property under the control of a family member, and sustained by local elites. The sacred building could become a monastic *cella*, connecting the family to the clientele of San Salvatore at Monte Amiata, already protected by the Carolingian emperors.[75]

69 CDMA 57 (806) = ChLA 61, no. 6.
70 CDMA 83 (819) = ChLA 61, no. 30.
71 CDMA 52 (803) = ChLA 61, no. 1.
72 The *aurifex* Petronius witnessed with his *signum manum* CDMA 57 (806) = ChLA 61, no. 6, next to the church of the *castellum* of Montepulciano; ChLA 61, no. 8, Olle/*Hoile* (807).
73 ChLA 61, no. 20 (812); ChLA 61, no. 30 (819).
74 ChLA 61, no. 8 (807); ChLA 61, no. 20 (812). Cf. A. Castagnetti, *Arimanni di Lucca e distinzione sociale nelle sepolture* (Verona: Daigo Press, 2015), pp. 116–22.
75 For connections with royal monasteries cf. Folcwin of Rankweil's presence in the Saint-Gall necrology and in the Reichenau confraternity book; Bullimore, 'Folcwin of Rankweil', 47–8.

This does not mean that it was always possible to keep a public office over a period of time. Such is the case of a *gastaldus* named Occhino, attested for the first time in 791 in the territory of Monte Amiata.[76] In 822 Immo and Imilfredo, two sons of the deceased Occhino, contested a donation made by a certain Vualcarius to San Salvatore, but on this occasion no office holders are recorded.[77] We should be cautious about supposing the permanence of positions of power over generations within the same family without certainty of their identity.

Local offices were not hereditary in a strict sense but there were certainly local or micro-regional elites from which office holders were chosen. This is evident when individuals appear performing different functions, such as Cristiano, attested in two originals as *centenarius*, *clericus* and *notarius*; or the *centenarius* Engilperht, who was also *sculdhaizus* and *vicarius*; or his colleague Liutprant, who also acted as the bishop's *defensor*, that is, advocate.[78]

Norms and lower-level public office holders

Normative texts transmitted from several parts of Europe do not contain clear rules as to how local office holders were to be nominated. They do, however, indicate that there were certain expectations regarding their qualifications, their hierarchies and the way they were supposed to fulfil their duties.

The most detailed evidence comes from Anglo-Saxon law codes. Here, kings seem to have expected reeves to be expert in law, capable of deciding which (written) laws applied in a given case and of providing the assemblies with legal knowledge.[79] They were held personally responsible for incorrect judgements based on their legal expertise; if this occurred for personal gain, they were to be severely punished.

This kind of knowledge about laws and procedures presupposed literacy: King Alfred, for example, expected his reeves to be able to read in the vernacular. This was seen as essential for all those who were

---

76   CDMA 39 (791) = ChLA 24, no. 765.
77   CDMA 91 (823) = ChLA 61, no. 37 (822). It has been suggested that Immo *bassus domno imperatoris* and Occhinus *bassus domno imperatoris*, attested in 838, were sons or nephews of the *gastaldus* (Bougard, *La justice*, p. 351) but a comparison of their handwriting in original charters excludes this identification.
78   TF 400b (819).
79   Lambert, *Law and Order*, p. 144.

INTERVENTIONS IN LOCAL SOCIETIES

invested with 'offices of power'.[80] Alfred also made it clear that royal office holders should study or risk losing office.[81] Shortly after the end of Alfred's reign, an early tenth-century law code issued by Edward the Elder, written in Old English, was addressed specifically to reeves. This is its prologue:

> King Edward commands all his reeves: that you pronounce such legal decisions as you know to be most just and in accordance with the written laws; you shall not for any cause fail to interpret the public law and at the same time it shall be your duty to provide that every case shall have a date fixed for its decision.[82]

The reference to 'written laws', literally, 'books of law' (*dombec*), clearly puts the requirement to learn to read, which had characterised Alfred's programme, into effect. The code itself deals with the regulation of purchasing and settlement of disputes, including the use of witnesses and oaths.

Early eighth-century Lombard normative texts depict a well-ordered hierarchy of regional and local office holders, for the Lombard kingdom was divided into duchies led by *duces* of the high aristocracy, from which kings were chosen. Kings had large fiscal properties, especially in the Po valley, but also in other territories such as southern Tuscany. Organised in *curtes regiae, curtes reginae, gualdi*,[83] they were administered by *gastaldi* and *actores regis*, also called *scarii*, who had policing functions and a role in administering justice, with the help of minor office holders.[84]

---

80   D. Pratt, *The Political Thought of King Alfred the Great* (Cambridge: Cambridge University Press, 2011), p. 121.
81   *Alfred the Great: Asser's Life of King Alfred and Other Contemporary Sources*, ed. and trans. S. Keynes and M. Lapidge (Harmondsworth: Penguin, 1983), nos 256, 259, pp. 110, 275.
82   I Edward, in *Die Gesetze der Angelsachsen*, ed. F. Liebermann, 3 vols (Halle: Niemeyer, 1903-16), vol. 1, p. 138; *The Laws of the Earliest English Kings*, ed. and trans. F. L. Attenborough (Cambridge: Cambridge University Press, 1922), p. 115.
83   On the significance of *waldo* as public land and not necessarily forest, see Tabacco, *I liberi del re*, pp. 113–38; C. Wickham, *Studi sulla società degli Appennini nell'alto medioevo. Contadini, signori e insediamento nel territorio di Valva (Sulmona)* (Bologna: CLUEB, 1999), p. 21.
84   Gasparri, 'Il regno longobardo in Italia', in S. Gasparri and P. Cammarosano (eds), *Langobardia* (Udine: Casamassima, 1990), pp. 237–305; S. Gasparri, *Italia longobarda. Il regno, i Franchi, il papato* (Rome/Bari: Laterza, 2012).

Laws issued by King Ratchis, *c*. 745, established the following hierarchy in the running of justice: *iudex* (*dux* or *gastald civitatis*),[85] *sculdhais/ sculdahis, centini* (*centenarii*), *locopositi* or other subordinate and unqualified people.[86] The operative efficiency of gastalds emerges once again in the record of the dispute between Siena and Arezzo over the boundaries of their dioceses. From the *breve de inquisitionis* of June 715 it is clear that gastalds in Siena used to intervene actively in ecclesiastical matters and controlled the mobility of ecclesiastics by issuing letters (*epistolae rogatoriae*), when clerics needed to leave Siena territory to reach bordering Arezzo. Continuity with the Lombard past in early Carolingian Italy is indicated by some early capitularies, in which minor local officers were still designated following the Lombard tradition, playing a central role in judicial proceedings; they were now tasked with aiding (Carolingian) *comites* instead of (Lombard) *duces*.[87]

For the Carolingian world north of the Alps, capitularies also provide some insight.[88] They, too, show a hierarchy, but less specific and multi-layered than in Lombard Italy.[89] They contain only passing references to access to office. A capitulary from the end of Charlemagne's reign refers to *centenarii* after counts but before *ceteri nobiles viri*, implying that *centenarii* were regarded as *nobiles* (in itself another unclear category).[90] A capitulary issued by Louis the Pious mentions them in a list: 'praepositus, advocatus, centenarius vel qualibet alia dignitate praedita libera persona', where *centenarii* and other office holders are presented as free men invested with a certain honour (*dignitas*).[91]

85 S. Gasparri, *I duchi longobardi* (Rome: ISIME, 1978), p. 28.
86 *Le leggi dei Longobardi*, Ratchis, no. 1, pp. 260–1.
87 *I capitolari italici. Storia e diritto della dominazione carolingia in Italia*, ed. C. Azzara and P. Moro (Rome: Viella, 1998), no. 5 (9) (*c*. 782), ch. 7, p. 60: 'De universali quidem populo quis, ubique iustitias quaesierit, suscipiat tam a comitibus suis quam etiam a castaldehis seu ab sculdaissihis vel loci positi iuxta ipsorum legem absque tarditate'.
88 M. Innes, *State and Society in the Early Middle Ages: The Middle Rhine Valley 400–1000* (Cambridge: Cambridge University Press, 2000), pp. 126–9.
89 On capitularies for Carolingian Italy, see *I capitolari italici*, ed. Azzara and Moro; the first should be redated after H. Mordek, 'Die Anfänge der fränkischer Gesetzgebung für Italien', *Quellen und Forschungen aus italienischen Archiven und Bibliotheken*, 85 (2005), 1–35.
90 *Capitulare missorum* (*a. 802/813*), ch. 3, in MGH Capit. 1, no. 60, p. 147.
91 *Capitulare missorum Wormatiense* (*a. 829*), ch. 10, in MGH Capit. 2, no. 192, p. 16.

A capitulary issued in Aachen in 809 mentions the 'appointment' of *centenarii* and other office holders involved in legal proceedings but only in a passive clause: they 'should be appointed to fulfil their duties'. From the perspective of the Carolingian court, qualification and character were essential: only the best and most God-fearing men were to be chosen for service.[92] This complements the prescription that *centenarii* could be removed from office by *missi* if they neglected their duties.[93]

According to Frankish norms, *centenarii* and other office holders were therefore expected to come from a social elite of a kind (*nobiles*), but to be placed in their positions according to qualification, and to be controlled in the exercise of their office by *missi*. While it is possible that chapter 40 of the capitulary of 802 indicates that Charlemagne thought of *centenarii* (like *comites*) as *ministeriales nostri*, 'our' servants, the source is problematic:[94] transmitted only in a tenth-century Italian manuscript, whose scribe misunderstood his ninth-century model, it is also possible that *ministerialibus nostris* was simply the third element of an enumeration.[95] In a capitulary from 826 Louis the Pious ordered an investigation by his *missi* and speaks of counts and 'their' *vicarii* and *centenarii*:[96] from the imperial court's perspective, local office holders were associated with a count and probably responsible to him. A similar clause occurs in a capitulary issued by Charlemagne in 811: *comites et eorum centenarios*.[97]

In these splinters of information issued by the royal courts of Europe, *centenarii*, royal reeves and other lower office holders are presented as the king's 'servants' (*ministeriales*) and therefore responsible to him – and, in the Frankish world, to the *missi* and counts appointed by the king. They appear to be placed in their offices from 'above' and removed from their

---

92 *Capitulare Aquisgranense (a. 809)*, ch. 11, in MGH Capit. 1, no. 61, p. 149: 'Ut iudices, advocati, praepositi, centenarii, scabinii, quales meliores inveniri possunt et Deum timentes, constituantur ad sua ministeria exercenda'.
93 *Capitulare missorum in Theodonis villa datum (a. 805)*, ch. 12, in MGH Capit. 1, no. 44, p. 124.
94 *Capitulare missorum generale (a. 802)*, ch. 40, in MGH Capit. 1, no. 33.
95 Ibid., ch. 39: nobody shall steal *feramina* from the king's forests. For the manuscript transmission, see S. Patzold, 'Normen im Buch. Überlegungen zu Geltungsansprüchen so genannter "Kapitularien"', *Frühmittelalterliche Studien*, 41 (2007), 331–50.
96 *Legationis capitulum*, in MGH Capit. 1, no. 152, p. 310: 'Et habeat unusquisque comes vicarios et centenarios suos secum'.
97 *Capitula de rebus exercitalibus in placito tractanda (a. 811)*, ch. 2, in MGH Capit. 1, p. 165.

offices from 'above'. However, laws and capitularies are a genre of texts that overemphasise a specific perspective: they tend to show an orderly tableau in which royal or court control over office holders is central. The same type of emphasis applies to Frankish *missi*, who appear in the capitularies as royal office holders sent from the centre to control officers in the peripheries of empire. However, prosopographical studies have shown how complex this was in practice.[98] We should assume that legal norms tend to present local office holders as royal office holders, overemphasising their link to the court.

Normative texts also make it clear that office holders of all ranks abused their position for their own interests, as we have already seen in the case of the Freising hundredman Engilperht and the brothers Erchanhart and Cartfrid, and perhaps Folcwin of Rankweil. Such rulings can already be found in the edict issued by the Lombard king Rothari, which clearly stated that if a *gastaldus* or any royal agent (*actor regis*) received a gift (*gairethinx*) from someone after appointment 'to administer the king's lands or royal matters', he could only keep them with the permission of the king.[99] The possibility of using one's office for personal interests in the localities of early medieval Europe came from one's position as mediator between higher levels and local society. For the Carolingian Empire, normative texts are again useful for tracing this. In 811 a capitulary issued by Charlemagne prohibits the practice of taking property from the 'poor' (*pauperes*) – bishops, abbots and their advocates as well as counts and their *centenarii* were accused of doing this. Chapter 3 of the capitulary explains how this could take place: if someone was unwilling to give his or her property to the bishop, abbot, judge or hundredman, then these office holders would look for a chance to sentence the poor person or to force a man to go to war again and again until he agreed to give or sell his property, while others, who had already given up their land, were allowed to remain at home.[100] A similar practice was decried at the Council of Arles soon afterwards in 813. Here, *centenarii* are explicitly mentioned

98 J. Hannig, 'Zentrale Kontrolle und regionale Machtbalance. Beobachtungen zum System der karolingischen Königsboten am Beispiel des Mittelrheingebietes', *Archiv für Kulturgeschichte*, 66 (1984), 1–46; J. Hannig, 'Zur Funktion der karolingischen "missi dominici" in Bayern und in den südöstlichen Grenzgebieten', *Zeitschrift der Savigny-Stiftung für Rechtsgeschichte: Germanistische Abteilung*, 101 (1984), 256–300.

99 *Le leggi dei Longobardi*, Rothari, no. 375, p. 108.

100 *Capitula de rebus exercitalibus in placito tractanda (a. 811)*, chs 2, 3, in MGH Capit. 1, no. 73, p. 165.

alongside counts and *iudices*.[101] To these examples one could add a capitulary issued by Louis the Pious in 829, which mentions *centenarii* 'who hold *placita* more out of avarice than for holding court and by this descend on the people too much'.[102] Immediately after this, two earlier capitularies are referred to. The first does not mention *centenarii*, but forbids holding too many *placita* (which involved payments, travel and absence from one's own property). The second, however, explicitly refers to local office holders.[103] By such means, local office holders were to be prevented from abusing their standing to gain control of property.

These cases of abuse indicate that all office holders (not just local office holders) had their own issues and interests in their areas of office. They also show their intermediate position. They were 'servants' of the king and they exercised special authority in the areas they were charged with administering. At the same time, they had property in this area, they were neighbours of the people they were in charge of as office holders, and members of the local and micro-regional elites. This brought the temptation to use their *ministerium* to further their own interests, material or otherwise, at the cost of their peers. This was true on all levels and in all regions, from bishops and counts to hundredmen and viscounts, from royal or other reeves in Anglo-Saxon England to *decani* and *sculdasci* in Italy.

We might conclude very carefully that we do not know exactly how great was the kings' or counts' agency in placing someone in office. Central powers in the Frankish Empire, in England and in Lombard and early Carolingian Italy certainly expected to be able to control these office holders and to remove them if necessary. This appears to be a strong contrast to northern Iberia – although, of course, at regional level landowners there had agents and one might expect similar behaviour with respect to them. Elsewhere, it seems that most office holders were chosen from

101 *Capitula e canonibus excerpta* [= *Council of Arles, a. 813*], ch. 22, in MGH Capit. 1, no. 78, p. 174: 'Ut comites vel vicarii seu iudices aut centenarii sub mala occasione vel ingenio res pauperum non emant nec vi tollant; sed quisque hoc comparare voluerit, in publico placito coram episcopo fiat'.
102 *Capitulare pro lege habendum Wormatiense (a. 829)*, ch. 5, in MGH Capit. 2, no. 193, p. 19 (followed by Ansegis, *Collectio capitularium*, MGH Capit. n.s. 1, lib. III, ch. 40 and lib. IV, ch. 55, which is identical with the text cited in the following footnote).
103 *Capitulare missorum (a. 819)*, ch. 14, in MGH Capit. 1, no. 141, p. 290: *placita* should be held three times per year and nobody should be forced to attend more than that.

the area in which they were to serve and that they belonged to important families from exactly these areas. This may have been a remnant of the Roman world that had left its impression on most parts of early medieval Europe: in the late Roman Empire there had already been systematic attempts to create ties between local elites and the imperial administration by giving members of these elites offices. As a result, local elites in Late Antiquity were neither purely local nor purely imperial. The local level of the *civitas* and imperial administration were inseparably interwoven.[104] The same principle is still visible after the fragmentation of the Empire in the West. Local office holders were not only legitimised by their service for the central powers, but were at the same time – as a rule – members of the elites in the very regions in which they were active as holders of an office (or several offices). This was doubtless instrumental within the dynamics of local societies and in the integration of the local and higher levels.[105]

Conclusion

Office holders were one mechanism by which the outside world demonstrated its presence in local societies and intervened throughout history. In a very general sense, this was true in most of the early medieval regions studied in this book, if not in all. Titles varied, as did roles and duties – from region to region, even within a realm, and also over time. There are, however, some common features. Lower-level office holders were local in the sense that they very often owned property in the places where they held office and had family ties. But – with very few exceptions, such as Italian *decani* or *locopositi*, some Iberian *saiones* and Frankish *maiores* – their duties and their authority extended well beyond the local sphere. In this sense, they were not local but micro-regional office holders. They were at the same time both members of communities and political leaders who had to balance their actions between the needs of their neighbours and demands from above. Their intermediary position meant that they

---

104 P. Heather, 'Senators and Senates', in A. Cameron and P. Garnsey (eds), *The Cambridge Ancient History* (Cambridge: Cambridge University Press, 1998), pp. 184–210, at p. 208.
105 C. Wickham, 'The changing composition of early elites', in F. Bougard, H.-W. Goetz and R. Le Jan (eds), *Théories et pratiques des élites au haut Moyen Âge. Actes du colloque de Hambourg, 10–13 septembre 2009* (Turnhout: Brepols, 2011), pp. 5–20.

were also nodes of communication linking the local to the higher levels of kingdom, duchy or county. In this, their role was similar to that of the local clergy discussed in Chapter 5.

It is remarkable that virtually all those with public duties and functions were involved in the exercise of justice in one way or another – *saiones* brought people to court, took oaths and organised proceedings; royal reeves and *iudices* presided over courts; *scabini* acted in juries; and *centenarii*, too, seem to have been involved in judicial proceedings, although we do not know in what way. This underlines the fact that courts were an important (and lucrative) way to exercise influence in local society, and it must be likely that any higher authority would try to establish control of practical proceedings through the office holders.

In spite of these similarities, there were great regional differences concerning both the types of office that existed and their development from the eighth to the early eleventh centuries. In Italy, office holders were clearly more important than elsewhere, as was true throughout the period. This does not mean there were no changes: titles such as *decanus* fell out of use, and others (*iudex*, *notarius*) gained importance. For the Frankish Empire, it is remarkable that we mostly find officer titles in those areas bordering on northern Italy, in Bavaria and Alemannia, although one would expect them to have been in use elsewhere, too, since they are mentioned in normative texts. Political changes of regime, such as the Carolingian takeover of both Lombard Italy and the duchies of Bavaria and Alemannia, did not have immediate consequences for scribal practice in the use of titles. This does not mean that political developments were irrelevant: when Charlemagne ordered the clergy to employ advocates to represent them in court and for other secular matters, he unwittingly set in motion a development by which abbots' and bishops' advocates became powerful office holders by the tenth century, at least in the east of the Frankish Empire. Since these advocates also administered justice within the property and immunities of the churches, their rise probably contributed to the disappearance of *centenarii* and other lower-level offices.

In Anglo-Saxon England and in Iberia, we find very little variation in the use of titles throughout the period. In England, royal reeves and their counterparts in the service of churches and aristocratic landowners had been important since the seventh century, and they remained so in the tenth. In Iberia, a few *saiones* are identified by rural settlement in the late tenth century, perhaps in association with the emergence of local *concilia* in some places, within a limited area.

The varying terminology, the wide range of possible tasks, the marked regional differences in early medieval practice and in the transmission of sources all make it necessary to widen the scope of this investigation. The holders of lower offices were only one of several groups who intervened in local societies. We must ask about other kinds of outside intervention and their consequences for local practice.

7

Interventions and interactions

External interventions in local society took place in very different ways in early medieval Europe. Their intensity depended, to a large degree, on the extent of claims made by central authorities and other powers, such as lay aristocrats or heads of religious institutions. In the early ninth century, for example, Frankish rulers of the Carolingian family attempted to control everyday life even within local society – a remarkable and far-reaching intention. The new norms written down for this purpose in capitularies, conciliar records and episcopal statutes are likely to have had consequences for interaction between neighbours in rural localities.[1] In Anglo-Saxon England, too, royal claims to local control permeated society, especially in the tenth century.[2] In other regions of Europe, such as northern Iberia or Brittany, central powers attempted far less at the local level and, with the gradual transformation of the Carolingian world across the long tenth century, royal power became less tangible in many parts of central and western Europe too, although not in England.[3] Even then, however, few rural settlements were self-contained islands, secluded from the outside world.

1 Cf. S. Esders, 'Amt und Bann: Weltliche Funktionsträger (*centenarii*, *vicarii*) als Teil ländlicher Gesellschaft im Karolingerreich', in T. Kohl, S. Patzold and B. Zeller (eds), *Kleine Welten. Lokale Gesellschaften im Karolingerreich* (Ostfildern: Thorbecke, 2019), pp. 255–307.
2 T. Lambert, *Law and Order in Anglo-Saxon England* (Oxford: Oxford University Press, 2017), ch. 3.
3 Cf. G. Althoff, 'Das ottonische Reich als regnum Francorum?', in J. Ehlers (ed.), *Deutschland und der Westen Europas* (Stuttgart: Thorbecke, 2002), pp. 235–61; H. Keller and G. Althoff, *Die Zeit der späten Karolinger und Ottonen* (Stuttgart: Klett-Cotta, 2008).

The aim of this chapter is to describe typical and widespread forms of external intervention into the local in the three fields of war, justice and property and to analyse their consequences on the ground. There are difficulties. Normative texts can provide very detailed evidence about the way interventions were supposed to happen from the perspective of political leaders, and reasonable assumptions can be made about the aims and intentions of the kings, aristocrats and clerical dignitaries who intervened locally. However, written sources are usually silent on the consequences of intervention in local contexts and on the social relations of groups and individuals within them. There are nevertheless a few spotlights, which we should resist attempting to combine into a coherent system that may never have existed. Rather, they are interesting, if isolated, cases.

The themes of war, property and justice structure the chapter. For each of the three topics, the practices and institutions through which intervention occurred will first be described, largely from the perspective of those who intervened, while also bearing in mind the social dynamics occasioned by these interventions at a local level.

War

In most areas of early medieval Europe war was not an exception but the rule.[4] For example, Carolingian kings ordered military expeditions almost every year, sustaining the goal – from around about 800 – of obtaining plunder and tribute, but not conquering regions as before;[5] Annals from the Frankish Empire explicitly noted when there had been no wars during the year.[6] Contemporary writers applauded their kings

---

4 See T. Reuter, 'Carolingian and Ottonian warfare', in M. H. Keen (ed.), *Medieval Warfare. A History* (Oxford: Oxford University Press, 1999), pp. 13–35; and for a different view, B. S. Bachrach, *Early Carolingian Warfare: Prelude to Empire* (Philadelphia, PA: University of Pennsylvania Press, 2001); B. S. Bachrach, 'Charlemagne and the Carolingian general staff', *The Journal of Military History*, 66 (2002), 313–57; cf. now C. Haack, *Die Krieger der Karolinger. Organisation von Kriegsdiensten als soziale Praxis um 800* (Berlin: De Gruyter, 2019).

5 T. Reuter, 'Plunder and tribute in the Carolingian empire', *Transactions of the Royal Historical Society*, 35 (1985), 75–94; pre-Carolingian: D. Jäger, *Plündern in Gallien 451–592: eine Studie zu der Relevanz einer Praktik für das Organisieren von Folgeleistungen* (Berlin: De Gruyter, 2017), and R. Keller and L. Sarti (eds), *Pillages, tributs, captifs. Prédation et sociétés de l'Antiquité tardive au haut Moyen Âge* (Paris: Éditions de la Sorbonne, 2018).

6 Cf. *Annales Laureshamenses*, s.a. 802, in MGH SS 1, p. 38: 'Eo anno demoravit domnus Caesar Carolus apud Aquis quietus cum Francis sine hoste'. For

for their wars: Einhard, for one, dedicated the first part of his biography of Charlemagne to his conquests;[7] and Regino of Prüm praised King Carloman, Charlemagne's great-grandson, with these words: 'Indeed, he led many wars together with his father [King Louis the German], and more still without his father into the kingdoms of the Slavs – and he always returned with the triumph of victory.'[8] Much the same could be said of Iberian rulers, with their constant campaigning, whether from north or south of the peninsula.[9] The northern chronicles are laconic but indicate campaigns year after year, such as the slaughter of thousands of Muslims noted by the Castilian Annals under the year 939;[10] southern texts are more expansive and detail directions and action taken, such as the ninety days of campaigning against Castile in the summer of 920, the Caliph with the army, concentrating on destroying the fruit and other resources of cultivated land, as reported by the Chronicle of 'Arīb ibn Sa'īd, a provincial governor for Caliph 'Abd al-Raḥman III and a court official for Caliph al-Ḥakam II.[11]

Most wars were not conflicts between large-scale political units or states, as would become common in Europe in the modern age. Rulers did not hold a monopoly on the exercise of violence because magnates also had retinues of armed men, trained to kill, and magnates fought against each other. Although in England the distinction tended to be maintained, there was not always a sharp distinction between war (*bellum*) and feud, designated in continental sources through words derived from Germanic vernacular, such as *faida* or *guerra*.[12] Feud was recognised as significant

an important reconsideration of these annals, see R. Pokorny, 'Die Annales Laureshamenses in einer neu aufgefundenen Teilüberlieferung', *Deutsches Archiv für Erforschung des Mittelalters*, 69 (2013), 1–44.

7 Einhard, *Vita Karoli magni imperatoris*, chs 5–15, MGH SS rer. Germ. [25], pp. 7–17.
8 Regino of Prüm, *Chronicon*, s.a. 880, MGH SS rer. Germ. [50], p. 116.
9 See above, pp. 39–40.
10 'Inuenerunt enim ibidem rex Ranemirus et eius comites qui er{an}t cum illo congregati cum suas ostes ... et alia multitudo acmina preliatores. Adiubante Deo, inruerunt super mauros et ceciderunt ad gladio in die illa quasi tria milia uel amplius, ibique est captus mauro Aboyahia ... dum perrexissent mauros {in} fuga et subtraxissent se exire de xpistiannorum terra'; J. C. Martín, 'Los *Annales Castellani Antiquiores* y *Annales Castellani Recentiores*: edición y traducción anotada', *Territorio, Sociedad y Poder*, 4 (2009), 203–26, at 209.
11 *La Crónica de 'Arīb sobre al-Andalus*, trans. J. Castilla Brazales (Granada: Impredisur, 1992), pp. 163–4.
12 *Karolomanni capitulare Vernense (a. 884)*, ch. 3, in MGH Capit. 2, no. 287, p. 372, line 40, for example. In Italy there is a mid sixth-century definition of

in Anglo-Saxon society, as attested in many law codes.[13] Kings did attempt to curb hostilities between magnates;[14] they used instruments such as payments in compensation for damages to the injured party (*wergild*)[15] as well as oaths and other rituals.[16] Kings themselves could be parties to such conflicts: King Otto I, for example, in the first two decades after his coronation in 936, fought several bloody wars against his sons Thankmar and Liudolf, his brother Henry, his son-in-law the duke of Lotharingia, and many other magnates and their men.[17] And quite apart from internal conflicts such as these, there were invasions from outside: Arab and Berber groups in Iberia, southern France and Italy; warrior bands from Scandinavia who led raids on Britain and Ireland and the continent; and the mobile Magyar groups who arrived on horseback across great swathes of central Europe, into present-day Switzerland, Lotharingia and Italy.[18]

There can be no doubt that war had consequences for life at the local level. In general, the aim of warfare was to harm the enemy, to loot and – explicitly in the case of al-Andalus but perhaps more widespread than this – to destroy enemy food supplies.[19] All had an obvious impact on local societies: the rural population might themselves be captured and

faida: 'ut faida, quod est inimicitia, post accepta suprascripta conpositione postponatur et amplius non requiratur, nec dolus teneatur, sed sit sibi causa finita, amicitia manentem'; *Edictus Rothari*, ch. 74, in MGH LL 4, pp. 23-4.

13 P. Hyams, 'Feud and the state in late Anglo-Saxon England', *The Journal of British Studies*, 40:1 (2001), 1–43; Lambert, *Law and Order*, chs 1, 3, 4, 5.

14 *Capitula legibus addenda (a. 818/19)*, ch. 13, in MGH Capit. 1, no. 136, p. 284, excerpted in Ansegis, *Collectio Capitularium* IV, 25, MGH Capit. n.s. 1, p. 637; cf. *Capitulare pro lege habendum Wormatiense (a. 829)*, ch. 8, in MGH Capit. 2, p. 20.

15 S. Esders, 'Wergeld und soziale Netzwerke im Frankenreich', in S. Patzold and K. Ubl (eds), *Verwandtschaft, Name und soziale Ordnung (300–1000)* (Berlin: De Gruyter, 2014), pp. 141–59; G. Ausenda and S. Barnish, 'A comparative discussion of Langobardic feud and blood-money compensation, with parallels from contemporary anthropology and from medieval history', in G. Ausenda and P. Delogu (eds), *The Langobards before the Frankish Conquest: An Ethnographic Perspective* (Woodbridge: Boydell Press, 2009), pp. 309–39.

16 Cf. G. Althoff, *Spielregeln der Politik im Mittelalter. Kommunikation in Frieden und Fehde* (Darmstadt: Primus, 1996); G. Althoff, *Die Macht der Rituale. Symbolik und Herrschaft im Mittelalter* (Darmstadt: Primus, 2003).

17 For an up-to-date guide to the events, see M. Becher, *Otto der Große. Kaiser und Reich. Eine Biographie* (Munich: Beck, 2012), pp. 120–39.

18 See above for detail, pp. 25–32, 33–4, 39.

19 *La Crónica de Arīb*, trans. Castilla Brazales, pp. 126, 131, 172, 175, 196, 210, 217.

sold as slaves;[20] they might witness the plundering of their possessions;[21] or they might quite simply lose the food on which they depended for survival. In Spain taking slaves is sometimes specified in detail: King Ordoño II gave the church of Santiago de Compostela thirty-four slaves captured from the 'Ishmaelites', that is, the Muslims of al-Andalus; prisoners from the north were led to Córdoba in chains after the 986 Andalusi attack on Simancas; and land near León was left unworked in the time of Vermudo II because the two owners had been captured by the Ishmaelites and taken off to Córdoba.[22] In Portugal a woman and her daughter captured by the Vikings were ransomed as they were about to sail off in a Viking boat.[23]

In Francia, in 884, the young Carolingian king Carloman attempted to limit the impact of magnates' raids in a capitulary. Its prologue is pessimistic: how could external enemies be defeated 'when our brothers' blood is dripping from our mouths and our hands are full of blood – and our arms are heavy under the weight of misery and robbery'? God would not answer their prayers, because they are drowned by 'the cries and laments and sighs of the poor and the orphans, the minors and the widows'.[24] The Franks were even told that plundering and forcing the poor into hunger and nakedness was equal to homicide. As for the impact of raids from outside, the evidence suggests that the repeated Magyar raids forced local populations to flee: it is probably no coincidence that early tenth-century charters from Salzburg repeatedly mention *loci deserti* ('deserted

---

20 Unfree dependants living in villages in eighth-century northern Lombard Italy, however, were regularly sold, bought and manumitted, even by non-aristocratic owners. See C. Wickham, 'Social structures in Lombard Italy', in Ausenda and Delogu (eds), *The Langobards*, pp. 118–48, at pp. 126–7; S. Gasparri, *Voci dai secoli oscuri. Un percorso nelle fonti dell'alto medioevo* (Rome: Carocci, 2017), pp. 57–80.
21 S. Coupland, 'Holy ground? Plundering and burning of churches by Vikings and Franks in the ninth century', *Viator*, 45 (2014), 73–98.
22 SantA 21 (911); SantA 52; Liii 737 (1015).
23 PMH DC 261 (1026); cf. A. Christys, *Vikings in the South. Voyages to Iberia and the Mediterranean* (London: Bloomsbury, 2015), p. 96.
24 *Karolomanni capitulare Vernense*, prol., p. 372: 'Et quomodo poterimus inimicos nostros devincere, cum sanguis fratrum nostrorum ab ore nostro distillat, et manus nostrae plenae sunt sanguine et brachia pondere miseriarum et rapinarum gravantur totaque virtus animi corporisque debilitatur? Preces nostrae a Deo non recipiuntur, quia clamores et ploratus atque suspiria pauperum et orphanorum, pupillorum atque viduarum praeoccupant et praeveniunt preces nostras'.

places').²⁵ Peasants fled the Viking raids to seek safety further inland in Francia, too, and some were apparently reluctant to return.²⁶

The authors who wrote about the many raids were not usually interested in individual victims and their reactions, but in their consequences for the powerful. In a sermon written around the year 900, for instance, the monk Abbo of Saint-Germain-des-Prés worried about the capture or killing of peasants (*villani*) in Viking raids, not for its own sake but for its impact on their lords: 'What shall we do without these people, we who do not know how to plough or to sow or to prune vines or to dig? What shall we do now?'²⁷ Such texts therefore do not tell us much about the local consequences of war. What happened in a settlement that had been devastated by a band of warriors? Did people stay or did they flee? Who buried the victims, who consoled the survivors? Who organised reconstruction? And which kinds of local solidarity were necessary for rebuilding? We can but ask; we usually cannot find the answers.

In his entries for the years 881 and 882, Regino of Prüm reports that the large army of Vikings led by Godfrid and Sigfrid plundered and burned the regions of Liège, Utrecht, the Rhineland near Cologne, and also Aachen, Kornelimünster, Stavelot and Malmedy (see figure 8.2).²⁸ On 6 January 882 the Northmen reached the monastery of Prüm and 'completely devastated the surrounding region'. According to Regino, an innumerable multitude of foot soldiers, gathered from the fields and villages, formed an army and attacked the Vikings. The 'ignoble commoners' (*ignobile vulgus*) were, however, slaughtered by the Northmen like animals on the butcher's table – not because they were unarmed, but because they lacked military capabilities (*militaris disciplina*).²⁹ The text

---

25 *Codex Oadalberti*, ed. W. Hauthaler, in *Salzburger Urkundenbuch*, vol. 1: *Traditionscodices* (Salzburg: Gesellschaft für Salzburger Landeskunde, 1910), nos 22 (early 927), 93 (933), 60 (930), 59 (925), 10 (927).
26 See above, p. 116.
27 *Abbo von Saint-Germain-des-Prés, 22 Predigten: kritische Ausgabe und Kommentar*, ed. U. Önnerfors (Frankfurt am Main: Peter Lang, 1985), p. 94: 'Quale opus habemus nos sine illis hominibus: nos non scimus neque terras arare neque seminare neque vineas putare aut fodere? Quid faciemus nos modo?'
28 Regino of Prüm, *Chronicon*, s.a. 881, p. 118.
29 Regino of Prüm, *Chronicon*, s.a. 882, p. 118: 'In quo loco innumera multitudo peditum ex agris et villis in unum agmen conglobata eos quasi pugnatura adgreditur. Sed Nortmanni cernentes ignobile vulgus non tantum inerme, quantum disciplina militari nudatum, super eos cum clamore irruunt tantaque caede prosternunt, ut bruta animalia, non homines mactari viderentur.'

is remarkable: if we accept Regino's wording, this was not an attack led by magnates, but a spontaneous reaction by the people living around Prüm. We may suppose that such self-organised forms of local resistance were common, although there are only rare glimpses of these activities in surviving texts. However, war had an impact on local groups across Europe in other ways. Who were the people – and how many – who usually went to war? This is an issue that has been keenly debated.[30] There must have been some shared expectations of the size of an army, given Paul the Deacon's account set in northern Italian Friuli in 663: when the invading Slavs saw Duke Wechtari coming from the walled city of Cividale del Friuli against them with only twenty-five men, 'they laughed, saying that the patriarch was advancing against them with his clergy'.[31] Recent excavation at Torksey in England has provided some evidence of the size of the Great Heathen Army in the 860s: it shows that the Viking force was probably as large as several thousands, with consequent implications for the size of the English armies they faced.[32] In fact there may have been no clear division between civilians and soldiers anywhere in Europe. From the end of the sixth century, the late Roman society of western Europe became increasingly militarised, and this must have had major consequences at a local level.[33] Who was forced to go to war, and when, depended on the scope of a military expedition – we might suppose that a villager from the Rhineland would not have been called up for Lothar's and Pippin's campaign in the Spanish March in 828, although there is a reference to one Rhineland villager who went to war in Italy.[34]

Wars were so frequent and widespread that recruitment must have been a common aspect of local experience. From the early ninth century,

---

30 Cf. Reuter, 'Carolingian and Ottonian warfare', pp. 25–30; for military obligations leading to potential army sizes of up to 100,000, see Bachrach, 'Charlemagne', 352–3.
31 Paul the Deacon, *Historia Langobardorum*, V, 23, MGH SS rer. Langob., p. 153. See F. Curta, 'Slavs in Fredegar and Paul the Deacon: medieval *gens* or "scourge of God"?', *Early Medieval Europe*, 6:2 (1997), 141–67, at 159.
32 D. Hadley and J. Richards, 'The winter camp of the Viking Great Army, AD 872-3, Torksey, Lincolnshire', *The Antiquaries Journal*, 96 (2016), 23–67.
33 L. Sarti, *Perceiving War and the Military in Early Christian Gaul (ca. 400–700 A.D.)* (Leiden: Brill, 2013); L. Sarti, 'Eine Militärelite im merowingischen Gallien? Versuch einer Eingrenzung, Zuordnung und Definition', *Mitteilungen des Instituts für Österreichische Geschichtsforschung*, 124 (2016), 271–95.
34 *Annales regni Francorum*, s.a. 828, MGH SS rer. Germ. [6], pp. 174–5; CL 257, vol. 2, p. 43.

English royal diplomas record with increasing frequency that all landed estates, including those belonging to ecclesiastical institutions, were obliged to provide the three so-called 'common burdens', namely, men for service in the army, bridge-work and the building of fortifications. Interestingly the formula used in charters from Christ Church and St Augustine's in Canterbury says explicitly that the three burdens were meant for fighting 'against the heathens', *contra paganos*.[35] A suggestion of the local organisation of army recruitment elsewhere is provided by a list of male names written in the area of Piacenza in northern Italy. Preserved in an early ninth-century south German manuscript, which includes both *leges barbarorum* and capitularies, the list comprises the names of men who had been asked to give their oath, best explained as a commitment to join the army.[36] The list, divided into five columns, was probably originally written in several stages; it is on a separate leaf, added to the codex. Seven office holders are mentioned, including two *gastaldi*, two *scabini* and notaries; some of these individuals can in fact be identified with persons known to have been living in Piacenza in 855. The list was perhaps compiled on the order of the local count *c.* 847, on the occasion of the campaign against the Saracens, and may also be connected with Lothar I's capitulary preparing for the expedition, in which the counts of Modena and Piacenza are mentioned fighting side by side.[37]

While we have no information on how the kings of northern Iberia secured military support, the Anglo-Saxon and Frankish realms imposed heavy fines on those who refused to join the army.[38] In England in the

35 N. Brooks, 'The development of military obligations in eighth- and ninth-century England', in P. Clemoes and K. Hughes (eds), *England Before the Conquest: Studies in Primary Sources presented to Dorothy Whitelock* (Cambridge: Cambridge University Press, 1971), pp. 69–84.

36 Sankt Paul im Lavanttal IV/1, fol. 184r; *Indiculus eorum qui sacramentum fidelitatis iuraverunt*, in MGH Capit. 1, no. 181, pp. 377–8. See H. Mordek, *Bibliotheca capitularium regum Francorum manuscripta. Überlieferung und Traditionszusammenhang der fränkischen Herrschererlasse* (Munich: MGH, 1995), pp. 685–95; S. Esders, M. Bassetti and W. Haubrichs, *Verwaltete Treue. Ein oberitalienisches Originalverzeichnis mit den Namen von 174 vereidigten Personen aus der Zeit Lothars I. und Ludwigs II.* (MGH Studien und Texte, forthcoming).

37 *Hlotharii capitulare de expeditione contra Sarracenos facienda (a. 846)*, in MGH Capit. 2, no. 203, pp. 65–8.

38 There are references to arms in Spanish charters, as an element of composite gifts or prices paid for property; for example, a shield Li 129 (939); swords S 166 (959), Lii 488 (944–82), the latter asssociated with horse, saddle and bridle, and

mid-Saxon period, King Ine's law code lists fines varying between 30 and 120 shillings according to the social status of the person.[39] The lowest fine was for ceorls, a category which would seem at this time to indicate free peasants. In the Frankish world, a fine of 60 *solidi*, called *haribannus*, had to be paid by those refusing to go to war.[40] However, both Anglo-Saxon and Frankish rulers made exceptions for those at the lower end of the social and economic scale. In the Frankish world, capitularies were issued during and after the great famines of 805/806 and the 820s, which allowed freemen to group together in order to support one of their number who would go to war on behalf of the others.[41] The oldest ruling that survives was probably issued in 808 and states that any man with more than four *mansi*, whether as property or as benefice, had to participate personally in campaigns – either accompanying his patron (*senior*), or if he was not going to war, with the count. A man who owned three *mansi* was ordered to join a man who owned only one *mansus*, who was to support the one who went to war. Similarly, two men owning two *mansi* each were to collaborate, with the one going to war supported by the other who remained at home; and four men owning one *mansus* each were expected to equip one of their number to join the campaign.[42] A comparable ruling may be found in late Anglo-Saxon England: only one man from every five hides was bound to go to war in the event of a royal expedition.[43]

We cannot be sure that such norms were always applied in practice, but rulers and their courts had an interest in enforcing their demands,

---

spurs. The precious sword in S 166 was the price paid to a woman by a priest and therefore looks more like a prestige object than a weapon.

39 Ine's law ch. 51, *Die Gesetze der Angelsachsen*, ed. F. Lieberman, 3 vols (Halle: Niemeyer, 1903–16), vol. 1, pp. 112–13.

40 Cf. A. Krah, 'Heerbann', in A. Erler and E. Kaufmann (eds), *Handwörterbuch zur deutschen Rechtsgeschichte*, 3 vols (Berlin: E. Schmidt, 2nd edn, 2008–16), vol. 2, cols 851–3.

41 Cf. C. Jörg, 'Die Besänftigung göttlichen Zorns in karolingischer Zeit. Kaiserliche Vorgaben zu Fasten, Gebet und Buße im Umfeld der Hungersnot von 805/06', *Das Mittelalter*, 15 (2010), 38–51; M. McCormick et al., 'Volcanoes and the climate forcing of Carolingian Europe, A.D. 750–950', *Speculum*, 82 (2007), 865–95, at 881–4.

42 *Capitulare missorum de exercitu promovendo*, ch. 1, in MGH Capit. 1, no. 50, p. 137.

43 R. Lavelle, *Alfred's Wars: Sources and Interpretations of Anglo-Saxon Warfare in the Viking Age* (Woodbridge: Boydell and Brewer, 2010), p. 67.

since gathering armies was not always easy.[44] Louis the Pious was forced to postpone an expedition to Brittany in 824 because of a famine – a real threat to a ruler's military capabilities.[45] Frankish central power sometimes became obsessed with details at the local level, as is visible in a normative text from 829: here, so-called *missi dominici*, that is, royal envoys with extensive powers, were charged with investigating how many free men could go to war themselves, and how many, incapable of going themselves, could support the service of others in groups of two or three. The *missi* were to draw up a list of men in both categories for each *centena* ('hundred') and deliver it to court.[46] The practice of forming small groups to support one of their members' military service remained in use in the following decades in the Frankish world. In his Edict of Pîtres, Charles the Bald reiterated his father's rulings on the subject.[47] And even in post-Carolingian times, King Henry I of east Francia drew on these examples in the 920s to improve defence against Hungarian raiders. According to Widukind of Corvey, Henry ordered that nine *agrarii milites* (farmer soldiers) on the eastern border of his realm should come together to support one of their number, so that he could live in a fort (*urbs*) permanently. In return, the man living in the fortress was to prepare lodgings (*habitacula*) for his eight comrades (*confamiliares*) and to store one-third of their harvest. Henry also ordered assemblies and feasts to be held in these forts, so that the people 'may learn in peace what they have to do against the enemies in times of peril'. According to Widukind, this was necessary because there had been neither walls nor fortifications there before.[48] In England, King Alfred's construction and maintenance of a network of

---

44 É. Renard, 'La politique militaire de Charlemagne et la paysannerie franque', *Francia*, 36 (2009), 1–34, at 1–3, suspects that the *mansus* unit was introduced for the purpose of military administration in the first place.

45 *Annales regni Francorum*, s.a. 824, p. 165: 'imperator vero iter, quod in Brittaniam facere paraverat, propter famem, quae adhuc praevalida erat, usque ad initium autumni adgredi distulit'.

46 *Capitulare pro lege habendum Wormatiense*, ch. 7, in MGH Capit. 2, no. 193, p. 20. For traces of court discussion: *Capitula ab episcopis in placito tranctanda*, ch. 7, in MGH Capit. 2, no. 186, p. 7; and *Capitulare missorum*, ch. 5, ibid., no. 188, p. 10 (transmitted in two different forms).

47 *Edictum Pistense (a. 864)*, ch. 27, in MGH Capit. 2, no. 273, p. 321.

48 Widukind of Corvey, *Rerum gestarum Saxonicarum libri tres*, I, 35, MGH SS rer. Germ. [60], pp. 48–9; for the interpretation of this much discussed passage, see M. Springer, 'Agrarii milites', *Niedersächsisches Jahrbuch für Landesgeschichte*, 66 (1994), 129–66.

fortresses, known as burhs, may well have had comparable effects on local populations, although Alfred's biographer, Asser, refers to people who had refused to build burhs.[49] We have little information about the social consequences of these rulings at the local level. Was the differing treatment of neighbours a source of tension? Did mutual support in going to war generate other forms of solidarity between the families involved? Would people help simply by giving a neighbour some of his military equipment, or would they help with practical work while the neighbour went to war? These group assignments must have necessitated either numerous agreements between peasant proprietors or very clear orders from the royal *missi*, the counts or other office holders about who was to go to war and who was allowed to remain at home.[50]

It is in this context that the complaints against office holders that appear several times in early ninth-century capitularies can be considered. According to these texts, counts and lower-level office holders abused their power of choosing specific men for army duty: they forced landowners to go to war again and again until they were ruined, in order to gain control of their lands.[51] We do not know how significant a problem this was, but it was clearly one of the factors that encouraged free proprietors to give their property to churches, so that as ecclesiastical tenants they could avoid further military service, paying dues to the churches instead.[52] An example of precisely this process at work can be seen in an addition to

49 R. Abels, *Alfred the Great: War, Kingship and Culture in Anglo-Saxon England* (London: Longman, 1998), pp. 194–207; *Alfred the Great. Asser's Life of King Alfred and Other Contemporary Sources*, trans. S. Keynes and M. Lapidge (Harmondsworth: Penguin, 1983), ch. 91, p. 102.
50 See above, p. 155, for Lombard Italy.
51 *Capitula de rebus exercitalibus in placito tractanda (a. 811)*, ch. 3, in MGH Capit. 1, no. 73, p. 165: 'Dicunt etiam, quod quicumque proprium suum episcopo, abbati vel comiti aut iudici vel centenario dare noluerit, occasiones quaerunt super illum pauperem, quomodo eum condempnare possint et illum semper in hostem faciant ire, usque dum pauper factus volens nolens suum proprium tradat aut vendat; alii vero qui traditum habent absque ullius inquietudine domi resideant'.
52 See the sceptical remarks of É. Renard, 'Une élite paysanne en crise? Le poids des charges militaires pour les petits alleutiers entre Loire et Rhin au IXe siècle', in F. Bougard, L. Feller and R. Le Jan (eds), *Les élites au haut Moyen Âge. Crises et renouvellements* (Turnhout: Brepols, 2006), pp. 315–36. Cf. A. Sigoillot, 'Les *liberi homines* dans le polyptyque de Saint-Germain-des-Prés', *Journal des Savants* (2008/2), 261–71, at 270–1.

the polyptyque of Saint-Germain-des-Prés near Paris, in which a group of farmers at Neauphlette donated their property to the monastery at some point in the late ninth century because 'they were not able to perform the king's military service'.[53] As members of the *familia* of a church, these people were exempt from going to war themselves, although they had to pay dues so that the churches could provide the military service required by the king. In this context we find evidence for comparable mechanisms of collective support. In the *Liber possessionum* of the monastery of Wissembourg, we learn that the inhabitants of Eyersheim were required to supply a quarter of an ox-drawn cart (*IIII pars carruce*) for military expeditions.[54] Here, too, we must imagine organisation and agreements at a local level in order to implement the requirement.

The fine levied for evading army service (*haribannus*) was prone to abuse by office holders, who might use it to extract unjustified revenues from local residents. Not everyone would have had a patron as influential as did the men who were asked to pay the *haribannus* by a *missus* of Louis the Pious in 832. Einhard, a powerful courtier and lay abbot of Saint-Bavo, whose tenants they were, became involved. He wrote a letter to the imperial envoy, brief but clear: 'I believed that you knew very well that our men in these areas were serving in the protection of the coast at the order of the emperor' (that is, they were involved in operations against potential Viking raids). Therefore, Einhard continued, it did not seem just that these men, who had only obeyed the emperor's orders, should now pay the *haribannus*. 'We thus ask your love that you may grant us a reprieve until our lord emperor arrives; we may admonish him with regard to his order and he will then issue a ruling, as it suits him.'[55] We do not know if Einhard's appeal to the emperor was successful, but it seems likely that those who did not have an intercessor as close to the king as Einhard could not have resisted a *missus* expecting them to pay a fine, even if it was unjustified.

A second letter written by Einhard shows us a different social dynamic introduced into local society by the recruitment of soldiers. Going to war could force men together who might be enemies at home. At some point

---

53 *Das Polyptychon von Saint-Germain-des-Prés*, ed. D. Hägermann (Cologne: Böhlau, 1993), pp. 23–4: 'quia militiam regis non valebant exercere'.
54 LPW, ch. 14, p. 109.
55 Einhard, *Epistolae*, MGH Epp. 5, no. 23, p. 121; trans. P. E. Dutton, *Charlemagne's Courtier: The Complete Einhard* (Toronto: University of Toronto Press, 2009), no. 22, p. 139.

between 822 and 840, Einhard wrote a letter to Hrabanus Maurus, the abbot of Fulda, interceding on behalf of one of the abbot's men named Gundhart, who was anxious not to go to war. Einhard wrote to Hrabanus:

> He assures that he is forced to remain at home by great necessity, namely the fact that he is feuding and does not dare to go on this expedition with his enemies and those attempting to kill him, especially with this count with whom he was ordered to go to war, and who is, as he assures, his mortal enemy.[56]

In Gundhart's case, the problem was exacerbated by the fact that his enemy was the count who was supposed to lead him into war. In order to avoid service, Gundhart not only offered to pay the *haribannus*, but also to organise the payment with the imperial office holders.

All in all, war was clearly an external factor that had important consequences for local residents in many regions of Europe – because their members became victims of violence and plunder and because locals joined military expeditions (whether voluntarily or involuntarily). Every expedition offered its participants a certain chance of material gain through looting or winning glory in battle, but it also evidently posed risks to health and life and hindered agricultural (or other) work at home. War could therefore introduce social differentiation within local society: as we have seen, it was significant in the Carolingian world of 808 whether one owned four *mansi* or less. But war could also dissolve social boundaries in local society: neighbours became victims of war together (and sometimes came to fight together, as the people of Prüm did in 882). And it could force men of different social ranks and vastly different resources together, sometimes, as the case of Gundhart implies, even mortal enemies.

Justice

In many regions of western Europe, local groups would have had their own social practices and institutions, which allowed them to resolve conflicts without outside involvement. These were for the most part, however, not recorded in writing and have therefore left few traces in the sources;[57] a notable exception lies in the corpus of charters from ninth-century eastern Brittany, which supplies plentiful evidence of the procedures used at

---

56 Einhard, *Epistolae*, no. 42, p. 131.
57 See above, pp. 99–106.

village level by villagers. Here we can find local courts, organised by and involving local people, often with no outside involvement; the procedures they used to present evidence, take oaths, find judgements and appoint sureties, however, were in essence the same as those used in higher-level courts across western Europe.[58]

Notwithstanding local social practice, the practice of the courts was one of the fields in which local residents could find themselves confronting interference from outside. In northern Iberia one of the well-documented court cases involved the monastery of Valdevimbre, south of León, and several people from San Juan en Vega. It was caused by an attempt on the part of the monastery to gain control of water to power its nearby mill. King Ramiro II and his court of bishops, judges and others sent out a group of royal judges, comprising a learned judge, two priests and an abbot, to investigate the matter. The delegation measured the water levels and found that there was sufficient water to power everyone's mills. Therefore, the king's court ruled in favour of the people of San Juan. A year or so later, the monks repeated their claim; once again, the king sent royal judges who found that the locals were not diverting too much water from the monastery's mill and that the monks' claim was ungrounded and 'malicious'. Nevertheless, the local people were ordered to assist in repairing the monks' mill when necessary. So, although the monastery had no valid claim, their access to the king's court brought them a small benefit. As in other parts of Europe, in this case outside forces were able to intervene directly in local relationships, although this seems to have happened less frequently in Spain than in other parts of Europe, and mostly in places – such as San Juan en Vega – that were very close to the centres of power (see figure 8.5).[59] A less direct, but nevertheless significant, form of intervention might come through the judging panels assembled to hear local cases in Iberia: far from decisions being made by people of the locality, it was often the case that members were aristocrats who might travel very considerable distances to attend; royal companions and royal judges, such as Pelayo

---

58 For detail, see W. Davies, 'Disputes, their conduct and their settlement in the village communities of East Brittany in the ninth century', *History and Anthropology*, 1:2 (1985), 289–312; for comparisons across western Europe, W. Davies, *Windows on Justice in Northern Iberia, 800–1000* (Abingdon: Routledge, 2016), ch. 9.

59 Li 128 (938). See above, p. 83; pp. 105–6 for further cases of monastic impact.

González, travelled the two hundred kilometres between León and Galicia.⁶⁰

Many courts in Europe were de facto smaller or larger assemblies, led by office holders, such as counts and reeves, or landowners, sometimes acting in the name of a king. However, as shown in Chapter 6, we must not think of office holders as neutral agents of a central power. They often had strong local ties themselves. A striking example of such ties comes from a court case held in Bavaria in 811. The point of contention was a church that had been built several years earlier at Hinterauerbach by a certain Priso, now deceased, and given to the church of Freising, although Priso's sons denied this and claimed the church for themselves (see figure 8.3). The case was treated in a 'public meeting of bishops, abbots and counts'; all Bavarian bishops of the time are named in the record. Archbishop Arn of Salzburg, a royal *missus*, led the proceedings, interviewing one of Priso's sons. The case took an unusual turn, because Arn then went on to state that he himself had been a witness of Priso's donation. Arn had grown up in this area and knew the parties involved.⁶¹ With the judge having declared his position, Priso's son unsurprisingly lost the case.⁶²

Many cases of conflict resolution are known from charters written after a court session. They usually recorded the outcome, that is, a decision by judges or a confession or an agreement to settle; and they often recorded the names of those held to have been present at the settlement and who could therefore be asked to testify that the outcome had, in fact, been as recorded. Some of these documents also contain a more or less detailed description of the proceedings, such as, for example, a charter documenting a conflict about the church of Saint Mary in the *villa* of Parignargues, in 898, in the diocese of Nîmes in southern France.⁶³

60 For example, in León and north-west Galicia respectively, the court cases Li 192 (946), LaC 59 (956); other appearances: Cel 256 (936), Cel 4 (938), S 129 (950), S 132 (951), Cel 54 (955), Lii 295 (956). On membership of Iberian judging panels, Davies, *Windows on Justice*, ch. 6.
61 On Arn, see M. Diesenberger, *Predigt und Politik im frühmittelalterlichen Bayern: Arn von Salzburg, Karl der Große und die Salzburger Sermones-Sammlung* (Berlin: De Gruyter, 2015), pp. 22–6; H. Dopsch, 'Arn von Salzburg (ca. 740–821)', in K. Weigand (ed.), *Große Gestalten der bayerischen Geschichte* (Munich: Utz, 2012), pp. 13–30.
62 TF 299.
63 *Cartulaire du chapitre de l'église cathédrale Notre-Dame de Nîmes (834–1156)*, ed. E. Germer-Durand (Nîmes: Catélan, 1874), no. 8, pp. 16–18.

Italian *placita* share distinctive features that are not common in other western European charters.[64] A typical example can be found in a *notitia iudicati* written at Trento on 26 February 845. Here the abbot of the monastery of S. Maria in Organo in Verona proceeded to court with a claim against several men whom he wanted to perform labour service for his monastery. The respondents denied that their condition was servile: after a long legal dispute, the Trento hearing reached what might be called a negotiated settlement. The *scabini* questioned witnesses about the basis on which respondents performed their *corvée* labour. By establishing that their labour service was linked to the properties on which they lived, rather than their persons, the *scabini* restored the rights of the abbot but at the same time protected the low-ranking freemen from being reduced to servile status.[65]

A generation later, in 876, Abbot Bertilus of Saint-Bénigne in Dijon, represented by his advocate Saifardus, complained to the court of Bishop Isaac of Langres against three men named Radulf, Archemrad and Bonefrid. The assembly was held on the balcony of the church of Saint-Étienne in Dijon in the presence of the *vicedominus* Brunardus, a certain Agano and 'very many others'. The three men were accused of being in possession of a *mansus* in Barges en Oscheret, which properly belonged to the monastery of Saint-Bénigne, and of seven *mancipia* named Odelbert, Jonas, Vetruda, Gotbalda, Flodolen, Natalia and Vuineran. The pivotal evidence was presented by the priest Agenbaldus: he testified that he himself had given the land and the serfs to the monastery of Saint-Bénigne. After this testimony, Radulf, Archemrad and Bonefrid returned the land and the people to the monastery.[66]

Examples of this kind could be multiplied for numerous other regions of Europe. For decades, historical research has used this rich material to reconstruct modes of conflict and conflict settlement in the early Middle Ages.[67] Yet however helpful court documents are for understanding

64   See above, p. 143, and below, pp. 226–7.
65   *I placiti*, vol. 1, no. 49, pp. 160–6; ChLA 59, no. 17; cf. G. Albertoni, 'Law and the peasant: rural society and justice in Carolingian Italy', *Early Medieval Europe*, 18:4 (2010), 417–45, at 417–33; A. Castagnetti, *'Teutisci' nella 'Langobardia' carolingia* (Verona: Libreria Universitaria, 1995).
66   *Chartes et documents de Saint-Bénigne de Dijon.* 1. *VIe–Xe siècles*, ed. R. Folz (Dijon: Société des Annales de Bourgogne, 1986), no. 96, pp. 128–9.
67   W. Davies and P. Fouracre (eds), *The Settlement of Disputes in Early Medieval Europe* (Cambridge: Cambridge University Press, 1986); *La giustizia nell'alto medioevo, secoli IX–XI*, 2 vols (Spoleto, 1997); W. C. Brown and P. Górecki

dispute resolution practice, they are not always useful for understanding the impact of external interventions on localities: they do not often document how judgements, confessions and agreements affected the social relationships of local people. Nevertheless, we can observe in some places that external intervention was itself a stimulus for local residents to come together and act collectively, as the people of five settlements along the river Arlanzón in northern Iberia did in the face of a challenge from the abbot of San Torcuato.[68] In eastern Brittany, despite the very local nature of courts, we can also see some external impact: usually a local machtiern (minor aristocrat) presided over court proceedings, but sometimes representatives of the Breton ruler (*princeps*) did so, or some combination of both. On four occasions representatives of the *princeps* presided;[69] and on two occasions a representative of the *princeps* and machtierns presided together.[70] Representatives of the *princeps* seem to feature at this level either when the *princeps* had personal property interests in the *plebs* or alternatively when the monastery of Redon appealed to the *princeps* for resolution of a dispute. As in northern Iberia, that appeal brought external agencies directly into local society. What is interesting about these cases is that we can see the external presence fomenting conflict within a single family as well as diverting customary dues to a powerful monastery; and we can see something of local peasant power play as when, for example, those who had given evidence against the unsuccessful litigant Anauhocar then became sureties for his acquiescence; in another case two of the judges themselves became sureties for a different unsuccessful litigant, Merchrit.[71]

The strong local ties of those who led assemblies, even if they were formally acting in the name of a king, the interests of those taking part, and presumably the local traditions of doing things a certain way, also meant that kings might find it difficult to manipulate local or micro-regional

(eds), *Conflict in Medieval Europe. Changing Perspectives on Society and Culture* (Aldershot: Ashgate, 2003). For Bavaria: W. C. Brown, *Unjust Seizure: Conflict, Interest, and Authority in an Early Medieval Society* (Ithaca, NY: Cornell University Press, 2001). For Tuscany: M. Stoffella, 'Condizionamenti politici e sociali nelle procedure di risoluzione dei conflitti nella Toscana occidentale tra età longobarda e carolingia', *Studi Medievali*, 59:1 (2018), 35–61.
68 C 22 (932); see Davies, *Windows on Justice*, ch. 8, for other Spanish examples.
69 CR 106 (843–51), CR 124 (843–4), CR 192 (834–7), and by implication CR 61 (842).
70 CR 139 (860), CR 180 (843–9).
71 E.g. CR 192; CR 106; CR 61 and CR 180.

assemblies. Indeed, we may interpret law-giving by kings – Lombard, Anglo-Saxon, Frankish – as an attempt to gain influence over the conduct of legal procedures in the localities.[72] In the second half of the tenth century, the introduction of hundredal courts, which were under direct royal control in England, may have been a conscious attempt to bypass unreliable reeves (and local assemblies) and to assure a more consistent way of doing justice.[73] Anglo-Saxon reeves were held responsible for judgements and were subject to punishment if they were found to be corrupt or incompetent.[74]

This also seems to have been true for the Carolingian world. Here regional and supra-regional elites and rulers were worried that social relationships between local neighbours could be a barrier to lordly penetration of their small worlds. There were many efforts to prevent solidarity and mutual obligations at a local level, especially in legal proceedings when fiscal or church property was the subject of dispute. Carolingian rulers and their bishops tended to be critical of all forms of horizontal cooperation and alliance, such as, especially, guilds, which were based on their members' promissory oaths.[75] Anglo-Saxon rulers were also

---

72 Lambert, *Law and Order*, pp. 142–7, for Anglo-Saxon England, but the point is valid for all law-giving kings. For English law-giving and its consequences, see P. Wormald, *The Making of English Law: King Alfred to the Twelfth Century, Volume I: Legislation and its Limits* (Oxford: Blackwell, 1999); vol. 2 published posthumously as P. Wormald, *Papers Preparatory to the Making of English Law: King Alfred to the Twelfth Century, Volume II: From God's Law to Common Law*, ed. S. Baxter and J. Hudson (London: University of London, 2014), http://www.earlyenglishlaws.ac.uk/reference/wormald/ (accessed 4 September 2019).

73 Lambert, *Law and Order*, p. 133. On the powerful role played by the late Anglo-Saxon state in the exercise of justice, including both high-level disputes and more local litigation, see P. Wormald, 'Charters, law and the settlement of disputes in Anglo-Saxon England', in Davies and Fouracre (eds), *The Settlement of Disputes*, pp. 149–68, at p. 167. Evidence for local disputes is limited: A. G. Kennedy, 'Disputes about *bocland*: the forum for their adjudication', *Anglo-Saxon England*, 14 (1985), 175–95, at 177; but characters such as the priest who steals a cloak touch the local level; P. Wormald, 'A handlist of Anglo-Saxon lawsuits', *Anglo-Saxon England*, 17 (1988), no. 127.

74 Lambert, *Law and Order*, pp. 144–5; Wormald, *Papers Preparatory to the Making of English Law*, pp. 151, 153, 156, 199.

75 See above, p. 90. O. G. Oexle, 'Conjuratio und Gilden im frühen Mittelalter. Ein Beitrag zur sozialen Kontinuität zwischen Antike und Mittelalter', in B. Schwineköper (ed.), *Gilden und Zünfte. Kaufmännische und gewerbliche Genossenschaften im frühen und hohen Mittelalter* (Sigmaringen:

concerned about horizontal solidarities, especially in cases when kinsmen were able to protect each other from the law.[76]

In the above examples, we have already seen that not only written evidence such as charters could be offered in legal proceedings, but also witness testimony, which could be supplied by the defendant, although not necessarily so.[77] If it was, it brought the risk that a court might make a decision on the basis of the prestige, social status and perhaps the liabilities that bound others from the locality to the defendant – as in court cases from many other periods and areas. The Carolingians responded to this challenge with several instruments. One solution was the appointment of *missi* to control comparatively large districts, in the name of the emperor, in which they monitored the counts and their officers. These *missi*, delegated to dispense justice and eradicate grievances of different kinds, generally worked in pairs, as a mutual control.[78] A court held at Rizana in 804, for instance, under the auspices of *missi* sent by Charlemagne, revealed how the Frankish official in charge of Istria, Duke John, had been exploiting the residents, using his authority to take over communal lands and rights.[79]

As a second instrument, *missi dominici* often placed local people under the obligation to act as *fideiussores*, sureties. These people personally

---

Thorbecke, 1985), pp. 151–214; O. G. Oexle, 'Gilden als soziale Gruppen in der Karolingerzeit', in H. Jankuhn (ed.), *Das Handwerk in vor- und frühgeschichtlicher Zeit. Teil I. Historische und rechtshistorische Beiträge und Untersuchungen zur Frühgeschichte der Gilde* (Göttingen: Vandenhoeck & Ruprecht, 1981), pp. 284–354.

76 See R. Abels, '"The crimes by which Wulfbald ruined himself with his lord": the limits of state action in late Anglo-Saxon England', *Reading Medieval Studies*, 40 (2014), 42–53, at 50–1.

77 *Cartulaire du chapitre de l'église cathédrale Notre-Dame de Nîmes*, ed. Germer-Durand, no. 8.

78 For the system and functions of *missi dominici*, see S. Kikuchi, *Untersuchungen zu den Missi dominici: Herrschaft, Delegation und Kommunikation in der Karolingerzeit* (Munich: Ludwig-Maximilians-Universität, 2013); J. Hannig, '"Pauperiores vassi de infra palatio?" Zur Entstehung der karolingischen Königsbotenorganisation', *Mitteilungen des Instituts für Österreichische Geschichtsforschung*, 91 (1983), 309–74; J. Hannig, 'Zentrale Kontrolle und regionale Machtbalance. Beobachtungen zum System der karolingischen Königsboten am Beispiel des Mittelrheingebietes', *Archiv für Kulturgeschichte*, 66 (1984), 1–46.

79 *I placiti*, vol. I, no. 17, pp. 48–56; French translation, Ph. Depreux, *Les sociétés occidentales du milieu du VIe à la fin du IXe siècle* (Rennes: Presses Universitaires de Rennes, 2002), pp. 293–9.

bore the risk of perjury, for they had to make sure that the defendant actually arrived at the royal court to be tried by the emperor in person, or they had to stand in for defendants who withdrew from proceedings brought by the *missi*.[80] References to sureties also occur frequently in Anglo-Saxon sources, including both legal codes and charters. In the second half of the tenth century suretyship became a major obligation in England, as all men had a legal duty to have sureties liable for any fine incurred.[81] Use of sureties was also extremely common in Brittany and in northern Iberia, but with an interesting difference: in both regions they were not appointed as a consequence of orders from rulers; rather, they were an important instrument of customary local practice. Hence, the many interactions and alliances we can see at local level in these cases tell us much more about how suretyship worked on the ground than about external impact.[82]

A third instrument was the use of so-called inquisition proceedings, at first only on fiscal lands but, from the reign of Louis the Pious onwards, also for church land. These represented a crucial innovation in process: in the course of their inquest (*inquisitio*), the emperor's *missi* could themselves determine from whom to take evidence locally.[83] This was a chance to prise open the web of solidarities and dependencies at the micro level (although possibly at the risk of some witnesses facing reprisals after the *missi* left). How exactly such an inquest took place is shown quite clearly in the above-mentioned Trento trial held at the beginning

80 *Capitulare missorum Wormatiense (a. 829)*, ch. 4, in MGH Capit. 2, no. 192, p. 15: 'Volumus, ut quicumque de scabinis deprehensus fuerit propter munera aut propter amicitiam vel inimicitiam iniuste iudicasse, ut per fideiussores missus ad praesentiam nostram veniat'; ibid., chs 6–7, p. 15; ch. 10, p. 16; *Capitulare Wormatiense (a. 829)*, chs 1, 10, ibid., no. 191, pp. 12, 14; *Capitulare pro lege habendum Wormatiense (a. 829)*, ch. 4, ibid., no. 193, p. 19. Esders, 'Amt und Bann'.

81 Lambert, *Law and Order*, p. 273. For examples of the role of witnesses and sureties in late Anglo-Saxon litigation, see A. Kennedy, 'Law and litigation in the Libellus Æthelwoldi episcopi', *Anglo-Saxon England*, 24 (1995), 131–83; and for other areas, T. Charles-Edwards, M. Owen and D. Walters (eds), *Lawyers and Laymen* (Cardiff: University of Wales Press, 1986), pp. 15–233.

82 For detail, see W. Davies, 'Suretyship in the *Cartulaire du Redon*', in Charles-Edwards, Owen and Walters (eds), *Lawyers and Laymen*, pp. 72–91; W. Davies, 'On suretyship in tenth-century northern Iberia', in J. Escalona and A. Reynolds (eds), *Scale and Scale Change: Western Europe in the First Millennium* (Turnhout: Brepols, 2011), pp. 133–52.

83 Cf. Esders, 'Amt und Bann'.

of 845. After complaints made by the abbot of S. Maria to Louis II, the king ordered an enquiry (*inquisitio*) through two royal *missi* – a royal *iudex* and a *locopositus* of the duke of Trento – in front of a large tribunal. Many minor office holders from different parts of the *comitatus* of Trento were also summoned: seven *scabini*, all associated with localities within the *comitatus*, four *sculdahi*, the two archdeacons of Verona and Trento, many *vassi dominici* and other freemen of middling or higher status.[84] However, this example also shows the limits of efforts to break horizontal solidarities: from the perspective of central authority the *scabini* were more of a problem than the witnesses, since it would seem that local *scabini* – through their knowledge of judicial procedures and as members of local communities – were sometimes able to moderate interventions from outside and stand for the rights of the community to which they belonged. The limits of the use of inquest are also shown in a rare example from north-west Spain: here, when questioned, two men from each of five settlements made responses about past practice in their locality that were so ambiguous that a test by ordeal had to be arranged.[85]

Interestingly, bishops in the Carolingian Empire developed an analogous instrument to the *inquisitio* during the later ninth century in order to be informed as accurately as possible about abuses in the parishes of their dioceses during their visitations:[86] the so-called 'Send', a special kind of episcopal court, is particularly vividly described in Regino of Prüm's *Libri duo de synodalibus causis* of the early tenth century. According to Regino, the bishop should address the whole local community when he held court, but then call seven 'mature, honourable and

---

84 See above, p. 196. Here, the *locopositus* is clearly a *missus* of the *comes*: *I capitolari italici. Storia e diritto della dominazione carolingia in Italia*, ed. C. Azzara and P. Moro (Rome: Viella, 1998), no. 10 (801), ch. 7, p. 77 (= MGH Capit. 1, no. 98, p. 205). Cf. A. Castagnetti, 'Lociservatores, locopositi, gastaldi e visconti a Milano in età carolingia', in P. Corrao and E. Igor Mineo (eds), *Dentro e fuori la Sicilia. Studi di storia per Vincenzo D'Alessandro* (Rome: Viella, 2009), pp. 45–78; M. Stoffella, 'Lociservatores nell'Italia carolingia: l'evidenza Toscana', in M. Bassetti et al. (eds), *Studi sul medioevo per Andrea Castagnetti* (Bologna: CLUEB, 2011), pp. 345–82.
85 Sob 109 (early 990s).
86 For the *inquisitio* by royal *missi* as a model for the episcopal 'Sendgericht', cf. R. Schieffer, 'Zur Entstehung des Sendgerichts im 9. Jahrhundert', in W. Müller and M. Sommar (eds), *Medieval Church Law and the Origins of the Western Legal Tradition. A Tribute to Kenneth Pennington* (Washington DC: Catholic University of America Press, 2006), pp. 50–6.

honest men' from the community, who each had to swear the following oath on holy relics:[87]

> From now on and henceforth: if you have learned or heard, or if you later determine that in this parish (*parrochia*) something has been done or is done in the future that happens to be against the will of God and against the right Christian way, then you may not conceal [...] it from the archbishop of Trier or his legate, whom the archbishop has ordered to investigate, neither for love nor for fear, nor for reward, nor because of kinship, whenever he asks you about it. So may God and these relics of the saints here help you.[88]

We can only guess the tensions triggered by being under oath to denounce one's neighbours, before the bishop, for all minor or major transgressions. The swearing-in as a witness at an ecclesiastical court cannot always have been very beneficial to the social life of those sworn in. However, the formulation of the oath is indicative of the fears and worries of the episcopate: love (*amor*), fear (*timor*), reward (*praemium*) and kinship (*parentela*) – with these four words the complex network of debts, obligations, solidarities, friendships and enmities is vividly described; from the point of view of regional and supra-regional elites, such networks were opposed to their control of local communities and to the establishment of law and God-given order at the local level. Sometimes, however, it looks as if bishops were unable to penetrate the local group. When Bishop Ermenraus of Châlons excommunicated the inhabitants (*incolae*) of a village around 860 for a murder they had not committed, it was presumably a kind of collective punishment intended to force the residents to produce the guilty party: a heavy-handed response that showed the limitations of the bishop's power as much as its strength.[89]

Such strategies may have changed the fabric of social relationships within a locality. We can see that supra-regional elites and rulers feared that material and immaterial obligations were forged in small settlements, where neighbours knew each other personally. Here, legal processes

---

87 Regino of Prüm, *Libri duo de synodalibus causis et disciplinis ecclesiasticis*, II, 2, *Das Sendhandbuch des Regino von Prüm*, ed. W. Hartmann (Darmstadt: Wissenschaftliche Buchgesellschaft, 2004), p. 236: 'honestiores atque veraciores viros in medio debet evocare'.
88 Ibid., II, 3, p. 236.
89 Flodoard, *Historiae Remensis ecclesiae*, III, 23, MGH SS 36, p. 305: register of a letter from Hincmar of Reims to Bishop Ercamraus, 'pro cuiusdam ville incolis, quos irrationabiliter ab omni consolatione divini ministerii propter quoddam homicidium non ab ipsis patratum'.

could fail because they were operated by public officials, who were themselves part of local society, because local networks of friendship and enmity were established, and because those accused could name their own character witnesses in order to limit liability.

Property

Transferring property – both landed property and serfs – was another way in which outsiders intervened in the affairs of the residential group. Of course, every transaction did not necessarily have consequences at the local level: in many cases it probably did not matter to local residents if the title to a plot of land was transferred from one distant aristocratic landowner to another. Hincmar of Reims, for example, wrote to the *familia* of a Reims estate in Thuringia, which had been transferred to the abbey of Corvey in Saxony, advising all of them to obey their new landlord, but without any indication that anything else was going to change.[90]

But sometimes these transfers did matter to residents. For example, in 829, a number of them complained to their former owner Bishop Baturich of Regensburg about the treatment they were receiving from their new owner. The bishop, who had exchanged the serfs for some land, entered into negotiations with their new owner, an abbot named Sigimot, who refused to make amends. As a consequence, the exchange was annulled and the serfs reverted to their former lord, the bishop.[91] Over a hundred years later, in 984, residents of the village of Bruoch near Metz similarly complained that their new landlord, the monastery of Gorze, had increased their obligations; the abbot agreed to return them to the levels they were at prior to the estate's transfer.[92]

Landowners often demonstrated great interest in anchoring property boundaries in local knowledge. Precise boundary descriptions are found in Italian,[93] Anglo-Saxon, Welsh and Spanish charters, but are

90 Flodoard, *Historia Remensis ecclesiae*, III, 24, p. 323: 'Familie quoque in eisdem rebus consistenti litteris mandans, quo eidem abbati obedientes in cunctis existerent'.
91 TR 25, p. 32.
92 See J.-P. Devroey, 'Confronter la coutume domaniale entre seigneurs et paysans en Lorraine au Xe siècle', in L. Jégou et al. (eds), *Faire lien. Aristocratie, réseaux et échanges compétitifs: Mélanges en l'honneur de Régine Le Jan* (Paris: Editions de la Sorbonne, 2015), pp. 155–78.
93 Even if notaries carefully described boundaries, in northern Italy *missi* of both parties to an exchange were sent to the locations in order to verify the exchange

rarer in parts of the Frankish realm north of the Alps prior to the tenth century.[94] Landowners were dependent on local knowledge in cases of disputes and so local people were called to witness the ritual transfer of land. When, for example, Hrandolf and his wife Theothrat gave their land in five villages to the monastery of Hersfeld on the border between Saxony and Francia, their representatives and the monastery's agents travelled to each of the places in order to carry out the transfer. By ritually and publicly investing the monks' agents with their new property, the transfer of ownership was entrenched in local memory and hopefully secured for the distant owners. The scribe listed the names of the local witnesses – most of them members of local elites – in every place.[95] So, likewise, in ninth-century Brittany, when property was given to the monastery of Redon, the monastery's agents often attended the transaction in the locality and witness names were noted.[96] Indeed, in cases of disputed ownership, we can sometimes see the witnesses and guarantors of earlier transactions called to give evidence, because we have the original charters as well as the records of subsequent disputes, as happened twice in the village of Ruffiac in the 860s.[97] And in one early eleventh-century English case of disputed ownership, involving the bishop of Hereford, those who had traced the bounds of the original sale to him were asked to do so again in order to resolve the dispute; as it

agreement; see F. Bougard, *La justice dans le royaume d'Italie de la fin du VIIIe siècle au début du XIe siècle* (Rome: École française de Rome, 1995), pp. 151, 179–91.

94 For a detailed analysis of surviving boundary descriptions from eastern Frankish territories, see E. Roberts, 'Boundary clauses and the use of the vernacular in eastern Frankish charters *c.*750–*c.*900', *Historical Research*, 91 (2018), 580–604. For the chronology of parish boundaries in the middle Rhine valley, see R. Deutinger, 'Die ältesten mittelrheinischen Zehntterminationen', *Archiv für mittelrheinische Kirchengeschichte*, 54 (2002), 11–36. For examples from Spain, and a useful discussion of the nature of 'local knowledge', see J. Escalona, 'Dense local knowledge: grounding local to supralocal relationships in tenth-century Castile', in J. Escalona Monge, O. Vesteinsson and S. Brookes (eds), *Polity and Neighbourhood in Early Medieval Europe* (Turnhout: Brepols, 2019), pp. 351–79.

95 UBH 26.

96 For example, CR 23 (859), CR 26 (857), CR 69 (860), CR 73 (859), CR 95 (861), CR 98 (866), CR 175 (858), CR 225 (868).

97 CR 138 (846) and CR 139 (860), in fact a case between peasants; CR 143 (851–7) and CR 144 (post 851–7); cf. the *senes* of Avessac providing local evidence against a peasant who questioned the monastery's ownership, CR 195 (840–1).

turned out, the original vendor and witnesses, the bishop, the challenger and his associates all rode the boundaries together and agreement was reached.[98] Rituals of transfer varied greatly, even within a region. In the case of the process held in Dijon, mentioned above, the defendants renounced their property *cum festuca* (that is, with a ritual in which a staff was given as a symbol of the land to be transferred).[99] Common rituals involved the new owner walking (or riding) along the boundary of the transferred property, or handing over a symbolic piece of the property such as a handful of earth for a gift of ploughland, or the altar cloth or bell cord for a gift of a church.[100] Spanish rituals emphasise the importance of crossing or marking the boundary too, at the moment of transfer, and one text implies that the entrance to a disputed property was marked with the judge's seal when restored to a successful claimant.[101] Sometimes, continental rituals were more elaborate. When Count Ratold gave his property to the church of Freising, in 839, the bishop himself came to his house. In front of his neighbours and relatives, the bishop asked Ratold, who was standing in the centre of his house wearing his sword, if he had the power to transfer the land. Since nobody denied that this was the case, Ratold invested the bishop with all his property over the doorstep and then left the house, letting the bishop and his men enter.[102] Since the recipient of Ratold's donation was technically not the bishop himself, but the altar of his church and relics within it, the bishop brought a reliquary with relics of the patron saints so that the saints and their altar were present in a real sense. In other

---

98 Sawyer 1460; see Wormald, 'Handlist of Anglo-Saxon lawsuits', no. 77; A. Langlands, 'Local places and local people in Anglo-Saxon Wessex', in Escalona, Vesteinsson and Brookes (eds), *Polity and Neighbourhood*, pp. 381–405, at p. 390.
99 See above, p. 196.
100 For examples from Bavaria, see T. Kohl, *Lokale Gesellschaften. Formen der Gemeinschaft in Bayern vom 8. bis zum 10. Jahrhundert* (Ostfildern: Thorbecke, 2010), pp. 75–85. For English examples, see S. Kelly, 'Anglo-Saxon lay society and the written word', in R. McKitterick (ed.), *The Uses of Literacy in Early Mediaeval Europe* (Cambridge: Cambridge University Press, 1990), pp. 36–62, at p. 44.
101 OD 73 (1007); see Davies, *Windows on Justice*, p. 166, n. 63. Irish rituals for taking control of property could involve lighting a fire or crossing a burial mound on the boundary; F. Kelly, *A Guide to Early Irish Law* (Dublin: Dublin Institute for Advanced Studies, 1988), pp. 186–9, 280.
102 TF 634.

cases, the bishop or his agents spent three days and nights in a house to affirm their control of a new property, and in one a piece of meadow was mown by the bishop's men immediately after it was donated.[103]

The impact at local level of the management of their possessions by an aristocrat or spiritual institution was not always that which was intended. A good example of accidental consequences, causing significant local social upheaval, is that generated by a court in Courtisols, documented in the polyptyque of the monastery of Saint-Remi in Reims.[104] The polyptyque, created shortly after 847 under Archbishop Hincmar of Reims (who was at the same time abbot of Saint-Remi), gives us a good idea of the structure of the population of Courtisols. Here 1,083 adults and children were recorded in the polyptyque as free (*ingenui*). Alongside them lived 127 *servi* and *ancillae*, each of whom had to give the monastery a due of 12 *denarii*. In addition, there are also eleven *cartularii* and 26 *ingenuitatem habentes per cartam*, that is, people who had been manumitted using a written process. One individual is called *franca*, but it is not clear how this woman was different from the *ingenui*. Finally, thirty persons are named without any indication of their legal status. The polyptyque even recorded a few with specialised occupations – namely, two artisans (*fabri*) who were unfree and shared an unfree tenure, four *berbiarii servi* and one *berbiaria ancilla* ('shepherds'). All the inhabitants of this place shared a total of 92.5 free tenures (*mansa ingenuilia*) and 35 unfree tenures (*mansa servilia*). These numbers alone indicate that there were significant social differences between the residents of Courtisols. One hundred and sixty-nine men and their families lived on the free tenures, with thirty-nine of them having a whole tenure (*mansum*) each. Only one single resident of Courtisols – the *scabinus* Geimfridus – is shown to have farmed two farmsteads. Fifty-six families had to share a single tenure with another family; fifty-one families shared their tenure with two others; twenty-one families even shared with three or four other families. We cannot see the totality of social difference in

---

103 TF 337, 455, 558; for the meadow, TF 538a.
104 See above, pp. 116–17. This case has been extensively examined; see, most recently, J.-P. Devroey, 'Libres et non-libres sur les terres de Saint-Remi de Reims: la notice judiciaire de Courtisols (13 mai 847) et le polyptyque d'Hincmar', *Journal des Savants* (2006/1), 65–103; J. Barbier, '"The praetor *does* concern himself with trifles": Hincmar, the polyptych of St-Remi and the slaves of Courtisols', in R. Stone and C. West (eds), *Hincmar of Rheims: Life and work* (Manchester: Manchester University Press, 2015), pp. 211–27.

this place, but these clues make it clear there were subtle local economic, social and legal internal differentiations.[105]

To create the polyptyque, monks from the monastery of Saint-Remi had to gather the necessary information. We can see that the act of documentation did not neutrally describe the state of affairs, but changed it: it required classifications that in practice seem to have been quite blurred. The endeavour thus resulted in a dispute over the legal status of some residents of Courtisols, documented in a text that was soon afterwards inserted into the polyptyque of Saint-Remi. According to the charter, a meeting of a public court (*placitum publicum*) was held on 13 May 847, in Courtisols itself, to negotiate the legal status of some of the inhabitants: Grimoldus, Vuarmherus, Leuthadus, Ostroldus, Adelardus, Iuoia and Hildiardis *filia* denied being unfree and said *ex nativitate ingenui esse debemus* ('from birth, we ought to be free'). Seven elders (*senissimi*) of the place testified that the grandmothers of those concerned – a Berta and an Avila – had been bought by the monastery and consequently their descendants were unfree (*servi et ancillae deberent esse*). The *scabini* who pronounced the verdict were Geimfridus (the most affluent man in the locality with his hold on two farmsteads), Ursoldus, Fredericus, Ursiaudus, Hroderaus, Herleherus, Ratbertus and Gislehardus. On closer inspection, it turns out that the case affected, on the one hand, precisely those four people who, according to the polyptyque, held free tenures (*mansa ingenuilia*) but were classified as *servi*. And on the other hand, there were three people holding unfree tenures, which they shared with free persons. We may suppose that for years these people had lived their daily lives in much the same way as their free neighbours – especially since the episcopal see of Reims had been vacant from 835 to 845. It was not until the monks of Saint-Remi decided to count all the inhabitants of Courtisols, and to classify them as 'free' or 'unfree', that an exact assignment to one of the categories became necessary. Here the recording process itself had side-effects on local society, as doubtless happened elsewhere too. Perhaps it was not only in the monastery's interest to categorise those affected as unfree; maybe, given the status of the *senissimi* and the role of the leading and more affluent free locals acting as *scabini*, who wanted to emphasise their local superiority, some free residents also became willing supporters of the effort.[106]

---

105 *Le polyptyque et les listes de cens de l'abbaye de Saint-Remi de Reims: IXe–XIe siècles*, ed. J.-P. Devroey (Reims: Académie nationale de Reims, 1984), pp. 16–29.
106 Cf. A. Rio, *Slavery after Rome, 500–1100* (Oxford: Oxford University Press, 2017), p. 197, for this point, and pp. 183–94 on the recording of status in Francia.

In many parts of western Europe, the land farmed by members of a local settlement was owned by people or institutions who also held property elsewhere and who did not interact on a daily basis with residents as local neighbours; any transfer of land and any description of possessions was an event that could trigger change in local relationships. At the same time, owners who did not live as neighbours had to rely on the knowledge embedded in a local society when managing their properties. The case of Courtisols shows that even unintended side-effects could have a strong impact on local residents – and it was sometimes the neighbours who did not want local people to change their social status.

In conclusion, interventions from outside were part of the everyday experience of people in many parts of western Europe. We have seen that war, justice and property were important areas in which such interventions were regularly felt by local people. However, we should be careful not to regard residents of rural settlements in the early Middle Ages merely as victims of the intervention of the 'powerful' and 'strangers'. The example of the Courtisols court case cautions us against any social romanticism. Individual members of local residential groups could often find supporters and mediators outside their small worlds – supporters who only intervened when expressly called upon to do so. And unless a ruler him- or herself had interests locally, local people could sometimes find a patron who was even more powerful and influential than any regional official whose demands they were struggling to oppose; hence, Einhard could contradict a *missus dominicus* and intervene in favour of his clients. Other cases include that of two unfree poachers who, threatened with corporal punishment, fled to Einhard's church in Seligenstadt and persuaded Einhard to intervene for them with the count. Einhard's wife Imma, in turn, interceded with a certain Blithrud in the name of an unfree man from Mosbach named Wenilo, who had married without the permission of his master Albuin – probably the husband of Blithrud.[107] External intervention into the local in the early Middle Ages could be an opportunity as well as a threat.

---

107 Einhard, *Epistolae*, no. 15, p. 128.

8

Neighbours, visitors and strangers: searching for the local

When Donadeo's son was caught thieving in northern Galicia in the early tenth century, he was taken to court, where he confessed and was committed to pay a fine valued at thirty cattle.[1] A group of six named sureties, including two priests, guaranteed that the son would not try to run away, but if he did then they, the sureties, would pay the court holder, Hermenegildo, twenty cattle; in that case, Donadeo and his wife Tidina would hand over their own property to the sureties. The wretched son (somewhat inappropriately called Salomon) did run away, releasing and taking with him both another thief, who was liable for a fine of three horses, and also Hermenegildo's servant Maurelo. The parents duly handed over their property, on 7 July 931, by the church in Codegio, a transaction witnessed by twelve people, including two of the sureties, and recorded by one Froilani.

This story occurs as a preface to a very standard donation charter. Without it, and similar prefaces, we would not see this set of personal relationships within a free peasant society: parents' responsibility for the wrongdoing of a son; the association between thieves; the gathering of a band of sureties rich enough to underwrite the fine (note the inclusion of two local priests); the need to ensure that the sureties suffered no personal loss; the benefit to the court holder, a person with servants (Hermenegildo was a significant landowner); not forgetting the expectation that a thief convicted with due process in a judicial court might run away, beyond the home community, and escape the penalty. A complexity of relationships within a face-to-face, small-scale rural society: Codegio was 3 kilometres from Sobrado, the location of the court and Hermenegildo's residence;

[1] Sob 21.

209

the priests, the scribe and some of the witnesses feature in other charters relating to that area at that time.[2]

The details of the story are important because the events occurred some twenty years before the foundation of the monastery which ultimately came to preserve the record. The charter was part of Hermenegildo's lay archive, which he handed over when he vacated his property and founded the monastery of Sobrado in 952.[3] It allows us to see peasant relationships, and peasant expectations, before the landscape was complicated by the interests of a powerful monastic institution, although one might say it was already complicated by the interests, and presence, of a powerful landowner. Here, in north-west Iberia, far beyond the reach of the legacy of the Carolingian Empire, we have elements of many of the themes that have recurred in this book.

It hardly needs saying that the source material available for the early Middle Ages does not allow reconstruction of the feelings and the nuances of personal relationships of individual peasants. There is a limit to what can be known. But that does not mean we see nothing: multiple actions, reactions, pressures and attitudes have been detailed in the chapters above, whether recorded in miracle collections, letters, histories or charters, as in the rich detail of the Sobrado story; there is material in estate records that derives from systematic local enquiries;[4] and the corpus of archaeological data provides increasing evidence of the varied complexion of residential space. There are gaps, of course, but there is enough to make some suggestions.

We could hardly expect that the residential group was the only group to which its members belonged or that such a grouping defined its single and only identity. Then, as now, people associated for different purposes and belonged to this group and that, depending on function, in discrete and overlapping combinations. Looking for a single social group – a core group – is neither useful nor relevant. Nor is it appropriate to look for social cohesion as understood in modern political or academic discourse: social cohesion is 'society's ability to secure the long-term well-being of all of its members, including equitable access to available resources, respect

---

2 Sob 28 (920); Sob 22, Sob 24, Sob 29 (all 931).
3 See A. J. Kosto, '*Sicut mos esse solet*: documentary practices in Christian Iberia, c. 700–1000', in W. C. Brown, M. Costambeys, M. Innes and A. J. Kosto (eds), *Documentary Culture and the Laity in the Early Middle Ages* (Cambridge: Cambridge University Press, 2013), pp. 259–82, at pp. 269–73.
4 See above, pp. 44–5.

for human dignity with due regard for diversity, personal and collective autonomy and responsible participation', runs one of many authoritative definitions.[5] The concern with equality and autonomy characteristic of modern discussion will not work for the early Middle Ages.[6] However, it may be worth looking for other presumed attributes, such as solidarity, shared values, shared beliefs and a sense of belonging.

One thing clearly emerges from this study: some kinds of group cohesion are identifiable in the regions of early medieval western Europe considered here, but they do not fit into a simple framework. And they certainly do not prefigure the structured and integrated communities of the later Middle Ages – whose place-based determinants contrast with developments before and after.[7] There is very little in the chapters above to suggest that group cohesion functioned within a single settlement, although residents could be identified by location; nor to suggest the single settlement as a unit of organisation. Cross-settlement networks are more significant.

Cross-settlement networks raise the questions of range and scale. For ease of reference, and consistency, we have used the convention of referring to the residents of a space of the order of 10-km diameter as a 'locality', that of the order of 30-km diameter as a 'micro-region' and that in the range of 80–150-km diameter, such as Tuscany and Galicia, as a 'region' (see figure 0.1). We stress that these are simply conventions; we do not imagine that 10-km, 30-km or 80-km units were any kind of norm; everywhere had a range of variations. There are several regions, however, in which an area the size of a locality was a meaningful unit of operation: the zone dependent on a baptismal church in Tuscany, with its several settlements and sometimes several churches, might be 3, 5, 10 or even 14 km across, depending on terrain and local circumstances;[8] the zone served by a priest in Bavaria might be very small indeed, but that served from a

---

5   *Concerted Development of Social Cohesion Indicators: Methodological Guide* (Strasbourg: Council of Europe, 2005), p. 23.
6   See A. Green, G. Janmaat and H. Cheng, 'Social cohesion: converging and diverging trends', *National Institute Economic Review*, 215 (2011), 6–22.
7   See above, pp. 8–9, 10.
8   See above, pp. 133, 156; M. Stoffella, 'Local priests in early medieval rural Tuscany', in S. Patzold and C. van Rhijn (eds), *Men in the Middle. Local Priests in Early Medieval Europe* (Berlin: De Gruyter, 2016), pp. 98–124. For a useful set of maps of Italian territories of this kind, see C. J. Wickham, *The Mountains and the City. The Tuscan Appennines in the Early Middle Ages* (Oxford: Clarendon Press, 1988), pp. 384–9, here 'pieval territories'.

baptismal church up to 8 km or more;[9] the zone served by the priests of the *plebs* in ninth-century Brittany was characteristically 6 or 7 km across, though it could be smaller or (rarely) twice the size.[10] There was variation, everywhere, in the size of these pastoral zones but the locality constituted a meaningful unit for the baptised. The locality, not the single settlement: all of these zones included several settlements.

The locality was also meaningful in other respects. In England the administrative and judicial unit of the hundred, which had a monthly court and through which responsibilities for peace-keeping were organised, was often of the order of 7 to 10 km across, although there were some much larger hundreds.[11] If Eythorne lay at the limit of the hundred, 7 km away from its functional centre at Eastry, then this suggests its scale in the ninth century.[12] From Catalonia comes evidence of the size of group deemed suitable to provide an oath in support of a monastery: here, in 913, 493 people (including 242 women) from the Vall de Sant Joan swore in support of the abbess of Sant Joan, all of their names being recorded on a single surviving parchment. The valley was about 10 km long and included twenty-one settlements.[13] And the Breton *plebs*, where civic functions were defined in relation to the *plebs*, fits the locality pattern too (see figure 8.1). The fact that it had associated secular institutions is not in itself so different from the hundred in later tenth-century England, although neither the institutions nor the source of their authority were the same. It is difficult to find evidence of comparabilities elsewhere and they may not have existed at this date. For example, northern Spain is an exception in several respects: there are a few settlements with associated *concilia* in the later tenth century. Those that had such associations were on the way to the institutionalisation of community

---

9 See T. Kohl, *Lokale Gesellschaften. Formen der Gemeinschaft in Bayern vom 8. bis zum 10. Jahrhundert* (Ostfildern: Thorbecke, 2010), esp. pp. 128–32, 267–9, maps pp. 208, 213, 218; T. Kohl, '*Presbyter in parochia sua*: local priests and their churches in early medieval Bavaria', in Patzold and van Rhijn (eds), *Men in the Middle*, pp. 50–77, at pp. 73–7, map p. 51.
10 W. Davies, *Small Worlds. The Village Community in Early Medieval Brittany* (London: Duckworth, 1988), p. 65.
11 See above, pp. 102–3.
12 See above, pp. 165–6; not cited as a hundred until the eleventh century.
13 J. Jarrett, *Rulers and Ruled in Frontier Catalonia, 880–1010: Pathways of Power* (Woodbridge: Boydell Press, 2010), pp. 34–42. There are inconsistencies, and errors, in recording the names, but the point remains that the abbess wanted the people from that zone to swear in support of her case.

decision-making.[14] While there is no way of assessing how many lesser settlements fell within the sphere of any one *concilium*, it is observable that Melgar, whose *concilium* was noted in 979, already had bounds cited in 950–67 which were 5 km from the main settlement, and it had settlements sited within its 'territory' in 964; people from several different settlements witnessed a major gift of property there in 959, including both smaller settlements from the neighbourhood of Melgar and larger settlements some 20 km distant.[15] Two of those larger settlements had their own legal officers, *saiones*; this might suggest that functioning centres in this area served 20-km zones, larger than a locality, as it also suggests that those officers had a competence wider than that of the locality. On the whole, the scale of association in northern Iberia appears to have been wider than any 10-km model, and judicial courts, which had no association with *concilia*, appear to have served areas significantly larger than that of the locality.

Breton practice has sometimes seemed different because functions focused on the village, a clearly nucleated settlement, usually with a church. But the village was not the only settlement in the *plebs*: there was a multiplicity of other, smaller settlements, whose residents were all *plebenses*. For example, in the ninth century there were at least thirty separate settlements within the *plebs* of Ruffiac but outside the *plebs* centre, and sub-districts of the *plebs* were identified: the villa of Loutinoc (the modern hamlet of Lodineu) lay in Lerniaco in the *plebs* of Ruffiac; Ranlouuinid was a villa that lay in Trebetuual in the *plebs* of Ruffiac.[16]

There is plenty of good evidence of group action, of one kind or another, and it is perfectly clear that different households could come together for agricultural purposes or to take legal action, whether by locality or settlement. As we have seen, in England a shift towards more intensive arable production meant that in some parts of the south midlands, arable fields began to be managed in strips in the later tenth century. This does not mean that open-field farming became a norm but it does imply that some farmers were cooperating for agricultural purposes.[17] Resources could also be shared between several households – woods,

14   See above, p. 105.
15   S 298, S 126, S 219, S 164 (all on single sheets).
16   CR 155 (830): 'villam Loutinoc sitam in condita plebe Rufiaco in loco nuncupante Lerniaco'; CR 152 (829–30): 'villam Rannlouuinid sitam in condita Rufiaco in loco nuncupante Trebetuual'. Some of the thirty look like isolated farms.
17   See above, p. 77.

water, grazing – as examples from England, the Ardennes, the Rhineland, around Lake Zurich, Bavaria and Spain all testify.[18] Households cooperated at the 'pinch points' of the agricultural year – harvest time, especially, but also in cases of disastrous climatic events such as flood and famine. And when tenants had regular obligations to landlords, especially from 900 onwards, collective ploughing and harvesting, and sometimes spinning and weaving, became common.[19] This does not mean that all members of all settlements engaged in collective agricultural practices, nor indeed that all members of any one settlement did, but it does mean that some households shared work in some circumstances.

It is also perfectly clear that households, or their heads, did sometimes join together to take or oppose legal action. In Francia there are early legal prescriptions requiring witnesses to be neighbours and there are some famous cases of groups of tenants opposing landlord demands – with equally famous 'odious backstabbing' by some of their neighbours.[20] Beyond Francia the residents of settlements in both Italy and Iberia came together in court to oppose landowner aggression – whether residents from a single named place or from a group of settlements.[21] In England, there is plentiful evidence of action by and against individuals in the context of the hundred court, but group action is more difficult to detect. In Brittany judicial process was organised at the – not uncomparable – level of the *plebs*; here it is clear that neither all residents of the central village nor all members of the *plebs* participated in any one set of judicial proceedings, as it is also clear that here too individual action is more evident than group action. Nevertheless, it is probably reasonable to suppose that the free *plebenses* recognised and supported the system.[22] There is no good evidence that groups of tenants (or dependants) were any more or less likely to associate for any of these purposes than groups of free peasant proprietors.

It is worth asking if differences in group behaviour are detectable on the basis of topography. Where there is credible evidence of group action that can be related to a precise locality, a group defined by a collective term, such as *plebs* or *concilium* or *collacio*, might be found in any kind of landscape, from the uplands (at 1,100 metres) of the Pardomino *plebes*

18 See above, pp. 83-4.
19 See above, pp. 88, 92-3.
20 See above, pp. 99-101, 206-7.
21 See above, pp. 194-5, 196.
22 See above, pp. 104, 197.

to the undulating landscapes of the eastern Breton *plebes* to the plateau valley of the Melgar *concilium*.[23] Where there is evidence of collective action involving building a church or making a group gift, then such groups tended to live on the plains or in rolling hills, such as the people of Dauendorf and of Marche-en-Famennes.[24] Where there is evidence of collective legal action – whether a group taken to court and fighting back, or a group consenting to transactions – then such groups tended to live in the uplands, such as Limonta and Oulx, or in undulating lands of mixed farming and plenty of arable, such as San Juan en Vega.[25] There is, then, nothing in the material surveyed to support the view that residential groups only developed any sense of group interest when they lived in open lands with predominantly arable farming. It is also useful to remember that discord and faction could occur within a group as well as joint action: we have only to look at the case of Courtisols, lying in the plains of Champagne, or Mitry farther west in the Paris basin, to be reminded of this.[26] Dissenting voices might be heard anywhere, as they clearly were in Breton communities, despite their strong sense of identity and their communal institutions.

As for shared values and beliefs, as demonstrated in Chapter 5, in the many areas with a network of local priests under the direction of a bishop, the duty of pastoral care necessarily meant that the same Christian message and the same exhortations to good behaviour and to care for neighbours were heard by every flock; the sphere of responsibility of the local priest (or group of priests) defined a community, many of whose members would meet and share the experience of regular and irregular public rituals. There were areas, such as northern Iberia, where ministry was neither so finely structured nor so explicitly inspected as it was in, for example, the Carolingian Empire, but even here the same messages were conveyed and values shared – as is quite clearly indicated by donations from individual peasants. Of course, we do not have to suppose that the message was always conveyed in perfect form, nor that everyone listened – in any area – as we see from the examples of priests who failed or who pursued self and/or family interest: the famous case of Trisingus associates priests

23 See above, pp. 70, 98, 104, 204 . The seven Pardomino *plebes* lie in a zone of at least 8 km diameter; there is no reason to suppose they were like Breton *plebes*. Italian *pievi*, areas dependent on a baptismal church, occupied all kinds of landscape.
24 See above, p. 98.
25 See above, pp. 81–2, 83, 105, 194–5.
26 See above, pp. 206–7.

with sexual impropriety, drunkenness and assault.[27] Nevertheless, reinforced by the practical priestly functions of lending, recording and translating, the reach of the local priest(s), particularly the priest of a baptismal church, shaped a community of a kind.[28]

As argued in Chapter 5, local priests were 'hinge people'; they brought knowledge of a world beyond the settlement to local residents and brought them into contact with individuals from that wider world. So too did the wide variety of officers with whom many locals interacted, as demonstrated in Chapter 6. These ranged from officers who collected and managed the payment of rents and dues for both secular and ecclesiastical landlords to office holders answerable to a higher political authority, who were involved in transmitting messages, in the conduct of property transactions and in managing the business of judicial courts, as also to the (sometimes temporary) judicial functions of the Spanish *saio*. These officers had properties themselves, and by their presence, their visits and their greater mobility they linked those whose lives were lived in one place with those who had greater economic resources and higher-level political activity. It is also the case that *centenarii* met and did things together, as did priests and even *saiones*, and such networks spanned localities and functioned in wider geographical arenas, reinforcing the paths of supra-local contact. Two clearly identifiable *centenarii* in the eastern part of the diocese of Freising, in Bavaria, for example, both operated within a zone of about 40-km diameter – undoubtedly at a micro-regional scale, apparently without any territorial distinction between them.[29] Italian *centenarii*, such as Cristiano, clearly operated within a comparable micro-region.[30] There were, however, significant regional differences in the distribution of officers, despite changes over time, with far more – at different levels – in Italy than elsewhere, and far fewer in Spain and Portugal than anywhere else. The number of officers within range, and the frequency of their visits, must have made a difference to the lived lives of peasant farmers: awareness of the world beyond must have been greater in England and Francia, and probably even more so in Italy, than in the Iberian case and perhaps in isolated pockets everywhere, just as the capacity of the world beyond to impact on peasant life must have been greater.

27 Pp. 136–7.
28 See above, pp. 140–8.
29 Kohl, *Lokale Gesellschaften*, pp. 294–9.
30 See above, pp. 156–7.

Within the single settlement, or indeed the locality, there is little to suggest shared beliefs and values beyond those of the Christian message, and the extent of any such sharing is difficult to assess. This is largely a source problem, though shared resistance to attack is sometimes evident, as described most clearly in Regino's account of resistance to the Viking onslaught from the fields and villages around Prüm.[31] Stories are often suggestive, especially the stories of miracle collections, although these are views of peasant values mediated through the perspective of a monastic scriptorium. The story of One Ox preferences cunning over neighbourliness, perhaps reflecting practice in opposition to a dominant Christian value, as also do stories of resistance to Sunday observance and of abandoned children.[32] There is also plenty of theft, its objects ranging from highly desirable precious goods to essential food for the starving: divine intervention against theft in miracle stories; fines and compensations for theft in charters, as began this chapter; normative prescriptions to combat theft in legal collections; formulas for oaths to deny theft. Some people clearly stole from their neighbours, as others fought or assaulted or raped them.[33] These may have been exceptions but they do not encourage us to suppose a shared view of social cohesion in every settlement or every locality. On the other hand, there is evidence of ritual, through which social memory would have been sustained: pre-eminently the rituals of the Christian church, uniting those people of a locality who looked to the baptismal church, but also the rituals associated with tenant obligations, as well as the occasional local feast, binding together, at least intermittently, the tenants of a landowner or the residents of a settlement.[34]

It is also very difficult to find evidence of any awareness of belonging to a group, or indeed of the existence of discrete groups recognisable to external observers, such as feature in eighth-century texts from England but disappear in later discourse – groups with names such as *Gyruii* and *Feppingas*.[35] Groups of people could be identified by listing personal names, a common Iberian practice, or occasionally by using a collective

---

31 See above, pp. 186–7.
32 See above, pp. 91; 90, 117.
33 For examples, see Davies, *Windows on Justice*, pp. 182–3, 191–9.
34 See above, pp. 128–31; 46, 91, 93.
35 HE III. 20, III. 21. See the many proper names of this type, including these two, in the so-called 'Tribal Hidage'; J. Blair, 'The Tribal Hidage', in M. Lapidge, J. Blair, S. Keynes and D. Scragg (eds), *The Wiley Blackwell Encyclopedia of Anglo-Saxon England* (Chichester: John Wiley and Sons, 2nd edn, 2014), pp. 473–5.

term, but using a distinctive proper name was very unusual. Scribes sometimes suggest that all the people of one place did this or that – *omnes de X* – but we do not know how often this represented reality. The normal method of referring to a group of residents, in most regions, was by placename, often literally as 'people of X', *homines de Argengeuve* or *homines de Lemonioni*, although as an external observation this cannot in itself imply any shared sense of belonging between the *homines*.[36] Indeed, while context is sometimes explicit, we do not always know if the place-name referred to a single settlement, a group of settlements or more. In many cases it must have referred to several settlements: in the extremely large estate of Courtisols, for example, it is perfectly clear that there must have been many settlements in the ninth century, just as it had many 'poles of power'.[37] A similar point could be made regarding those places associated with *concilia* on the Spanish *meseta*, such as Melgar – the indications are that members of several settlements participated in collective deliberation, just as happened at meetings of a Breton *plebs*.

Next, we consider insiders and outsiders. Perhaps surprisingly, there are many indications of the integration of immigrants in settlements and localities, especially in England and Iberia, particularly within agricultural communities.[38] The point at which invaders could become legitimate and accepted settlers is obscure, though this clearly did happen, as with the deviant Christian Vikings of Normandy; we can track high-level political agreements, such as Alfred and Guthrum's Peace in late ninth-century England, but we do not know how acceptance was effected at ground level.[39] Besides evidence of inclusion, there are different kinds of evidence of exclusion, from the temporary exclusion of the penitent to the permanent exclusion of the unwanted.[40] The excluded Moors of northern Iberia may for the most part have been captives, or their

---

36 W 527 (867), a royal charter; Sob 129 (942). Despite the comments of T. Lazzari, 'Comunità rurali nell'alto medioevo: pratiche di descrizione e spie lessicali nella documentazione scritta', in P. Galetti (ed.), *Paesaggi, comunità, villaggi medievali*, 2 vols (Spoleto: Fondazione CISAM, 2012), vol. 2, pp. 405–23, at pp. 410–11.
37 See J.-P. Devroey, 'Libres et non-libres sur les terres de Saint-Remi de Reims: la notice judiciaire de Courtisols (13 mai 847) et le polyptyque d'Hincmar', *Journal des Savants* (2006/1), 65–103, at 67–8, 92–3.
38 See above, pp. 110–11, 112–13.
39 See above, pp. 33–4.
40 See above, pp. 131–2. Cf. the formulas for letters to be carried by penitents; for example, the 'Tracturia in perigrinatione' of *Formulae Salicae Lindenbrogianae*, no. 17, in MGH Formulae, pp. 278–9.

descendants – representatives of the adversarial phases of invasion. The possibility that strangers might arrive and be permitted to settle within a group is envisaged by early Frankish law, as also that they might not be so permitted. Although the initiative for exclusion could be individual, as argued strongly above, the decision was essentially a group decision.[41] An act of group exclusion must lie behind the fate of those who ended up in execution cemeteries on boundaries, although we usually cannot know what led to their exclusion – whether as wrongdoer or simply as stranger. It is highly unlikely that every member of a settlement, or locality, or any other group, contributed to the decision to exclude, however, unless it was an extremely small group: we know for certain that there were groupings that did not include all residents and, where decisions were taken on behalf of a community, it was interested and active members who took them rather than all members.[42] And remember thieves: a major concern for rule makers, storytellers and victims. While it might seem simple to suppose that all thieves were outsiders, arriving from afar by night, and making a swift getaway if lucky, it is clear from examples such as that with which this chapter began that thieves could be members of the local social group, with parents known and family property available. It is also clear that, once convicted, if not restrained they might range beyond the home group, at once both insider and outsider.

Local priests had a foot in the world beyond but were, for the most part, insiders, members of a local group with local property interests and often with family associations. Secular officers usually would have had similar local and family associations, at least in one part of their zone of operation, but they must have been outsiders in many parts of that zone; outsiders, but familiar outsiders and in many cases tolerated, though by no means always.[43] Once again, the insider/outsider dichotomy is complex, overlapping and multi-layered: outsiders were welcomed, opposed and tolerated, and they could mediate between local people and distant interests; insiders could be excluded.

Lastly, the insights that come from comparison. At macro level, it is obvious that relationships between political leaders and local groups could vary enormously. The kind of attention paid by Carolingian rulers

---

41 See above, pp. 110, 114–15.
42 See above, p. 214, and Davies, *Windows on Justice*, pp. 213–15.
43 For conflicts between local residents and officers, see above, pp. 108–9, 161–2, 199–201.

and Carolingian bishops to the lives of their peasant subjects is not echoed by the actions of Spanish rulers or bishops: life in a farming settlement in northern Iberia must have been free from that kind of micro-management, although peasants probably heard the same moral messages from their priests. England, especially in the tenth century, was more comparable to the Carolingian world in this respect, and Italy even more so, with a greater range of officers to put prescription into effect. Brittany shared Carolingian attention for a short period in the ninth century but was dissimilar for most of our period.

Landlord impact was in some ways more similar between regions and in some ways more diverse. In every region there was land worked for landlords in the context of large estates and also land worked by free peasant proprietors or leaseholders.[44] Landlords did not always dominate: free peasants existed and in some regions they determined the character of discrete areas. We do not usually know the proportions of estate land to free, although we can see that areas such as the Frankish heartland, and to a lesser extent Galicia, had a high proportion of large estates. Diversity was itself a norm. But that very fact means that landlord presence and landlord power could be as significant in parts of northern Iberia as it was in parts of England, Francia or Italy, just as it means that the intervention of landlords' agents and the power of patronage were irrelevant in free peasant zones, whether in Spain or Francia.

There is no basis for suggesting any regional differences in group behaviour at a local level, other than the collaboration required for military purposes in the Frankish, and to some extent the English, worlds.[45] Stable institutions for the conduct of local lay business are rare in this period, with the notable regional exceptions of Brittany in the ninth century, England in the tenth and the early steps towards institutionalisation in a few parts of later tenth-century Spain. We do not often find established structures of local association anywhere in western Europe in this period. People came to meetings as and when business impelled them.

We end, as we began, with diversity – between regions, within regions, within micro-regions, within localities, within settlements – association and discord, shared tasks and individual enterprise, peasants

---

44 See above, pp. 70–3; J.-P. Devroey and A. Wilkin (eds), *Autour de Yoshiki Morimoto. Les structures agricoles en dehors du monde carolingien, formes et genèse* (Brussels: Le Livre Timperman, 2012).

45 See above, pp. 188–91

and aristocrats, insiders and outsiders. There was no single kind of association nor line of development in western Europe in the early Middle Ages. Evidence for social cohesion within single settlements or larger units is extremely limited, as is evidence of any awareness of group identity. That does not mean that no one collaborated: rather, people joined together in different kinds of group, for different purposes, across larger and smaller areas. In some regions, for some purposes, the locality was a meaningful unit of association, as it could be for pastoral and judicial purposes, and in other regions wider units could perform those roles. Groups might in any case overlap and some associations were played out through networks – networks of priests and of local lay officers are especially notable, but people of lesser status collaborated through networks too, most obviously networks of family connections. Collective action certainly happened, particularly for agricultural or legal purposes, but we should not assume that all residents participated nor that the collectivity remained active across many years. And there is nothing to suggest that group identity crystallised in areas of predominantly arable farming nor that it failed do so in other kinds of landscape. As for common values, there is good evidence of their existence in the delivery of the Christian message and in the sustained efforts to support that message across very wide areas, although there are also plenty of indications that in practice every individual did not follow those values and that some valued self-interest above neighbourliness. In the end, despite the norm of the Christian message throughout the areas surveyed here, there were nevertheless some strong regional contrasts in local practice and experience: the attempted micro-management of Frankish rulers in Carolingian times stands alongside the complete absence of any such attempts by Spanish rulers; the plethora of local officers in northern Italy is matched by the paucity of such people in northern Iberia. The worlds of middle men and of rulers could impact very differently on local people: it depended where you were.

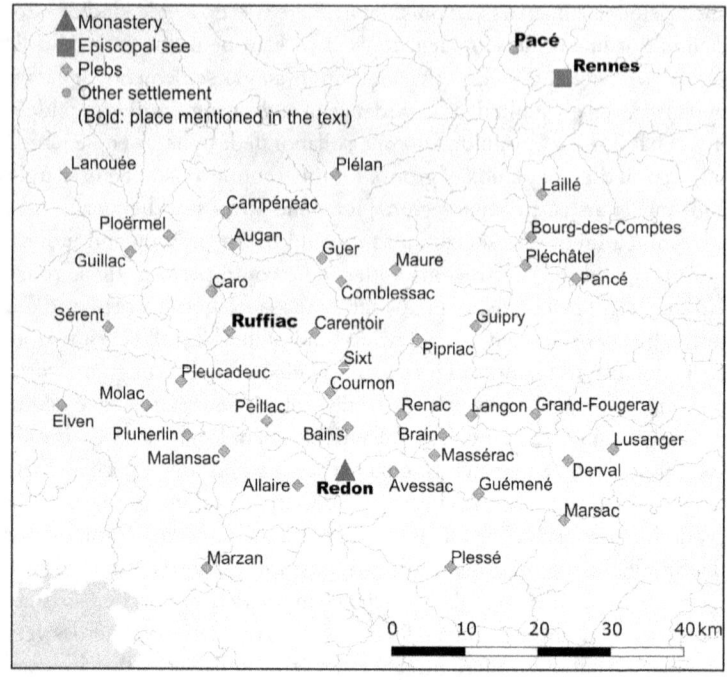

Figure 8.1 Eastern Brittany

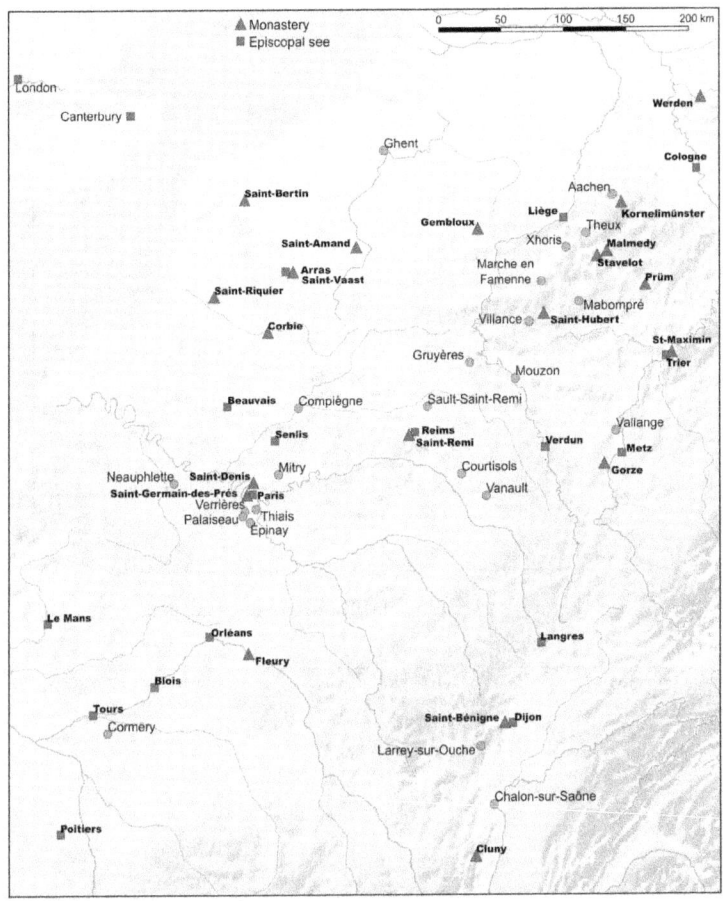

Figure 8.2   Northern France/Belgium

NEIGHBOURS AND STRANGERS

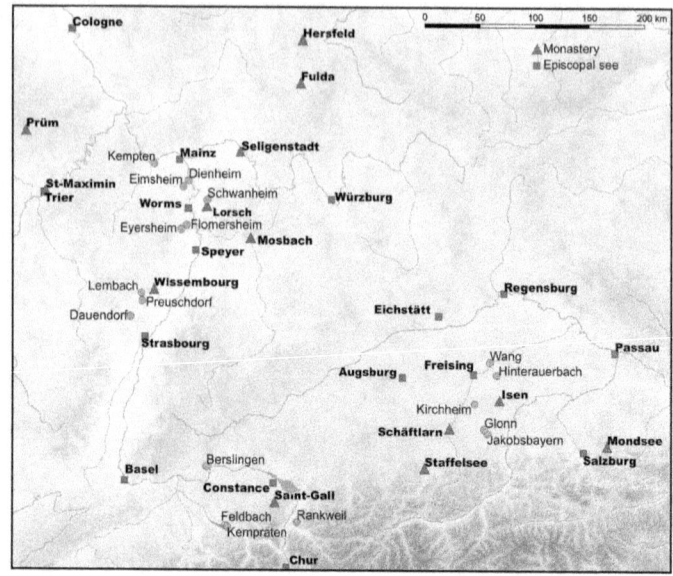

Figure 8.3 Rhineland/Bavaria/Saint-Gall area

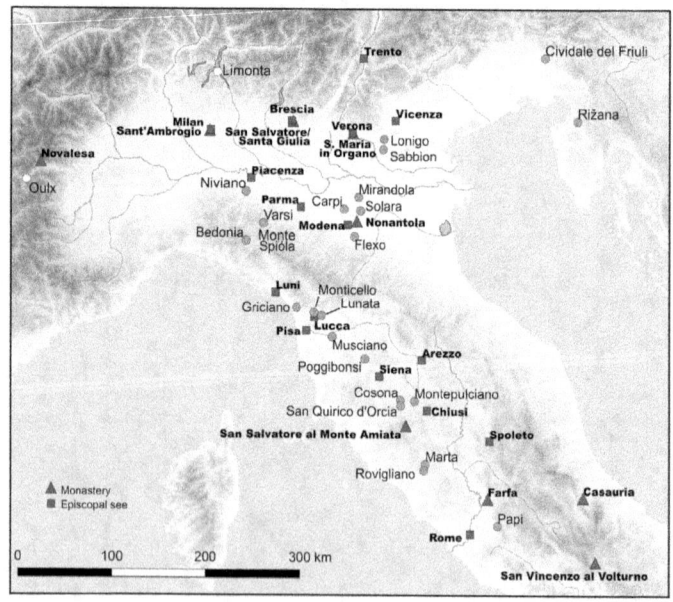

Figure 8.4 Northern Italy

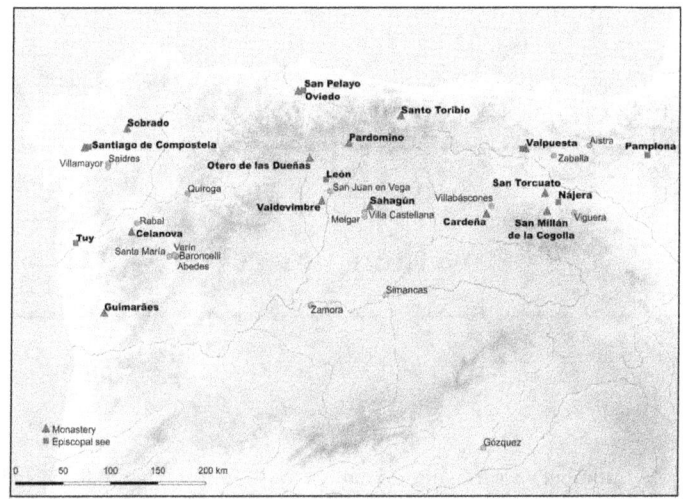

Figure 8.5   Northern Iberia

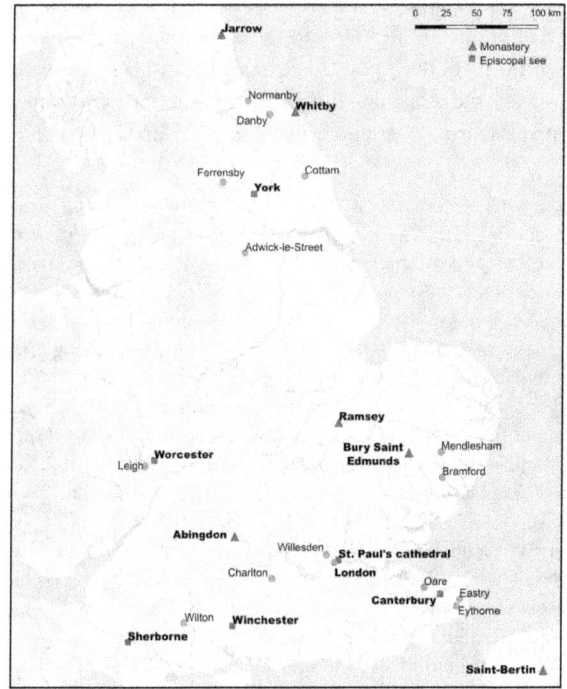

Figure 8.6   England

Appendix: written sources

Charters

The number of surviving private charters from early medieval Italy, whether on single sheets or in cartularies, is exceptional. There are about 7,500 documents from northern and central Italy, from the years between c. 680 and 1000, that were not issued by a public authority;[1] yet more involve public authorities and there are many more from southern Italy.[2] Two-thirds of the 7,500 from the north and centre are documents on single sheets, the remaining third coming from cartularies such as those of Farfa and Casauria – over 900 from Casauria.[3] More than half of Tuscan

---

1 F. Bougard, 'Actes privés et transferts patrimoniaux en Italie centro-septentrionale (VIIIe –Xe siècle)', in F. Bougard (ed.), *Les transferts patrimoniaux en Europe occidentale, VIIIe–Xe siècle (I). Actes de la table ronde de Rome, 6, 7 et 8 mai 1999, Mélanges de l'École française de Rome. Moyen-Âge*, 111:2 (1999), pp. 539–62, at p. 539. Northern Italian charters, from 680, in CDL; but see also publications of ChLA, 2nd series, listed at https://www.urs-graf-verlag.com/index.php?funktion=cla_uebersicht.

2 For charters involving a public authority, from 774 onwards, see *I placiti*. For one of the largest southern collections, that of Santissima Trinità at Cava de Tirreni, with 536 charters from late eighth century to 1000, see *Codex Diplomaticus Cavensis*, vols 1–3 of 12 vols, ed. M. Morcaldi et al. (Naples: Piazzi, 1873–76).

3 Gregory of Catino, *Regestum Farfense*, in *Regesto di Farfa*, ed. I Giorgi and U. Balzani, 5 vols (Rome: R. Società di Storia Patria, 1879–1914); *Liber instrumentorum seu chronicorum monasterii Casauriensis seu Chronicon Casauriense*, ed. A. Pratesi and P. Cherubini, 3 vols (Rome: ISIME, 2017–18); see L. Feller, 'Le cartulaire-chronique de San Clemente a Casauria', in O. Guyotjeannin, L. Morelle and M. Parisse (eds), *Les cartulaires* (Paris: Droz et H. Champion, 1993), pp. 261–77. See also M. Costambeys, 'The laity, the clergy, the scribes and their

charters come from the single diocese of Lucca, with over 1,800 pre-eleventh-century documents, mostly on single sheets, this being the largest Italian repository.[4] In southern Tuscany the archive of San Salvatore al Monte Amiata, now at the State Archive of Siena, is one of the richest, including nearly 220 original charters.[5] Many Italian charters were written on parchment by professional writers (both lay and clerical notaries), with witnesses adding their *signum manus* or endorsement in their own hand; this is important because it can allow us to identify the hands of different witnesses, essential for establishing the identity of individuals who appear in different documents.

Outside Italy, a major collection is the 750 or so pre-eleventh-century private charters of the former abbey of Saint-Gall (in modern Switzerland), preserved on early medieval single sheets. The Saint-Gall private charters represent an extraordinary – and for regions north of the Alps unique – collection. They relate to much of early medieval Alemannia and Raetia, that is, to modern Switzerland, southern Germany and western Austria.[6]

archives: the documentary record of eighth and ninth-century Italy', in W. C. Brown, M. Costambeys, M. Innes and A. J. Kosto (eds), *Documentary Culture and the Laity in the Early Middle Ages* (Cambridge: Cambridge University Press, 2013), pp. 231–58, at pp. 237–43.

4 On Lucca's ecclesiastical archives, see H. Schwarzmaier, *Lucca und das Reich bis zum Ende des XI. Jahrhunderts. Studien zur Sozialstruktur einer Herzogsstadt in der Toskana* (Tübingen: Niemeyer, 1972); A. Mailloux, 'Modalités de constitution du patrimoine épiscopal de Lucques, VIIIe–Xe siècle', in Bougard (ed.), *Les transferts patrimoniaux*, pp. 701–23; S. M. Pagano and P. Piatti (eds), *Il patrimonio documentario della Chiesa di Lucca: Prospettive di ricerca* (Florence: SISMEL, 2010). See also Costambeys, 'The laity, the clergy, the scribes and their archives'; M. Mersiowsky, *Die Urkunde in der Karolingerzeit. Originale, Urkundenpraxis und politische Kommunikation*, 2 vols (Wiesbaden: Harrassowitz, 2015), vol. I, pp. 360–1.

5 F. Bougard, *La justice dans le royaume d'Italie de la fin du VIIIe siècle au début du XIIe siècle* (Rome: École française de Rome, 1995), pp. 95–102; CDMA.

6 W; ChLA 100–111. See H. Fichtenau, *Das Urkundenwesen in Österreich vom 8. bis zum frühen 13. Jahrhundert* (Vienna/Cologne/Graz: Böhlau, 1971), pp. 38–55; R. McKitterick, *The Carolingians and the Written Word* (Cambridge: Cambridge University Press, 1989), pp. 76–134; P. Erhart and J. Kleindinst, *Urkundenlandschaft Rätien* (Vienna: Österreichische Akademie der Wissenschaften, 2004); B. Zeller, 'Urkunden und Urkundenschreiber des Klosters St. Gallen bis ca. 840', and K. Heidecker, 'Urkunden schreiben im alemannischen Umfeld des Klosters St. Gallen', both in P. Erhart, K. Heidecker and B. Zeller (eds), *Die Privaturkunden der Karolingerzeit* (Dietikon-Zurich: Urs Graf, 2009), pp. 173–82, 183–92.

APPENDIX

The 1,300 pre-eleventh-century charters of the episcopal see of Freising in Bavaria are comparable, although these have been transmitted in copies collected in early medieval cartularies. The earliest surviving manuscript of a cartulary contains about 570 records and was composed in the first half of the ninth century by the priest Cozroh.[7] From Fulda in the Rhine-Main region, approximately the same number of charters has survived, although only two of the ten books of Fulda's original ninth-century cartulary have been preserved.[8] There is a smaller collection of documents in the Liber Traditionum of Wissembourg in Alsace, compiled in the 860s. It has about 270 charters and, like the two volumes of the Fulda cartulary, contains only part of the original monastic collection.[9] Other examples come from the monasteries and episcopal churches of Passau, Mondsee, Schäftlarn and Regensburg in Bavaria, and Werden in the Rhineland. In Freising a codex recording exchanges was also made.[10] Many early medieval charter collections from north of the Alps, such as the charters from Lorsch, Stavelot-Malmedy and Gorze, are contained in later cartularies; that of Gorze was destroyed in 1944, which means that we are dependent on a nineteenth-century edition to access its contents.[11]

7 TF; A. Krah, 'Die Handschrift des Cozroh: Einblicke in die kopiale Überlieferung der verlorenen ältesten Archivbestände des Hochstifts Freising', *Archivalische Zeitschrift*, 89 (2007), 407–31; H. Hummer, 'The production and preservation of documents in Francia: the evidence of cartularies', in Brown et al. (eds), *Documentary Culture*, pp. 189–230, at pp. 193–201.

8 UBF; CDF. See also the twelfth-century digest of the Fulda cartulary: H. Meyer zu Ermgassen, *Der Codex Eberhardi des Klosters Fulda*, 4 vols (Marburg: Elwert, 1995–2009); Hummer, 'The production', p. 193.

9 TW; F. Staab, 'Noch einmal zur Diplomatik der Weißenburger Traditionen', *Archiv für mittelrheinische Kirchengeschichte*, 44 (1992), 311–22; L. A. Doll, 'Ist die Diplomatik der Weißenburger Urkunden geklärt? Eine Erwiderung auf Franz Staab, Noch einmal zur Diplomatik der Weißenburger Traditionen', *Archiv für mittelrheinische Kirchengeschichte*, 45 (1993), 439–47; Hummer, 'The production'.

10 *Die Traditionen des Hochstiftes Passau*, ed. M. Heuwieser (Munich: Rieger, 1930); TR; *Die Traditionen des Klosters Schäftlarn 760–1305*, ed. A. Weissthanner (Munich: Beck, 1953); *De oudste particuliere oorkonden van het klooster Werden: een diplomatische studie met enige uitweidingen over het ontstaan van dit soort oorkonden in het algemeen*, ed. D. P. Blok (Assen: Van Gorcum, 1960); *Das älteste Traditionsbuch des Klosters Mondsee*, ed. G. Rath and E. Reiter (Linz: Oberösterreichisches Landesarchiv, 1989); Hummer, 'The production', pp. 191–3.

11 CL; *Cartulaire de l'abbaye de Gorze. Ms. 826 de la Bibliothèque de Metz*, ed. A. D'Herbomez (Paris: Klincksieck, 1898); HR.

APPENDIX

Nowhere demonstrates the value of nineteenth-century editions and of transcripts made by early modern antiquaries better than does the region that became France. Fewer single sheets survive from west Francia than east Francia, because of exceptional levels of archival destruction at the time of the French Revolution, but the texts of thousands of charters survive in important seventeenth- and eighteenth-century transcripts, many of which were published in the nineteenth-century series Collection de Documents inédits sur l'Histoire de France, often now available online.[12] These include transcripts of cartularies and of collections of charters embedded in *Gesta Abbatum*, such as those of Saint-Bertin copied by Folquin in 962.[13] The archives of the monastery of Cluny in Burgundy were once vast, Lambert de Barive copying about 5,000 records in the late eighteenth century; 300 single sheets remain and texts of 1,941 charters from pre-994 relating to Cluny are available.[14] Indeed, Burgundian charters constitute 30 per cent of the 11,353 French charters available from the period 600–999, however they be preserved.[15] Charters from the monastery of Saint-Denis, in present-day Paris, constitute another major

12 For original French charters of pre-1121, see the ARTEM database: http://www.cn-telma.fr//originaux/index/ (accessed 4 September 2019). See also B.-M. Tock, 'L'acte privé en France, VIIe siècle – milieu du Xe siècle', *Mélanges de l'École française de Rome. Moyen Âge*, 111 (1999), 499–537; M. Innes, 'Archives, documents and landowners in Carolingian Francia', in Brown et al. (eds), *Documentary Culture*, pp. 152–88, at pp. 173–88.

13 *Cartulaire de l'abbaye de Saint-Bertin*, ed. M. Guérard (Paris: Imprimerie royale, 1840); R. F. Berkhofer III, *Day of Reckoning: Power and Accountability in Medieval France* (Philadelphia, PA: University of Pennsylvania Press, 2004), pp. 18–19.

14 *Recueil des chartes de l'abbaye de Cluny*, ed. A. Bernard and A. Bruel, 6 vols (Paris: Imprimerie Nationale, 1876–1903); *Les plus anciens documents originaux de l'abbaye de Cluny*, vols 1–3, ed. H. Atsma, S. Barret and J. Vezin (Brepols: Turnhout, 1997–2002). See B. H. Rosenwein, *To be the Neighbor of Saint Peter: The Social Meaning of Cluny's Property, 909–1049* (Ithaca, NY: Cornell University Press, 1989), pp. 14–20.

15 The numbers relate to modern France, including Lorraine and Alsace; there are 1,213 'originals'. Grateful thanks to Nicolas Perreaux, who supplied them (21 December 2017) from the database *Cartae Europeae Medii Aevi* (*CEMA*), compiled during his doctoral study, 'L'écriture du monde. Dynamique, perception, catégorisation du mundus au Moyen Âge (VIIe–XIIIe siècles). Recherche à partir de bases de données numérisées', Université de Bourgogne, Dijon, 2014; see N. Perreaux, 'L'écriture du monde (I)', *Bulletin du centre d'études médiévales d'Auxerre | BUCEMA*, 19.2 (2015), doi: 10.4000/cem.14264, http://journals.openedition.org/cem/14264 (accessed 27 June 2018).

collection, with 267 pre-eleventh-century texts preserved on single sheets (including some papyri), in cartularies and in other kinds of source such as the *Gesta Dagoberti* and a ninth-century formulary; royal patronage of Saint-Denis means that many of these documents, which include a famous series of forgeries, are of supposed royal or imperial origin, although they include private charters too, such as those of 797 and 832-33.[16] Other collections derive from eleventh-century and later cartularies, *gesta*, narratives, formularies and inventories: for example, eighth- and ninth-century private charters from the lost early eleventh-century cartulary of Perrecy in Burgundy survive in later cartularies from Fleury; and La Grasse, in the far south-west, south of Carcassonne, has 86 pre-eleventh-century charters (including *faux*) culled from miscellaneous sources.[17] The eleventh-century cartulary of the monastery of Redon, however, survives, except for nearly fifty missing folios, and contains 283 (mostly private) charters of the ninth or early tenth centuries and five post-1000 records; a further 103 charters, including two of the tenth century, were added by later hands; and another 62 ninth-century Redon charters are known from early modern transcripts and are believed to derive from the missing folios of the original cartulary.[18]

The corpus of charters from Catalonia constitutes over 6,000 pre-eleventh-century documents, in cartularies and on single sheets, from Pallars and Ribagorça in the west to Barcelona on the Mediterranean coast, largely of the ninth and tenth centuries.[19] From the rest of northern

16 See D. Sonzogni, 'Le chartrier de l'abbaye de Saint-Denis en France au haut Moyen Âge: essai de reconstitution', *Pecia*, 3 (2003), 9–210, and D. Sonzogni, *Les actes du fonds d'archives de Saint-Denis, VIe-Xe siècle: étude critique et catalogue raisonné* (2016–17), nos 147, 176, http://saint-denis.enc.sorbonne.fr/les-textes/actes-du-haut-moyen-age/introduction.html (accessed 27 June 2018); a long series of papers by Hartmut Atsma and Jean Vezin unravelled the *faux*, e.g. 'Le dossier suspect des possessions de Saint-Denis en Angleterre revisité (VIIIe-IXe siècle)', in *Fälschungen im Mittelalter*, 5 vols (Hanover, 1988), vol. 4, *Diplomatische Fälschungen* (II), pp. 211–36.

17 *Recueil des chartes de l'abbaye de Saint-Benoît-sur-Loire*, ed. M. Prou and A. Vidier, 2 vols (Paris: Picard, 1900–12); see Innes, 'Archives, documents and landowners', pp. 173–82. *Recueil des chartes de l'abbaye de La Grasse*, vol. 1 (779–1119), ed. E. Magnou-Nortier and A.-M. Magnou (Paris: Comité des travaux historiques et scientifiques, 1996).

18 CR; facsimile in *Cartulaire de l'abbaye Saint-Sauveur de Redon* (Rennes: Amis des Archives historiques du diocèse de Rennes, Dol et Saint-Malo, 1998).

19 There is no single modern edition of Catalan charters, although the *Catalunya Carolíngia* series of separate volumes, in progress since 1926, aims to publish all

Iberia, excluding Catalonia, about 2,700 pre-eleventh-century charters have survived from different collections, in cartulary copies or on single sheets. The largest surviving collections, which include many single sheets, are those of the episcopal and diocesan archives of León, with nearly 600 pre-eleventh-century records, while that of the monastery of Sahagún has nearly 400 records on single sheets and in a cartulary.[20] Other important large collections, in cartularies, come from the monasteries of Celanova and Sobrado in Galicia,[21] Cardeña in Castile and San Millán de la Cogolla in La Rioja.[22] The corpus of charters from Portugal is also significant, and includes 236 records on single sheets and in cartularies, from many different episcopal and monastic sources.[23] Beyond that there are smaller collections from across the north. Some of these are especially important, such as those from the monastery of Santo Toribio on the edge of the Liébana valley in the far north, in an early fourteenth-century cartulary which includes a significant proportion of ninth-century charters (77 pre-1000); from the cathedral of Oviedo and the monastery of San Pelayo beside it (with single sheets in both collections, 34 and 26 records respectively); 49 charters from Otero de las Dueñas on the northern edge of the *meseta* – very important because virtually all of its pre-eleventh-century charters are original single sheets from lay archives; and 47 records from Valpuesta in Castile (in two cartularies, of which the earlier includes folios written in tenth-century hands).[24] Although there are a few charters from the Visigothic period and the eighth century, and 200 from the ninth century, the majority are of the tenth century.

Extant Anglo-Saxon charters comprise about 1,500 documents, dating from the seventh century to the Norman Conquest of 1066; of these, approximately 300 survive as single sheets, while the others are known through later medieval and modern copies, mostly contained in monastic

---

pre-1000 charters (Barcelona: Institut d'Estudis Catalans) – e.g. two volumes on the counties of Pallars and Ribagorça, published in 1955. There are many different editions of individual (part) collections, and many sets of charters published in, for example, the journal *Urgellia. Anuari d'estudis històrics dels antics comtats de Cerdanya, Urgell i Pallars, d'Andorra i la Vall d'Aran.*

20 Li, Lii, Liii; S.
21 Cel; Sob.
22 C; SM, BG.
23 PMH DC.
24 T; Ov; OvC; OD; V.

cartularies.[25] The two oldest Anglo-Saxon cartularies (and fragments of a third) come from Worcester cathedral and were compiled in the eleventh century; there are many later cartularies, of which those originating from Abingdon, Sherborne, Wilton and Winchester are especially important.[26] Cartularies of the later Middle Ages and early modern period, for example those from Burton, Crowland, St Paul's (London) and Muchelney, often provide unique witness to Anglo-Saxon texts.[27]

The earliest surviving examples of Anglo-Saxon charters are royal diplomas, in Latin, dating from the late seventh century. Royal diplomas constitute roughly 1,000 of the extant Anglo-Saxon documents. A further 100 are Old English royal writs (largely dating from the eleventh century and comparable to the continental mandate, that is, an instruction to royal officials). Anglo-Saxon private charters were clearly influenced by royal diplomas; the earliest surviving examples are in Latin but later private documents were increasingly written partly or entirely in Old English. They consist of roughly eighty grants by the laity and 150 grants by bishops; remaining documents include wills, leases, memoranda, records of disputes and agreements.[28]

Estate records

The polyptyque of the Parisian monastery of Saint-Germain-des-Prés ('Irminon's Polyptyque'), which was compiled on the orders of Abbot Irminon during the 820s, is the oldest and most detailed of the ninth-century polyptyques and has partly survived in a ninth-century copy; part was destroyed in a fire in the eighteenth century. It describes the

---

25 For individual charters, see Sawyer. For cartularies, the standard reference work is G. R. C. Davis, *Medieval Cartularies of Great Britain and Ireland* (London: Longmans, Green, 1958), rev. C. Breay, J. Harrison and D. M. Smith (London: British Library, 2010).

26 See F. Tinti, *Sustaining Belief: The Church of Worcester from c. 870 to c. 1100* (Farnham: Ashgate, 2010), pp. 85–150; Davis, *Medieval Cartularies*, pp. 1–2, 179–80, 210, 211–14.

27 Davis, *Medieval Cartularies*, pp. 22–3, 61–2, 119–20, 137.

28 S. Kelly, 'Anglo-Saxon lay society and the written word', in R. McKitterick (ed.), *The Uses of Literacy in Early Medieval Europe* (Cambridge: Cambridge University Press, 1990), pp. 36–62; S. Keynes, 'Royal government and the written word in late Anglo-Saxon England', in McKitterick (ed.), *The Uses of Literacy*, pp. 226–57; C. Insley, 'Archives and lay documentary practice in the Anglo-Saxon world', in Brown et al. (eds), *Documentary Culture*, pp. 336–62.

holdings of the monastery, namely twenty-five villas, comprising 1,700 *mansi* of land and woods, and it provides not only the tenants' names, but also their social status and family relationships.[29] The set of dossiers from Saint-Remi in Reims, including extracts from a polyptyque made while Hincmar was archbishop of Reims (845–82) and abbot of this monastery, describes estates in the region of Reims and Champagne. The polyptyque of Prüm, composed in 893 by the monks of the local monastery, is extant in a thirteenth-century copy. It concerns estates situated in a wide area, from the north Rhine to beyond Metz and from Verdun to Worms, roughly 120 small estates that covered about 1,750 *mansi* of land.[30]

Several of the Italian polyptyques relate to Tuscany, and to Lucca in particular.[31] The polyptyque of Santa Giulia di Brescia, in Lombardy, is particularly interesting, though incomplete, and survives as twelve parchment sheets sewn together, written by three ninth- or tenth-century scribes; the text must have been compiled at some point after 879 and a dorsal note cites a date of 906; what survives covers eighty-five widely scattered estates (*curtes* and *curticellae*).[32]

29 A *mansus* was a unit of land, comparable to the hide, sufficient to support a household. *Polyptyque de l'abbé Irminon*, ed. B. Guérard, 2 vols (Paris: L'imprimerie royale, 1844); *Polyptyque de l'Abbaye de Saint-Germain-des-Prés rédigé au temps de l'abbé Irminon*, ed. A. Longnon, 2 vols (Paris: Champion, 1895); *Das Polyptychon von Saint-Germain-des-Prés*, ed. D. Hägermann (Cologne: Böhlau, 1993); J.-P. Devroey, 'Problèmes de critique autour du polyptyque de l'abbaye de Saint-Germain-des-Prés', in H. Atsma (ed.), *La Neustrie. Les pays au nord de la Loire de 650 à 850*, 2 vols (Sigmaringen: Thorbecke, 1989), vol. 1, pp. 441–65.

30 *Polyptyque de l'abbaye de Saint-Remi de Reims*, ed. B. Guérard (Paris: L'imprimerie royale, 1853); *Le polyptyque et les listes de cens de l'Abbaye de Saint-Remi de Reims: IX–XI siècles*, ed. J.-P. Devroey (Reims: Académie nationale de Reims, 1984); *Das Prümer Urbar*, ed. I. Schwab (Düsseldorf: Droste, 1983). See University of Leicester homepage of Carolingian polyptyques, https://www.le.ac.uk/hi/polyptyques/ (accessed 4 September 2019).

31 *Inventari del vescovato, della cattedrale e di altre chiese di Lucca*, ed. P. Guidi and E. Pellegrinetti (Rome: Biblioteca Vaticana, 1921), fasc. 2, pp. 13–20; M. Luzzati, 'Lucca', I, in *Inventari altomedievali di terre, coloni e redditi*, ed. A. Castagnetti, M. Luzzati, G. Pasquali and A. Vasina (Rome: ISIME, 1979), pp. 205–24; P. Tomei, 'Un nuovo "polittico" lucchese del IX secolo. Il *breve de multis pensionibus*', *Studi Medievali*, 53:2 (2012), 567–602.

32 'S. Giulia di Brescia', ed. G. Pasquali, in *Inventari altomedievali di terre*, ed. Castagnetti et al., pp. 41–94.

APPENDIX

One collection of the primary records that lie behind the English Domesday Book remains extant in the Exon Domesday, relating to southwest England, which survives in its original form.[33]

Narrative sources

The most important collections of Frankish annals are the Royal Frankish Annals (*Annales Regni Francorum*), written at the Carolingian court and running from the mid-eighth century to 829; the Annals of Saint-Bertin, which cover events in the Carolingian world from a west Frankish perspective, from 830 to 882, partly written by Archbishop Hincmar of Reims; and the multi-authored Annals of Fulda, from an east Frankish perspective, running from 838 to 901.[34] Some sets of annals, such as the so-called Annales Guelferbytani, draw on local sources, combining local information with material drawn from texts originating in political centres.[35] Regino of Prüm's Chronicle, which also contains local information, was more of a universal history than a set of annals, beginning with the Incarnation of Christ and running to 908, drawing upon a wide range of existing written sources and covering the entire history of the Carolingian Empire in some detail; it was probably completed round about 908 when Regino (d. 915) was in Trier.[36] On a different scale, the 'Casus sancti Galli'

---

33   https://www.exondomesday.ac.uk/ (accessed 27 June 2018). This project, led by Professor Julia Crick, Kings College London, is establishing a website that will include a complete digital facsimile, with new codicological and palaeographical descriptions, together with a full new text and translation.

34   *Annales regni Francorum inde a. 741 usque ad a. 829*, ed. F. Kurze, MGH SS rer. Germ. 6 (Hanover: Hahn, 1895); *Les annales de Saint-Bertin*, ed. F. Grat, J. Vielliard and S. Clémencet (Paris: Klincksieck, 1964); *The Annals of St-Bertin*, trans. J. L. Nelson (Manchester: Manchester University Press, 1991); *Annales Fuldenses*, ed. F. Kurze, MGH SS rer. Germ. 7 (Hanover: Hahn, 1891); *The Annals of Fulda*, trans. T. Reuter (Manchester: Manchester University Press, 1992).

35   I. H. Garipzanov, 'Annales Guelferbytani: changing perspectives of a local narrative', in R. Corradini and M. Diesenberger (eds), *Zwischen Niederschrift und Wiederschrift: Frühmittelalterliche Hagiographie und Historiographie im Spannungsfeld von Kompendienüberlieferung und Editionstechnik* (Vienna: Österreichische Akademie der Wissenschaften, 2009), pp. 123-38.

36   *Regino of Prüm, Chronicon*, ed. F. Kurze, MGH SS rer. Germ. [50] (Hanover: Hahn, 1890); trans. S. MacLean, *History and Politics in Late Carolingian and Ottonian Europe. The Chronicle of Regino of Prüm and Adalbert of Magdeburg* (Manchester: Manchester University Press, 2009), pp. 1-60.

were started as a kind of *Gesta Abbatum* by Ratpert of Saint-Gall in the late ninth century and continued by Ekkehard (IV) in the eleventh century in more of a chronicle style.[37] In England the Anglo-Saxon Chronicle, or more properly chronicles, took its form in the reign of King Alfred c. 890-92 and was then developed in different ways at different centres until the later eleventh century, MS E continuing into the mid-twelfth.[38] The Alfredian core drew widely from existing sets of annals and thereby offers access to pre-ninth-century written sources too, although the principal manuscripts made different selections from the available annals.[39]

---

37 Ekkehard IV, *Casus sancti Galli*, ed. H. F. Haefele (Darmstadt: Wissenschaftliche Buchgesellschaft, 3rd edn, 1991).
38 *The Anglo-Saxon Chronicle: A Collaborative Edition*, general ed. D. Dumville and S. Keynes (Cambridge: D. S. Brewer, 1983–); in progress but see especially vols 3-8 (1983-2004) for MSS A, B, C, D, E, F; trans. M. Swanton, *The Anglo-Saxon Chronicles* (London: Phoenix, 1996, rev. edn, 2000).
39 There are seven principal manuscripts: S. Keynes, 'Manuscripts of the *Anglo-Saxon Chronicle*', in R. Gameson (ed.), *The Cambridge History of the Book in Britain. Volume 1: c. 400-1100* (Cambridge: Cambridge University Press, 2012), pp. 537-52; P. Stafford, 'The making of chronicles and the making of England: the Anglo-Saxon Chronicles after Alfred', *Transactions of the Royal Historical Society*, 27 (2017), 65-86.

GLOSSARY

Actor, pl. *actores* A minor officer appointed by kings or queens (especially in Lombard and early Carolingian Italy), who was responsible for the administration of local fiscal estates.

Arimannus, pl. *arimanni* The ordinary Lombard soldier (*exercitalis, vir devotus*), who was a freeman. In Carolingian and post-Carolingian periods, the word *arimanni* designated free small and medium landowners, who were entitled to participate in local affairs, were summoned to law courts and could claim public rights as a group and therefore receive ***diplomata*** from kings. Used until the end of the eleventh century.

Beneficium 'Good deed' or 'favour'. In the early Middle Ages, the term was frequently used for a grant of land, often in return for rent and/or services, and thus a synonym for ***precarium***.

Bookland In Anglo-Saxon England, land held through a *landboc*, that is, a royal charter which granted tenure in perpetuity, free from worldly dues, although from the eighth-ninth century those who held bookland were expected to provide the so-called 'three common burdens', that is, bridge-work, fortress-work and service on military expeditions.

Brittonic A term for the P-Celtic languages of Britain and Brittany (as distinct from the Q-Celtic languages of Ireland, Scotland and the Isle of Man): Breton, Cornish, Cumbric and Welsh.

Catechumen Candidate for baptism. Catechumens were taught by a cleric about Christian beliefs and rituals, for a set period of time, before they became full members of the Christian community by undergoing the ritual of baptism. The length of the catechumenate (the period in which catechumens were taught) seems to have varied across early medieval Europe, but could take up to a year.

Centenarius, pl. *centenarii* Title of a lower-level office holder in the Frankish realm, subject to the *comes*, deriving from Latin *centena*, 'hundred', the area or group of people in his care (hence 'hundred-man'). Several other titles were used for the same (or similar) lower-level offices: ***sculdhais, vicarius, vicecomes, tribunus, prepositus***. See also ***decanus***.

GLOSSARY

Comes*, pl. *comites Common title for a high officer in the Frankish world and Carolingian and post-Carolingian Italy, usually translated as 'count'. Tasks generally included the administration of justice in a certain area and civil and military functions. In northern Iberia a powerful landed aristocrat, without office in the period here considered.

Comitatus The sphere of authority of a *comes*, at times territorialised.

Consors*, pl. *consortes Inhabitants of a certain locality, or a group of people with family ties, who held customary or confirmed rights over land, which they exercised as a group.

***Corvée* labour** Labour services (carting, ploughing, harvesting, etc.) owed to lords, often as a form of rent, for which no payment was received.

Curtis*, pl. *curtes regiae/reginae Estate. In Lombard Italy, the administrative centres of large fiscal estates normally, but not necessarily, centred in the most important cities and seats of duchies. Controlled by the king through the appointment of gastalds, they supplied the king's palace and its officers with necessities. *Curtes reginae*, concentrated in the Po valley and administered by minor officers, supplied the queen's household.

Decanus*, pl. *decani In the Lombard kingdom, the title of a lower-level office holder who, together with ***centenarii***, was responsible for an area or a group of people; subject to a duke (*dux*). According to the Lombard laws, *decani* could exempt free people from joining the army.

Demesne Land within an estate that was not handed over to tenants but was cultivated directly for the owner, whether by wage labour or more often by ***corvée* labour**.

Diploma*, pl. *diplomata A term favoured in some historiographical traditions to refer to more formal types of charter, usually issued by an emperor or a king.

Eigenkirche Term introduced in 1894 by the historian Ulrich Stutz to describe a church owned by an early medieval (lay) person and often founded on his or her own land. Such churches, also known as proprietary churches, are considered to have been a source of conflict because owners claimed rights to **tithes** and to appoint clerics, which according to canon law was the prerogative of the local bishop.

Elemosina Alms or gifts given by Christians to the poor as an act of charity. Almsgiving was a Christian duty, and it could contribute to **penance** for one's sins.

Emirate A term for the sphere of authority of an emir, an Arabic or Islamic ruler.

Familia A term with a wide range of meanings, including the members of a household; hence, the Englishman Bede's Latin word for vernacular **hide**. Widely used to designate the aggregate of dependants of different kinds, attached to different estates, who were subservient to a lord.

Farmstead A cluster consisting of a homestead, other buildings (e.g. storage facilities) and infrastructures (e.g. hearths or wells) that was isolated or formed a unit within a settlement. Farmsteads could be delimited by an enclosure and often appear to have operated as sites for both housing and productive activity (e.g. farming, craft). Cf. **household**.

Fealty From Latin *fidelitas*, meaning 'faithfulness', it describes the allegiance of one person to another, sometimes sealed by an oath. Fealty often found expression in the rendering of services, especially military service. Cf. ***fideles***.

Fideles Free followers or companions of a, usually secular, patron who served her/him loyally and rendered services, especially military service. In Spanish texts it can mean 'surety', 'oath-helper' and 'trusted person' or 'witness', that is, oathworthy person.

Formulary A collection of texts for use as models in preparing legal or quasi-legal documents. It could include charters, contracts, letters, prayers or oaths and could cover subjects such as marriage settlements, transfer of property, testamentary disposition, treatment of slaves and hire of labour.

Franchises In the later Middle Ages, an agreement between the residents of an estate and its lord which set out in writing the obligations of each to the other.

Free/unfree status In Roman law, the distinction between free and unfree marks the difference between free individuals and slaves. In early medieval societies, the free/unfree distinction was maintained, but its social significance became increasingly complex: in some contexts, fully fledged slavery persisted; in others the social and economic conditions of the unfree improved, while some free individuals became subservient to a lord. These trends also led to the emergence of the intermediary status of 'lesser free' or 'half-free' (e.g. *colliberti, barscalci, accolae, aldii*).

Gastaldus*, pl. *gastaldi* (gastalds)** The Lombard royal administrative and judicial officer in each district (*civitas*), immediately subordinate to the king. The title is also used in Carolingian and post-Carolingian Italy to designate local public officers such as ***vicecomites.

Gentiles A term used to refer to non-Christian invaders, including Vikings, in early medieval texts.

Gerefa Old English term for office holders with a range of administrative responsibilities (reeves). Royal reeves, for example, were initially in charge of royal estates but later had responsibilities relating to the administration of justice.

Gesta Abbatum Narrative accounts of the deeds of one or more abbots; may include documents such as charters or letters.

Gualdus*, pl. *gualdi Marginal, often wooded but not uninhabited land in Lombard Italy; cf. *forestis* or *silvae* in Francia. In Lombard and Carolingian Italy some of the *gualdi/vualdi* owned by the king could be given to groups of *arimanni* to feed the horses they were supposed to ride when summoned to the king's army.

Guild An association between people, normally of a comparable social status, usually confirmed by sworn oaths.

Hall, seigneurial Exceptional large building owned by a king or lord, whether isolated or part of a larger settlement. It could fulfil different functions (e.g. lordly residence, reception of visitors, hosting of judicial courts or feasts), which influenced its architecture.

Hide Described by Bede as 'the land of one family'. In Anglo-Saxon England, it originally designated the basic property unit of a nuclear family (a couple, their children and, on occasion, further family members and/or slaves); cf. **household**, ***mansus***. Throughout the Anglo-Saxon period important as the unit of assessment for public obligations such as taxation, rent or services.

Hoba Germanic term, often used as a synonym for ***mansus***.

Household In rural sociology, a household is a physical and economic unit (a farmstead) associated with a social unit (usually a nuclear family, i.e. a couple with children, occasionally further family members and/or slaves). In the early Middle Ages farming was always part of the household's economy, but it could be combined with complementary non-farming activities.

Hundred In late Anglo-Saxon England an administrative unit. See also ***centenarius***.

Iudex*, pl. *iudices 'Judge', generic title for office holders of all ranks in the Frankish world and Italy, where it was used for dukes and gastalds. From the first half of the tenth century especially, its use was reserved in northern Italy for office holders who could administer justice and who mainly wrote documents. In northern Iberia it often designated a person with legal expertise.

GLOSSARY

Labour service See *corvée* **labour**.

Locopositus Mentioned for the first time in the Lombard laws issued by King Liutprand, a synonym used to designate a local officer appointed by the king and intended to head a minor law court.

Mansus*, pl. *mansi (also ***mansum*, pl. *mansa***) (**manse**) In Francia and Carolingian Italy, originally a house but increasingly a peasant homestead and the land holding that supported it. In the ninth and tenth centuries, the basis of organisation of large estates (*curtes*). See **hide**, **household**.

Maior*, pl. *maiores Agent charged with administering property for a landowner. Other terms for this function are *villicus* or *vicedominus*.

Mallus A Frankish judicial court, operating at a micro-regional or regional level.

Missus*, pl. *missi Agent(s). In Francia in the Carolingian period, appointed by a ruler specifically to inspect a count's administration in a group of counties (*missaticum*). Ninth-century *missi dominici* were often regional magnates, sometimes a bishop or an abbot and a count together. There is evidence of more minor *missi*, representing bishops or counts in localities, for example.

Open field Arable field containing several unenclosed parcels that belonged to different owners but were cultivated following the same crop rotation and treated as common pasture after harvest.

Pagenses A term used to label people residing in a *pagus*, roughly equivalent to a county.

Penance Period of repentance that followed a sinner's confession to a priest. During this period the sinner was excluded from church and the Christian community and was to live on bread and water. Once the sinner had fulfilled penance, he or she was considered to be forgiven by God and ritually received back into the church and its community.

Penitential Handbook of penance. Such books generally list many different kinds of sin, and state the length and the specific kind of **penance** the sinner should undergo.

Placitum*, pl. *placita A word used by historians to refer to a specific type of document recording the final composition at the end of a lawsuit. By the eighth century in Francia and Italy it came to mean a public court hearing, later the whole of a public court case and also documents recording the case. In other regions the range of meaning is wider, without the specific Frankish/Italian usage.

Precarium*, *-ia In Francia and Italy, a grant of land on revocable tenure, usually but not always in return for rent or service; also, by extension, a charter making such a grant. How far such grants were in practice revocable varied considerably. See *beneficium*.

Ran, pl. *rannou* In Brittany, the basic property unit. It included a house, arable land, on occasion meadow, pasture and/or access to uncultivated land. Cf. **household**.

Saio, pl. *saiones* In early medieval northern Iberia, an executive officer of a judicial court.

Scabinus, pl. *scabini* Minor judicial officers introduced in local administration in Carolingian Francia and in Italy during the last decades of the eighth century, often an element of judging panels in public court hearings. In northern Italy, from *c.* 900, they were progressively replaced by public notaries and *iudices*.

Sculdhais A Lombard local officer representing the king, responsible to the *gastaldus*. Also found in Carolingian and post-Carolingian Italy, the term was occasionally used north of the Alps in the early Carolingian period. According to the Lombard laws, he could exempt free people from joining the army. See also **centenarius**.

Seigneurialisation Processes that led to the formation and/or extension of lordly domination (e.g. turning independent owners into tenants, increasing the weight of rent and labour services, extending the competences and/or spatial range of a law court). Beyond its social and legal dimensions, seigneurialisation could also have material consequences for settlements and landscapes (e.g. the construction of castles).

Settlement Place where people live and interact. In European early medieval rural societies, farmsteads were a fundamental unit of settlement. They could occur in relative isolation (dispersed settlement pattern) or in a cluster with other farmsteads (concentrated settlement pattern). See **farmstead**.

Signum manus Often abbreviated (*Sig*, *S*, *Sign* + *m*) or realised as a simple cross, and always linked to a (personal) name, a mark intended to represent the act of signing a legal document by those involved. In practice many such marks were not made by issuers or witnesses but by the scribe who wrote the document, although autograph marks do occur.

Sureties Or guarantors. People who guaranteed the fulfilment of obligations by other parties, appointed when an agreement was made (such as a sale transaction) or a dispute settled. Execution of their responsibilities could involve payment from their own resources, distraint on a defaulter's property or forcible seizure of the defaulter's person.

GLOSSARY

Tenure Farmstead and/or land held from a landowner by an individual (the tenant) in exchange for rent in kind and/or money and/or labour services. See also *corvée* **labour**.

Thegn Thegns belonged to the highest social ranks of Anglo-Saxon England, forming part of the landed aristocracy. They provided administrative and military services for the king, had local power and moved easily between the localities and the centre.

Tithe Tenth part of the harvest and other product; every Christian to give it to his church every year.

Tribunus Widely used for a minor local officer, without precise definition. See also *centenarius*.

Vassal, *vassus/bassus* Dependant, retainer, usually of free status.

Vicarius In general, a representative. In Francia and Italy, often a minor local officer; see *centenarius*.

Vicecomes, pl. vicecomites A minor local officer in Francia and Italy, normally subject to a count within the district of a county, representing the local count when temporarily absent. During the tenth century *vicecomites* could be chosen from local magnates and reach almost comital status. See *comes*.

Vicedominus A figure, lay or cleric (especially a deacon), subordinate to bishops and cathedral chapters, with, from the beginning of the ninth century, administrative duties within a diocese. The role of the *vicedominus* expanded during the early Carolingian period, when bishops were often involved in matters outside their dioceses. These officers continued to appear in charters of the tenth and eleventh centuries.

Vir devotus A title especially used in eighth-century Lombard private charters in order to define free people who were supposed to join the king's army; sometimes used of *arimanni*.

Visitation, episcopal Visit by the bishop to every church in his diocese, in principle once a year, in order to perform rituals that were restricted to his own competence (e.g. dedication of altars, confirmation of the baptised, reconciliation of penitents) as well as to ensure that local pastoral care was up to standard and that clergy and laity lived good Christian lives.

BIBLIOGRAPHY

Primary sources

Abbo of Saint-Germain-des-Prés, 22 Predigten: kritische Ausgabe und Kommentar, ed. U. Önnefors, Lateinische Sprache und Literatur des Mittelalters, 16 (Frankfurt am Main: Peter Lang, 1985)

Les actes de consagracions d'esglésies de l'antic bisbat d'Urgell (segles IX–XII), ed. C. Baraut (Urgell: Societat Cultural Urgel·litana, 1986).

Adalhard of Corbie, *Consuetudines Corbeienses*, ed. J. Semmler, in *Initia consuetudinis benedictinae*, ed. Hallinger, pp. 355–418.

Adalhard of Corbie, 'Customs of Corbie', trans. C. W. Jones, in *The Plan of St. Gall*, ed. W. Horn and E. Born (Berkeley, CA: University of California Press, 1979), pp. 91–131.

Die Admonitio generalis Karls des Großen, ed. H. Mordek, K. Zechiel-Eckes and M. Glatthaar, MGH Fontes iuris germanici antiqui in us. schol., 16 (Hanover: Hahn, 2012).

Agobard of Lyon, *Œuvres*, trans. M. Rubellin (Paris: Cerf, 2016).

Agobard of Lyon, *De grandine et tonitruis*, ed. L. van Acker, in *Agobardi Lugdunensis opera omnia*, CCCM 52 (Turnhout: Brepols, 1981), pp. 3–15.

Alfred the Great: Asser's Life of King Alfred and Other Contemporary Sources, ed. and trans. S. Keynes and M. Lapidge (Harmondsworth: Penguin, 1983).

Amalarius, *Opera liturgica omnia*, ed. J. M. Hanssens, vol. 3 (Vatican City: Biblioteca Apostolica Vaticana, 1950).

Amolo of Lyons, *Epistola*, in Agobard of Lyon, *Œuvres*, trans. M. Rubellin (Paris: Cerf, 2016), pp. 428–57.

Angilbert, *Institutio sancti Angilberti abbatis de diversitate officiorum (800–811)*, ed. K. Hallinger, D. M. Wegener and D. H. Frank, in Hallinger (ed.), *Initia consuetudinis benedictinae*, pp. 283–303.

The Anglo-Saxon Chronicle: A Collaborative Edition, general ed. D. Dumville and S. Keynes (Cambridge: D. S. Brewer, 1983–).

The Anglo-Saxon Chronicles, trans. M. Swanton (London: Phoenix, 1996, rev. edn, 2000).

Anglo-Saxon Wills, ed. and trans. D. Whitelock (Cambridge: Cambridge University Press, 1930, repr. 2011).

'Los *Annales Castellani Antiquiores* y *Annales Castellani Recentiores*: edición y traducción anotada', ed. J. C. Martín, *Territorio, Sociedad y Poder*, 4 (2009), 203–26.

Annales Fuldenses, ed. F. Kurze, MGH SS rer. Germ. [7] (Hanover: Hahn, 1891); trans. T. Reuter, *The Annals of Fulda* (Manchester: Manchester University Press, 1992).

BIBLIOGRAPHY

Annales Laureshamenses, ed. G. H. Pertz, in MGH SS 1 (Hanover: Hahn, 1826), pp. 19–39.
Annales regni Francorum inde a. 741 usque ad a. 829, ed. F. Kurze, MGH SS rer. Germ. [6] (Hanover: Hahn, 1895).
Les annales de Saint-Bertin, ed. F. Grat, J. Vielliard and S. Clémencet (Paris: Klincksieck, 1964); trans. J. L. Nelson, *The Annals of St-Bertin* (Manchester: Manchester University Press, 1991).
Ansegis, *Collectio Capitularium*, ed. G. Schmitz, MGH Capit. n.s. 1 (Hanover: Hahn, 1996).
Augustine, *Opera omnia* V/1, PL 36 (Paris, 1841).
Augustine, *Opera omnia* IX, PL 40 (Paris, 1865).
Bede, *Ecclesiastical History of the English People*, ed. and trans. B. Colgrave and R. A. B. Mynors, Oxford Medieval Texts (Oxford: Clarendon Press, 1969).
Bede, *Opera omnia*, ed. C. Plummer, 2 vols (Oxford: Clarendon Press, 1896).
Caesarius of Arles, *Sermones, nunc primum in unum collecti et ad leges artis critiae ex innumeris mss recogniti*, ed. G. Morin, CCSL 103 (Turnhout: Brepols, 2nd edn, 1953).
Capitulare de villis, ed. A. Boretius, in MGH Capit. 1, no. 32, pp. 82–91; ed. C. Brühl in *Cod. Guelf. 254 Helmst. der Herzog August Bibliothek Wolfenbüttel* (Stuttgart: Müller and Schindler, 1971).
Cartulaire de l'abbaye de Gorze. Ms. 826 de la bibliothèque de Metz, ed. A. D'Herbomez (Paris: Klincksieck, 1898).
Cartulaire de l'abbaye de Saint-Bertin, ed. M. Guérard (Paris: L'imprimerie royale, 1840).
Cartulaire de l'abbaye Saint-Sauveur de Redon (Rennes: Amis des Archives historiques du diocèse de Rennes, Dol et Saint-Malo, 1998).
Cartulaire du chapitre de l'église cathédrale Notre-Dame de Nîmes (834–1156), ed. E. Germer-Durand (Nîmes: Catélan, 1874).
Cartulario del Infantado de Covarrubias, ed. L. Serrano (Valladolid: Cuesta, 1907).
Chartae Latinae Antiquiores. Facsimile-Edition of the Latin Charters, 2nd series: Ninth Century, vols 100–111, ed. P. Erhart, B. Zeller and K. Heidecker (Dietikon-Zurich: Urs Graf, 2006–18).
Chartes et documents de Saint-Bénigne de Dijon. 1. VIe–Xe siècles, ed. R. Folz (Dijon: Société des Annales de Bourgogne, 1986).
Charters of Christ Church Canterbury, ed. N. P. Brooks and S. E. Kelly, Anglo-Saxon Charters, 17, 18, 2 vols (Oxford: Oxford University Press for the British Academy, 2013).
Chronicon Mosomense, ed. and trans. M. Bur (Paris: CNRS, 1989).
Codex Carolinus, ed. W. Gundlach, in *Epistolae Merowingici et Karolini aevi*, vol. 1, MGH Epp. 3 (Berlin, 1957), pp. 469–657.
Codex diplomaticus Cavensis, ed. M. Morcaldi et al., 12 vols (Naples: Piazzi, 1873–76).
Codex Oadalberti, ed. W. Hauthaler, *Salzburger Urkundenbuch*, vol. 1: *Traditionscodices* (Salzburg: Gesellschaft für Salzburger Landeskunde, 1910).

BIBLIOGRAPHY

Councils and Synods with other Documents Relating to the English Church, Volume 1 A.D. 871-1204, Part 1 871-1066, ed. D. Whitelock, M. Brett and C. N. L. Brooke (Oxford: Clarendon Press, 1981).

La Crónica de Ārīb sobre al-Andalus, trans. J. Castilla Brazales (Granada: Impredisur, 1992).

Crónicas Asturianas, ed. and trans. J. Gil Fernández, J. L. Moralejo and J. I. Ruiz de la Peña (Oviedo: Universidad de Oviedo, 1985).

Decretio Childeberti, ed. K. A. Eckard, in MGH LL nat. Germ. 4, 1 (Hanover: Hahn, 1962), pp. 267-9.

Domesday book, seu Liber censualis Willelmi primi regis Angliæ, ed. A. Farley, 2 vols (London: [Record Commission], 1783).

Domesday Book, 38 vols, general ed. J. Morris (Chichester: Phillimore, 1975-92).

Domesday Book: A Complete Translation, ed. A. Williams and G. H. Martin (London: Penguin, 2002).

Edictum de expeditione Corsicana, ed. G. H. Pertz, in MGH LL 1 (Hanover: Hahn, 1835), p. 242; Italian trans., *I capitolari italici*, ed. C. Azzara and P. Moro (Rome: Viella, 1998), p. 124.

Edictus Rothari, ed. F. Bluhme, in MGH LL 4 (Hanover: Hahn, 1868), pp. 1-90.

Einhard, *Epistolae*, ed. K. Hampe, in MGH Epp. 5 (Berlin: Weidmann, 1899), pp. 105-45; trans. P. E. Dutton, *Charlemagne's Courtier: The Complete Einhard* (Toronto: University of Toronto Press, 2009).

Einhard, *Vita Karoli magni imperatoris*, ed. O. Holder-Egger, MGH SS rer. Germ. [25] (Hanover/Leipzig: Hahn, 1911).

Einhards Briefe. Mobilität und Kommunikation im Frühmittelalter, ed. A. Grabowsky, C. Haack, T. Kohl and S. Patzold (Seligenstadt: Einhard-Gesellschaft, 2018).

Ekkehard IV, *Casus sancti Galli*, ed. H. F. Haefele, Ausgewählte Quellen zur deutschen Geschichte des Mittelalters. Freiherr vom Stein-Gedächtnisausgabe, 10 (Darmstadt: Wissenschaftliche Buchgesellschaft, 3rd edn, 1991).

Flodoard, *Historiae Remensis ecclesiae*, ed. M. Stratmann, MGH SS 36 (Hanover: Hahn, 1998).

Gerefa, ed. and trans. T. Gobbitt, *Early English Laws*, online edition www.earlyenglishlaws.ac.uk/laws/texts/rect

Die Gesetze der Angelsachsen, ed. F. Lieberman, 3 vols (Halle: Niemeyer, 1903-16).

Gregory of Catino, *Regestum Farfense*, in *Regesto di Farfa*, ed. I. Giorgi and U. Balzani, 5 vols (Rome: Società di Storia Patria, 1879-1914).

Heiric of Auxerre, *Miracula Sancti Germani*, AASS, 31 jul, vol. 7 (Antwerp: Du Moulin, 1781), pp. 255-83 (repr. Paris/Rome: Palmé, 1868, pp. 266-94).

Heriveus of Reims, Letter to Archbishop Wido of Rouen, in PL 132, pp. 661-74.

Hincmar of Reims, *Collectio de ecclesiis et capellis*, ed. M. Stratmann, MGH Fontes iuris, 14 (Hanover: Hahn, 1990).

Hincmar of Reims, *De presbiteris criminosis*, ed. G. Schmitz, MGH Studien und Texte, 34 (Hanover: Hahn, 2004).

Hincmar of Reims, *Vita Remigii*, ed. B. Krusch, MGH SS rer. Merov. 3 (Hanover: Hahn, 1896), pp. 239-349.

245

Hupertus, *Apparitio sancti Vedasti*, AASS, 6 feb, vol. 1 (Antwerp: Iacob Meursium, 1658), pp. 803–5 (repr. Paris/Rome: Palmé, 1863, pp. 812–13).

Initia consuetudinis benedictinae. Consuetudines saeculi octavi et noni, ed. K. Hallinger (Siegburg: Schmitt, 1963).

Inventari altomedievali di terre, coloni e redditi, ed. A. Castagnetti, M. Luzzati, G. Pasquali and A. Vasina (Rome: ISIME, 1979).

Inventari del vescovato, della cattedrale e di altre chiese di Lucca, ed. P. Guidi and E. Pellegrinetti, Studi e Testi pubblicati per cura degli scrittori della Biblioteca Vaticana, 34, 2 fasc. (Rome: Biblioteca Vaticana, 1921).

The Laws of the Earliest English Kings, ed. and trans. F. L. Attenborough (Cambridge: Cambridge University Press, 1922).

The Laws of the Salian Franks (Pactus legis Salicae), trans. K. Fischer-Drew (Philadelphia: University of Pennsylvania Press, 1991).

Leges Langobardorum, 643–866, ed. F. Beyerle (Witzenhausen: Deutschrechtlicher Instituts-Verlag, 2nd edn, 1962).

Lex Baiwariorum, ed. Ernst von Schwind, MGH LL nat. Germ. 5, 2 (Hanover: Hahn, 1926).

Lex Salica, ed. K. A. Eckhardt, MGH LL nat. Germ. 4, 2 (Hanover: Hahn, 1964).

Lex Visigothorum, ed. K. Zeumer, MGH LL nat. Germ. 1, 1 (Hanover: Hahn, 1902).

Liber instrumentorum seu chronicorum monasterii Casauriensis seu Chronicon Casauriense, ed. A. Pratesi and P. Cherubini, 3 vols (Rome: ISIME, 2017–18).

Liber Ordinum Sacerdotal (Cod. Silos, Arch. Monástico, 3), ed. J. Janini (Silos: Abadía de Silos, 1981).

Miracula Sancti Huberti, AASS, 3 nov, vol. 1 (Paris: Palmé, 1887), pp. 819–29.

Miracula Sancti Remacli, AASS, 3 sept, vol. 1 (Antwerp: van der Plasche, 1746), pp. 696–721 (repr. Paris/Rome: Palmé, 1868, pp. 696–721).

Miracula Sancti Germani Parisiensis, AASS, 28 may, vol. 6 (Paris/Rome: Palmé, 1866), pp. 786–94.

Miracula Sancti Maximini, AASS, 29 may, vol. 7 (Antwerp: Cnobar, 1688), pp. 25–33 (repr. Paris/Rome: Palmé, 1866, pp. 25–33).

Miracula Sancti Riquarii, AASS, 26 apr, vol. 3 (Antwerp: Cnobar, 1675), pp. 447–57 (repr. Paris/Rome: Palmé, 1866, pp. 451–61).

De oudste particuliere oorkonden van het klooster Werden: een diplomatische studie met enige uitweidingen over het ontstaan van dit soort oorkonden in het algemeen, ed. D. P. Blok (Assen: Van Gorcum, 1960).

Pactus legis Salicae, ed. K. A. Eckhardt, MGH LL nat. Germ. 4, 1 (Hanover: Hahn, 1962).

Paenitentiale pseudo-Theodori, ed. C. van Rhijn, CCSL 156B (Turnhout: Brepols, 2009).

Paul the Deacon, *Historia Langobardorum*, ed. L. Bethmann and G. Waitz, MGH SS rer. Langob. (Hanover: Hahn, 1878), pp. 12–187.

Pérez de Urbel, J., *Sampiro. Su crónica y la monarquía leonesa en el siglo x* (Madrid: Consejo Superior de Investigaciones Científicas, 1952).

Les plus anciens documents originaux de l'abbaye de Cluny, vols 1–3, ed. H. Atsma, S. Barret and J. Vezin (Brepols: Turnhout, 1997–2002).

BIBLIOGRAPHY

Das Polyptychon von Saint-Germain-des-Prés, ed. D. Hägermann (Cologne: Böhlau, 1993).
Polyptyque de l'Abbaye de Saint-Germain-des-Prés rédigé au temps de l'abbé Irminon, ed. A. Longnon, 2 vols (Paris: Champion, 1895).
Polyptyque de l'abbé Irminon, ed. B. Guérard, 2 vols (Paris: L'imprimerie royale, 1844).
Polyptyque de l'abbaye de Saint-Remi de Reims, ed. B. Guérard (Paris: L'imprimerie royale, 1853).
Le polyptyque et les listes de cens de l'abbaye de Saint-Remi de Reims: IX–XI siècles, ed. J.-P. Devroey, Travaux de l'Académie Nationale de Reims, 163 (Reims: Académie nationale de Reims, 1984).
Das Prümer Urbar, ed. I. Schwab, Publikationen der Gesellschaft für Rheinische Geschichtskunde, 20 (Düsseldorf: Droste, 1983).
Ratramnus of Corbie, *Epistolae*, ed. E. Dümmler, in *Epistolae Karolini aevi*, vol. 4, MGH Epp. 6 (Berlin: Weidemann, 1925), pp. 149–58.
Recueil des actes de Charles II le Chauve, roi de France, ed. G. Tessier, 3 vols (Paris: L'imprimerie nationale, 1943).
Recueil des chartes de l'abbaye de Cluny, ed. A. Bernard and A. Bruel, 6 vols (Paris: L'imprimerie nationale, 1876–1903).
Recueil des chartes de l'abbaye de La Grasse, vol. 1 (779–1119), ed. E. Magnou-Nortier and A.-M. Magnou (Paris: Comité des travaux historiques et scientifiques, 1996).
Recueil des chartes de l'abbaye de Saint-Benoît-sur-Loire, ed. M. Prou and A. Vidier, 2 vols (Paris: Picard, 1900–12).
Regino of Prüm, *Chronicon*, ed. F. Kurze, MGH SS rer. Germ. [50] (Hanover: Hahn, 1890); trans. S. MacLean in S. MacLean, *History and Politics in Late Carolingian and Ottonian Europe. The Chronicle of Regino of Prüm and Adalbert of Magdeburg* (Manchester: Manchester University Press, 2009), pp. 61–231.
Regino of Prüm, *Libri duo de synodalibus causis et disciplinis ecclesiasticis, Das Sendhandbuch des Regino von Prüm*, ed. W. Hartmann, Ausgewählte Quellen zur deutschen Geschichte des Mittelalters. Freiherr vom Stein-Gedächtnisausgabe, 42 (Darmstadt: Wissenschaftliche Buchgesellschaft, 2004).
Rudolf of Fulda, *Miracula sanctorum in Fuldenses ecclesias translatorum*, ed. Georg Waitz, MGH SS 15, 1 (Hanover: Hahn, 1887), pp. 328–41.
Die Traditionen des Hochstiftes Passau, ed. M. Heuwieser, Quellen und Erörterungen zur bayerischen Geschichte, n.s. 6 (Munich: Rieger, 1930).
Die Traditionen des Klosters Schäftlarn 760–1305, ed. A. Weissthanner, Quellen und Erörterungen zur bayerischen Geschichte, n.s. 10/1 (Munich: Beck, 1953).
Das älteste Traditionsbuch des Klosters Mondsee, ed. G. Rath and E. Reiter, Forschungen zur Geschichte Oberösterreichs, 16 (Linz: Oberösterreichisches Landesarchiv, 1989).
Die Urkunden der Merowinger, ed. Th. Kölzer with M. Hartmann and A. Stieldorf, MGH DD (Hanover: Hahn, 2001).
Versus de Unibove, La Beffa di Unibos, ed. and (Italian) trans. F. Bertini and F. Mosetti Casaretto (Alessandria: Edizione dell'Orso, 2000).
Vita sancti Geraldi Auriliacensis, ed. A.-M. Bultot-Verleysen (Brussels: Société des Bollandistes, 2009).

Wandalbert of Prüm, *De mensium duodecim*, ed. E. Dümmler, MGH poetae Latini medii aevi, 2 (Weidemann: Berlin, 1884), pp. 604–33; trans. in C. Hammer, *Charlemagne's Months and their Bavarian Labors: The Politics of the Seasons in the Carolingian Empire* (Oxford: British Archaeological Reports, 1997), pp. 53–70.

Widukind of Corvey, *Rerum gestarum Saxonicarum libri tres*, ed. P. Hirsch and H.-E. Lohmann, MGH SS rer. Germ. 60 (Hanover: Hahn, 1935).

William of Jumièges, *Gesta Normannorum Ducum*, ed. and trans. E. van Houts, 2 vols (Oxford: Oxford University Press, 1992–95).

Secondary works

Abels, R., *Alfred the Great: War, Kingship and Culture in Anglo-Saxon England* (London: Longman, 1998).

Abels, R., '"The crimes by which Wulfbald ruined himself with his lord": the limits of state action in late Anglo-Saxon England', *Reading Medieval Studies*, 40 (2014), 42–53.

Abrams, L., 'Early Normandy', *Anglo-Norman Studies*, 35 (2013), 45–64.

Aillet, C., *Les mozarabes. Christianisme, islamisation et arabisation en péninsule ibérique (IXe–XIIe siècle)*, Bibliothèque de la Casa de Velázquez, 45 (Madrid: Casa de Velázquez, 2010).

Albertoni, G., 'Law and the peasant: rural society and justice in Carolingian Italy', *Early Medieval Europe*, 18:4 (2010), 417–45.

Althoff, G., *Otto III.*, Gestalten des Mittelalters und der Renaissance (Darmstadt: Wissenschaftliche Buchgesellschaft, 1997).

Althoff, G., *Spielregeln der Politik im Mittelalter. Kommunikation in Frieden und Fehde* (Darmstadt: Primus, 1997).

Althoff, G., 'Saxony and the Elbe Slavs', in Reuter (ed.), *The New Cambridge Medieval History, Volume III*, pp. 267–92.

Althoff, G., 'Das ottonische Reich als regnum Francorum?', in J. Ehlers (ed.), *Deutschland und der Westen Europas* (Stuttgart: Thorbecke, 2002), pp. 235–61.

Althoff, G., *Die Macht der Rituale. Symbolik und Herrschaft im Mittelalter* (Darmstadt: Primus, 2003).

Althoff, G., *Die Zeit der späten Karolinger und Ottonen* (Stuttgart: Klett-Cotta, 2008).

Amari, M., *Storia dei musulmani di Sicilia*, 3 vols (Florence: Le Monnier, 1854).

Amorim, G. E. G. et al., 'Understanding 6th-century barbarian social organization and migration through paleogenomics', *Nature Communications*, 9 (2018), doi: 10.1038/s41467-018-06024-4.

Andreolli, B., and M. Montanari, *L'azienda curtense in Italia: proprietà della terra e lavoro contadino nei secoli VIII–XI* (Bologna: CLUEB, 1985).

Andreolli, B., V. Fumagalli and M. Montanari (eds), *Le campagne italiane prima e dopo il Mille. Una società in trasformazione* (Bologna: CLUEB, 1985).

Angenendt, A., 'Taufe und Politik im frühen Mittelalter', *Frühmittelalterliche Studien*, 7 (1973), 143–68.

Astill, G., 'Anglo-Saxon attitudes: how should post-AD 700 burials be interpreted?', in D. Sayer and H. Williams (eds), *Mortuary Practices and Social Identities in the*

BIBLIOGRAPHY

Middle Ages: Essays in Burial Archaeology in Honour of Heinrich Härke (Exeter: University of Exeter Press, 2009), pp. 222–35.

Atsma H. (ed.), *La Neustrie. Les pays au nord de la Loire de 650 à 850, Francia*, Beiheft, 16, 2 vols (Sigmaringen: Thorbecke, 1989).

Atsma, H., and J. Vezin, 'Le dossier suspect des possessions de Saint-Denis en Angleterre revisité (VIIIe–IXe siècle)', in *Fälschungen im Mittelalter*, vol. 4: *Diplomatische Fälschungen (II)*, MGH Schriften, 33 (Hanover: Hahn, 1988), pp. 211–36.

Augenti, A., *Archeologia dell'Italia medievale* (Rome/Bari: Laterza, 2016).

Ausenda, G., and S. Barnish, 'A comparative discussion of Langobardic feud and blood-money compensation, with parallels from contemporary anthropology and from medieval history', in G. Ausenda and P. Delogu (eds), *The Langobards before the Frankish Conquest: An Ethnographic Perspective* (Woodbridge: Boydell Press, 2009), pp. 309–39.

Bachrach, B. S., *Early Carolingian Warfare: Prelude to Empire* (Philadelphia, PA: University of Pennsylvania Press, 2001).

Bachrach, B. S., 'Charlemagne and the Carolingian general staff', *The Journal of Military History*, 66 (2002), 313–57.

Bader, K. S., *Studien zur Rechtsgeschichte des mittelalterlichen Dorfes*, 3 vols (Vienna/Cologne/Graz: Böhlau, 1957–73).

Bakay, K., 'Hungary', in Reuter (ed.), *The New Cambridge Medieval History, Volume III*, pp. 536–52.

Banham, D., and R. Faith, *Anglo-Saxon Farms and Farming* (Oxford: Oxford University Press, 2014).

Banks, R. A., 'A study of the Old English versions of the Lord's Prayer, the Creeds, the Gloria and some prayers found in British Museum MS. Cotton Galba A. xiv, together with a new examination of the place of liturgy in the literature of Anglo-Saxon magic and medicine', PhD thesis, Queen Mary College, University of London, 1968.

Banniard, M. *Viva voce: communication orale du IVe au IXe siècle en occident latin* (Paris: Institut des études augustiniennes, 1992).

Barbero, A., and M. Vigil, *La formación del feudalismo en la Península Ibérica* (Barcelona: Crítica, 1978).

Barbier, J., '*De minimis curat praetor*: Hincmar, le polyptyque de Saint-Remi de Reims et les esclaves de Courtisols', in G. Constable and M. Rouche (eds), *Auctoritas: Mélanges offerts à Olivier Guillot* (Paris: PUPS, 2006), pp. 267–79.

Barbier, J., '"The praetor *does* concern himself with trifles": Hincmar, the polyptych of St-Remi and the slaves of Courtisols', in R. Stone and C. West (eds), *Hincmar of Rheims: Life and Work* (Manchester: Manchester University Press, 2015), pp. 211–27.

Barnwell, T., 'The early Frankish *mallus*: its nature, participants and practices', in Pantos and Semple (eds), *Assembly Places and Practices*, pp. 233–46.

Barrett, G., 'The written and the world in early medieval Iberia', DPhil thesis, University of Oxford, 2015.

Barrow, J., *The Clergy in the Medieval World: Secular Clerics, their Families and Careers in North-Western Europe, c.800–c.1200* (Cambridge: Cambridge University Press, 2015).
Barrow, J., 'The clergy in English dioceses, c. 900–c. 1066', in Tinti (ed.), *Pastoral Care*, pp. 17–26.
Barton, S., and R. Portass (eds), *Beyond the Reconquista: Essays on the Politics, Society and Culture of Medieval Iberia, 800–1200* (Leiden: Brill, forthcoming).
Bassett S. (ed.), *The Origins of Anglo-Saxon Kingdoms* (London: Leicester University Press, 1989).
Bassetti, M., and M. Stoffella (eds), *Gli ufficiali minori in Italia nell'alto medioevo (VIII–XI secolo)* (Spoleto: Fondazione CISAM, forthcoming).
Bauduin, P., *La première Normandie (Xe–XIe siècles): sur les frontières de la Haute Normandie, identité et construction d'une principauté* (Caen: Presses Universitaires de Caen, 2004).
Baxter, S., *The Earls of Mercia. Lordship and Power in Late Anglo-Saxon England* (Oxford: Oxford University Press, 2007).
Becher, M., *Otto der Große. Kaiser und Reich. Eine Biographie* (Munich: Beck, 2012).
Becker, L., *Hispano-romanisches Namenbuch. Untersuchung der Personennamen vorrömischer, griechischer und lateinisch-romanischer Etymologie auf der Iberischen Halbinsel im Mittelalter (6.–12. Jahrhundert)* (Berlin: De Gruyter, 2009).
Berkhofer, III, R. F., *Day of Reckoning: Power and Accountability in Medieval France* (Philadelphia, PA: University of Pennsylvania Press, 2004).
Bianchi, G., 'Building, inhabiting and "perceiving" private houses in early medieval Italy', in Quirós Castillo (ed.), *Arqueología de la arquitectura y arquitectura del espacio doméstico*, pp. 195–212.
Bianchi, G., 'Analyzing fragmentation in the early Middle Ages: the Tuscan model and the countryside in central-northern Italy', in S. Gelichi and R. Hodges (eds), *New Directions in Early Medieval Archaeology: Spain and Italy Compared* (Turnhout: Brepols, 2015), pp. 301–33.
Blair, J., *The Church in Anglo-Saxon Society* (Oxford: Oxford University Press, 2005).
Blair, J., 'The Tribal Hidage', in M. Lapidge, J. Blair, S. Keynes and D. Scragg, *The Wiley Blackwell Encyclopedia of Anglo-Saxon England* (Chichester: John Wiley and Sons, 2nd edn, 2014), pp. 473–5.
Blair, J., *Building Anglo-Saxon England* (Princeton, NJ: Princeton University Press, 2018).
Blaise, A., *Dictionnaire latin-français des auteurs crétiens* (Turnhout: Brepols, 1954–67).
Blickle, P., *Kommunalismus. Skizzen einer gesellschaftlichen Organisationsform*, 2 vols (Munich: Oldenburg, 2000).
Bloch, M., *Les caractères originaux de l'histoire rurale française*, Instituttet for sammenlignende kulturforskning, serie B: skrifter, 19 (Oslo: Aschehoug, 1931).
Bloch, M., 'The rise of dependent cultivation and seigniorial institutions', in J. H. Clapham and E. Power (eds), *The Cambridge Economic History of Europe, vol. I: The Agrarian Life of the Middle Ages* (London: Cambridge University Press, 1941), pp. 224–75.

BIBLIOGRAPHY

Bobrycki, S., 'The flailing women of Dijon: crowds in ninth-century Europe', *Past and Present*, 240 (2018), 2–44.

Bonnassie, P., *La Catalogne du milieu du Xe à la fin du XIe siècle: croissance et mutations d'une société*, 2 vols (Toulouse: Université de Toulouse-Le Mirail, 1975–76).

Borgolte, M., *Geschichte der Grafschaften Alemanniens in fränkischer Zeit*, Vorträge und Forschungen, Sonderband, 31 (Sigmaringen: Thorbecke, 1984).

Borst, A., *Schriften zur Komputistik im Frankenreich von 721 bis 818*, vol. 1 (Hanover: Hahn, 2006).

Bosl, K., *Frühformen der Gesellschaft im mittelalterlichen Europa. Ausgewählte Beiträge zu einer Strukturanalyse der mittelalterlichen Welt* (Munich/Vienna: Oldenbourg, 1964).

Bougard, F., 'Entre Gandolfingi et Obertenghi: les comtes de Plaisance aux Xe et XIe siècles', *Mélanges de l'École française de Rome. Moyen Âge*, 101 (1989), 11–66.

Bougard, F., *La justice dans le royaume d'Italie de la fin du VIIIe siècle au début du XIe siècle*, Bibliothèque des écoles françaises d'Athènes et de Rome, 291 (Rome: École française de Rome, 1995).

Bougard, F., 'Pierre de Niviano, dit le Spolétin, et le gouvernement du comté de Plaisance à l'époque carolingienne', *Journal des Savants* (1996/2), 291–337.

Bougard, F., 'Actes privés et transferts patrimoniaux en Italie centro-septentrionale (VIIIe–Xe siècle)', in Bougard (ed.), *Les transfers patrimoniaux*, pp. 539–62.

Bougard, F., 'L'église de Varsi', in D. Chamboduc de Saint Pulgent and M. Dejoux (eds), *La fabrique des sociétés médiévales méditerranéenes. Le Moyen Âge de François Menant* (Paris: Editions de la Sorbonne, 2018), pp. 421–31.

Bougard F. (ed.), *Les transferts patrimoniaux en Europe occidentale, VIIIe–Xe siècle (I). Actes de la table ronde de Rome, 6, 7 et 8 mai 1999, Mélanges de l'École française de Rome. Moyen-Âge*, 111:2 (1999).

Bougard, F., L. Feller and R. Le Jan (eds), *Les élites au haut Moyen Âge. Crises et renouvellements*, Collection Haut Moyen Âge, 1 (Turnhout: Brepols, 2006).

Boüard, A. de, *Manuel de diplomatique française et pontificale, Volume II: L'acte privé* (Paris: Picard, 1948).

Brogiolo, G. P., D. E. Angelucci, A. Colecchia and F. Remondino (eds), *APSAT 1. Teoria e metodi della ricerca sui paesaggi di altura* (Florence: All'Insegna del Giglio, 2011).

Brooks, N., 'The development of military obligations in eighth- and ninth-century England', in P. Clemoes and K. Hughes (eds), *England Before the Conquest: Studies in Primary Sources presented to Dorothy Whitelock* (Cambridge: Cambridge University Press, 1971), pp. 69–84.

Brown, P., *The Cult of the Saints, its Rise and Function in Latin Christianity* (Chicago: University of Chicago Press, 1981).

Brown, M. P., and C. A. Farr (eds), *Mercia: An Anglo-Saxon Kingdom in Europe* (London: Leicester University Press, 2001).

Brown, W. C., *Unjust Seizure: Conflict, Interest, and Authority in an Early Medieval Society* (Ithaca, NY: Cornell University Press, 2001).

Brown, W. C., M. Costambeys, M. Innes and A. J. Kosto (eds), *Documentary Culture and the Laity in the Early Middle Ages* (Cambridge: Cambridge University Press, 2013).

Brown, W. C., and P. Górecki (eds), *Conflict in Medieval Europe. Changing Perspectives on Society and Culture* (Aldershot: Ashgate, 2003).

Bruand, O., *Les origines de la société féodale: l'exemple de l'Autunois* (Dijon: Editions Universitaires de Dijon, 2009).

Bruce, S., 'Hagiography as monstrous ethnography: a note on Ratramnus of Corbie's letter concerning the conversion of the Cynocephali', in G. Wieland, C. Ruff and R. G. Arthur (eds), *Insignis Sophiae Arcator: Medieval Latin Studies in Honour of Michael Herren on his 65th Birthday* (Turnhout: Brepols, 2006), pp. 45–56.

Brunterc'h, J.-P., 'Le duché du Maine et la marche de Bretagne', in Atsma (ed.), *La Neustrie*, vol. 1, pp. 29–127.

Bullimore, K., 'Folcwin of Rankweil: the world of a Carolingian local official', *Early Medieval Europe*, 13:1 (2005), 43–77.

Cameron, K., 'Scandinavian settlement in the territory of the five boroughs: the place-name evidence', in K. Cameron (ed.), *Place-Name Evidence for the Anglo-Saxon Invasions and Scandinavian Settlements* (Nottingham: English Place-Name Society, 1975), pp. 115–71.

Cammarosano, P., *Nobili e re. L'Italia politica nell'alto medioevo* (Rome/Bari: Laterza, 1998).

Campana, S., C. Felici and L. Marasco, 'Progetto valle dell'Asso: Resoconto di otto anni di indagini', in S. Campana, C. Felici, R. Francovich and F. Gabbrielli (eds), *Chiese e insediamenti nei secoli di formazione dei paesaggi medievali della Toscana (V–X secolo): Atti del seminario San Giovanni d'Asso-Montisi, 10–11 novembre 2006* (Florence: All'Insegna del Giglio, 2008), pp. 7–35.

Caro, G., 'Zwei Elsässer Dörfer zur Zeit Karls des Großen. Ein Beitrag zur wirtschafts-geschichtlichen Verwertung der *Traditiones Wizenburgenses*', *Zeitschrift für die Geschichte des Oberrheins*, 56, n.s. 17 (1902), 450–79, 563–87.

Carocci, S., 'Signoria rurale e mutazione feudale: una discussione', *Storica*, 8 (1997), 49–91.

Cartron, I., 'Avant le cimetière au village: la diversité des espaces funéraires. Historiographie et perspectives', in Treffort (ed.), *Le cimetière au village dans l'Europe médiévale et moderne*, pp. 23–39.

Carvajal Castro, Á., *Bajo la máscara del* regnum. *La monarquía asturleonesa en León (854–1037)*, Biblioteca de Historia, 85 (Madrid: Consejo Superior de Investigaciones Científicas, 2017).

Castagnetti, A., *L'organizzazione del territorio rurale nel Medioevo. Circoscrizioni ecclesiastiche e civili nella 'Langobardia' e nella 'Romania'* (Bologna: Pàtron, 2nd edn, 1982), pp. 71–87.

Castagnetti, A., 'Flexo e Carpi nell'alto medioevo. La storia dei territori come verifica di teorie e ricerca di radici delle autonomie', in *Mirandola e le terre del Basso Secchia* (Modena: Aedes Muratoriana, 1984), pp. 13–27.

Castagnetti, A., *Il Veneto nell'alto medioevo* (Verona: Libreria Universitaria, 1990).

Castagnetti, A., *'Teutisci' nella 'Langobardia' carolingia* (Verona: Libreria Universitaria, 1995).
Castagnetti, A., 'Il conte Anselmo I: l'invenzione di un conte carolingio', in *Studi storici Luigi Simeoni*, 56 (2006), 9-60.
Castagnetti, A., 'Lociservatores, locopositi, gastaldi e visconti a Milano in età carolingia', in P. Corrao and E. Igor Mineo (eds), *Dentro e fuori la Sicilia. Studi di storia per Vincenzo D'Alessandro* (Rome: Viella, 2009), pp. 45-78.
Castagnetti, A., *Preistoria di Onorio II antipapa. Cadalo diacono nella società italica della prima metà del secolo XI* (Spoleto: Fondazione CISAM, 2014).
Castagnetti, A., *Arimanni di Lucca e distinzione sociale nelle sepolture* (Verona: Daigo Press, 2015).
Castellanos, S., and I. Martín Viso, 'The local articulation of central power in the north of the Iberian peninsula (500-1000)', *Early Medieval Europe*, 13:1 (2005), 1-42.
Catteddu, I., *Archéologie médiévale en France*, 2 vols (Paris: La Découverte, 2009).
Chalmeta Gendrón, P., *Invasión e islamización: la sumisión de Hispania y la formación de al-Andalus* (Madrid: Mapfre, 1994).
Chetwood, J., 'Re-evaluating English personal naming on the eve of the Conquest', *Early Medieval Europe*, 26:4 (2018), 518-47.
Chibnall, M., *The Debate on the Norman Conquest* (Manchester: Manchester University Press, 1999).
Christlein, R., 'Kirchheim bei München, Oberbayern', *Das Archäologische Jahr in Bayern*, 1980 (1981), 162-3.
Christys, A., *Christians in Al-Andalus (711-1000)* (Richmond: Curzon Press, 2002).
Christys, A., *Vikings in the South. Voyages to Iberia and the Mediterranean* (London: Bloomsbury, 2015).
Coleman, E. R., 'Medieval marriage characteristics: a neglected factor in the history of medieval serfdom', *The Journal of Interdisciplinary History*, 2:2 (1980), 205-19.
Collins, R., 'The Spanish kingdoms', in Reuter (ed.), *The New Cambridge Medieval History, Volume III*, pp. 670-91.
Collins, R., *Visigothic Spain, 409-711* (Oxford: Blackwell, 2004).
Concerted Development of Social Cohesion Indicators: Methodological Guide (Strasbourg: Council of Europe, 2005).
Conde, F. J. F., 'Poblaciones foráneas: mozárabe, musulmana y judía en el reino de León', in *Monarquía y sociedad en el reino de León. De Alfonso III a Alfonso VII* (León: Centro de Estudios e Investigación San Isidoro, 2007), pp. 763-891.
Conti, E., *La formazione della struttura agraria moderna nel contado fiorentino*, 3 vols (Rome: ISIME, 1965-66).
Córdoba, R., 'Technology, craft, and industry', in Graham-Campbell and Valor (eds), *The Archaeology of Medieval Europe*, pp. 208-30.
Costambeys, M., 'The laity, the clergy, the scribes and their archives: the documentary record of eighth and ninth-century Italy', in Brown et al. (eds), *Documentary Culture*, pp. 231-58.
Coupland, S., 'Holy ground? Plundering and burning of churches by Vikings and Franks in the ninth century', *Viator*, 45 (2014), 73-98.

Crouch, D., *The Normans: The History of a Dynasty* (London: Hambledon, 2002).
Cubitt, C., 'Unity and diversity in the early Anglo-Saxon liturgy', in Swanson (ed.), *Unity and Diversity*, pp. 45–57.
Cursente B. (ed.), *L'Habitat dispersé dans l'Europe médiévale et moderne. Actes des XVIIIes Journées Internationales d'Histoire de l'Abbaye de Flaran 15–17 Septembre 1996*, Flaran, 18 (Toulouse: Presses Universitaires Le Mirail-Toulouse, 1999).
Curta, F., 'Slavs in Fredegar and Paul the Deacon: medieval *gens* or "scourge of God"?', *Early Medieval Europe*, 6:2 (1997), 141–67.
Curta, F., *Southeastern Europe in the Middle Ages, 500–1250* (Cambridge: Cambridge University Press, 2006).
Czock, M., 'Practices of property and the salvation of one's soul: priests as men in the middle in the Wissembourg material', in Patzold and van Rhijn (eds), *Men in the Middle*, pp. 11–31.
Dannenbauer, H., 'Adel, Burg und Herrschaft bei den Germanen', *Historisches Jahrbuch*, 61 (1941), 1–50.
Dannenbauer, H., 'Hundertschaft, Centena und Huntari', *Historisches Jahrbuch*, 62/69 (1942/1949), 155–219.
Dark, K. R., *Civitas to Kingdom. British Political Continuity 300–800* (London: Leicester University Press, 1994).
Davies, W., 'Priests and rural communities in east Brittany in the ninth century', *Études Celtiques*, 20 (1983), 177–93.
Davies, W., 'Disputes, their conduct and their settlement in the village communities of East Brittany in the ninth century', *History and Anthropology*, 1:2 (1985), 289–312.
Davies, W., 'Suretyship in the *Cartulaire du Redon*', in T. Charles-Edwards, M. Owen and D. Walters (eds), *Lawyers and Laymen. Studies in the History of Law presented to Professor Dafydd Jenkins on his Seventy-Fifth Birthday* (Cardiff: University of Wales Press, 1986), pp. 72–91.
Davies, W., *Small Worlds. The Village Community in Early Medieval Brittany* (London: Duckworth, 1988).
Davies, W., *Acts of Giving: Individual, Community, and Church in Tenth-Century Spain* (Oxford: Oxford University Press, 2007).
Davies, W., 'Where are the parishes? Where are the minsters? The organization of the Spanish church in the tenth century', in D. Rollason, C. Leyser and H. Williams (eds), *England and the Continent in the Tenth Century: Studies in Honour of Wilhelm Levison (1876–1947)* (Turnhout: Brepols, 2010), pp. 379–97.
Davies, W., 'On suretyship in tenth-century northern Iberia', in J. Escalona and A. Reynolds (eds), *Scale and Scale Change: Western Europe in the First Millennium*, The Medieval Countryside, 6 (Turnhout: Brepols, 2011), pp. 133–52.
Davies, W., 'Free peasants and large landowners in the west', *Revue belge de philologie et d'histoire*, 90 (2012), 361–80.
Davies, W., 'Local priests and the writing of charters in northern Iberia in the tenth century', in J. Escalona and H. Sirantoine (eds), *Chartes et cartulaires comme instruments de pouvoir. Espagne et Occident chrétien (VIIIe–XIIe siècles)* (Toulouse: Université de Toulouse-Le Mirail, 2013), pp. 29–43.

BIBLIOGRAPHY

Davies, W., *Windows on Justice in Northern Iberia 800-1000* (Abingdon: Routledge, 2016).
Davies, W., 'Local priests in northern Iberia', in Patzold and van Rhijn (eds), *Men in the Middle*, pp. 125-44.
Davies, W., and P. J. Fouracre (eds), *The Settlement of Disputes in Early Medieval Europe* (Cambridge: Cambridge University Press, 1986).
Davis, G. R. C., *Medieval Cartularies of Great Britain and Ireland* (London: Longmans, Green, 1958), rev. C. Breay, J. Harrison and D. M. Smith (London: British Library, 2010).
Declercq, G., 'Originals and cartularies: the organisation of archival memory (ninth-eleventh centuries)', in K. Heidecker (ed.), *Charters and the Use of the Written Word in Medieval Society*, Utrecht Studies in Medieval Literacy, 5 (Turnhout: Brepols, 2000), pp. 147-70.
Delogu, P., 'Lombard and Carolingian Italy', in McKitterick (ed.), *The New Cambridge Medieval History, Volume II*, pp. 290-319.
Demade, J., 'The medieval countryside in German-language historiography since the 1930s', in I. Afonso (ed.), *The Rural History of Medieval European Societies* (Turnhout: Brepols, 2007), pp. 173-252.
Depreux, Ph., *Les sociétés occidentales du milieu du VIe à la fin du IXe siècle* (Rennes: Presses Universitaires de Rennes, 2002).
Depreux, Ph., 'Zur Nützlichkeit bzw. Nutzlosigkeit von Kunsttiteln für Kapitularien (am Beispiel der Nummern 134-135, 143-145 und 178 aus der Boretius-Edition)', *Deutsches Archiv für Erforschung des Mittelalters*, 70 (2014), 87-106.
Deutinger, R., 'Die ältesten mittelrheinischen Zehntterminationen', *Archiv für mittelrheinische Kirchengeschichte*, 54 (2002), 11-36.
Devroey, J.-P., 'Problèmes de critique autour du polyptyque de l'abbaye de Saint-Germain-des-Prés', in Atsma (ed.), *La Neustrie*, vol. 1, pp. 441-65.
Devroey, J.-P., 'La démographie du polyptyque de Saint-Rémi de Reims', in P. Demouy and Ch. Vulliez (eds), *Compter les Champenois. Actes du colloque (avril 1996, Reims)* (Reims: Université de Reims, 1998), pp. 81-94.
Devroey, J.-P., *Économie rurale et société dans l'Europe franque (VIe-IXe siècles). 1. Fondements matériels, échanges et lien social* (Paris: Belin, 2003).
Devroey, J.-P., 'Communiquer et signifier entre seigneurs et paysans', in *Comunicare e significare nell'alto medioevo*, Settimane di studio del centro italiano di studi sull'alto Medioevo, 52 (Spoleto: Fondazione CISAM, 2005), pp. 121-53.
Devroey, J.-P., 'Libres et non-libres sur les terres de Saint-Remi de Reims: la notice judiciaire de Courtisols (13 Mai 847) et le polyptyque d'Hincmar', *Journal des Savants* (2006/1), 65-103.
Devroey, J.-P., *Puissants et misérables. Système social et monde paysan dans l'Europe des Francs (VIe-IXe siècles)*, Mémoire de la Classe des Lettres, Collection in-8°, 3rd ser., 40 (Brussels: Académie Royale de Belgique, 2006).
Devroey, J.-P., 'Peasant mobility and settlement', in Kasten (ed.), *Tätigkeitsfelder*, pp. 37-48.
Devroey, J.-P., 'La hiérarchisation des pôles habités et l'espace rural. Autour des possessions de l'abbaye de Prüm (893) en Ardenne belge', in M. Gaillard

et al. (eds), *De la mer du Nord à la Méditerranée. Francia Media. Une région au coeur de l'Europe (c. 840–c. 1050)*. *Actes du colloque international (Metz, Luxembourg, Trèves, 8–11 février 2006)*, Publications du Centre luxembourgeois de documentation et d'études médiévales, 25 (Luxembourg: CLUDEM, 2011), pp. 175–206.

Devroey, J.-P., 'Perception de la nature productive et aspects des paysages ruraux à Saint-Remi de Reims au IXe siècle', *Revue belge de philologie et d'histoire*, 89 (2011), 267–94.

Devroey, J.-P., 'L'introduction de la dîme en Occident: entre espaces ecclésiaux et territoires seigneuriaux à l'époque Carolingienne', in M. Lauwer (ed.), *La dîme, l'église et la société féodale* (Turnhout: Brepols, 2012), pp. 87–106.

Devroey, J.-P., 'Mise en valeur du sol et cycles de culture dans le système domanial (VIIIe–Xe siècle) entre Seine et Rhin', in R. Viader and C. Rendu (eds), *Cultures temporaires et féodalité. Les rotations culturales et l'appropriation du sol dans l'Europe médiévale et moderne. Actes des XXXIIIIes Journées internationales d'histoire de l'abbaye de Flaran, 12 et 13 octobre 2012* (Toulouse: Presses Universitaires du Mirail, 2014), pp. 33–57.

Devroey, J.-P., 'Du grand domaine carolingien à la "seigneurie monastique". Saint-Remi de Reims, Gorze, Saint-Vanne de Verdun (880–1050)', in Iogna-Prat et al. (eds), *Cluny. Les moines et la société*, pp. 279–98.

Devroey, J.-P., 'Confronter la coutume domaniale entre seigneurs et paysans en Lorraine au Xe siècle', in Jégou et al. (eds), *Faire lien*, pp. 155–78.

Devroey, J.-P., 'Le petit monde des seigneuries domaniales: seigneurs, notables et officiers dans les seigneuries royales et ecclésiastiques à l'époque carolingienne', in Kohl, Patzold and Zeller (eds), *Kleine Welten*, pp. 165–203.

Devroey, J.-P., and N. Schroeder, 'Beyond royal estates and monasteries: landownership in the early medieval Ardennes', *Early Medieval Europe*, 20:1 (2012), 39–69.

Devroey, J.-P., and N. Schroeder, 'Land, oxen, and brooches. Local societies, inequality, and large estates in the early medieval Ardennes (c. 850–c. 900)', in J. A. Quirós Castillo (ed.), *Social Inequality in Early Medieval Europe: Local Societies and Beyond*, HAMA 39 (Turnhout: Brepols, 2019), pp. 177–202.

Devroey, J.-P., and A. Wilkin (eds), *Autour de Yoshiki Morimoto. Les structures agricoles en dehors du monde carolingien, formes et genèse* (Brussels: Le Livre Timperman, 2012).

Dickinson, T., 'The formation of a folk district in the kingdom of Kent: Eastry and its early Anglo-Saxon archaeology', in R. Jones and S. Semple (eds), *Sense of Place in Anglo-Saxon England* (Donington: Shaun Tyas, 2012), pp. 147–67.

Dickinson, T., C. Fern and A. Richardson, 'Early Anglo-Saxon Eastry: archaeological evidence and the development of a district centre in the kingdom of Kent', *Anglo-Saxon Studies in Archaeology and History*, 17 (2011), 1–86.

Dierkens, A., and C. Treffort, 'Le cimetière au village dans l'Europe médiévale et moderne: rapport introductif', in Treffort (ed.), *Le cimetière au village dans l'Europe médiévale et moderne*, pp. 8–19.

Dierkens, A., N. Schroeder and A. Wilkin (eds), *Penser la paysannerie médiévale, un défi impossible?* (Paris: Editions de la Sorbonne, 2017).

Diesenberger, M., *Predigt und Politik im frühmittelalterlichen Bayern: Arn von Salzburg, Karl der Große und die Salzburger Sermones-Sammlung*, Millenium-Studien, 58 (Berlin: De Gruyter, 2015).

Diesenberger, M., Y. Hen and M. Pollheimer (eds), *Sermo doctorum: Compilers, Preachers and their Audiences in the Early Middle Ages* (Turnhout: Brepols, 2013).

Dohrmann, W., *Die Vögte des Klosters St. Gallen in der Karolingerzeit*, Bochumer historische Studien (Bochum: Brockmeyer, 1985).

Doll, L. A., 'Ist die Diplomatik der Weißenburger Urkunden geklärt? Eine Erwiderung auf Franz Staab, Noch einmal zur Diplomatik der Weißenburger Traditionen', *Archiv für mittelrheinische Kirchengeschichte*, 45 (1993), 439-47.

Donat, P., *Haus, Hof und Dorf in Mitteleuropa vom siebten bis zwölften Jahrhundert: Archäologische Beiträge zur Entwicklung und Struktur der bäuerlichen Siedlung*, Schriften zur Ur- und Frühgeschichte, 33 (Berlin: Akademie Verlag, 1980).

Dopsch, H., 'Arn von Salzburg (ca. 740-821)', in K. Weigan (ed.), *Große Gestalten der bayerischen Geschichte* (Munich: Utz, 2012), pp. 13-30.

Drews, W., *The Unknown Neighbor: The Jew in the Thought of Isidore of Seville*, The Medieval Mediterranean, 59 (Leiden: Brill, 2006).

Duby, G., *La société aux XIe et XIIe siècles dans la région mâconnaise* (Paris: SEVPEN, 1953).

Duby, G., *L'économie rurale et la vie des campagnes dans l'occident médiéval (France, Angleterre, Empire IX-XV siècles)*, 2 vols (Paris: Aubier, 1962).

Duby, G., *Guerriers et paysans, VIIe-XIIe siècle. Premier essor de l'économie européenne*, Bibliothèque des histoires (Paris: Gallimard, 1973).

Dutton, P. E., *Carolingian Civilization: A Reader* (Peterborough, Ont.: Broadview Press, 1993).

Edwards, C., 'German vernacular literature: a survey', in R. McKitterick (ed.), *Carolingian Culture: Emulation and Innovation* (Cambridge: Cambridge University Press, 1993), pp. 141-70.

Engels, F., 'Die Mark', in K. Marx and F. Engels, *Werke*, vol. 19/4 (Berlin: Dietz, 1962), pp. 315-30.

Erhart, P., and J. Kleindinst, *Urkundenlandschaft Rätien*, Forschungen zur Geschichte des Mittelalters, 7 (Vienna: Österreichische Akademie der Wissenschaften, 2004).

Erhart, P. '"... und mit alter briefen urkund (dorin gemischlet) bestäht". Der frühmittelalterliche Urkundenschatz des Klosters St. Gallen in den Händen Vadians', in R. Gampe (ed.), *Vadian als Geschichtsschreiber* (Saint-Gall: Sabon, 2006), pp. 69-98.

Erhart, P., K. Heidecker and B. Zeller (eds), *Die Privaturkunden der Karolingerzeit* (Dietikon-Zurich: Urs Graf, 2009).

Escalona Monge, J., *Sociedad y territorio en la alta edad media castellana. La formación del alfoz de Lara*, BAR International Series, 1079 (Oxford: Archaeopress, 2002).

Escalona Monge, J., 'Mapping scale change: hierarchization and fission in Castilian rural communities during the tenth and eleventh centuries', in W. Davies, G. Halsall and A. Reynolds (eds), *People and Space in the Middle Ages, 300-1300* (Turnhout: Brepols, 2006), pp. 143-66.

Escalona Monge, J., O. Vesteinsson and S. Brookes (eds), *Polity and Neighbourhood in Early Medieval Europe* (Turnhout: Brepols, 2019).

Escalona Monge, J., 'Dense local knowledge: grounding local to supralocal relationships in tenth-century Castile', in Escalona, Vesteinsson and Brookes (eds), *Polity and Neighbourhood*, pp. 351–79.

Esders, S., *Die Formierung der Zensualität. Zur kirchlichen Transformation des spätrömischen Patronatswesens im früheren Mittelalter* (Ostfildern: Thorbecke, 2010).

Esders, S., 'Wergeld und soziale Netzwerke im Frankreich', in S. Patzold and K. Ubl (eds), *Verwandtschaft, Name und soziale Ordnung (300–1000)*, Ergänzungsband zum Reallexikon der Germanischen Altertumskunde, 90 (Berlin: De Gruyter, 2014), pp. 141–59.

Esders, S., 'Die "Capitula de expeditione Corsicana" Lothars I. vom Februar 825. Überlieferung, historischer Kontext, Textrekonstruktion und Rechtsinhalt', *Quellen und Forschungen aus italienischen Archiven und Bibliotheken*, 98:1 (2018), 91–144.

Esders, S., 'Amt und Bann: Weltliche Funktionsträger (*centenarii, vicarii*) als Teil ländlicher Gesellschaften im Karolingerreich', in Kohl, Patzold and Zeller (eds), *Kleine Welten*, pp. 255–307.

Esders, S., and H. J. Mierau, *Der althochdeutsche Klerikereid: Bischöfliche Diözesangewalt, Kirchliches Benefizialwesen und volkssprachliche Rechtspraxis im frühmittelalterlichen Baiern* (Hanover: Hahn, 2000).

Esders, S., M. Bassetti and W. Haubrichs, *Verwaltete Treue. Ein oberitalienisches Originalverzeichnis mit den Namen von 174 vereidigten Personen aus der Zeit Lothars I. und Ludwigs II.*, MGH Studien und Texte (Hanover: Hahn, forthcoming).

Esders S. (ed.), *Rechtsverständnis und Konfliktbewältigung. Gerichtliche und außergerichtliche Strategien im Mittelalter* (Cologne: Böhlau, 2007).

Estepa Díez, C., 'Formación y consolidación del feudalismo en Castilla y León', in *En torno al feudalismo hispánico. I congreso de estudios medievales* (Ávila: Fundación Sánchez-Albornoz, 1989), pp. 157–256.

Étaix, R., 'Un manuel de pastorale de l'époque carolingienne (Clm 27152)', *Revue Bénédictine*, 91 (1981), 105–30.

Everett, N., *Literacy in Lombard Italy, c. 568–774* (Cambridge: Cambridge University Press, 2003).

Ewig, E., *Die Merowinger und das Frankenreich*, Urban-Taschenbücher, 392 (Stuttgart: Kohlhammer, 6th edn, 2012).

Faith, R., *The English Peasantry and the Growth of Lordship*, Studies in the Early History of Britain (London: Leicester University Press, 1997).

Fees, I., and Ph. Depreux (eds), *Tauschgeschäft und Tauschurkunde vom 8. bis zum 12. Jahrhundert / L'acte d'échange, du VIIIe au XIIe siècle*, Archiv für Diplomatik, Beiheft, 13 (Cologne: Böhlau, 2013).

Feller, L., 'Le cartulaire-chronique de San Clemente a Casauria', in O. Guyotjeannin, L. Morelle and M. Parisse (eds), *Les cartulaires* (Paris: Droz et Champion, 1993), pp. 261–77.

BIBLIOGRAPHY

Feller, L., A. Gramain and F. Weber, *La fortune de Karol: Marché de la terre et liens personnels dans les Abruzzes au haut Moyen Âge* (Rome: École française de Rome, 2005).
Fernández Flórez, J. A., 'Los documentos y sus *scriptores*', in J. M. Fernández Catón (ed.), *Monarquía y sociedad en el Reino de León. De Alfonso III a Alfonso VII*, 2 vols (León: Centro de Estudios e Investigación 'San Isidoro', 2007), vol. 2, pp. 97–139.
Fichtenau, H., *Das Urkundenwesen in Österreich vom 8. bis zum frühen 13. Jahrhundert*, Mitteilungen des Instituts für Österreichische Geschichtsforschung, Ergänzungsband, 23 (Vienna/Cologne/Graz: Böhlau, 1971).
Fleming, R., *Domesday Book and the Law: Society and Legal Custom in Early Medieval England* (Cambridge: Cambridge University Press, 1998).
Fossier, R., *Enfance de l'Europe. Xe–XIIe siècles. Aspects économiques et sociaux*, 2 vols (Paris: Presses Universitaires de France, 1982).
Fossier, R., and J. Chapelot, *Le village et la maison au moyen âge* (Paris: Hachette littérature, 1980).
Fouracre, P., 'Frankish Gaul to 814', in McKitterick (ed.), *The New Cambridge Medieval History, Volume II*, pp. 85–109.
Fouracre, P., 'The use of the term *beneficium* in Frankish sources: a society based on favours', in W. Davies and P. Fouracre (eds), *The Languages of Gift in the Early Middle Ages* (Cambridge: Cambridge University Press, 2010), pp. 62–88.
Fouracre P. (ed.), *The New Cambridge Medieval History, Volume I, c.500–c.700* (Cambridge: Cambridge University Press, 2005).
Fowler, P., *Farming in the First Millennium* (Cambridge: Cambridge University Press, 2002).
Francovich, R., and M. Ginatempo (eds), *Castelli: storia e archeologia del potere nella Toscana medievale* (Florence: All'Insegna del Giglio, 2000).
Francovich, R., and R. Hodges, *Villa to Village. The Transformation of the Roman Countryside in Italy, c. 400–1000* (London: Duckworth, 2003).
Freedman, P., *Images of the Medieval Peasant* (Stanford, CA: Stanford University Press, 1999).
Freudenberg, S., Trado atque dono: *Die frühmittelalterliche private Grundherrschaft in Ostfranken im Spiegel der Traditionsurkunden der Klöster Lorsch und Fulda (750 bis 900)*, Vierteljahresschrift für Sozial- und Wirtschaftsgeschichte, Beiheft, 224 (Stuttgart: Steiner, 2013).
Fumagalli, V., *Terra e società nell'Italia padana. I secoli IX e X* (Bologna: Università degli studi, Istituto di storia medievale e moderna e di paleografia e diplomatica, 1974).
Fumagalli, V., 'Precarietà dell'economia contadina e affermazione della grande azienda fondiaria nell'Italia settentrionale dall'VIII all'XI secolo', *Rivista di storia dell'agricoltura*, 15 (1975), 3–27.
Galetti, P., 'Paesaggi, comunità, villaggi nell'Europa medievale', in Galetti (ed.), *Paesaggi, comunità, villaggi medievali*, vol. 1, pp. 1–22.
Galetti P. (ed.), *Paesaggi, comunità, villaggi medievali. Atti del Convegno internazionale di studio, Bologna, 14–16 gennaio 2010*, 2 vols (Spoleto: Fondazione CISAM, 2012).

BIBLIOGRAPHY

Ganshof, F. L., *Recherches sur les capitulaires* (Paris: Sirey, 1958).

Ganz, D., 'The Old French sermon on Jonah: the nature of the text', in Diesenberger, Hen and Pollheimer (eds), *Sermo doctorum*, pp. 427–39.

García de Cortázar y Ruiz de Aguirre, J. A., *El dominio del monasterio de San Millán de la Cogolla (siglos X a XIII). Introducción a la historia rural de Castilla altomedieval*, Acta Salmanticensia, Filosofia y Letras, 59 (Salamanca: Universidad de Salamanca, 1969).

Garipzanov, I. H., 'Annales Guelferbytani: changing perspectives of a local narrative', in R. Corradini and M. Diesenberger (eds), *Zwischen Niederschrift und Wiederschrift: Frühmittelalterliche Hagiographie und Historiographie im Spannungsfeld von Kompendienüberlieferung und Editionstechnik*, Forschungen zur Geschichte des Mittelalters, 15 (Vienna: Österreichische Akademie der Wissenschaften, 2009).

Gasparri, S., *I duchi longobardi* (Rome: ISIME, 1978).

Gasparri, S., 'La questione degli arimanni', *Bullettino dell'Istituto Storico Italiano per il Medio Evo e Archivio Muratoriano*, 87 (1978), 121–53.

Gasparri, S. 'Il regno longobardo in Italia. Struttura e funzionamento di uno stato altomedievale', in Gasparri and Cammarosano (eds), *Langobardia*, pp. 237–305; repr. in Gasparri (ed.), *Il regno dei Longobardi*, pp. 1–92.

Gasparri, S., *Italia longobarda. Il regno, i Franchi, il papato* (Rome/Bari: Laterza, 2012).

Gasparri, S., *Voci dai secoli oscuri. Un percorso nelle fonti dell'alto medioevo* (Rome: Carocci, 2017).

Gasparri S. (ed.), *Il regno dei Longobardi in Italia. Archeologia, società e istituzioni* (Spoleto: Fondazione CISAM, 2004).

Gasparri, S., and P. Cammarosano (eds), *Langobardia* (Udine: Casamassima, 1990).

Geary, P. J., *Furta Sacra. Thefts of Relics in the Central Middle Ages* (Princeton, NJ: Princeton University Press, 1978, 2nd edn, 1990).

Geary, P., *Phantoms of Remembrance: Memory and Oblivion at the End of the First Millennium* (Princeton, NJ: Princeton University Press, 1994).

Génicot, L., *L'économie rurale Namuroise au bas moyen âge, 1199–1429*, 4 vols (Louvain: Bibliothèque de l'Université, 1943–95).

Génicot, L., 'La communauté rurale en Belgique jusqu'au XIIIe siècle', in *Les Structures du pouvoir dans les communautés rurales en Belgique et dans les pays limitrophes (12e-19e siècle). 13e Colloque international, Spa, 3-5 septembre 1986* (Brussels: Crédit communal, 1988), pp. 17–44.

Génicot, L., *Rural Communities in the Medieval West* (Baltimore, MD: Johns Hopkins University Press, 1990).

Gérard, F., 'La structuration du village pour une économie agraire planifiée à la fin du IXe siècle en Lorraine. Les sites de Vitry-sur-Orne et de Demange-aux-Eaux', *Archéopages*, 34 (2012), 38–47.

Ghignoli, A., 'Su due famosi documenti pisani del secolo VIII', *Bullettino dell'Istituto Storico Italiano per il Medio Evo*, 106 (2004), 1–69.

Gittos, H., 'Is there any evidence for the liturgy of parish churches in late Anglo-Saxon England? The Red Book of Darley and the status of Old English', in Tinti (ed.), *Pastoral Care*, pp. 63–82.

Gittos, H., 'The audience for Old English texts: Ælfric, rhetoric and the edification of the simple', *Anglo-Saxon England*, 43 (2014), 231–66.

La giustizia nell'alto medioevo, secoli IX–XI, Settimane di studio del centro italiano di studi sull'alto medioevo, 44, 2 vols (Spoleto: Fondazione CISAM, 1997).

Godding, R., *Prêtres en Gaule Mérovingien* (Brussels: Société des Bollandistes, 2001).

Goetz, H.-W., 'Herrschaft und Recht in der frühmittelalterlichen Grundherrschaft', *Historisches Jahrbuch*, 104 (1984), 392–410.

Goetz, H.-W., 'Beobachtungen zur Grundherrschaftsentwicklung der Abtei St. Gallen vom 8. zum 10. Jahrhundert', in W. Rösener (ed.), *Strukturen der Grundherrschaft im frühen Mittelalter*, Veröffentlichungen des Max-Planck-Instituts für Geschichte, 92 (Göttingen: Vandenhoeck & Ruprecht, 1989), pp. 197–246.

Goetz, H.-W., 'Serfdom and the beginnings of a "seigneurial system" in the Carolingian period: a survey of the evidence', *Early Medieval Europe*, 2:1 (1993), 29–51.

Goosmann, E., 'Aristocratic exploitation of ecclesiastical property in the ninth century. The case of the villa Gendt', *Francia*, 45 (2018), 27–59.

Goullet, M., and M. Heinzelmann (eds), *La réécriture hagiographique dans l'Occident médiéval: transformations formelles et idéologiques* (Ostfildern: Thorbecke, 2003).

Graham-Campbell, J. A., and M. Valor (eds), *The Archaeology of Medieval Europe*, 2 vols (Århus: Aarhus University Press, 2007).

Green, A., G. Janmaat and H. Cheng, 'Social cohesion: converging and diverging trends', *National Institute Economic Review*, 215 (2011), 6–22.

Große, R., and M. Sot (eds), *Charlemagne: les temps, les espaces, les hommes. Construction et déconstruction d'un règne*, Collection Haut Moyen Age, 34 (Turnhout: Brepols, 2018).

Guillot, O., and R. Favreau (eds), *Pays de Loire et Aquitaine de Robert le Fort aux premiers Capétiens. Actes du colloque scientifique international tenu à Angers en septembre 1987*, Mémoires de la Société des Antiquaires de l'Ouest, 5th ser., vol. 4, 1996 (Poitiers: Société des Antiquaires de l'Ouest, 1997).

Guyotjeannin, O., L. Morelle and M. Parisse (eds), *Les cartulaires* (Paris: Droz et H. Champion, 1993).

Haack, C., *Die Krieger der Karolinger. Organisation von Kriegsdiensten als soziale Praxis um 800* (Berlin: De Gruyter, 2019).

Hadley, D., and J. Richards, 'The winter camp of the Viking Great Army, AD 872–3, Torksey, Lincolnshire', *The Antiquaries Journal*, 96 (2016), 23–67.

Hadley, D. M., and J. D. Richards (eds), *Cultures in Contact: Scandinavian Settlement in England in the Ninth and Tenth Centuries* (Turnhout: Brepols, 2000).

Halsall, G., *Warfare and Society in the Barbarian West, 450–900* (London: Routledge, 2003).

Halsall, G., 'The barbarian invasions', in Fouracre (ed.), *The New Cambridge Medieval History, Volume I*, pp. 35–55.

Hamerow, H., *Early Medieval Settlements. The Archaeology of Rural Communities in Northwest Europe, 400–900* (Oxford: Oxford University Press, 2002).

Hamerow, H., *Rural Settlements and Society in Anglo-Saxon England* (Oxford: Oxford University Press, 2012).

Hammer, C. I., 'Land sales in eighth- and ninth-century Bavaria: legal, economic and social aspects', *Early Medieval Europe*, 6:1 (1997), 47–76.

Hannig, J., '"Pauperiores vassi de infra palatio?" Zur Entstehung der karolingischen Königsbotenorganisation', *Mitteilungen des Instituts für Österreichische Geschichtsforschung*, 91 (1983), 309–74.

Hannig, J., 'Zur Funktion der karolingischen "missi dominici" in Bayern und in den südöstlichen Grenzgebieten', *Zeitschrift der Savigny-Stiftung für Rechtsgeschichte: Germanistische Abteilung*, 101 (1984), 256–300.

Hannig, J., 'Zentrale Kontrolle und regionale Machtbalance. Beobachtungen zum System der karolingischen Königsboten am Beispiel des Mittelrheingebietes', *Archiv für Kulturgeschichte*, 66 (1984), 1–46.

Härke, H., '"Warrior graves"? The background of the Anglo-Saxon weapon burial rite', *Past and Present*, 126 (1990), 22–43.

Härke, H., 'Anglo-Saxon immigration and ethnogenesis', *Medieval Archaeology*, 55 (2011), 1–28.

Härtel, R., *Notarielle und kirchliche Urkunden im frühen und hohen Mittelalter*, Historische Hilfswissenschaften, 4 (Vienna: Böhlau, 2011).

Hartmann, W., 'Neue Texte zur bischöflichen Reformgesetzgebung aus den Jahren 829/31: Vier Diözesansynoden Halitgars von Cambrai', *Deutsches Archiv für Erforschung des Mittelalters*, 35 (1979), 368–94.

Heather, P., 'Senators and Senates', in A. Cameron and P. Garnsey (eds), *The Cambridge Ancient History* (Cambridge: Cambridge University Press, 1998), pp. 184–210.

Hechberger, W., *Adel im fränkisch-deutschen Mittelalter. Zur Anatomie eines Forschungsproblems*, Mittelalter-Forschungen, 17 (Ostfildern: Thorbecke, 2005).

Heidecker, K., 'Urkunden schreiben im alemannischen Umfeld des Klosters St. Gallen', in Erhart, Heidecker and Zeller (eds), *Die Privaturkunden*, pp. 183–92.

Hen, Y., *Culture and Religion in Merovingian Gaul, AD 481–751* (Leiden: Brill, 1995).

Hen, Y., 'Rome, Anglo-Saxon England and the formation of the Frankish liturgy', *Revue Bénédictine*, 112 (2002), 301–22.

Hen, Y., 'Priests and books in the Merovingian period', in Patzold and van Rhijn (eds), *Men in the Middle*, pp. 162–76.

Hines, J., 'The becoming of the English: identity, material culture and language in early Anglo-Saxon England', *Anglo-Saxon Studies in Archaeology and History*, 7 (1994), 49–59.

Hodges, R., *Dark Age Economics. A New Audit* (London: Bloomsbury, 2012).

Hodges R. (ed.), *San Vincenzo al Volturno 1: The 1980–86 Excavations Part 1* and *San Vincenzo al Volturno 2: The 1980–86 Excavations Part 2* (London: The British School at Rome, 1993, 1995).

Howe, J., *Before the Gregorian Reform: The Latin Church at the Turn of the First Millennium* (Ithaca, NY: Cornell University Press, 2016).
Hoyt, S., 'Farm of the manor and community of the vill in Domesday Book', *Speculum*, 30 (1955), 147–69.
Hübner, R., 'Gerichtsurkunden der fränkischen Zeit', *Zeitschrift der Savigny-Stiftung für Rechtsgeschichte: Germanistische Abteilung*, 12 (1891), 1–118, and 14 (1893), 1–152.
Huglo, M., *Fonti e paleografia del canto ambrosiano* (Milan: Archivio Ambrosiano, 1956).
Hummer, H., 'The production and preservation of documents in Francia: the evidence of cartularies', in Brown et al. (eds), *Documentary Culture*, pp. 189–230.
Hyams, P., 'Feud and the state in late Anglo-Saxon England', *The Journal of British Studies*, 40:1 (2001), 1–43.
Innes, M., *State and Society in the Early Middle Ages: The Middle Rhine Valley 400–1000* (Cambridge: Cambridge University Press, 2000).
Innes, M., 'Charlemagne's government', in J. Story (ed.), *Charlemagne. Empire and Society* (Manchester: Manchester University Press, 2005), pp. 71–89.
Innes, M., 'On the material culture of legal documents: charters and their preservation in the Cluny archive, ninth to eleventh centuries', in Brown et al. (eds), *Documentary Culture*, pp. 283–320.
Innes, M., 'Archives, documents and landowners in Carolingian Francia', in Brown et al. (eds), *Documentary Culture*, pp. 152–88.
Innes, M., and C. West, 'Saints and demons in the Carolingian countryside', in Kohl, Patzold and Zeller (eds), *Kleine Welten*, pp. 67–99.
Insley, C., 'Archives and lay documentary practice in the Anglo-Saxon world', in Brown et al. (eds), *Documentary Culture*, pp. 336–62.
Iogna-Prat, D., M. Lauwers, F. Mazel and I. Rosé (eds), *Cluny. Les moines et la société au premier âge féodal* (Rennes: Presses Universitaires de Rennes, 2013).
Isaïa, M.-C., *Remi de Reims: mémoire d'un saint, histoire d'une église* (Paris: Cerf, 2010).
Isaïa, M.-C., 'Hagiographie et pastorale: la collection canonique d'Hervé, archevêque de Reims († 922)', *Mélanges de Science Religieuse*, 67:3 (2010), 27–48.
Isla Frez, A., *La alta edad media. Siglos VIII–XI* (Madrid: Síntesis, 2002).
Jäger, D., *Plündern in Gallien 451–592: eine Studie zu der Relevanz einer Praktik für das Organisieren von Folgeleistungen*, Ergänzungsband zum Reallexikon der Germanischen Altertumskunde, 103 (Berlin: De Gruyter, 2017).
Jarnut, J., U. Nonn and M. Richter (eds), *Karl Martell in seiner Zeit*, Francia, Beiheft, 37 (Sigmaringen: Thorbecke, 1994).
Jégou, L., S. Joye, T. Lienhard and J. Schneider (eds), *Faire lien. Aristocratie, réseaux et échanges compétitifs: Mélanges en l'honneur de Régine Le Jan* (Paris: Editions de la Sorbonne, 2015).
Jarrett, J., *Rulers and Ruled in Frontier Catalonia, 880–1010: Pathways of Power* (Woodbridge: Boydell Press, 2010).
Jörg, C., 'Die Besänftigung göttlichen Zorns in karolingischer Zeit. Kaiserliche Vorgaben zu Fasten, Gebet und Buße im Umfeld der Hungersnot von 805/06', *Das Mittelalter*, 15 (2010), 38–51.

John, E., *Land Tenure in Early England: A Discussion of Some Problems*, Studies in Early English History, 1 (Leicester: Leicester University Press, 1960).

John, E., *Orbis Britanniae and Other Studies*, Studies in Early English History, 4 (Leicester: Leicester University Press, 1966).

Jones, R., and M. Page, *Medieval Villages in an English Landscape. Beginnings and Ends* (Macclesfield: Windgather Press, 2006).

de Jong, M., '"Ecclesia" and the early medieval polity', in S. Airlie, W. Pohl and H. Reimitz (eds), *Staat im frühen Mittelalter*, Forschungen zur Geschichte des Mittelalters, 11 (Vienna: Österreichische Akademie der Wissenschaften, 2006), pp. 113–26.

de Jong, M., *The Penitential State. Authority and Atonement in the Age of Louis the Pious, 814–840* (Cambridge: Cambridge University Press, 2009).

de Jong, M., 'The state of the church: *ecclesia* and early medieval state formation', in W. Pohl and V. Wieser (eds), *Der frühmittelalterliche Staat – europäische Perspektiven*, Forschungen zur Geschichte des Mittelalters, 16 (Vienna: Österreichische Akademie der Wissenschaften, 2009), pp. 241–54.

de Jong, M., 'Hincmar, priests and Pseudo-Isodore: the case of Trising in context', in R. Stone and C. West (eds), *Hincmar of Rheims: Life and Work* (Manchester: Manchester University Press, 2015), pp. 268–88.

Kasten, B., 'Beneficium zwischen Landleihe und Lehen – eine alte Frage, neu gestellt', in D. R. Bauer, R. Hiestand, B. Kasten and S. Lorenz (eds), *Mönchtum – Kirche – Herrschaft, 750–1000, Josef Semmler zum 65. Geburtstag* (Sigmaringen: Thorbecke, 1998), pp. 243–60.

Kasten, B., 'Agrarische Innovationen durch Prekarien', in Kasten (ed.), *Tätigkeitsfelder*, pp. 139–54.

Kasten B. (ed.), *Tätigkeitsfelder und Erfahrungshorizonte des ländlichen Menschen in der frühmittelalterlichen Grundherrschaft (bis ca. 1000)* (Stuttgart: Steiner, 2006).

Keefe, S. A., 'Carolingian baptismal expositions: a handlist of tracts and manuscripts', in U.-R. Blumenthal (ed.), *Carolingian Essays: Andrew W. Mellon Lectures in Early Christian Studies* (Washington DC: Catholic University of America Press, 1983), pp. 169–237.

Keefe, S. A., *Water and the Word: Baptism and the Education of the Clergy in the Carolingian Empire*, 2 vols (Notre Dame, IN: University of Notre Dame Press, 2002).

Keefe, S. A., *A Catalogue of Works Pertaining to the Explanation of the Creed in Carolingian Manuscripts* (Turnhout: Brepols, 2012).

Keller, H., 'Der Gerichtsort in oberitalienischen und toskanischen Städten', *Quellen und Forschungen aus italienischen Archiven und Bibliotheken*, 49 (1969), 1–72.

Keller, H., and G. Althoff, *Die Zeit der späten Karolinger und Ottonen: Krisen und Konsolidierungen, 888–1024*, Gebhardt Handbuch der deutschen Geschichte, 3 (Stuttgart: Klett-Cotta, 2008).

Kellner, M. G., *Die Ungarneinfälle im Bild der Quellen bis 1150: von der 'Gens detestanda' zur 'Gens ad fidem Christi conversa'*, Studia Hungarica, 46 (Munich: Ungarisches Institut, 1997).

Keller, R., and L. Sarti (eds), *Pillages, tributs, captifs. Prédation et sociétés de l'Antiquité tardive au haut Moyen Âge* (Paris: Editions de la Sorbonne, 2018).
Kelly, F., *A Guide to Early Irish Law* (Dublin: Dublin Institute for Advanced Studies, 1988).
Kelly, T. F., *The Beneventan Chant* (Cambridge: Cambridge University Press, 1989).
Kelly, S., 'Anglo-Saxon lay society and the written word', in McKitterick (ed.), *The Uses of Literacy in Early Mediaeval Europe*, pp. 36-62.
Kemble, J. M., *The Saxons in England. A history of the English Commonwealth till the period of the Norman conquest*, 2 vols (London: Longmans, Green, 1849).
Kennedy, A. G., 'Disputes about *bocland*: the forum for their adjudication', *Anglo-Saxon England*, 14 (1985), 175-95.
Kennedy, A., 'Law and litigation in the Libellus Æthelwoldi episcopi', *Anglo-Saxon England*, 24 (1995), 131-83.
Kennedy, H., *Muslim Spain and Portugal: A Political History of al-Andalus* (London: Routledge, 1996).
Kershaw, J., *Viking Identities. Scandinavian Jewellery in England* (Oxford: Oxford University Press, 2013).
Kéry, L., *Canonical Collections of the Early Middle Ages (ca. 400-1140). A Bibliographical Guide to the Manuscripts and Literature* (Washington DC: Catholic University of America Press, 1999).
Keynes, S., 'Manuscripts of the *Anglo-Saxon Chronicle*', in R. Gameson (ed.), *The Cambridge History of the Book in Britain. Volume 1: c. 400-1100* (Cambridge: Cambridge University Press, 2012), pp. 537-52.
Kikuchi, S., *Untersuchungen zu den Missi dominici: Herrschaft, Delegation und Kommunikation in der Karolingerzeit* (Munich: Ludwig-Maximilians-Universität, 2013).
Klápště, J., and A. Nissen-Jaubert, 'Rural settlement', in Graham-Campbell and Valor (eds), *The Archaeology of Medieval Europe*, vol. 1, pp. 76-110.
Klápště J. (ed.), *Agrarian Technology in the Medieval Landscape: Agrartechnik in mittelalterlichen Landschaften. Technologie agraire dans le paysage médiéval. Ruralia X. 9th-15th September 2013, Smolenice, Slovakia*, Ruralia, 10 (Turnhout: Brepols, 2016).
Kohl, T., 'Gemeinde vor der Gemeinde? Dienheim in karolingischer Zeit', in A. Gruel (ed.), *Die ländliche Gemeinde im Spätmittelalter* (Berlin: Weidler, 2005), pp. 185-204.
Kohl, T., *Lokale Gesellschaften. Formen der Gemeinschaft in Bayern vom 8. bis zum 10. Jahrhundert*, Mittelalter-Forschungen, 29 (Ostfildern: Thorbecke, 2010).
Kohl, T., '*Presbyter in parochia sua*: local priests and their churches in early medieval Bavaria', in Patzold and van Rhijn (eds), *Men in the Middle*, pp. 50-77.
Kohl, T., 'Ländliche Gesellschaft, lokale Eliten und das Reich - der Wormsgau in der Karolingerzeit', in Kohl, Patzold and Zeller (eds), *Kleine Welten*, pp. 309-36.
Kohl, T., S. Patzold and B. Zeller (eds), *Kleine Welten. Ländliche Gesellschaften im Karolingerreich*, Vorträge und Forschungen (Ostfildern: Thorbecke, 2019).

Kosto, A. J., '*Sicut mos esse solet*: documentary practices in Christian Iberia, *c.* 700–1000', in Brown et al. (eds), *Documentary Culture*, pp. 259–82.

Krah, A., 'Die Handschrift des Cozroh: Einblicke in die kopiale Überlieferung der verlorenen ältesten Archivbestände des Hochstifts Freising', *Archivalische Zeitschrift*, 89 (2007), 407–31.

Krah, A., 'Heerbann', in A. Erler and E. Kaufmann (eds), *Handwörterbuch zur deutschen Rechtsgeschichte*, 3 vols (Berlin: Erich Schmidt, 2nd edn, 2008–16), vol. 2, cols 851–3.

Kreutz, B. M., *Before the Normans: Southern Italy in the Ninth and Tenth Centuries* (Philadelphia, PA: University of Pennsylvania Press, 1992).

Krönert, K., 'Les "Miracula Sancti Maximini" (BHL 5826): entre hagiographie et historiographie', *Revue Bénédictine*, 115 (2005), 112–50.

Krug, H., 'Untersuchungen zum Amt des "Centenarius"-Schultheiß. Teil I und II', *Zeitschrift der Savigny-Stiftung für Rechtsgeschichte. Germanistische Abteilung*, 87/88 (1970/1971), 1–31, 29–109.

Kuchenbuch, L., *Bäuerliche Gesellschaft und Klosterherrschaft im 9. Jahrhundert: Studien zur Sozialstruktur der Familia der Abtei Prüm*, Vierteljahrschrift für Sozial- und Wirtschaftsgeschichte, Beiheft, 66 (Wiesbaden: Steiner, 1978).

Kuchenbuch, L., 'Opus feminile. Das Geschlechterverhältnis im Spiegel von Frauenarbeiten im früheren Mittelalter', in H.-W. Goetz (ed.), *Weibliche Lebensgestaltung im frühen Mittelalter* (Cologne/Weimar/Vienna: Böhlau, 1991), pp. 139–75.

Kuchenbuch, L., '*Porcus donativus*: language use and gifting in seigniorial records between the eighth and the twelfth centuries', in G. Algazi et al. (eds), *Negotiating the Gift. Pre-modern Figurations of Exchange*, Veröffentlichungen des Max-Planck-Instituts für Geschichte, 188 (Göttingen: Vandenhoeck & Ruprecht, 2003), pp. 193–246.

Kuchenbuch, L., 'Abschied von der Grundherrschaft – Ein Prüfgang durch das ostfränkisch-deutsche Reich 950–1050', *Zeitschrift der Savigny-Stiftung für Rechtsgeschichte, Germanistische Abteilung*, 121 (2004), 1–99.

Kümin, B., *The Communal Age in Western Europe c. 1100–1800. Towns, Villages and Parishes in Pre-Modern Society* (Basingstoke: Palgrave Macmillan, 2013).

Kurze, W., 'I momenti principali della storia di San Salvatore al Monte Amiata', in M. Ascheri and W. Kurze (eds), *L'Amiata nel medioevo* (Rome: Viella, 1989), pp. 33–48.

Lambert, T., *Law and Order in Anglo-Saxon England* (Oxford: Oxford University Press, 2017).

Langlands, A., 'Local places and local people in Anglo-Saxon Wessex', in Escalona, Vesteinsson and Brookes (eds), *Polity and Neighbourhood*, pp. 381–405.

Lapidge, M., J. Blair, S. Keynes and D. Scragg (eds), *The Wiley Blackwell Encyclopedia of Anglo-Saxon England* (Chichester: John Wiley and Sons, 2nd edn, 2014).

Lauwers, M., 'De l'incastellamento à l'inecclesiamento. Monachisme et logiques spatiales du féodalisme', in Iogna-Prat et al. (eds), *Cluny. Les moines et la société*, pp. 315–38.

BIBLIOGRAPHY

Lauwers, M., 'Le cimetière au village ou le village au cimetière? Spatialisation et communautarisation des rapports sociaux dans l'occident médiéval', in Treffort (ed.), *Le cimetière au village dans l'Europe médiévale et moderne*, pp. 41–60.

Lauwers, M., 'Le "travail" sans la domination?', in Dierkens, Schroeder and Wilkin (eds), *Penser la paysannerie médiévale*, pp. 303–32.

Larrea, J. J., *La Navarre du IVe au XIIe siècle* (Paris/Brussels: De Boeck Supérieur, 1998).

Lavelle, R., *Alfred's Wars: Sources and Interpretations of Anglo-Saxon Warfare in the Viking Age* (Woodbridge: Boydell and Brewer, 2010).

Lazzari, T., 'Comunità rurali nell'alto medioevo: pratiche di descrizione e spie lessicali nella documentazione scritta', in Galetti (ed.), *Paesaggi, comunità, villaggi medievali*, vol. 2, pp. 405–23.

Le Boulanger, F., *Pacé (Ille-et-Vilaine) – ZAC Beausoleil. Une unité agricole du haut Moyen Âge dans un environnement mis en valeur anciennement*, Rapport d'opération. Fouille archéologique (Cesson-Sévigné: INRAP Grand Ouest, 2011).

Le Jan, E., L. Feller and J.-P. Devroey (eds), *Les élites et la richesse au Haut Moyen Âge* (Turnhout: Brepols, 2010).

Leicht, P. S., 'L'archivio di Alahis', in A. Giuffrè (ed.), *Studi di storia e diritto in onore di Enrico Besta per il suo XL compleanno*, vol. 2 (Milan: Giuffrè, 1937), pp. 29–36; repr. in Leicht, *Scritti di storia del diritto italiano*, vol. 2/1 (Milan: Giuffrè, 1948), pp. 233–9.

Lemesle, B., *Conflits et justice au moyen âge. Normes, loi et résolution des conflits en Anjou aux XIe et XIIe siècles* (Paris: Presses Universitaires de France, 2008).

Leyser, K. J., *Rule and Conflict in an Early Medieval Society: Ottonian Saxony* (London: Edward Arnold, 1979).

Leyser, K. J., 'The Battle at the Lech, 955. A study in tenth-century warfare', in K. J. Leyser, *Medieval Germany and its Neighbours 900–1250* (London: Hambledon, 1982), pp. 43–67.

Liebs, D., *Römische Jurisprudenz in Gallien (2. bis 8. Jahrhundert)* (Berlin: Duncker & Humblot, 2002).

Loring, M. I., D. Pérez and P. Fuentes, *La Hispania tardorromana y visigoda, siglos V–VIII* (Madrid: Síntesis, 2007).

Loveluck, C., and D. Tys, 'Coastal societies, exchange and identity along the Channel and southern North Sea shores of Europe, AD 600–1000', *Journal of Maritime Archaeology*, 1 (2006), 140–69.

Lynch, J. H., *Godparents and Kinship in Early Medieval Europe* (Princeton, NJ: Princeton University Press, 1986).

MacLean, S., *Kingship and Politics in the Late Ninth Century: Charles the Fat and the End of the Carolingian Empire* (Cambridge: Cambridge University Press, 2003).

Mailloux, A., 'Modalités de constitution du patrimoine épiscopal de Lucques, VIIIe–Xe siècle', in Bougard (ed.), *Les transferts patrimoniaux*, pp. 701–23.

Mancassola, N., *Società e istituzioni pubbliche locali. Gli ufficiali minori del comitato di Piacenza in età carolingia* (Spoleto: Fondazione CISAM, 2017).

Manzano Moreno, E., *Conquistadores, emires y califas. Los omeyas y la formación de al-Andalus* (Barcelona: Crítica, 2006).

Marrocchi, M., *Monaci scrittori. San Salvatore al monte Amiata tra Impero e Papato (secoli VIII–XIII)* (Florence: Florence University Press, 2014).
Martín Viso, I., *Fragmentos del Leviatán. La articulación política del espacio zamorano en la alta edad media* (Zamora: Instituto de estudios zamoranos, 2002).
Marx, K., *Grundrisse der Kritik der politischen Ökonomie* (Berlin: Dietz, 1953).
Marx, K., *Pre-Capitalist Economic Formations*, trans. J. Cohen, ed. E. J. Hobsbawm (London: Lawrence and Wishart, 1964).
Maurer, G. L. von, *Geschichte der Markenverfassung in Deutschland* (Erlangen: Enke, 1856).
Mayer, Th., 'Die Entstehung des "modernen" Staates im Mittelalter und die freien Bauern', *Zeitschrift der Savigny-Stiftung für Rechtsgeschichte, Germanistische Abteilung*, 57 (1937), 210–88.
Mayer, Th., 'Adel und Bauern im Staat des deutschen Mittelalters', in Th. Mayer (ed.), *Adel und Bauern im deutschen Staat des Mittelalters* (Leipzig: Koehler & Amelang, 1943), pp. 1–21.
McCormick, M. et al., 'Volcanoes and the climate forcing of Carolingian Europe, A.D. 750–950', *Speculum*, 82 (2007), 865–95.
McCune, J., 'The sermon collection in the Carolingian clerical handbook, Paris, Bibliothèque nationale de France, lat 1012', *Mediaeval Studies*, 75 (2013), 35–91.
McCune, J., 'The preacher's audience, c.800–c.950', in Diesenberger, Hen and Pollheimer (eds), *Sermo doctorum*, pp. 283–338.
McKitterick, R., *The Frankish Church and the Carolingian Reforms, 789-895* (London: Royal Historical Society, 1977).
McKitterick, R., *The Carolingians and the Written Word* (Cambridge: Cambridge University Press, 1989).
McKitterick, R., 'Zur Herstellung von Kapitularien. Die Arbeit des Leges-Skriptoriums', *Mitteilungen des Instituts für Österreichische Geschichtsforschung*, 101 (1993), 3–16.
McKitterick, R., 'Unity and diversity in the Carolingian church', in Swanson (ed.), *Unity and Diversity in the Church*, pp. 59–82.
McKitterick R. (ed.), *The Uses of Literacy in Early Mediaeval Europe* (Cambridge: Cambridge University Press, 1990).
McKitterick R. (ed.), *The New Cambridge Medieval History, Volume II, c.700–c.900* (Cambridge: Cambridge University Press, 1995).
Meens, R., *Penance in Medieval Europe* (Cambridge: Cambridge University Press, 2015).
Meens, R., 'Conclusions: early medieval priests – some further thoughts', in Patzold and van Rhijn (eds), *Men in the Middle*, pp. 222–8.
Mériaux, C., '*Boni agricolae in agro Domini*: Prêtres et société à l'époque carolingienne (VIIIe-Xe siècle)', Dossier d'Habilitation à diriger des Recherches II, Université Charles de Gaulle, Lille 3, 2014.
Mériaux, C., 'Ideal and reality: Carolingian priests in northern Francia', in Patzold and van Rhijn (eds), *Men in the Middle*, pp. 78–97.

BIBLIOGRAPHY

Mersiowsky, M., *Die Urkunde in der Karolingerzeit. Originale, Urkundenpraxis und politische Kommunikation*, MGH Schriften, 60, 2 vols (Wiesbaden: Harrassowitz, 2015).

Meyer zu Ermgassen, H., *Der Codex Eberhardi des Klosters Fulda*, 4 vols (Marburg: Elwert, 1995-2009).

Mignot, P., and N. Schroeder, 'Agrarian practices and landscape in the estate of Wellin (Belgium) from the early Middle Ages to the modern period: archaeology and history', in Klápště (ed.), *Agrarian Technology in the Medieval Landscape*, pp. 267-78.

Mínguez Fernández, J. M., *El dominio del monasterio de Sahagún en el siglo X*, Acta Salmanticensia, Filosofia y Letras, 119 (Salamanca: Universidad de Salamanca, 1980).

Molyneaux, G., *The Formation of the English Kingdom in the Tenth Century* (Oxford: Oxford University Press, 2015).

Moorhouse, S., and J. Bond, 'An approach to understanding medieval field systems', in Klápště (ed.), *Agrarian Technology in the Medieval Landscape*, pp. 1-48.

Mordek, H., *Bibliotheca capitularium regum Francorum manuscripta. Überlieferung und Traditionszusammenhang der fränkischen Herrschererlasse*, MGH Hilfsmittel, 15 (Munich: MGH, 1995).

Mordek, H., *Studien zur fränkischen Herrschergesetzgebung: Aufsätze über Kapitularien und Kapitulariensammlungen ausgewählt zum 60. Geburtstag* (Frankfurt am Main: Peter Lang, 2000).

Mordek, H., 'Die Anfänge der fränkischer Gesetzgebung für Italien', *Quellen und Forschungen aus italienischen Archiven und Bibliotheken*, 85 (2005), 1-35.

Morgan, L. H., *Ancient Society* (New York: H. Holt, 1878).

Morsel J. (ed.), *Communautés d'habitants au moyen âge (XIe-XVe siècles)* (Paris: Editions de la Sorbonne, 2018).

Müller-Mertens, E., 'The Ottonians as kings and emperors', in Reuter (ed.), *The New Cambridge Medieval History, Volume III*, pp. 233-66.

Nelson, J. L., 'Dispute settlement in Carolingian West Francia', in Davies and Fouracre (eds), *The Settlement of Disputes*, pp. 45-64.

Nelson, J. L., 'Making ends meet: wealth and poverty in the Carolingian church', *Studies in Church History*, 24 (1987), 25-36.

Nelson, J. L., 'The Frankish kingdoms, 814-898: the West', in McKitterick (ed.), *The New Cambridge Medieval History, Volume II*, pp. 110-41.

Nelson, J. L., 'Rulers and government', in Reuter (ed.), *The New Cambridge Medieval History, Volume III*, pp. 95-129.

Nelson, J. L., 'England and the continent in the ninth century III: rights and rituals', *Transactions of the Royal Historical Society*, 14 (2004), 1-24.

Neumann, M., 'Die bairische Volksordnung zur Karolingerzeit auf Grund genealogischer Untersuchungen', PhD dissertation, University of Erlangen, 1947.

Neveux, F., 'La fondation de la Normandie et les Bretons (911-933)', in C. Laurent, B. Merdrignac and D. Pichot (eds), *Mondes de l'Ouest et villes du monde: Mélanges en l'honneur d'André Chédeville* (Rennes: Presses Universitaires de Rennes, 1998), pp. 297-309.

Nissen-Jaubert, A., 'Habitats ruraux et communautés rurales', in J. Fridrich, J. Klápšte, Z. Smetánka and P. Sommer (eds), *Ruralia II. Spa, 1st–7th September 1997, Památky archeologické.* Supplementum, 11, Ruralia, 2 (Prague: Archeologický ústav, 1998), pp. 213–25.

Nitz, H.-J., 'The Church as colonist: the Benedictine abbey of Lorsch and planned *Waldhufen* colonization in the Odenwald', *Journal of Historical Geography*, 9 (1983), 105–26.

Nitz, H.-J., 'Settlement structures and settlement systems of the Frankish central state in Carolingian and Ottonian times', in D. Hook (ed.), *Anglo-Saxon Settlements* (Oxford: Blackwell, 1988), pp. 249–73.

Noël, R., 'A la recherche du village médiéval: Hier et aujourd'hui', in J.-M. Yante and A.-M. Bultot-Verleysen (eds), *Autour du 'village'. Établissements humains, finages et communautés rurales entre Seine et Rhin (IVe–XIIIe siècles). Actes du colloque international de Louvain-la-Neuve, 16–17 mai 2003* (Louvain-la-Neuve: Université catholique de Louvain, 2010), pp. 3–75.

Nonn, U., *Pagus und Comitatus in Niederlothringen. Untersuchungen zur politischen Raumgliederung im frühen Mittelalter* (Bonn: Röhrscheid, 1983).

Obermeier, M., *"Ancilla". Beiträge zur Geschichte der unfreien Frauen im Frühmittelalter* (Pfaffenweiler: Centaurus, 1996).

Oexle, O. G., 'Gilden als soziale Gruppen in der Karolingerzeit', in H. Jankuhn (ed.), *Das Handwerk in vor- und frühgeschichtlicher Zeit. Teil I. Historische und rechtshistorische Beiträge und Untersuchungen zur Frühgeschichte der Gilde*, Abhandlungen der Akademie der Wissenschaften in Göttingen. Philologisch-Historische Klasse, 122 (Göttingen: Vandenhoeck & Ruprecht, 1981), pp. 284–354.

Oexle, O. G., 'Conjuratio und Gilden im frühen Mittelalter. Ein Beitrag der sozialen Kontinuität zwischen Antike und Mittelalter', in B. Schwineköper (ed.), *Gilden und Zünfte. Kaufmännische und gewerbliche Genossenschaften im frühen und hohen Mittelalter*, Vorträge und Forschungen, 29 (Sigmaringen: Thorbecke, 1985), pp. 151–214.

Pagano, S. M., and P. Piatti (eds), *Il patrimonio documentario della Chiesa di Lucca: Prospettive di ricerca. Atti del convegno internazionale di studi (Lucca, Archivio Arcivescovile, 14–15 novembre 2008)* (Florence: SISMEL, 2010).

Pallares Méndez, M. del C., *Ilduara, una aristócrata del siglo X* (La Coruña: Ediciós Do Castro, 1998).

Pallares, M. del C., and E. Portela Silva, 'El lugar de los campesinos. De repobladores a repoblados', in A. Rodríguez (ed.), *El lugar del campesino. En torno a la obra de Reyna Pastor* (València: Consejo Superior de Investigaciones Científicas, 2007), pp. 61–87.

Pantos, A., 'The location and form of Anglo-Saxon assembly-places: some "moot points"', in Pantos and Semple (eds), *Assembly Places and Practices*, pp. 155–80.

Pantos, A., and S. Semple (eds), *Assembly Places and Practices in Medieval Europe* (Dublin: Four Courts Press, 2004).

Parkes, H., *The Making of Liturgy in the Ottonian Church. Books, Music and Ritual in Mainz, 950–1050* (Cambridge: Cambridge University Press, 2015).

Pasquali, G., 'L'azienda curtense e l'economia rurale dei secoli VI-XI', in A. Cortonesi, G. Pasquali and G. Piccinni (eds), *Uomini e campagne nell'Italia medievale* (Rome/Bari: Laterza, 2002), pp. 5-71.

Pastor, R., *Resistencias y luchas campesinas en la época del crecimiento y consolidación de la formación feudal. Castilla y León, siglos X-XIII* (Madrid: Siglo Veintiuno de España, 1980).

Pastor, R., 'Sur la genèse du féodalisme en Castille et dans le León, Xe-XIIe siècles. Point de départ pour une histoire comparative', in H. Atsma and A. Burguière (eds), *Marc Bloch aujourd'hui. Histoire comparée et sciences sociales* (Paris: École des hautes études en sciences sociales, 1990), pp. 259-70.

Patzold, S., 'Normen im Buch. Überlegungen zu Geltungsansprüchen so genannter "Kapitularien"', *Frühmittelalterliche Studien*, 41 (2007), 331-50.

Patzold, S., *Episcopus: Wissen über Bischöfe im Frankenreich des späten 8. bis frühen 10. Jahrhunderts* (Ostfildern: Thorbecke, 2008).

Patzold, S., 'Bildung und Wissen einer lokalen Elite des Frühmittelalters: das Beispiel der Landpfarrer im Frankenreich des 9. Jahrhunderts', in F. Bougard, R. Le Jan and R. McKitterick (eds), *La culture du Haut Moyen Âge, une question d'élites?* (Turnhout: Brepols, 2009), pp. 377-91.

Patzold, S., '*Pater noster*: priests and the religious instruction of the laity in the Carolingian *populus christianus*', in Patzold and van Rhijn (eds), *Men in the Middle*, pp. 199-228.

Patzold, S., and C. van Rhijn (eds), *Men in the Middle. Local Priests in Early Medieval Europe* (Berlin: De Gruyter, 2016).

Pauler, R., *Das Regnum Italiae in ottonischer Zeit. Markgrafen, Grafen und Bischöfe als politische Kräfte*, Bibliothek des Deutschen Historischen Instituts in Rom, 54 (Tübingen: Niemeyer, 1982).

Pearce, S., *The Kingdom of Dumnonia. Studies in History and Tradition in South-Western Britain AD 350-1150* (Padstow: Lodenek Press, 1978).

Pellegrini, L., '*Plebs* e *populus* in ambito rurale nell'Italia altomedievale', in *Società, istituzioni, spiritualità. Studi in onore di Cinzio Violante*, 2 vols (Spoleto: Fondazione CISAM, 1994), vol. 1, pp. 599-632.

Pelteret, D. A. E., *Slavery in Early Mediaeval England: From the Reign of Alfred until the Twelfth Century* (Woodbridge: Boydell Press, 1995).

Perreaux, N., 'L'écriture du monde. Dynamique, perception, catégorisation du mundus au Moyen Âge (VIIe-XIIIe siècles). Recherche à partir de bases de données numérisées', PhD dissertation, Université de Bourgogne, Dijon, 2014.

Perreaux, N., 'L'écriture du monde (I)', *BUCEMA. Bulletin du centre d'etudes médiévales d'Auxerre*, 19:2 (2015), 1-37, http://journals.openedition.org/cem/14264 (accessed 27 June 2018), doi: 10.4000/cem.14264

Perrin, C. E., *Recherches sur la seigneurie rurale en Lorraine d'après les plus anciens censiers (IXe-XIIe siècle)*, Publications de la Faculté des Lettres de l'Université de Strasbourg, 71 (Paris: Les Belles Lettres, 1935).

Petrucci, A., and C. Romeo, '*Scriptores in urbibus*': *Alfabetismo e cultura scritta nell'Italia altomedievale* (Bologna: Il Mulino, 1992).

Peytremann, E., *Archéologie de l'habitat rural dans le nord de la France du IVe au XIIe siècle*, 2 vols, Mémoires de l'association française d'archéologie mérovingienne, 13 (Saint-Germain-en-Laye: AFAM, 2003).
Phelan, O. M., *The Formation of Christian Europe: The Carolingians, Baptism, and the Imperium Christianum* (Oxford: Oxford University Press, 2014).
Pirie, F., and J. Scheele (eds), *Legalism: Community and Justice* (Oxford: Oxford University Press, 2014).
Pohl, W., *Die Awaren. Ein Steppenvolk in Mitteleuropa 567–822 n. Chr.* (Munich: Beck, 3rd edn, 2015).
Pokorny, R., 'Die Annales Laureshamenses in einer neu aufgefundenen Teilüberlieferung', *Deutsches Archiv für Erforschung des Mittelalters*, 69 (2013), 1–44.
Portass, R., *The Village World of Early Medieval Northern Spain. Local Community and the Land Market*, Royal Historical Society Studies in History (Woodbridge: Boydell Press, 2017).
Pratt, D., *The Political Thought of King Alfred the Great* (Cambridge: Cambridge University Press, 2011).
Provero, L., 'Forty years of rural history for the Italian Middle Ages', in I. Alfonso (ed.), *The Rural History of Medieval European Societies. Trends and Perspectives* (Turnhout: Brepols, 2007), pp. 141–72.
Provero, L., 'Le comunità rurali nel medioevo: qualche prospettiva', in R. Bordone, P. Guglielmotti, S. Lombardini and A. Torre (eds), *Lo spazio politico locale in età medievale, moderna e contemporanea. Ricerche italiane e riferimenti europei* (Alessandria: Orso, 2007), pp. 335–40.
Provero, L., 'Abitare e appartenere: percorsi dell'identità comunitaria nei villaggi piemontesi dei secoli XII–XIII', in Galetti (ed.), *Paesaggi, comunità, villaggi medievali*, vol. 1, pp. 309–25.
Quirós Castillo, J. A., 'Early medieval landscapes in north-west Spain: local powers and communities, fifth–tenth centuries', *Early Medieval Europe*, 19:3 (2011), 285–311.
Quirós Castillo, J. A. (ed.), *Arqueología de la arquitectura y arquitectura del espacio doméstico en la alta Edad Media Europea*, Arqueología de la Arquitectura, 9 (Madrid/Vitoria: CSIC, 2012).
Quirós Castillo, J. A., 'Archaeology of power and hierarchies in early medieval villages in Northern Spain', in J. Klápště (ed.), *Hierarchies in Rural Settlements. Ruralia IX. 26th September–2nd October 2011. Götzis, Austria*, Ruralia, 9 (Turnhout: Brepols, 2013), pp. 199–212.
Quirós Castillo, J. A., and A. Vigil-Escalera, 'Networks of peasant villages between Toledo and Uelegia Alabense, Northwestern Spain (Vth–Xth centuries)', *Archeologia Medievale*, 33 (2006), 79–128.
Quirós Castillo, J. A. (ed.), *Social Complexity in Early Medieval Rural Communities. The North-Western Iberia Archaeological Record* (Oxford: Oxbow Books, 2016).
Rabe, S., *Faith, Art and Politics at Saint-Riquier* (Philadelphia, PA: University of Pennsylvania Press, 1995).

Redlich, O., *Die Privaturkunden des Mittelalters*, Handbuch der mittelalterlichen und neueren Geschichte, 4, 3 (Munich/Berlin: Oldenbourg, 1911).

Rembold, I., *Conquest and Christianization. Saxony and the Carolingian World, 772–888* (Cambridge: Cambridge University Press, 2018).

Renard, É., 'Une elite paysanne en crise? Le poids des charges militaires pour les petits alleutiers entre Loire et Rhin au IXe siècle', in Bougard, Feller and Le Jan (eds), *Les élites au haut Moyen Âge*, pp. 315–36.

Renard, É., 'La politique militaire de Charlemagne et la paysannerie franque', *Francia*, 36 (2009), 1–34.

Renes, H., 'Grainlands. The landscape of open fields in a European perspective', *Landscape History*, 31:2 (2010), 37–70.

Reuter, T., 'Plunder and tribute in the Carolingian empire', *Transactions of the Royal Historical Society*, 35 (1985), 75–94.

Reuter, T., *Germany in the Early Middle Ages, c.800–1056* (London: Longman, 1991).

Reuter, T., 'Debate: The "feudal revolution"', *Past and Present*, 155 (1997), 177–95.

Reuter, T., 'Carolingian and Ottonian warfare', in M. H. Keen (ed.), *Medieval Warfare. A History* (Oxford: Oxford University Press, 1999), pp. 13–35.

Reuter T. (ed.), *The New Cambridge Medieval History, Volume III, c.900–c.1024* (Cambridge: Cambridge University Press, 1999).

Reuter T. (ed.), *Alfred the Great. Papers from the Eleventh-Centenary Conferences* (Aldershot: Ashgate, 2003).

Reynolds, A., *Anglo-Saxon Deviant Burial Customs* (Oxford: Oxford University Press, 2009).

Reynolds, S., *Kingdoms and Communities in Western Europe, 900–1300* (Oxford: Oxford University Press, 1984).

van Rhijn, C., *Shepherds of the Lord. Priests and Episcopal Statutes in the Carolingian Period* (Turnhout: Brepols, 2007).

van Rhijn, C., 'The local church, priests' handbooks, and pastoral care in the Carolingian period', in *Chiese locali e chiese regionali nell'alto medioevo*, Settimane di studio del centro italiano di studi sull'alto medioevo, 61 (Spoleto: Fondazione CISAM, 2014), pp. 689–706.

van Rhijn, C., 'Manuscripts for local priests and the Carolingian reforms', in Patzold and van Rhijn (eds), *Men in the Middle*, pp. 177–98.

van Rhijn, C., and S. Patzold, 'Introduction', in Patzold and van Rhijn (eds), *Men in the Middle*, pp. 1–10.

Richter, M., '"... quisquis scit scribere, nullum potat abere labore". Zur Laienschriftlichkeit im 8. Jahrhundert', in J. Jarnut, U. Nonn and M. Richter (eds), *Karl Martell in seiner Zeit* (Sigmaringen: Thorbecke, 1994), pp. 393–404.

Rio, A., *The Formularies of Angers and Marculf. Two Merovingian Legal Handbooks* (Liverpool: Liverpool University Press, 2008).

Rio, A., *Legal Practice and the Written Word in the Early Middle Ages: Frankish Formulae, c. 500–1000* (Cambridge: Cambridge University Press, 2009).

Rio, A., *Slavery after Rome, 500–1100* (Oxford: Oxford University Press, 2017).

Roach, L., *Æthelred the Unready* (New Haven, CT: Yale University Press, 2016).

Roberts, E., 'Boundary clauses and the use of the vernacular in eastern Frankish charters *c.*750–*c.*900', *Historical Research*, 91 (2018), 580–604.
Rohr, Ch. (ed.), *Tassilo III. von Bayern* (Regensburg: Pustet, 2005).
Rösener, W., *Grundherrschaft im Wandel. Untersuchungen zur Entwicklung geistlicher Grundherrschaften im südwestdeutschen Raum vom 9. bis 14. Jahrhundert*, Veröffentlichungen des Max-Planck-Instituts für Geschichte, 102 (Göttingen: Vandenhoeck & Ruprecht, 1991).
Rollason, D., *Saints and Relics in Anglo-Saxon England* (Oxford: Blackwell, 1989).
Rosenwein, B. H., *To be the Neighbor of Saint Peter: The Social Meaning of Cluny's Property, 909–1049* (Ithaca, NY: Cornell University Press, 1989).
Rosenwein, B. H., *Negotiating Space: Power, Restraint, and Privileges of Immunity in Early Medieval Europe* (Manchester: Manchester University Press, 1999).
Salrach, J. M., 'Les féodalités méridionales: des Alpes à la Galice', in E. Bournazel and J.-P. Poly (eds), *Les féodalités* (Paris: Presses Universitaires de France, 1998), pp. 313–88.
Salrach, J. M., *Justícia i poder a Catalunya abans de l'any mil* (Vic: Eumo, 2013).
Sánchez-Albornoz, C., 'Las behetrías: la encomendación en Asturias, León y Castilla', *Anuario de Historia del Derecho Español*, 1 (1924), 158–336; repr. in C. Sánchez-Albornoz, *Viejos y nuevos estudios sobre las instituciones medievales españolas*, 3 vols (Madrid: Espasa-Calpe, 1976–80), vol. 1, pp. 15–191.
Sánchez-Albornoz, C., *Despoblación y repoblación del valle del Duero* (Buenos Aires: Instituto de Historia de España, 1966).
Sarti, L., *Perceiving War and the Military in Early Christian Gaul (ca. 400–700 A.D.)*, Brill's Series on the Early Middle Ages, 22 (Leiden: Brill, 2013).
Sarti, L., 'Eine Militärelite im merowingischen Gallien? Versuch einer Eingrenzung, Zuordnung und Definition', *Mitteilungen des Instituts für Österreichische Geschichtsforschung*, 124 (2016), 271–95.
Sawyer, P. H., 'The density of the Danish settlement in England', *University of Birmingham Historical Journal*, 6 (1957–58), 1–17.
Sawyer, P. H., *Kings and Vikings: Scandinavia and Europe, AD 700–1100* (London: Methuen, 1982).
Schieffer, R., 'Zur Entstehung des Sendgerichts im 9. Jahrhundert', in W. Müller and M. Sommar (eds), *Medieval Church Law and the Origins of the Western Legal Tradition. A Tribute to Kenneth Pennington* (Washington DC: Catholic University of America Press, 2006), pp. 50–6.
Schieffer R. (ed.), *Schriftkultur und Reichsverwaltung unter den Karolingern*, Abhandlungen der Rheinisch-Westfälischen Akademie der Wissenschaften, 97 (Opladen: Springer, 1996).
Schlesinger, W., *Die Entstehung der Landesherrschaft. Untersuchung vorwiegend nach mitteldeutschen Quellen* (Dresden: Wissenschaftliche Buchgesellschaft, 1941).
Schneider, J., *Auf der Suche nach dem verlorenen Reich. Lotharingien im 9. und 10. Jahrhundert*, Publications du CLUDEM, 30 (Cologne/Weimar/Vienna: Böhlau, 2010).

Schneidmüller, B., *Karolingische Tradition und frühes französisches Königtum. Untersuchungen zur Herrschaftslegitimierung der westfränkisch-französischen Monarchie im 10. Jahrhundert*, Frankfurter historische Abhandlungen, 22 (Wiesbaden: Steiner, 1979).

Schneidmüller, B., 'Karl III. ("der Einfältige"), 893/898-923/929', in J. Ehlers, H. Müller and B. Schneidmüller (eds), *Die französischen Könige des Mittelalters*, Beck'sche Reihe, 1723 (Munich: Beck, 2006), pp. 22-35.

Schreg, R., 'Farmsteads in early medieval Germany – architecture and organisation', in Quirós Castillo (ed.), *Arqueología de la arquitectura y arquitectura del espacio doméstico*, pp. 247-65.

Schroeder, N., *Les hommes et la terre de saint Remacle. Histoire sociale et économique et sociale de l'abbaye de Stavelot-Malmedy, VIIe-XIVe siècle* (Brussels: Université de Bruxelles, 2015).

Schroeder, N., 'Der Odenwald in Früh- und Hochmittelalter. Siedlung, Landschaft und Grundherrschaft in einem Mittelgebirge', *Siedlungsforschung. Archäologie, Geschichte, Geographie*, 33 (2016), 355-87.

Schroeder, N., 'Medieval and modern open fields in southern Belgium: a summary review and new perspectives', in C. Dyer, E. Thoen and T. Williamson (eds), *Peasants and their Fields. The Rationale of Open-Field Agriculture* (Turnhout: Brepols, 2018), pp. 183-206.

Schulze, H. K., *Die Grafschaftsverfassung der Karolingerzeit in den Gebieten östlich des Rheins* (Berlin: Duncker & Humblot, 1973).

Schupfer, F., *Le istituzioni politiche longobardiche* (Florence: Le Monnier, 1863).

Schwarzmaier, H., *Lucca und das Reich bis zum Ende des XI. Jahrhunderts. Studien zur Sozialstruktur einer Herzogsstadt in der Toskana* (Tübingen: Niemeyer, 1972).

Schwind, F., 'Beobachtungen zur inneren Struktur des Dorfes in karolingischer Zeit', in H. Jankuhn, R. Schützeichel and F. Schwind (eds), *Das Dorf der Eisenzeit und des frühen Mittelalters – wirtschaftliche Funktion – soziale Struktur. Bericht über die Kolloquien der Kommission für die Altertumskunde Mittel- und Nordeuropas in den Jahren 1973 und 1974*, Abhandlungen der Akademie der Wissenschaft in Göttingen. Phil.-hist. Klasse, 3rd ser., 101 (Göttingen: Vandenhoeck & Ruprecht, 1977), pp. 444-93.

Scragg, D., 'Homilies', in Lapidge et al. (eds), *The Wiley Blackwell Encyclopaedia of Anglo-Saxon England*, pp. 247-8.

Scragg, D., 'A ninth-century Old English homily from Northumbria', *Anglo-Saxon England*, 45 (2016), 39-49.

Segschneider, M. (ed.), *Ringwälle und verwandte Strukturen des ersten Jahrtausends n. Chr. an Nord- und Ostsee* (Neumünster: Wachholtz, 2009).

Seibert, H., 'Eines großen Vaters glückloser Sohn? Die neue Politik Ottos II.', in B. Schneidmüller and S. Weinfurter (eds), *Ottonische Neuanfänge. Symposium zur Ausstellung 'Otto der Große, Magdeburg und Europa'* (Mainz: von Zabern, 2001), pp. 293-320.

Sergi, G., 'Lo sviluppo signorile e l'inquadramento feudale', in N. Tranfaglia and M. Firpo (eds), *La storia. I grandi problemi dal Medioevo all'età contemporanea*, vol. 2 (Turin: UTET, 1986), pp. 369-94.

Sergi G. (ed.), *Curtis e signoria rurale: interferenze fra due strutture medievali* (Turin: Scriptorium, 1993).
Settia, A. A., *Castelli e villaggi nell'Italia padana: popolamento, potere e sicurezza fra IX e XIII secolo* (Naples: Liguori, 1984).
Sigoillot, A., 'Les *Liberi homines* dans le polyptyque de Saint-Germain-des-Prés', *Journal des Savants* (2008/2), 261–71.
Smith, J. M. H., 'Religion and lay society', in McKitterick (ed.), *The New Cambridge Medieval History, Volume II*, pp. 654–78.
Smyth, A. P., *Scandinavian Kings in the British Isles, 850–880* (Oxford: Oxford University Press, 1977).
Sonnlechner, C., 'The establishment of new units of production in Carolingian times: making early medieval sources relevant for environmental history', *Viator*, 35 (2004), 21–48.
Sonzogni, D., 'Le chartrier de l'abbaye de Saint-Denis en France au haut Moyen Âge: essai de reconstitution', *Pecia*, 3 (2003), 9–210.
Sonzogni, D., *Les actes du fonds d'archives de Saint-Denis, VIe–Xe siècle: étude critique et catalogue raisonné* (2016–17), http://saint-denis.enc.sorbonne.fr/les-textes/actes-du-haut-moyen-age/introduction.html (accessed 27 June 2018).
Spinei, V., *The Great Migrations in the East and South East of Europe from the Ninth to the Thirteenth Century*, trans. D. Bădulescu (Cluj-Napoca: Romanian Cultural Institute, Museum of Brăila Istros, 2003).
Sprandel, R., *Das Kloster Sankt Gallen in der Verfassung des karolingischen Reiches* (Freiburg: Eberhard Albert, 1958).
Springer, M., 'Agrarii milites', *Niedersächsisches Jahrbuch für Landesgeschichte*, 66 (1994), 129–66.
Staab, F., *Untersuchungen zur Gesellschaft am Mittelrhein in der Karolingerzeit*, Geschichtliche Landeskunde (Wiesbaden: Steiner, 1975).
Staab, F., 'Noch einmal zur Diplomatik der Weißenburger Traditionen', *Archiv für mittelrheinische Kirchengeschichte*, 44 (1992), 311–22.
Stafford, P., *Unification and Conquest: A Political and Social History of England in the Tenth and Eleventh Centuries* (London: Edward Arnold, 1989).
Stafford, P., 'Reeve', in Lapidge et al. (eds), *The Wiley Blackwell Encyclopaedia of Anglo-Saxon England*, pp. 397–398.
Stafford, P., 'The making of chronicles and the making of England: the Anglo-Saxon Chronicles after Alfred', *Transactions of the Royal Historical Society*, 27 (2017), 65–86.
Stocking, R., 'Forced converts, "crypto-Judaism", and children: religious identification in Visigothic Spain', in J. V. Tolan, N. de Lange, L. Foschia and C. Nemo-Pekelman (eds), *Jews in Early Christian Law: Byzantium and the Latin West, 6th–11th Centuries* (Turnhout: Brepols, 2014), pp. 243–65.
Stoffella, M., 'Lociservatores nell'Italia carolingia: l'evidenza Toscana', in M. Bassetti et al. (eds), *Studi sul medioevo per Andrea Castagnetti* (Bologna: CLUEB, 2011), pp. 345–82.
Stoffella, M., 'Local priests in early medieval rural Tuscany', in Patzold and van Rhijn (eds), *Men in the Middle*, pp. 98–124.

Stoffella, M., 'In a periphery of the Empire: Tuscany between the Lombards and the Carolingians', in Große and Sot (eds), *Charlemagne. Les temps, les espaces, les hommes*, pp. 319–36.

Stoffella, M., 'Condizionamenti politici e sociali nelle procedure di risoluzione dei conflitti nella Toscana occidentale tra età longobarda e carolingia', *Studi Medievali*, 3rd ser., 59:1 (2018), 35–61.

Stoffella, M., 'Gli ufficiali pubblici minori nella Toscana carolingia e postcarolingia', in M. Bassetti and M. Stoffella (eds), *Gli ufficiali minori in Italia nell'alto medioevo (VIII–XI secolo)* (Spoleto: Fondazione CISAM, forthcoming).

Stone, R., 'Exploring minor clerics in early medieval Tuscany', *Reti Medievali Rivista*, 18:1 (2017), doi: 10.6092/1593-2214/5076.

Swan, M., 'Memorialised readings: manuscript evidence for Old English homily composition', in P. Pulsiano and E. M. Treharne (eds), *Anglo-Saxon Manuscripts and their Heritage* (Ashgate: Aldershot, 1998), pp. 205–17.

Swanson, R. N. (ed.), *Unity and Diversity in the Church*, Studies in Church History, 32 (Oxford: Blackwell, 1996).

Tabacco, G., *I liberi del re nell'Italia carolingia e postcarolingia* (Spoleto: Fondazione CISAM, 1966).

Tabacco, G., 'L'avvento dei Carolingi nel regno dei Longobardi', in Gasparri and Cammarosano (eds), *Langobardia*, pp. 375–403; repr. in Gasparri (ed.), *Il regno dei Longobardi*, pp. 443–79.

Tabacco, G., *Sperimentazioni del potere nell'alto medioevo* (Turin: Einaudi, 1993).

Tabacco, G., *Dai re ai signori: forme di trasmissione del potere nel Medioevo* (Turin: Bollati Boringhieri, 2000).

Tejerizo García, C., 'Settlement patterns and social inequality: the Duero basin in early Middle Ages (4th–8th centuries)', in Quirós Castillo (ed.), *Social Complexity in Early Medieval Rural Communities*, pp. 17–34.

Teuscher, S., *Lords' Rights and Peasant Stories. Writing and the Formation of Tradition in the Later Middle Ages* (Philadelphia, PA: University of Philadelphia Press, 2012).

Thompson, V., 'The pastoral contract in late Anglo-Saxon England: priest and parishioner in Oxford, Bodleian Library, MS Laud Miscellaneous 482', in Tinti (ed.), *Pastoral Care*, pp. 106–20.

Tinti, F., 'The "costs" of pastoral care: church dues in Anglo-Saxon England', in Tinti (ed.), *Pastoral Care*, pp. 27–51.

Tinti, F., 'Introduction', in Tinti (ed.), *Pastoral Care*, pp. 1–16.

Tinti, F., *Sustaining Belief: The Church of Worcester from c. 870 to c. 1100* (Farnham: Ashgate, 2010).

Tinti, F., 'Looking for local priests in Anglo-Saxon England', in Patzold and van Rhijn (eds), *Men in the Middle*, pp. 145–61.

Tinti F. (ed.), *Pastoral Care in Late Anglo-Saxon England*, Anglo-Saxon Studies, 6 (Woodbridge: Boydell Press, 2005).

Tock, B.-M., 'L'acte privé en France, VIIe siècle–milieu du Xe siècle', *Mélanges de l'École française de Rome. Moyen Âge*, 111 (1999), 499–537.

Tomei, P., 'Un nuovo "polittico" lucchese del IX secolo. Il *breve de multis pensionibus*', *Studi Medievali*, 53:2 (2012), 567–602.

Toubert, P., *Les structures du Latium médiéval: le Latium méridional et la Sabine du IXe siècle a la fin du XIIe siècle*, Bibliothèque des écoles françaises d'Athènes et de Rome, 221, 2 vols (Rome: École française de Rome, 1973).

Toubert, P., *L'Europe dans sa première croissance: de Charlemagne à l'an mil* (Paris: Fayard, 2004).

Townend, M., *Viking Age Yorkshire* (Pickering: Blackthorn Press, 2014).

Treffort C. (ed.), *Le cimetière au village dans l'Europe médiévale et moderne: actes des XXXVes journées internationales d'histoire de l'abbaye de Flaran 11 et 12 octobre 2013* (Toulouse: Presses Universitaires du Midi, 2015).

Tsuda, T., 'War die Zeit Karls des Großen "die eigentliche Ära der Kapitularien"?', *Frühmittelalterliche Studien*, 49 (2016), 21–48.

Ubl, K., 'Gab es das Leges-Skriptorium Ludwigs des Frommen?', *Deutsches Archiv für Erforschung des Mittelalters*, 70 (2014), 43–65.

Ubl, K., *Lex Salica. Sinnstiftungen eines Rechtsbuchs. Die Lex Salica im Frankenreich* (Ostfildern: Thorbecke, 2017).

Valenti, M., 'Architecture and infrastructure in the early medieval village: the case of Tuscany', in L. Lavan, E. Zanini and A. Sarantis (eds), *Technology in Transition A.D. 300–650* (Leiden: Brill, 2007), pp. 451–90.

van Uytfanghe, M., 'The consciousness of a linguistic dichotomy (Latin-Romance) in Carolingian Gaul: the contradictions of the sources and their interpretation', in R. Wright (ed.), *Latin and the Romance Languages in the Early Middle Ages* (London: Routledge, 1991), pp. 114–29.

Vauchez, A., *La Sainteté en Occident aux derniers siècles du moyen age. Après les procès de canonisation et les documents hagiographiques* (Rome: École française de Rome, 1988).

Viader, R., 'Les grandes charrues. Cultures temporaires, communautés rurales et corvées de labour', in Dierkens, Schroeder and Wilkin (eds), *Penser la paysannerie médiévale*, pp. 363–85.

Vigil-Escalera Guirado, A., 'Invisible social inequalities in early medieval communities: the bare bones of household slavery', in Quirós Castillo (ed.), *Social Complexity in Early Medieval Rural Communities*, pp. 113–24.

Vigil-Escalera Guirado, A., M. Moreno-García, L. Peña-Chocarro, A. Morales Muñiz, L. Llorente Rodríguez, D. Sabato and M. Ucchesu, 'Productive strategies and consumption patterns in the early medieval village of Gózquez (Madrid, Spain)', *Quaternary International*, 346 (2014), 7–19.

Vigil-Escalera Guirado, A., G. Bianchi and J. A. Quirós Castillo (eds), *Horrea, Barns and Silos. Storage and Incomes in Early Medieval Europe* (Bilbao: Universidad del País Vasco, 2013).

Vinogradoff, P., *Villainage in England. Essays in English Mediaeval History* (Oxford: Clarendon Press, 1892).

Violante, C., *La società milanese nell'età precomunale* (Bari: Laterza, 1953).

Violante, C., 'La signoria "territoriale" come quadro delle strutture organizzative del contado nella Lombardia del secolo XII', in W. Paravicini and K. F. Werner (eds),

Histoire comparée de l'administration (IVe–XVIIIe siècles), Francia, Beiheft, 9 (Zurich/Munich: Artemis, 1980), pp. 333-44.

Vivas, M., 'La privation de sépulture au Moyen Âge. L'exemple de la province ecclésiastique de Bordeaux (Xe–début du XIVe siècles)', *Revue historique de Bordeaux et du département de la Gironde*, 19 (2013), 238-41.

Vogel, C., *Medieval Liturgy: An Introduction to the Sources*, rev. and trans. W. G. Storey and N. K. Rasmussen (Washington DC: Pastoral Press, 1986).

Vogler, W., *Kostbarkeiten aus dem Stiftsarchiv St. Gallen in Abbildungen und Texten* (Saint-Gall: Verlagsgemeinschaft St. Gallen, 1987).

Waitz, G., *Deutsche Verfassungsgeschichte*, vols 1-2 (Kiel: Schwers, 1844-47).

Weinrich, L., 'Tradition und Individualität in den Quellen zur Lechfeldschlacht', *Deutsches Archiv für Erforschung des Mittelalters*, 27 (1971), 291-313.

West, C., 'The significance of the Carolingian advocate', *Early Medieval Europe*, 17:2 (2009), 186-206.

West, C., *Reframing the Feudal Revolution: Political and Social Transformation Between Marne and Moselle, c. 800–c. 1100* (Cambridge: Cambridge University Press, 2013).

West, C., 'Le saint, le charpentier et le prêtre: l'Apparitio Sancti Vedasti et les élites dans la Francie du IXe siècle', in Jégou et al. (eds), *Faire lien*, pp. 237-48.

West, C., 'Visions in a ninth-century village: an early medieval microhistory', *History Workshop Journal*, 81:1 (2016), 1-16.

West, C., 'Carolingian kingship and the peasants of Le Mans: the *Capitulum in cenomannico pago datum*', in Große and Sot (eds), *Charlemagne: les temps, les espaces, les hommes*, pp. 227-44.

West, C., 'Exclusion et la paysannerie au XIe siècle au miroir des Versus de Unibove', in S. Joye, S. Gioanni and R. Le Jan (eds), *Richesse, pauvreté et exclusion dans les sociétés du haut Moyen Âge* (Turnhout: Brepols, forthcoming).

West, J., 'Into German: the language of the earliest German literature', in B. Murdoch (ed.), *German Literature of the Early Middle Ages* (Woodbridge: Boydell Press, 2004), pp. 35-56.

Wickham, C., *Early Medieval Italy: Central Power and Local Society, 400-1000* (London: Macmillan, 1981).

Wickham, C., 'Land disputes and their social framework in Lombard-Carolingian Italy, 700-900', in Davies and Fouracre (eds), *The Settlement of Disputes*, pp. 105-24; repr. in Wickham, *Land and Power. Studies in Italian and European Social History, 400-1200* (London: British School at Rome, 1994), pp. 229-56.

Wickham, C., *The Mountains and the City. The Tuscan Appennines in the Early Middle Ages* (Oxford: Clarendon Press, 1988).

Wickham, C., 'Paesaggi sepolti: insediamento e incastellamento sull'Amiata 750-1250', in M. Ascheri and W. Kurze (eds), *L'Amiata nel medioevo* (Rome: Viella, 1989), pp. 101-37.

Wickham, C., 'European forests in the early Middle Ages: landscape and land clearance', in *L'ambiente vegetale nell'alto medioevo*, Settimane di studio del centro italiano di studi sull'alto medioevo, 37 (Spoleto: Fondazione CISAM, 1990), pp. 479-548.

BIBLIOGRAPHY

Wickham, C., 'Problems of comparing rural societies in early medieval western Europe', *Transactions of the Royal Historical Society*, 2 (1992), 221–46.

Wickham, C., *Community and Clientele in Twelfth-century Tuscany. The Origins of the Rural Commune in the Plain of Lucca* (Oxford: Oxford University Press, 1998) (first published in Italian, 1995).

Wickham, C., 'La signoria rurale in Toscana', in G. Dilcher and C. Violante (eds), *Strutture e trasformazioni della signoria rurale nei secoli X–XIII (Atti della XXXVII Settimana di studio dell'Istituto storico italo-germanico in Trento, 12–16 settembre 1994)* (Bologna: Il Mulino, 1996), pp. 343–409.

Wickham, C., *Studi sulla società degli Appennini nell'alto medioevo. Contadini, signori e insediamento nel territorio di Valva (Sulmona)* (Bologna: CLUEB, 1999).

Wickham, C., 'Space and society in early medieval peasant conflicts', in *Uomo e spazio nell'alto Medioevo*, Settimane di studio del centro italiano di studi sull'alto Medioevo, 50 (Spoleto: Fondazione CISAM, 2003), pp. 551–86.

Wickham, C., *Framing the Early Middle Ages. Europe and the Mediterranean 400–800* (Oxford: Oxford University Press, 2005).

Wickham, C., 'Rethinking the structure of the early medieval economy', in J. R. Davis and M. McCormick (eds), *The Long Morning of Medieval Europe. New Directions in Early Medieval Studies* (Aldershot: Ashgate, 2008), pp. 19–31.

Wickham, C., 'Bounding the city: concepts of urban–rural difference in the West in the early Middle Ages', in *Città e campagna nei secoli altomedievali*, 2 vols (Spoleto: Fondazione CISAM, 2009), vol. 1, pp. 61–80.

Wickham, C., *The Inheritance of Rome: A History of Europe from 400 to 1000* (London: Penguin, 2009).

Wickham, C., 'Social structures in Lombard Italy', in G. Ausenda and P. Delogu (eds), *The Langobards before the Frankish Conquest: An Ethnographic Perspective* (Woodbridge: Boydell Press, 2009), pp. 118–48.

Wickham, C., 'Aristocratic wealth in Tuscany and Lazio, 700–1050: elements for a comparison', in Le Jan, Feller and Devroey (eds), *Les élites et la richesse*, pp. 251–63.

Wickham, C., 'The changing composition of early elites', in F. Bougard, H.-W. Goetz and R. Le Jan (eds), *Théories et pratiques des élites au haut Moyen Âge. Actes du colloque de Hambourg, 10–13 septembre 2009* (Turnhout: Brepols, 2011), pp. 5–20.

Wickham, C., 'Looking forward: peasant revolts in Europe, 600–1200', in J. Firnhaber-Baker (ed.), *The Routledge History Handbook of Medieval Revolt* (London: Routledge, 2016), pp. 155–67.

Wickham, C., 'The Tivoli *breve* of 945', in Dierkens, Schroeder and Wilkin (eds), *Penser la paysannerie médiévale*, pp. 161–76.

Wilkin, A., 'Le patrimoine foncier des élites dans la région de la Meuse moyenne jusqu'au XIe siècle', in Le Jan, Devroey and Feller (eds), *Les élites et la richesse*, pp. 327–43.

Wolfram, H., *Salzburg, Bayern, Österreich. Die Conversio Bagoariorum et Carantanorum und die Quellen ihrer Zeit*, Mitteilungen des Instituts für

Österreichische Geschichtsforschung, Ergänzungsband, 31 (Vienna/Munich: Oldenbourg, 1995).
Wolfram, H., 'Bavaria in the tenth and early eleventh centuries', in Reuter (ed.), *The New Cambridge Medieval History, Volume III*, pp. 293-309.
Wood, I. N., *The Merovingian Kingdoms 450-751* (New York: Longman, 1994).
Wood, S., *The Proprietary Church in the Medieval West* (Oxford: Oxford University Press, 2006).
Wormald, P., 'The age of Offa and Alcuin', in J. Campbell (ed.), *The Anglo-Saxons* (Oxford: Phaidon Press, 1982), pp. 101-28.
Wormald, P., 'A handlist of Anglo-Saxon lawsuits', *Anglo-Saxon England*, 17 (1988), 247-81.
Wormald, P., 'Charters, law and the settlement of disputes in Anglo-Saxon England', in Davies and Fouracre (eds), *The Settlement of Disputes*, pp. 149-68.
Wormald, P., *The Making of English Law. King Alfred to the Twelfth Century, Volume I: Legislation and its Limits* (Oxford: Blackwell, 1999).
Wormald, P., *Papers Preparatory to the Making of English Law: King Alfred to the Twelfth Century, Volume II: From God's Law to Common Law*, ed. S. Baxter and J. Hudson (London: University of London, 2014), http://www.earlyenglishlaws.ac.uk/reference/wormald/ (accessed 3 September 2019).
Wright, C. D., and R. Wright, 'Additions to the Bobbio Missal: *De dies malus* and *Joca monachorum* (fols. 6r-8v)', in Y. Hen and R. Meens (eds), *The Bobbio Missal: Liturgy and Religious Culture in Merovingian Gaul* (Cambridge: Cambridge University Press, 2004), pp. 79-139.
Wright, R., *Late Latin and Early Romance in Spain and Carolingian France* (Liverpool: Francis Cairns, 1982).
Wright, R., *A Sociophilological Study of Late Latin* (Turnhout: Brepols, 2002).
Yorke, B., *Kings and Kingdoms of Early Anglo-Saxon England* (London: B. A. Seaby, 1990).
Zadora-Rio, E., 'The making of churchyards and parish territories in the early medieval landscape of France and England in the 7th-12th centuries: a reconsideration', *Medieval Archaeology*, 47 (2003), 1-19.
Zeller, B., 'Urkunden und Urkundenschreiber des Klosters St. Gallen bis ca. 840', in Erhart, Heidecker and Zeller (eds), *Die Privaturkunden*, pp. 173-82.
Zeller, B., 'Writing charters as a public activity: the example of the Carolingian charters of St Gall', in M. Mostert and P. S. Barnwell (eds), *Medieval Legal Process: Physical, Spoken and Written Performance in the Middle Ages* (Turnhout: Brepols, 2011), pp. 27-37.
Zeller, B., 'Local priests in early medieval Alemannia', in Patzold and van Rhijn (eds), *Men in the Middle*, pp. 32-49.
Zeller, B., 'Language, formulae, and Carolingian reforms: the case of the Alemannic charters from St Gall', in R. Gallagher, E. Roberts and F. Tinti (eds), *The Languages of Early Medieval Charters: Latin, Germanic Vernaculars and the Written Word* (Leiden: Brill, forthcoming).

INDEX

abuses 142, 159, 176, 177, 191-2, 199
Admonitio generalis 47, 49, 120n.2
adultery 127, 131, 132
advocates 158, 162-3, 176, 179
Ælfric of Eynsham 50, 124n.12, 130n.37
Æthelnoth, reeve 165-6
Agobard of Lyon, archbishop 115-16
al-Andalus 37, 39, 110, 183, 185
Alemannia 22, *23*, 27, 101, 144, 160-3, 227
Alfred, king 33, 172-3, 190-1, 218, 235
alms 126n.19, 136, 138, 237
Alpine regions xvi, 19-20, 22, 31
Alsace xvi, 20, 22, 75, 228
annals 46, 47, 117, 234, 235
arable *see* land
Arabs 30-2, 37, 39, 111, 184
archaeology, evidence from 11, 12-13, 16, 52-64, 112-13, 166, 187
Ardennes 17, 19, 21, 46, 73, 75, 76, 78, 108, 214
arimanni 70, 236, 239
aristocrats 6, 32, 40, 71, 72, 173, 194-5
   conflict between 28, 183-4, 185
   demand by 61
   property of 67, 73-4, 78, 106
Arlanzón, river 83, 106, 197
armies, size of 187
army service 155, 176, 187-92, 220, 239, 241
Arn, archbishop of Salzburg 123n.9, 195
assemblies 47, 48, 107, 151, 165, 195, 197-8, 220

baptism 50, 51, 112, 128-9
Bavaria xvi, 19-20, 24, 28, 67, 71, 72, 80, 101, 145, 211
   office holders in 162, 163, 168-9
   settlements in 58, 62

behaviour, Christian 127-8, 130-1, 215-16, 217
Belgium xvi, 2, 10, *223*
Benevento, duchy of 23, 24, 32
Berbers 30, 37, 184
Berengar, king 28, 157, 169
bishops 49, 70, 97, 148n.110, 201-2, 203, 205
   control by 132n.45, 133-5, 137, 140
   see also Agobard; Arn; Canterbury; courts; Freising; Hincmar; Santiago de Compostela; statutes; Theodulf; Worcester; Wulfstan
boundaries, property 75, 89, 105-6, 174, 203-5
Brittany 2, 67, 119, 138, 140, 181, 193-4, 197, 200, *222*
   see also plebes
Bruoch 100, 203
burial 50, 51, 95, 108, 118
   see also cemeteries

Canterbury, archbishop of 166
capitularies xvi, 47-8, 92, 101, 120n.2, 137-8, 174-5, 189, 191-2
   Capitulare de villis 93, 152, 164
   see also Admonitio generalis
cartularies 42, 43, 226, 228, 230, 231, 232
cash 13, 65, 140
Catalonia 28, 38, 212
   charters from 97-8, 230
catechumens 128-9, 130, 236
   see also baptism
Celanova, monastery of 69, 110, *225*, 231
cemeteries 55, 60, 62, 130n.38, 219

INDEX

centenarii 101, 152, 174, 175, 176–7, 216, 236
  in Bavaria 158, 159, 160, 168, 171
  in Italy 155, 156
  Charlemagne, king and emperor 23, 24, 25, 68, 108, 162, 175
  prohibitions by 66, 91, 176
  Charles the Bald, king 25, 26, 69, 116, 140, 190
  charters 4, 40–4, 99, 103, 195, 196, 199, 203, 226–32
  forged 42, 230
  see also Catalonia; England; Saint-Gall
children 45, 69, 116, 117, 129, 206
Christianity *see* behaviour, Christian; bishops; churches; faith, Christian; priests
chronicles 46–7, 234–5
churches
  local 51, 62, 95, 138, 144, 209, 215
  baptismal 156, 170n.66, 170n.67, 211–12, 216
  ownership of 97, 133
  see also priests
cives 84, 86n.1, 99, 108
clientship 17, 65, 160, 169, 171, 208
climate 21, 22, 214
clothing 112, 113
collective action 17, 202, 214–15, 221
  agricultural 77, 88–90, 213–14
  legal 99–107, 197, 214
  religious 95–8, 215
collective obligations 92–5, 214
coloni 68, 69
concilia 105, 179, 212–13, 215, 218
  see also councils, church
confession (religious) 123, 130, 131–2, 240
Córdoba 37, 39, 185
Cosona 154–5, 170–1, *224*
councils, church 84, 96, 118, 124, 136n.59, 140, 151, 176
  see also Tribur, Council of
counts 26, 39, 106, 115, 152, 167, 175, 205, 237
  in Italy 24, 31, 157–8, 169, 188
court cases 99–100, 103–4, 106, 132, 159, 194–6, 199, 201, 206

courts, episcopal 201–2
Courtisols 68, 78, 116–17, 206–8, 215, 218, *223*

Dauendorf 98, 215, *224*
decani 152, 154, 155, 158, 170, 178, 237
demesne 76, 79, 82, 94, 163, 237
dependants 7, 46, 65, 66, 93, 110, 165, 185n.20, 238
  see also serfs; status
Dienheim 76, 87, 145, *224*
disputes 107–8, 115, 136–7
  judicial 99, 132, 139, 141, 174, 194–7, 207
  see also court cases; justice, administration of
Domesday Book 44, 45, 94, 102–3, 139, 234
Duero basin 19, 21, 58
dues 68, 93, 99, 140, 163, 191, 192
  see also rents
dukes 24, 29, 159, 174, 199, 201, 237, 239

East Francia 28–30, *29*, *31*, 144, 107, 190, 229
Eastry 165–6, 212, *225*
Eigenkirche 121, 237
  see also churches
Eimsheim *76*, *224*
Einhard 164, 183, 192–3, 208
Ekkehard IV 164, 235
emperors *see* Charlemagne; Louis the Pious; Otto I; Otto II; Otto III
enclosures 55, 56, 58, 62
Engilperht 158–9, 159–60, 168, 172, 176
England xvi, *34*, *35*, 58, 62, 102–3, 124, 188, 200, 212, *225*
  charters from 231–2
  land in 22, 77, 84
  office holders in 164–6
  political trends in 32–6
  status in 67, 71, 216
estates 7, 11, 72, 78, 81, 155, 188, 220
  growth of 14, 15, 41
  see also landownership; property
exclusion, social 116–18, 202, 218–19
exercitales 71, 155, 170n.67, 236

283

INDEX

faith, Christian 25, 131, 215, 221
families 71, 79, 117, 129, 159–60, 168, 206, 209, 221
   nuclear 55, 74, 239
   priests' 132–7, 139, 142
   see also relationships
familiae 65, 82, 93, 100, 163, 192, 203, 238
farming 60, 77, 88–91, 111, 119, 215
farmsteads 54–5, 56–7, 58, 59–60, 74, 206, 238
fields 60, 76, 77, 89
   open 8, 77, 89, 213, 240
field-systems 60
fines 165, 188–9, 192, 193, 209
fiscal land 171, 173, 198, 200, 236, 237
Flexo 103, 154, *224*
Folcwin 43, 161–2, 171n.75, 176
formularies 99, 101, 145, 146, 148, 230, 238
fortifications 39, 188, 190, 191
France 53n.1, 58, 62, 93, 120, 184, *223*, 229
Francia *23, 26, 29, 31*, 41, 49, 95, 124, 141, 162, 179
   judicial disputes in 99–102, 200–2
   political trends in 22–32, 185, 234
   property in 71, 72, 79, 163
   status in 66, 216
   see also East Francia; West Francia
freedom 5–6, 64–6, 155
   see also proprietors, free; status
Freising, episcopal see of 145, 158–9, 160, 168–9, 195, 205, 216, 228
Fulda, monastery of 28, 43, 145, 153, 193, 228

gastalds 43, 152, 157, 161, 169, 171–4, 176, 188, 238
geography
   physical xvii, 19–22
   political xvii, 22–51
Germany xvi, 6, 27, 40, 53n.1, 59, *224*, 227
   see also Francia; East Francia
Gesta Abbatum 47, 229, 235, 239
gifts 41, 93, 98, 138, 160, 176, 195, 205, 215
Gorze, monastery of 82, 100, 203, 228

groups, residential 1–2, 9, 36, 46, 87–8, 210–11, 214–15, 219
   names of 109, 211, 217–18
Gruyères 108, 114, *223*
guilds 91, 107, 198–9, 239

hagiography 4, 45–6, 107–8
haribannus see fines
Henry I, king of East Francia 29, 30, 190
hides 79, 189, 238, 239
Hincmar of Reims, archbishop 91, 135–6, 142, 203, 206, 233, 234
historiography
   English 8–10
   French 10–11, 16
   German 5–7, 16
   Italian 12–14
   Spanish 14–16
homilies 50, 123–8, 131
households 55, 80, 89, 90, 107, 213–14, 239
houses 52–64, 239
hundreds 102–4, 165, 166, 190, 198, 212, 214, 236, 239

Iberia 21, 62, 74, 80, 124, 148n.110, *225*, 231
   court cases in 104–6, 194–5, 200
   office holders in 150, 166–7, 213
   political trends in 36–40, 177, 181
   status in 67, 69–70, 72
   see also Portugal; Spain
identity 109–10
   group 1–2, 210, 221
   political 28, *33*, 38
   regional 22, 27, 40
immigrants, integration of 111–14, 114–15, 116, 218–19
incastellamento 12, 13, 63
inheritance *see* families; office; priests; property
inquests 132, 200–2
   local 45, 210
institutions, communal 7, 12, 18, 70n.83
investiture 173, 204, 205
Ireland *see* rituals

284

INDEX

Italy 66, 143, *224*, 226-7
  kingdom of 29, *29*, 32, 103-4
  office holders in 153-8, 162, 163, 169, 203n.*93*, 216, 225
  political trends in 22-32
  see also Tuscany
iudices 11, 152, 160, 174, 201, 239

Jews 109-10
judgement finders 105, 194-5
  see also scabini
judicial procedures 3, 174, 179, 194, 195, 197, 212-14, 240
  see also court cases; courts; sureties; witnesses
justice, administration of 155, 163, 166-7, 173-4, 179, 216

Kempraten 161, *224*
Kempten 117, *224*
kingdoms
  English 32-3, 35-6, 181
  Lombard 23-4, 173
  Spanish 37-9, 83, 194
  see also Italy; kings; Middle Kingdom; *regnum*
kings 6, 72, 155, 170, 173, 175, 183, 184, 192
  control by 162, 164, 176, 177, 197-8, 237
  see also Alfred; Berengar; Charlemagne; Charles the Bald; Henry I; law codes; Otto I; Otto II; Otto III
Kirchheim 54-5, *56*, 60, *224*

labour 15, 90, 116, 163
  service 14, 44, 65, 92, 164, 165, 196, 237
laity 41, 43, 95, 121, 123, 128, 143, 210
land
  arable 20, 77, 80, 81, 213, 215, 221
  management of 14, 69, 77, 92, 163-4, 165, 206
  units 79-80, 81-2
  see also estates; property
landownership 74-6, 78-9, 82, 89, 177, 178, 204, 208, 220
  see also priests; property; proprietors

landscape 19-22, 62-4, 74-7, 82-4, 214-15
language 126
  Arabic 37, 110, 111
  English 32, 34, 49, 50, 130, 172-3, 232
  Latin xv, 125-6, 130, 144, 147-8, 232
  Norse 34, 112-14
  vernacular 124-5, 129-30, 147-8
Larrey-sur-Ouche 99, *223*
law 172-8
  canon 48, 131, 135
  customary 49, 200
  law codes 48-9
  English 36n.47, 49, 102, 116, 141, 165, 172-3, 184, 189
  Lex Baiuuariorum 48, 101, 115
  Lex Salica 48, 102, 114-15
  Lombard 173-4, 237, 240, 241
  Visigothic 37, 48, 110, 166
León 21, 38-9, 70, 109, *225*, 231
letters 86, 136, 145, 164, 174, 192-3
literacy 143, 147, 149, 172-3
liturgy 49-51
  see also ordines
localities xiv, 90, 93, 96, 102, 103, 142, 170, 199, 211-13, 221
locopositi 152, 174, 178, 201, 240
Lombards *see* Benevento; kingdoms; law codes; Spoleto
lordship 6-7, 8, 10, 11, 15, 16, 17, 44, 69, 186
Lord's Prayer, the 125, 129, 130, 146
Lorsch, monastery of 42-3, 68, 145, 153, *224*, 228
Lotharingia 25, 28, *29*, 184
Louis the Pious, emperor 25, 83, 101, 136, 138, 174, 177, 190
Lucca 24, 31, 71, 138, 139, *224*, 227, 233

Mabompré 78, 79, *223*
Magyars 28-30, 184, 185-6, 190
maiores see mayors
mancipia 66-7, 68, 168, 196
  see also dependants

285

INDEX

mansa, mansi 78, 79, 80, 81, 138, 189, 193, 233, 240
manuscripts 125, 134, 145
  priests' xvi, 50, 126–7, 131
Marche-en-Famennes 97, 215, *223*
marches, Carolingian 24, 38–9, 187
Markgenossenschaften 6, 8
marriage 51, 65, 66, 116, 137n.62, 151
Mass 50, 95, 127, 130, 145
mayors 69, 163–4, 178, 240
Melgar 98, 105, 215, 218, *225*
meseta 16, 19, 80, 105, 21
micro-regions xiv, 71, 101, 172, 177, 178, 216, 220, 221, 240
Middle Kingdom 25, 27
Middle Rhineland *see* Rhineland
military expeditions 32, 33, 183, 187–9, 192, 193
mills 60, 83, 106, 110
miracula 45, 46, 89, 90, 93, 161, 167, 217
missi 68, 83, 175, 176, 195, 200, 201, 240
  dominici 190, 199, 208
Mitry 69, 100, 215, *223*
monasteries 68, 69
  claims by 83, 212
  demands of 92, 93
  property of 65, 70, 78, 82, 87, 233
  see also Celanova; Fulda; Gorze; Lorsch; Pardomino; Prüm; Redon; Sahagún; Saint-Bénigne; Saint-Denis; Saint-Gall; Saint-Germain-des-Prés; Saint-Remi; San Salvatore; Sobrado; Stavelot-Malmedy; Wissembourg
Moors 39, 110, 111, 218–19
Mozarabs 110–11
Musciano 98, 156, *224*
Muslims 14, 15, 16, 30, 183, 185
  emirates of 32, 37

neighbours *see vicini*
networks 17, 58, 75, 150, 168, 190, 211, 216, 221
notarii 43, 156, 158, 172, 179, 188, 227
  see also scribal practice; scribes

oaths 84, 91, 188, 198, 202, 212
office holders 34, 48, 109, 150–80, 195, 201, 216, 219, 225
office, succession to 135–6, 159–60, 167–72, 175
ordeals 132, 167, 201
ordines 50–1, 96, 129
orthography xv, 147
Otto I, king and emperor 30, 32, 157, 184
Otto II, king and emperor 30, 32
Otto III, king and emperor 30, 32, 47
outsiders 108–18, 128–9, 150, 203, 218, 219

Pacé 55–6, *57, 222*
Papi 89, *224*
Pardomino, monastery of 70, 106, 214, *225*
Paris basin xvi, 21, 67, 68, 73, 76, 78, 81, 215
parishes 10, 95, 130n.38, 202
  see also priests
pastoral care 120–1, 122–32, 137, 148–9, 215
pasture 77, 82, 83, 99, 240, 241
peasants 11, 94, 111, 186, 191, 216, 220
  practice of 3, 210
  uprisings of 107–8
  see also proprietors; status
penitentials 130n.39, 131–2, 136, 149, 240
Perahtger 161, 167–8, 169
Peringer, priest 167–8
Petrus *de Niviano* 156, 157, 169, 170
Piacenza 97, 104, 143, 156, 157, 169, 188, *224*
pigs 84, 164, 165
place-names 79, 112, 113–14, 218
placita 177, 207, 240
plebes 95, 98, 104
  Breton 2, 104, 212, 213, 214, 218
ploughing 86, 90, 91, 92, 214
plunder 182, 185, 186, 193
Poggibonsi 60, *61, 224*
polyptyques 44–5, 81, 87, 206–7, 232–3

286

INDEX

popes 23, 24, 30, 136
Portugal xvi, 38, 39, 43, 185, 216, 231
priests, local 2, 43, 50, 51, 132–7, 143–9, 151, 209, 216
  appointment of 133
  areas of responsibility of 120, 156, 211–12, 215
  examination of 133n.46, 146
  preaching by 123–6
  property of 137–43
  see also families; manuscripts; pastoral care; Peringer; Trisingus
property 8, 39, 41, 65, 72, 76–84, 101, 135, 151, 162–3, 203–8
  see also land; landownership; priests
proprietors, free 8, 14, 16, 68, 70–1, 72–3, 111, 189, 191–2, 220
proximi 126–8, 131
Prüm, monastery of 27, 87, 92, 186–7, 224, 233
public
  authority 93, 226
  sense of the 6–7, 151, 173
  see also baptism; court cases; office holders; rituals

quasi-presbiteri 133n.46

Raetia 23, 43, 158n.25, 160–2, 227
Rankweil 43, 162, 224
Redon, monastery of 104, 197, 204, 222, 230
reeves 84, 152, 164–6, 172–3, 179, 198, 239
Regino of Prüm 136n.57, 183, 186–7, 201–2, 234
'regions' xiv, 17, 19, 21, 27, 71, 76, 148, 158, 161, 168, 211, 221
regna 25, 27, 28–30, 40
regnum Francorum 22–3, 23, 24–5
relationships
  family 167–9, 170–1, 178
  vertical 5, 7, 9–10, 16
relics 45, 95, 108, 161, 202, 205
rents 66, 68, 70, 93, 105, 163, 165
Rhineland 68, 75, 78, 83, 186, 187, 214, 224
  Middle xvi, 20, 71, 72, 145

rituals 7, 46, 204–6, 217
  Irish 205n.101
  see also baptism
Rome 12, 24, 28, 32, 137
Rovigliano 153–4, 224
Ruffiac 138, 204, 213, 222
rulers 35, 189–90, 197
  Carolingian 25, 181, 220, 221
  see also aristocrats; kings

Sahagún, monastery of 15, 94, 109, 225, 231
Saint-Bénigne of Dijon, monastery of 99, 196, 223
Saint-Denis, monastery of 69, 100, 223, 229–30
Saint-Gall, monastery of 4, 20, 65, 84, 99, 224
  charters from 43, 48, 79, 138–9, 144, 147, 227
Saint-Germain-des-Prés, monastery of 80, 117, 163, 192, 223, 232–3
Saint-Remi of Reims, monastery of 68, 78, 93, 206–7, 223, 233
Saints' Lives *see* hagiography
saiones 132, 152, 166–7, 179, 213, 216, 241
sales 41, 66, 138, 145, 171, 204
San Juan en Vega 83, 194, 215, 225
San Salvatore al Monte Amiata 153–5, 157n.20, 171, 172, 224, 227
Santiago de Compostela 184, 225
  bishop of 39
Saxony 23, 27, 29, 30, 115, 204
scabini 152, 154, 158, 169, 179, 196, 201, 206, 207, 241
scale 11, 19, 101, 103, 107, 152, 212, 213, 216
Scandinavians *see* Vikings
schools *see* training
sculdhaisi 152, 154, 155–6, 158, 159, 161–2, 169, 174, 241
scribal practice 144, 152, 170, 179, 204, 218, 227
  see also signum manus
scribes 4, 43–4, 97, 143–8, 167, 175, 233
seigneurialisation 60, 63, 64, 69, 79, 241

287

INDEX

seigneuries 11, 13
serfs 15, 65–7, 116–17, 139n.70, 196, 203, 206–7
sermons *see* homilies
services 65, 66, 69, 92, 148, 155, 236, 238, 242
   see also army; labour
settlements, rural 52–64, 211
   character of 1, 54, 59, 241
   nucleated 7, 10, 17, 58, 62, 213
   pattern of 57–9, 63, 104, 218
signum manus 171, 227, 241
silos 53, 56, 62
slaves 31, 40, 64–5, 67, 145, 185, 238
   see also status
Slavs 30, *31*, 183, 187
Sobrado, monastery of 209–10, *225*, 231
social cohesion 1, 3, 10–11, 210–11, 217, 221
soils 21, 22, 81
source material, written xvii, *3*, 40–51, 90, 123, 138, 146, 182, 226–35
Spain xvi, 14–15, 19, 53n.1, *133*, 185, 201, 212–13, 216
Spoleto 23, *31*, *32*, 157, 169, *224*
status 5, 8, 17, 100, 104, 238
   free 12, 14, 16, 64–5, 70–1, 74, 87, 116, 189, 207
   lesser free 67, 160, 196
   legal 64–73, 206–7
   unfree 67–8, 74, 117, 163, 185n.20, 196, 207
statutes, episcopal 49, 122, 135, 145, 151
Stavelot-Malmedy, monastery of 27, 46, 83, 89, 100, 164, 186, *223*, 228
stratification, social 70–5
sureties 70, 102, 104, 199–200, 204, 209, 241

tenants 11, 14, 65–6, 68, 74, 76, 80–2, 117, 191, 192, 214, 217
tenures 67, 79, 80, 82, 206–7, 242
theft 36n.47, 49, 131, 217
thegns 71, 141, 242
Theodulf of Orléans, bishop 121n.3, 129n.34, 134

thieves 36n.47, 103, 116, 117, 209
tithes 92, 95, 97, 121, 136, 140–2, 242
tithings 36n.47, 102
training 134, 135, 144, 145, 173
transactions 66, 71, 101, 139, 144, 146, 147, 159, 160, 203, 208
   recording of 4, 43, 146–7, 204
   see also charters; scribes
   see also gifts, sales
Trento 196, 201, *224*
tribuni 152, 160, 242
Tribur, Council of 118, 120n.2
Trisingus, priest 136–7, 215–16
Tuscany xvi, *29*, *31*, 58, 67, 70, 75, 124, 211, *233*
   office holders in 153–5, 170–1
   physical character of 19, *20*, 21

Vallange 59–60, *59*, *223*
Varsi 96, 98, *224*
Verín 105–6, *225*
Verona 157, 158, 196, 201, *224*
vicarii 152, 158, 159, 160, 168, 175, 242
vicecomites 152, 157, 158, 242
vicini 101, 102, 115, 117, 126–8, 131
Vikings 35, 218, 239
   raids by 25–7, *33*, 39–40, 184, 185, 186
   settlements of 33–4, 112–13
Villance 74, 81, 87, *223*
villici 11, 151, 163, 164, 240
vineyards 70, 76, 80, 109, 111
vir devotus 71, 155, 236, 242
war 182–93
   see also military expeditions
water rights 80, 82, 83, 105, 106, 194, 214
wealth 64, 74, 85, 87
West Francia 27–8, *29*, *31*, 107, 116, 229
Wickham, C. J. 9–10, 18, 75
Wissembourg, monastery of xvi, 43, 66, 80, 84, 92, 152n.4, 192, *224*, 228
witnesses 71, 101, 102, 115, 199, 202, 204, 210, 214, 227, 241

witness lists 101, 105, 159, 161, 169
women 40, 68, 95, 108, 112, 113, 151, 212
   farmers 90
   labour by 92–3
   landowners 73, 75

woodland 21, 65, 82, 83, 84, 88, 99, 107
Worcester *225*, 232
   bishop of 84
Wulfstan, archbishop 125n.12, 130n.37

Xhoris 100, 164, *223*

EU authorised representative for GPSR:
Easy Access System Europe, Mustamäe tee 50,
10621 Tallinn, Estonia
gpsr.requests@easproject.com

www.ingramcontent.com/pod-product-compliance
Lightning Source LLC
Chambersburg PA
CBHW071829230426
43672CB00013B/2792